Dream and Image

Dream and Image

by

Bettina L. Knapp

Whitston Publishing Company

Troy, New York

1977

To Anaïs Nin

with

affection

and

admiration

My gratitude goes to the Guggenheim Foundation for awarding me a Fellowship which made *Dream and Image* possible. My thanks also goes to my research assistant, Joseph Marthan, for his conscientious aid.

The most mysterious Power enshrouded in the limitless clave, as it were, without cleaving its void, remaining wholly unknowable until from the force of the stroke there shone forth a supernal and mysterious point. Beyond that point there is no knowable, and therefore it is called Beginning, the creative utterance which is the starting point of all.

Zohar I.

PREFACE

The remote and nearby echoes of Image, the fabulous worlds of Dream, reach us through the pages of this vivid and profound book.

Bettina Knapp, whom Henri Peyre, a master of international scholarship, salutes as "one of the finest scholar teachers of literature in American Universities", offers us here a rich blend of learning and feeling.

Bettina Knapp proceeds with an acute look, large strides, and warmth. She walks on solid paths. No steps are groundless; every pace is sealed in reality, in life itself. Day to day life; and also, untrapped life. Total, intense life, with all its breath, and the multiple streams of the unconscious. "Man must ever again escape into the unconscious, for there live his roots." (Goethe)

Leading the reader through the 17th, 18th, 19th century, from Descartes to Mallarmé; focusing her study upon thirteen prominent French authors, Bettina Knapp escorts and questions writers as diverse as Balzac and Rimbaud, Charles Nodier and Karl Huysmans, Diderot and Baudelaire. Bettina Knapp has good reasons for this choice; she has lived in France, she understands France, and is thoroughly acquainted with French literature.

This captivating book examines a selection of writings in which the presence of "dream and image" are striking. Yet these sharp explorations, in a specific range of works, manage to enlighten the whole production and entire personality of their authors.

With knowledge and sensibility, Bettina Knapp puts mystery within our touch, without exhausting it; digs new galleries in the core of creation.

Her frequentation of psychoanalysis, her interest in Jung's theories, her vast culture contribute to enlarge the reader's outlook. Through the diversity of civilizations, she unfolds legends, pantheons, archetypal schemes, which appear rumbling with analogies. Disclosing worlds within words, her observations are meticulous, her sweep is always wide.

By degree, harmony rises from antagonistic or entangled figures. Out of the savana of the unconscious, an inner lane is traced. "Bettina Knapp has an unusually lucid mind," writes Anaïs Nin, "and a clear, sharp focus upon chaotic and diffuse materials. She has a gift for extracting the essential."

In this important volume, the sense of unity is never lost. An inner stride, an underlying current, a constant rythm, emerge out of the turmoil of men and time. Very justly, Bettina Knapp herself views "these vast and underlying movements as part of a whole picture; as eternal and universal frescoes coming into view at certain periods in history and in an individual's personal development."

It is a rewarding adventure to be led through these pages by such a guide. By a cartesian and dyonisian mind, with whom we can witness the finite nature of man in a non-stop transformative process. Man (everyone of us) at times in rupture, at other times in unison with the infinite nature of the universe.

Using "learning" as an excellent tool, Bettina Knapp fathoms its limits. So that we may behold the realms of self and the sustaining motions of inner life, she discards the "opaque curtains" of habit.

At the meeting point of emotion and ideas, of analysis and synthesis, this is a creative and uplifting book. "That which is in opposition to itself is at the same time in harmony with itself", claims Heraclitus in one of his sayings.

This is a book full of substance. Through our encounters with Descartes, Racine, Diderot, Cazotte, Nodier, Nerval, Balzac, Gautier, Baudelaire, Hugo, Huysmans, Rimbaud and Mallarmé, artists who are "forerunners of what is to be", we discover and experience our own living forces.

Andrée Chédid

TABLE OF CONTENTS

PREFACE i

Introduction 1

Section I: The Seventeenth Century
    Chapter 1: René Descartes—"The Dreams Came
        From Above" 25
    Chapter 2: Jean Racine—*Athaliah:* The Premonitory
        Dream and the Prophetic Vision 61

Section II: The Eighteenth Century
    Chapter 3: Denis Diderot—*D'Alembert's Dream:*
        The Relating of a Myth 85
    Chapter 4: Jacques Cazotte—*The Devil in Love:*
        A Dream Initiation 103

Section III: The Nineteenth Century
    Chapter 5: Charles Nodier—*The Crumb Fairy: A
        Hieros Gamos* or a Sacred Marriage of
        Sun and Moon 129
    Chapter 6: Gérard de Nerval—Soliman, Sheba,
        Adoniram and the Occult 151
    Chapter 7: Honoré de Balzac—*Louis Lambert:* The
        Legend of the Thinking Man 183
    Chapter 8: Théophile Gautier—*Arria Marcella:* The
        Greek Versus the Christian Way 203
    Chapter 9: Charles Baudelaire—"Parisian Dream":
        The Drama of the Poetic Process. 223
    Chapter 10: Victor Hugo—"What the Mouth of Dark-
        ness Says": The Dark Night of the Soul . . .257
    Chapter 11: Joris-Karl Huysmans—*Down There:*
        Satanism and the Male Psyche—The Black
        Mass and the Female Principle. 283
    Chapter 12: Arthur Rimbaud—"After the Flood":
        From Chaos to Cosmos 313

Table of Contents

Chapter 13: Stéphane Mallarmé—*Igitur* or *Elbehnon's Folly* the Depersonalization Process and the Creative Encounter 355

Conclusion 401

Bibliography 403

Thus the esthetically sensitive man stands in the same relation to the reality of dreams as the philosopher does to the reality of existence; he is a close and willing observer, for these pictures afford him an interpretation of life, and it is by these processes that he trains himself for life.

(*Friedrich Nietzsche*, The Birth of Tragedy.)

INTRODUCTION

Dreams and images are manifestations of man's arcane world. At times they emerge from the unconscious into consciousness with ease; at other instances they rise forth with volcanic force, thereby disrupting heretofore smooth-running orientation. The fresh material entering the rational sphere may take the form of disjointed images, as concretized, for example, by a Picasso painting; or it may be a series of seemingly inexplicable events, as delineated by Nerval in *Aurélia;* or a burst of heteroclite colors, as splashed onto canvases by Matisse; or Stravinsky-like cacophonies; or an array of numbers in the Pythagorean sense. The impact of these new visualizations introduces chaos or change into what had been formerly a stratified, ossified, and comprehensible outlook. For the writer or artist who lives in close rapport with his unconscious, the emergence of these unvitiated forms may, if he is discerning, enable him to discover unfamiliar directions, untried paths, and unfelt sensations in the manner of a Balzac or a Hugo in an effort, as Teilhard de Chardin wrote, to "discover Man unto his depths."[1] Dreams and images are the *prima materia* for the creative individual.

Since the beginning of time, man has sought to understand the forces of nature both within him and outside of his being; he has attempted to fathom the logic of patterns that seem to have been repeated *ad infinitum* during the course of history; he has tried to account for the factor of chance in the so-called rational flow of things. Man is unwilling to see himself as a victim in a world of contingencies, as these intrude every now and then in the collective sphere in the form of floods, wars, storms, famines, droughts, and in the individual domain as dreams and images. Although he lives amid imponderables, he is forever attempting to decipher the invisible, to devise some technical or aesthetic means by which he can understand or at least transform that which escapes him into some viable or workable entity. To manipulate what is beyond his comprehension, to dominate the unforseeable has been and perhaps will always be one of man's goals. In his attempt to reduce the infinite to the finite or to divine the Divine, man has interpreted arcane relationships with which he is confronted. In ancient China he took to reading plants and turtle scales, in Africa to throwing bones, in Chaldea to elucidating astral and natural signs. In Mesopotamia, where astrology, oneiromancy, and necromancy were *de rigueur*, oblique allusions as well as human and animal sounds were conceived of as fortuitous indications of some outer-worldly force. In Egypt, Babylonia, Palestine, Greece, and Rome, speech patterns and personality traits, sand drawings, and crystal gazing were studied in order to discern ways to break the fatal life-death cycle. Plato, who believed in reincarnation, suggested that the universal soul chose a human form into which it incarnated itself and that outer signs (body, mind) were the clue to what lay hidden. Telesthesia and synesthesia were considered expressions of that residual substance left over from a previous mode of existence. Heraclitus expressed this notion in terms of transformation: nothing is lost in the cosmos, all is in a state of eternal flux. "Fire finds repose in change," he wrote; or, "One cannot bathe twice in the same river."[2]

The material feeding the prophets' prognostications, the philosophers' credos, and the creative individuals' works emerges from what C. G. Jung termed the collective unconscious. Its contents become discernible to the individual in the form of archetypal imagery. The visualizations thus emerging may be used by the creative person as source material for his work, thus expanding his conscious frame of reference. Balzac's dazzling imagination was forever activated by his dreams. Descartes' mathematical discoveries were likewise conceived after three dreams. F. A. Kekulé had tried for many years to express molecular structure of trimethylbenzene graphically. He succeeded in his endeavor only after dreaming the following images:

> Long rows much more densely put together, all in motion, twisting and squirming like snakes. And, lo! What was that? Why, one of the snakes has taken hold of its own tail, and the configuration whirls arrogantly before my eyes. As if lightning had struck, I awoke, and this time I spent the rest of the night working out the consequences of my hypothesis.[3]

The unconscious as a helping device in man's artistic and scientific quest may be looked upon as a function of the mind or as a new world—a kind of fourth dimension in which a new space-time orientation comes into existence. The information furnished him by his unconscious in the form of dreams and images may shape his work and thus, to a certain extent, his destiny. For twentieth-century man who has traveled in space and broken the sound barrier, the unconscious has not only become accessible to him, but also exists as a productive force in his life when used with direction.

Like the stratosphere, biosphere, noosphere, and geno-sphere, I shall call that area in which dreams and images become discernible to the individual the *oneirosphere.* It is in this region, which includes both the personal and collective unconscious, that visualizations congregate, grow, and live inchoate. The oneirosphere is approachable as is a photograph in the process of development: from an invisible imprint on paper it is trans-formed with the aid of chemicals and time into recognizable forms and shapes. So it is with the unformed mass in the oneiro-sphere. The individual's creative impulse becomes the catalyzing agent. It triggers off the electric charge necessary to arouse the energy inherent in the evolving image, thus enabling it to catapult into consciousness.

It is the goal of *Dream and Image* to show how certain French writers experienced their *oneirosphere,* how they probed and dissected it, and how in their novels, poems, philosophical, and scientific works they made viable some of the shapes and forms emerging from it. Each chapter in *Dream and Image* may therefore be read as a single unit or as part of an evolving pro-cess: the creative individual's spiritual and artistic development in his perpetually altering rapport with his oneirosphere—from Descartes' unwitting Godsent experience to Mallarmé's willed ascesis.

The dreams and images, as they appear to the conscious mind of the writers under scrutiny, are interpreted in the light of the rational and orderly functioning world. Thus they are categorized into premonitory, anxiety, individuation, prodromal dreams; or labeled according to the events delineated and the mythical figures portrayed: Oedipus, Electra, Cassandra. When interpreting dreams as they appear in poems, novels, or essays, one cannot help but perceive them in the light of one's own psychological, aesthetic, and philosophical frame of reference. Nevertheless, an effort has been made to see these vast underlying movements as part of a whole picture; as eternal and universal frescoes coming into view at certain periods in history and in an individual's personal development. Whatever the dream or image, it is viewed as a ripple in an ocean, important to the individual experiencing the form, the shape, and the energy it generates, but not exclusive of the symbols therein revealed and their impact on the work and the world in general. To limit and codify dreams may lead to severe distortions. What is emphasized is the connecting principle involved in each manifestation of the unconscious which, for certain writers, may fall into specific motifs or patterns, as in the case of Rimbaud, who repeatedly used fire and water images, or Mallarmé, who frequently depicted spider webs in all shapes, forms, and allusions.

Before attempting an analysis of the dreams and images emanating from the oneirosphere of the thirteen writers whose works will be explicated in this volume, let us take a brief sampling of the role dreams and images have played since earliest times.

The ancient Egyptians believed dreams to be evidence of occult forces at work. Dreams were considered premonitory in nature, frequently revealing the words and intentions of the Egyptian Trinity of Gods (Osiris, Isis, Horus) and thus a means of communication between the living and the dead. The goddess Bess was the guardian of the dreamer. The Chester Beatty Papyrus found in Thebes (2052-1778 B.C.) is the first extant record of dreams. The techniques used by the ancient Egyptians with respect to dream interpretation are startling in their modernity. Dreams were not only recorded, but information regarding the individual's background, character, and physical appearance was also included. Dream association, allegorical material, puns, and interpretation via contraries were used in an attempt to discover the secrets hidden within the universe. The dreams recorded in the Chester Beatty Papyrus were divided into two categories: those dealing with good and bad people, and those dealing with favorable and unfavorable types; for example:

> When a man chews lotus flowers—it is good, it announces a happy event.

> When a man enters a room with wet clothes—it is bad, it portends a fight.[4]

The Egyptians, for whom earthly existence was considered of minor importance in comparison with the eternal life granted after death, were convinced that during dream periods the Ba (soul) was detached from the body and blended into the universal pleroma. The individual during these moments was permitted to enter into communication with the gods, the dead, and demons, thus becoming privy to his own destiny. Thutmose IV (1450 B.C.), for example, dreamed that a great god had visited him during his sleep and spoke the following:

> Look, my son Thutmose, I am your father Harmachis-Chepri-Re-Atum who is going to give you, the most honored of the living, a "terrestrial" kingdom.[5]

Thutmose was told that if this gift were granted, he would have to clear away the sands from the huge Sphinx at Gizeh. He carried out the god's will and then became the world's most powerful monarch.

Proper interpretation of the images and symbols thrust into the dreamer's mind by cosmic forces was deemed essential. Not everyone was capable of understanding such portents. Rigorous and lengthy training in the Egyptian mystery schools was required. *The Book of the Dead* was studied, among other sacred texts, and experienced as a vital document capable of acquainting the living with the world beyond. Although dream interpreters were not elevated to the rank of priests, they were, nonetheless, considered half priests or "Scribes of the Double House of Life"[6] and were referred to as *Katochoi* ("those retained" by the god of the house). They lived in sanctuaries, the most famous of which was located in Memphis in Thebes.

Incubation or healing dreams were very popular in ancient Egypt. Imhotep (2980-2950 B.C.), during his life a well-known doctor, architect, and priest of Ra, was deified after his death and became the patron of the sick. The ill would come to his sanctuary and go through a series of rituals and magic rites including cleansing, feasting, and imbibing of medicines and potions. These would inevitably provoke a certain type of dream in which Imhotep or another powerful deity appeared. If the dream was deemed positive by the Katochoi, the patient was cured; if not, he had to remain in the sanctuary until such time as his visual experience was deemed effective.

Dreams were also regarded as signs of encouragement sent by a particular god. An inscription dating from the thirteenth century B.C. engraved on the sanctuary at Karnak told this story: the pharaoh, fearing an invasion from the east, wanted to build a vigorous defense. "It seemed to his Majesty that he saw the statue of Ptah before Him who extended his sword and said: 'Take it! Rid yourself of your fear!' " The pharaoh interpreted this dream as the deity's support of his endeavor. He related it to his armies who were encouraged by this outer-worldly manifestation. They were victorious in their battle.[7]

The Assyrians and Babylonians, in contrast to the Egyptians, looked upon the world as a hostile entity. Destructive forces were always ready and able to impede man's way. Dreams, which were considered to be mysterious indications emanating from another world, were given great credence. Experts—priests, magicians, dervishes, fortune-tellers—were forever called upon to interpret these outer-worldly signs. Dreams were grouped according to types: relating to the completion of a task, the making of an object, to drinking, eating, sexual life, and so on. A well-known building dream was recorded by King Gudea (2500 B.C.): "I saw in my dream a man as tall as the sky, resembling a god, his wings were like the bird Imduged [a divine animal with an eagle's body and a lion's head]." This god ordered King Gudea to construct a temple in his honor, going so far as to trace its architecture for the king.[8]

The oldest exant dreams recorded on clay tablets date back to the time of Hammurabi (1728-1686 B.C.) Ashurbanipal (669-626 B.C.) also kept a dream book. On one occasion, it was said, Ashurbanipal and his soldiers experienced a collective dream. The goddess Ishtar appeared to them and said: "I will precede Ashurbanipal whom I created myself." The Babylonian armies encouraged by this protent, fought valiantly and won their battle.[9] Perhaps the most famous dreams of all are those related in the Babylonian epic *Gilgamesh*. The cosmic man

Gilgamesh related what he thought to be a very painful dream to his mother. He saw falling stars coming toward him which resembled flamboyant warriors. These finally took the shape of an immense man who then dropped to earth and began fighting with him. Gilgamesh, the stronger of the two, subdued him and took him to his mother, who greeted the man as if he were her own son. Gilgamesh's mother interpreted the dream that a stranger would come and fight with Gilgamesh, and she would adopt him as her son. The two would then become fast friends for life. Time passed. The savage strong man, Enkidu, came to Gilgamesh and all happened as the dream predicted.

Unlike other ancient peoples, the Hebrews believed they had a covenant with the Lord. To dream, then, was to experience God's commandments. With the passing of centuries and with powerful influences from neighboring countries, the Hebrew credo altered: dreams were thought to be sent by other forces, namely demons and the dead. The Talmud compares the soul to "a winged grasshopper with its feet attached to a chain which is in turn linked to its spinal column."[10] While the dreamer slept, the soul (a connection between man and God) escaped, flew around the universe, and then returned.

The Bible makes mention of many important dreams. In Genesis, for example, after Jacob was blessed by his father and sent out from Beersheba to Padan-aram, he had a premonitory vision.

> And he dreamed, and behold a ladder set up on the earth, and the top of it reached to heaven: and behold the angels of God ascending and descending on it. (28:12)

Before Joseph, Jacob's favorite son, was sold into slavery by his jealous brothers, he also had a prophetic dream.

> For, behold, we were binding sheaves in the field, and, lo, my sheaf arose, and also stood upright; and, behold, your sheaves stood round about, and made obeisance to my sheaf.
>
> And his brethren said to him, Shalt thou indeed reign over us? or shalt thou indeed have dominion over us? And they hated him yet the more for his dreams, and for his words. (37:7, 8)

In Egypt Joseph was imprisoned because his master's wife (Potiphar) had accused him wrongly; but he was later released after he interpreted the Pharaoh's dream (Genesis: 41:2-7 and 42:26-27). Because of his insight into the dream, Joseph had saved Egypt from a terrible famine. In return for his remarkable knowledge, the Pharaoh made him governor of Egypt, and after a time Joseph was reunited with his father and brothers whom he also had saved during the years of hunger.

Other examples of Biblical dreams are recorded in the Book of Daniel. When Daniel was taken into captivity in Babylon by Nebuchadnezzar, he was imprisoned in the lion's den for praying to his God. But because he was endowed with "understanding in all visions and dreams" (1:17), Daniel interpreted Nebuchadnezzar's terrifying dreams and the handwriting on the wall, and was freed. Saul, the first king of the Hebrews, a man who had once been heroic in battle but eventually proved unworthy of the power vested in him, believed in necromancy. When fighting the Philistines in Gilboa, he feared his enemy and prayed to God to come to him in a dream; however, God did not send the vision. Saul then consulted the medium at Endor and asked her to "bring up Samuel's spirit." Samuel predicted Saul's death in that very battle (I Samuel 28:11).

The concept of dream interpretation as expressed by the Hebrews in the Talmud is modern. Dreams are viewed as reflections of the tensions of man's daily activities, his longings, desires, needs, and aggressions—those he is either unable or unwilling to express during his waking hours. Unlike the Christians, the Hebrews were lenient with regard to sexuality. They believed that masculine demons (incubus) and feminine ones (succubus) visited dreamers. They did not consider relations with demons in the dream state as sinful nor as an indication of concubinage. The Hebrews, consequently, never searched for witches nor did they torture or burn their dreamers at the stake. Conversely, such activities were common during the Inquisitions in the Middle Ages, during the Renaissance in Europe, as well as in colonial Protestant America.[11]

For the Greeks, dreams had prophetic, prodromic, and therapeutic values. Dreams could be provoked by herbs, potions, gases, sacrifices, or by lying on the tomb of an ancestor. Hesiod called dreams "Sons of night and brothers of sleep." Homer, in his *Odyssey,* spoke of two doors leading to the dreamworld.

> One pair of gates is made of horn, and one of ivory. Those of the dreams which issue through the gate of sawn ivory, these are deceptive dreams, their message is never accomplished. But those that come into the open through the gates of the polished horn accomplished the truth for any mortal who sees them.[12]

The Greeks brought the incubation dream to its apogee. Patients who sought a cure through the dream had to go through rigorous rites, similar in some respects to modern shock treatment. First, the patient had to bathe in an icy cold river; then he had to offer certain animal sacrifices. The priests then interpreted the configuration of the animals's intestines to determine whether the time was favorable for the patient to go through his ordeal or not. If the signs were deemed right, two thirteen-year-old boys took the sick man to a river and performed further ablutions and unctions. The priests then had him drink the waters from a special spring, that of forgetfulness (lethe) and remembrance (mnemosyne), to forget his past but to remember the dream he would have. After the patient was shown the statue of Aesculapius and told to remove his garments, he was then wrapped in white swaddling clothes adorned with ribbons, reminiscent of a baby's attire.[13] The most terrifying part of his ordeal was now to take place: the man was hoisted feet first into a deep, dark, and narrow grotto inhabited by snakes and other venomous creatures, there to remain until he dreamed a healing dream. He was then promptly permitted to return to earth, feet first (like a breach birth, an omen of good luck and symbolic of rebirth), and related his dream or dreams to the priests who interpreted them. Frequently unconscious after his days and nights of terror and the narration of his dreams, he was carried to the sanctuary where he remained until his fright had worn off. Other treatments were also prescribed: the patient would lie down in a sanctuary on a bed called *kline* (the name *clinic* is derived from it) until such time as he dreamed of the god Aesculapius, his serpent, or his dog. The miracle of healing would then occur.[14] There were more than four hundred incubation centers in Greece devoted to Aesculapius. These flourished until the fifth century A.D. The most famous center of the Aesculapius cult was in Epidaurus. Instances of miraculous healing have been recorded: the blind were able to see, the paralyzed could walk, the dead were resurrected. Like Christ, Aesculapius was the most venerated healer of antiquity. Analogies have been made between the miracles he worked and those of Christ. Indeed, Aesculapius was the church's greatest foe. Some pagans claimed the name *Jesus* was derived from "Jaso" (the daughter of Aesculapius) and "Iashtai" (to heal) and that Jesus's miracles were in fact those of Aesculapius.[15]

The Greeks were also innovative in terms of dream analysis. Hippocrates (5th century B.C.) was the first to speak of "dissociation" in dreams. He believed the soul retained its thinking and feeling faculties during sleep but severed all links with the organs of sensation. He examined prodromic dreams and was convinced that the symptoms of a future sickness were revealed in the visual experience. He used patients' dreams when giving his medical diagnoses.[16] Democritus, the "father of nuclear science," asserted that dreams emanated from people as well as from objects, and in this sense he could be considered a forerunner of telepathic concepts.[17] He further declared that dreams were interpretations of what individuals had been or had experienced and were not sent to them by some outerworldly force. Plato wrote that dreams were "compensating" forces for "repressed" desires. In his *Republic* he stated: "In all of us, even in good men, there is a lawless wild beast nature, which peers out in sleep."[18] Reason, therefore, does not reign during sleeping hours. Aristotle wrote in *On Divination* that doctors should really pay attention to the dreams told to them by their patients. In his essays *On Sleep and Dreams, On Sleep, On Divination through Sleep,* Aristotle further subsumed that despite the fact that the senses are relatively inactive during sleep, "residual sensory activity continues."

> The residuary movements are like these: they are within the soul potentially, but actualize themselves only when the impediment to their doing so has been relaxed; and according as they are thus set free, they begin to move in the blood which remains in the sensory organs, and which is now but scanty, while they possess verisimilitude after the manner of cloud-shapes, which in their rapid metamorphoses one compares now to human beings and a moment afterwards to centaurs.[19]

The eye, for example, continues to move during sleep, producing images that are not the result of external stimuli. These visions or images are thought to be real objects by the dreamer though they are not. Judging perceptions (reason) and having them (dreams, illusions) are distinct functions. Therefore, to experience images is one factor, to carry them out in reality is yet another. Man continually experiences sensations but is frequently unaware of them during his waking hours because he is busy with so many other things. The dream, Aristotle believed, affects individuals even after they are awake.[20]

The Greek Artemidorus (134-200 A.D.) wrote the most complete volume on dream interpretation, *Oneirocritica*. He commented on and attempted to explicate the symbolic meanings of three thousand dreams. All types of fantasies were included: embarrassing ones in which the dreamer sees himself in the nude in front of other people, death wishes, visions of birth, incest, and theft; images of serpents, sticks, armaments, and water. Modern psychiatrists have seen illustrations of almost all types of complexes, ranging from Oedipal to Narcissus, in the *Oneirocritica*.[21]

The Romans were also fascinated by dream interpretations, the occult, and magic—all that went beyond the rational. Emperor Augustus was convinced that most of his dreams were premonitory in nature. During one of his battles, it was said, he had decided to rest in his tent because he was not feeling well. After a dream told him to leave his tent, he did so secretly. A few minutes later his enemies, believing he was still in it, destroyed the tent.[22] Tiberius, Caligula, and Domitian had preminotory dreams in which they witnessed their own demise. Nero was plagued with nightmares in which he saw himself covered with ants and being dragged bodily into dark areas, and being imprisoned. When Constantine I wanted to convert pagans to Christianity, he dreamed of a flaming cross above which the words *"in hoc signo vinces"* ("By this sign you will conquer") were written.

The Arabians, always at the mercy of obscure, terrifying demons, listened to the credo of Mohammed who believed most fervently in the profound meaning of dreams. He felt they were of such great significance that he had his disciples recount their dreams to him daily. The Koran, he asserted, had been revealed to him through a dream sent to him by the Angel Gabriel.

> During my sleep, the archangel Gabriel appeared to me carrying
> a cover of silk brocade upon which something had been written.
> And he said: "Read!" I read: "I don't know how to read." He
> pressed the brocade cover so close to my body that I thought
> my death was near. After that, he let me go and said: "Read!"
> And thus I read out loud and he finally left. And I awakened
> and it was as if these words had been branded with a red-hot
> iron in my heart. It was then that I heard a voice come from
> heaven and say: "Oh! Mohammed! You are the messenger of
> Allah, and I am Gabriel." I raised my face toward heaven and
> then I saw Gabriel in a human form, his feet at the side of
> heaven.[23]

Buddha's mother, Maya, had a dream of an elephant before
she became pregnant.[24] Buddha himself had dreams that prepared him for the great events in his life and work. In one dream
he saw four different birds and four different colors fly toward
him from the four corners of the world. As they dropped to his
feet, they turned white. These birds, he considered, were symbols representing his four future disciples.[25] Dreams are given
prominence in Brihadarmyaka-Upanishad (1000 B.D.). Chuang-
tzu (350 B.C.) believed if there were a difference between the
so-called world of reality and that of illusion, the distinction to
be made was tenuous.

> While men are dreaming, they do not perceive that it is a dream.
> Some will even have a dream in a dream, and only when they
> awake they know it was all a dream. And so, when the Great
> Awakening comes upon us, shall we know this life to be a great
> dream. Fools believe themselves to be awake now.
>
> Once upon a time, I Chuang-tzu dreamed I was a butterfly,
> fluttering hither and thither, to all intents and purposes a
> butterfly. I was conscious only of following my fancies as a
> butterfly, and was unconscious of my individuality as a butter-
> fly. Suddenly I was awakened, and there I was myself again.
> Now I do not know whether I was a man dreaming I was a
> butterfly, or whether I am a butterfly now dreaming I am a
> man.[26]

Many dreams are recorded in the New Testament. St.
Matthew (1:20) relates Joseph's prophetic dreams: "behold,
the angel of the Lord appeared unto him in a dream, saying,

Joseph, thou son of David, fear not to take unto thee Mary thy wife: for that which is conceived in her is of the Holy Ghost." The flight of the Holy Family into Egypt and their return to Palestine was the result of three dreams (Matthew 2:12, 13, 19). Strangely enough, the church's attitude toward dream interpretation during the Middle Ages and Renaissance was confused. Although the church tried to rid itself of the superstitious elements in oneiromancy, it could not condemn what had been written in the Bible: the dreams of Jacob, Daniel, Isaiah, Jeremiah, Joseph. Pope Gregory (715-731) condemned dream interpretation under penalty of death. Yet, the Holy Inquisition analyzed the dreams of those accused of acting against the Catholic Church, and if their visions were deemed to have been Devil-sent, the victims were condemned to death.[27] Magic, mystery, and fright surrounded dreams and their interpretations.

St. Augustine, who had been plagued with feelings of guilt throughout his life, in his *Confessions* related his mother's dream which foretold his conversion to Christianity.

> For whence was that dream with which Thou consolest her, so that she permitted me to live with her, and to have my meals at the same table in the house, which she had begun to avoid, hating and detesting the blasphemies of my error?[28]

St. Augustine was convinced that once he had opted for the new religion, his anguishes would vanish. They did not and nightmares continued to harass him. Although he could not fully believe in the reality of the evil spirits which engulfed his sleeping hours, he could not reject their presences.

St. Thomas Aquinas was convinced of the divine nature of dreams and in their premonitory messages. In his *Summa Theologica* he stated that God teaches men through dreams.

> What appears in dreams is seen by imaginative apprehension. Now angels reveal things in dreams, as witness the angel who appeared to Joseph in a dream. Therefore angels can change the imagination.[29]

Dreams were so important to Charlemagne that he hired a *maistre* whose sole function it was to interpret them. As recounted in *The Song of Roland*, Charlemagne had dreamed of the impending feud between two of his valiant knights, Roland and Oliver. In the dream Roland was the falcon and Oliver the vulture, and, according to *The Song of Roland,* they became good friends after this incident. Charlemagne also dreamed of the betrayal of one of his nobles, Ganelon, his condemnation, and the deaths of Roland and Oliver.

Whether narrated in the legends of King Arthur or Tristan, in the *Lays* of Marie de France, in miracle or mystery plays such as *The Miracle of St. Nicolas* or *Jeu de Theophilus* or Boccaccio's *The Decameron,* Chaucer's *The Nun's* and *The Priest's Tale,* Francesco Colonna's *The Dream of Poliphilus* and Dante's *Divine Comedy,* dreams were not only considered manifestations of occult forces but were also to become material for and essential to the creative process. The dream enabled writers and painters to enter into a world in which deeper perceptions could be experienced and a whole new range of feelings and sensations could be known.

Fascination with the dream as a creative force was apparent in the works of such sixteenth-century writers as Rabelais, who traced the history of dream interpretation in *Gargantua and Pantagruel* from antiquity to Artemidorus. Montaigne also wrote of the dream, which he approached with circumspection yet could not discount entirely. Shakespeare made much of dream visions in *Hamlet, Julius Caesar, Macbeth,* and *Richard III.* Bosch's pictorial fantasies are replete with diabolical figures; Dürer's "Doctor's Dreams" is an indication of his interest in the unknown. Matthias Grünewald's "The Temptation of St. Anthony" features a concrete manifestation of his unconscious visions—a world of blood and dismemberment. The mathematician and doctor Jerome Cardan had a recurring dream that ordered him to write what subsequently become *De Subtilitate Rerum.* The dream also revealed the plan of his volume and informed him how it must be written. Whenever Cardan was lax in his writing habits, the dream reoccurred, forcefully. However, once the volume was completed, the dream ceased.[30]

As a source of creativity, the dream has been attested to by writers, artists, musicians, and scientists such as René Descartes, Charlotte Brontë, Gérard de Nerval, Charles Lamb, Edgar Allan Poe, Charles Baudelaire, Arthur Rimbaud, Paul Valéry, Henri Poincaré, Richard Wagner, Sergey Rachmanioff, Odilon Redon,

William Hogarth, Henry James, James Ensor, Henri Fuseli, as well as many others. According to Samuel Taylor Coleridge, he wrote the entire "Kubla Kahn" after waking from a deep sleep one night in the summer of 1797. Robert Louis Stevenson had been trying to write the story of *The Strange Case of Dr. Jekyll and Mr. Hyde* for some weeks: "to find a body, a vehicle for that strong sense of man's double being which must at times come in upon and overwhelm the mind of every thinking creature. For two days I went about racking my brains for a plot of any sort; and on the second night I dreamed the scene at the window, and a scene afterward split in two in which Hyde, pursued for some crime, took the powder and underwent the change in the presence of his pursuers. All the rest was made awake and consciously."[31] When Giuseppe Tartini was in the process of composing what had been considered his greatest work, he dreamed he had made a pact with the Devil. In return he heard the Devil "play a solo so singularly beautiful and executed with such superior taste and precision that it surpassed all that he had ever heard or conceived in his life."[32] The Devil's Trill was the outcome of Tartini's visual experience. Marie Jean de Condorcet succeeded in solving a complicated mathematical problem only after a dream. William Blake discovered the way to engrave his design after his dead brother, Robert, came to him in a dream and showed him the way. Emerson believed dreams revealed character: "Judge of your natural character by what you do in your dreams."

Great significance has been given to premonitory dreams throughout the centuries. Calpurnia, for example, had a vision of Julius Caesar's death. Several days before his murder, Abraham Lincoln described a dream in which he was walking through the White House and saw a coffin around which "soldiers were acting as guards; and there was a throng of people, some gazing mournfully upon the corpse, whose face was covered, others weeping pitifully. 'Who is dead in the White House?' I demanded of one of the soldiers. 'The President,' was his answer; 'he was killed by an assassin!' Then came a loud burst of grief from the crowd, which awoke me from my dream. I slept no more that night."[33]

Dream and Image will attempt an analysis and an evaluation of the mythical, psychological, and philosophical factors present in certain key dreams as narrated by French writers of the seventeenth, eighteenth, and nineteenth centuries.

Dreams of all types (premonitory, prodromal, anxiety, etc.) found their way into the creative works of seventeenth-century writers, such as Pauline's dream in Corneille's *Polyeucte,* Saint-Amant's in his *Visions,* and Tristan's nightmares in *Nocturnal Terrors.* Pascal was so moved by his dreams that he felt they could have been drawn from reality. La Fontaine poetized dream sequences in "Two Friends", in "The Vaux Dream," and in "The Dream of an Inhabitant from Mogulia."

My choice of seventeenth-century dreams was limited to those recounted by Descartes and Racine. Descartes interpreted his three dreams as mysterious and enigmatic signs of encouragement sent to him by God. So important did he believe these dreams to be that he vowed to go on a pilgrimage to Loreto on foot from Venice. The meditations that followed his dreams (Nov. 16 to March 20) are the basis upon which he constructed his mechanistic system, including his arguments against Fermat, Harvey, Pascal, and Gassendi. Athaliah's dream in Jean Racine's play makes us privy to three important factors, each of which sheds light not only on some of Racine's torments and those of his contemporaries, but also on problems that plague us today: the dangers involved in an excessive case of mother-daughter identification; the cruelties that may arise in a matriarchal society when interests center so excessively on material satisfactions; and, perhaps the most important question of all, the concept of good and evil in Judaism and Christianity.

To define the eighteenth century as the Age of Englightenment only is to neglect its estoeric side. To be sure, in *D'Alembert's Dream,* Diderot used the dream as an ideal formula to exploit scientific and philosophical ideas. Moreover, writers—and this certainly was true for many of the Encyclopedists—were interested in the dream as a kind of scientific phenomenon and tried to analyze its structure and mechanism. Formey's *Essay on Dreams* and Father Richard's *Theory of Dreams* are examples of such physiological studies. But even among the great rationalists, such as Voltaire, the dreamworld was considered of great import. It was purported that Voltaire dreamed a canto of his poem "The Henriade." Rousseau, of course, bathed in the waking dream or reverie, thus expanding his universe and paving the way for the emphasis on the unconscious during the centuries to come. For the Illuminists, a mystical group that flourished during the eighteenth century, the world of the dream and the occult took precedence to a great extent over the existential domain. Jacques Cazotte, for example, believed his own premonitory dreams, one of which rightly predicted his beheading during the French Revolution. He wrote his popular novel, *The Devil in Love*, after having dreamed its plot.

Dreams and images in the literary works of the nineteenth-century writers flourished. Emotion, sensitivity, and imagination became important values enabling the creative writer to communicate with cosmic spheres. Nodier longed to transcend the world of appearances and matter and withdraw into his own domain of fantasy and joy. He succeeded by way of the waking and sleeping dream. His short story *The Crumb Fairy* may be considered the literary expression of a prolonged reverie that introduced the new concept of "moon-man psychology."

Gérard de Nerval's *Voyage in the Orient*, which arose for the most part from his active fantasy life, included a reworking of the Queen of Sheba legend. He introduced a new character, Adoniram, into the events, the prototype of the innovator and artist. Adoniram epitomizes the suffering, the inner turmoil and anguish experienced by creative people from time immemorial as they attempt to fashion and give birth to the new (whether it be form or idea). It is the leap the artist must take from the Uncreated (the world in *potentia*) to the Created (a concretization of the amorphous content) that makes for both his excoriating pain as well as for his sense of achievement and fulfillment which follow. We learn why the great artist (always ahead of his time) can never be understood by his contemporaries and why he is to be a solitary and lonely figure.

Balzac's *Louis Lambert,* and the Swedenborgian credo outlined therein, serves as an illustration to explicate the fine dividing line that exists between the dream and the creative vision of the mystic and the ragings of the insane. What are the differences? the similarities? Does insanity imply an ability to commune more deeply with the forces of the unconscious? with the cosmos? What is the significance of religious visions as reported by mystics such as St. Theresa of Avila, St. John of the Cross, Meister Eckhart, Jakob Boehme, Moses de Leon, and the Mirkabah mystics? What are the dangers awaiting the thinking man who overemphasizes the intellect while minimizing the physical world?

The parapsychological experience narrated in Gautier's short story "Arria Marcella" reveals the author's fundamental conflict between the way of the ancient Greeks and Romans and the attitude of Christianity as it manifested itself in nineteenth-century France. Paganism emphasized terrestrial joys and the beauty of the human body; Christianity, on the other hand, stressed ascetic attitudes, earthly suffering, repentence for sin, and subjugation of natural instinct in order to win paradise in afterlife. Gautier's conflict became precise and linear in his subliminal realm.

In "Parisian Dream" Baudelaire attempted to heal the ferocious schism inhabiting him—which was eroding his very being. Baudelaire may be regarded as the living incarnation of the Dioscori; twin forces burgeoned within his depths and welded together only in the work of art. The phenomenological world bred antagonism—the poem transcended this duality.

Hugo experienced a religious crisis particularly during his years of exile. He lived in "the somber, gray, violent, terribly stormy, severe" world of reality and in a nocturnal regime. From his oneirosphere emerged a series of complex and intimate symbols—an entire cosmogonic system—which he incorporated in one of his great mystical poems, "What the Mouth of Darkness Says."

Huysmans, plagued with the continuous pull of demonic forces within him, portrayed them at war with each other in his novel *Down There*. Since the concept of Satan is archetypal, it stems from the collective unconscious and is, therefore, eternal and universal. Huysmans described this phenomenon in the masculine practice of Satanism and in its feminine counterpart, the Black Mass.

Rimbaud's prose poem "After the Flood" delineates a violent, hallucinatory, creative experience—an act that takes him from chaos to cosmos. "After the Flood" may be viewed as a psychodrama in which the poet stages his plunge into freedom. The water image used throughout the poem reveals his desperate need to participate in the *illo tempore*. The moon figure, an important protagonist in "After the Flood," is viewed as the Great Female Archetype who imposes her authority wherever she chooses. In Rimbaud's oneirosphere the moon is no longer considered the benevolent force that figures in Romantic poetry, but has become a destructive element in that she is a perpetrator of illusions, thus reducing the man who believes in her to a state of dependency.

Igitur is perhaps the most perfect example of how the creative artist tackles his own mythical depths and how he deals with the forces of Thanatos in a positive manner in terms of the creative process. *Igitur* is a dream-meditation that took Mallarmé into the ever-deepening folds of his unconscious—that area termed super consciousness where universal and eternal truths cohabit. It is from this limitless realm he created his hero Igitur and recounted the depersonalization process, the ego dismemberment that enabled him to emerge from a psychological death bearing his secret treasure—the complex revelations inherent in the poetic experience. Mallarmé thus linked the fruit of his labor with such eternal documents as the Bible, the Kabbalah, the I Ching, the Upanishads, the Sutras, and the alchemical tracts. His Dantesque journey opened the door to what mystics call that primordial point, where nothingness becomes something, the void is transformed into the creation—the one into the multiple.

The active relationship the creative individual establishes with his oneirosphere creates a dynamism that enables him to live comfortably, if he so chooses, in two worlds. Such an expanded universe may serve to enrich his experience, furnish him with the material for his literary or scientific work, and perhaps add a dimension to his existential existence—paving the way for a profounder understanding of himself and his fellow man.

NOTES

[1]Pierre Teilhard de Chardin, *Le Phénomène humain*, p. 26.

[2]Jean Brun, *Héraclite*, p. 153.

[3]Bertram D. Lewin, *Dreams and the Uses of Regression*, p. 47.

[4]M. Pongracz et Santner, *Les Rêves à travers les ages*, p. 16.

[5]*Ibid.*, p. 20.

[6]Norman MacKenzie, *Dreams and Dreaming*, p. 30.

[7]Pongrecz et Santner, p. 20.

[8]*Ibid.*, p. 37.

[9]*Ibid.*, p. 39.

[10]*Ibid.*, p. 74.

[11]*Ibid.*, p. 79.

[12]Richmond Lattimore, *The Odyssey of Homer*, chapt. 19, line 560.

[13]MacKenzie, p. 43.

[14]Pongracz et Santner, p. 49.

[15]*Ibid.*, p. 55.

[16]*Ibid.*, p. 58.

[17]*Ibid.*, p. 59.

[18]*The Works of Plato*, p. 347.

[19]Richard McKeon, *The Basic Works of Aristotle*, p. 623.

[20]MacKenzie, p. 49.

[21]Pongracz et Santner, p. 64.

[22]*Ibid.*, p. 67.

[23]*Ibid.*, p. 87.

[24]*The Teachings of Buddha*, p. 4.

[25]MacKenzie, p. 58.

[26]*Ibid.*

[27]*Ibid.*, p. 95.

[28]St. Augustine, *The Confessions*, p. 57.

[29]St. Thomas Aquinas, *Summa Theologiae*, p. 27.

[30]MacKenzie, p. 73.

[31]Brian Hill, *Such Stuff as Dreams*, p. 164.

[32]*Ibid.*, p. 45.

[33]*Ibid.*, p. 28.

SECTION I

THE SEVENTEENTH CENTURY

1. *René Descartes—"The Dreams Came From Above"*

2. *Jean Racine—Athaliah: The Premonitory Dream and The Prophetic Vision*

CHAPTER 1

René Descartes: "The Dreams Came From Above"

> *Descartes, the father of rationalism (and conse-*
> *quently the father of the Revolution) who recog-*
> *nized only the authority of reason.*
> *(Friedrich Nietzsche,* Beyond Good and Evil.*)*

René Descartes, the originator of analytical geometry, the proponent of methodical doubt, of rational ontology, and of deductive physics held reason to be the only valid God-given instrument capable of leading man to truth and to enlightenment. Descartes' influence on philosophical thought during the centuries to follow was fundamental: Malebranche, Spinoza, Leibniz, Kant, and movements such as Positivism, Scientism, Intellectualism. According to Nietzsche, Descartes' overemphasis on the power of the rational function in man (a continuation of the Stoic and Christian traditions with their concomitant denigration of the physical man) was an important factor leading to the bloody eruption known as the French Revolution.

It is ironic, indeed, that Descartes, the proponent of rationalism, should have received the "revelation" of his scientific and philosophical system from the irrational domain—the oneirosphere. He believed the three dreams he had on November 10, 1619, "came to him from above," that they were Godsent. The visual perceptions and intuitions disclosed in the dreams he considered basic to his future creative efforts. So grateful was he to God for having enabled him to experience these insights that he vowed to make a pilgrimage to Our Lady of Loreto, which, it is said, he carried out five years later.

Descartes was not the only mathematician or physicist to have been stimulated by sensory images emanating from the oneirosphere. Jules Henri Poincaré (1854-1912), who enlarged the field of physics by research on the theory of functions and distinguished himself in the field of astronomical theory of orbits, had been unable to find a solution to a mathematical problem. He succeeded in his endeavor after perceiving the image in his mind's eye, which he described as follows: "Most striking at first is this appearance of sudden illumination, a manifest sign of long, unconscious prior work. The role of this unconscious work in mathematical invention appears to me incontestable."[1]

Albert Einstein when questioned as to how he had come upon his most original concepts, answered that he did not think in words. "A thought comes, and I may try to express it in words afterwards." His concepts first appeared to him through "physical entities"—certain signs and more or less clear images he could produce and combine. These elements were "of visual and some of muscular type...words are applied in the secondary stage, when the mentioned associative play is sufficiently established and can be reproduced at will."[2]

1. Descartes' Philosophy

The Discourse on Method (1637), The Meditations (1641), The Principles of Philosophy (1644), and The Passions of the Soul (1649) are perhaps Descartes' most celebrated works.

As a scientist, Descartes broke with the medieval doctors who accepted Aristotle's dicta blindly and who adhered to the sclerotic syllogism to prove their propositions rather than trying "to search for something better."[3] Descartes likewise criticized the educational methods to which he had been exposed at La Flèche, which were popular throughout France at this period and which relied mainly upon memory and feeling. In The Discourse on Method he later confessed, "As soon as I reached an age which allowed me to emerge from the tutelage of my teachers, I abandoned the study of letters altogether."[4] Descartes declared: "I could not do better than to devote all my life to the cultivation of my reason, and to progress as much as possible in the knowledge of truth, following the method I had prescribed for myself."[5]

Descartes rejected the emphasis placed on the humanities in the schools. They are misleading since they are based on the senses. Science, conversely, is based on evidence. Descartes chose mathematics (arithmetic and geometry) as the highest form of scientific thought: for the clarity of ideas required to pursue the rigorous thought processes necessary to solve problems, for the part played by intuition and deductive reasoning. The sciences as a whole must be studied, he insisted, not as separate entities, but as facets of a unified whole. There is but one science. There is but one method.

Descartes set down four precepts he would use to direct and perfect his thinking faculties with regard to a practical rather than to a theoretical point of view.

> The first was never to accept anything as true that I did not know to be evidently so: that is to say, carefully to avoid precipitancy and prejudice, and to include in my judgments nothing more than what presented itself so clearly and so distinctly to my mind that I might have no occasion to place it in doubt.
>
> The second, to divide each of the difficulties that I was examining into as many parts as might be possible and necessary in order best to solve it.
>
> The third, to conduct my thoughts in an orderly way, beginning with the simplest objects and the easiest to know in order to climb gradually, as by degrees, as far as the knowledge of the most complex, and even supposing some order among those objects which do not precede each other naturally.
>
> And the last, everywhere to make such complete enumeration and such general reviews that I would be sure to have omitted nothing.[6]

And Descartes continued, "I have constructed a method which, I think, enables me gradually to increase my knowledge and to raise it little by little to the highest point which the mediocrity of my mind and the short span of my life will allow it to reach."[7]

Descartes' method expounded deductive or *a priori* reasoning. He set out to discover a truth so evident that it could not be reduced to a smaller part and yet could be proven with relative ease. His first step in creating his method was to doubt the existence of everything and anything. "I resolved to pretend that nothing which had ever entered my mind was any more true than the illusions of my dreams."[8]

Before long Descartes concluded that the one thing he could not doubt was the existence of doubt itself. Since doubt is the produce of thought, then thinking exists, and since this faculty is a reality, so is the thinking being.

> But immediately afterward I became aware that while I de-
> cided thus to think that everything was false, it followed nec-
> essarily that I who thought thus must be something.[9]

He then formulated his celebrated dictum: *Cogito, ergo sum*
("I think, therefore I am").

Descartes proceeded to use the ontological proof of the
existence of God, the same one used by St. Anselm in the eleventh century. Because man is a thinking substance and has
within him the concept of the perfect being, that perfect being,
which could only be God, exists. A perfect being would not
resort to deception since deceit would make Him imperfect.
God then is perfect, just, omniscient, and omnipotent.

> ...with the result that it remained that it must have been put
> into me by a being whose nature was truly more perfect than
> mine and which even had in itself all the perfections of which
> I could have any idea, that is to say, in a single word, which was
> God.[10]

If man had created himself, Descartes believed, and there was no
God, man would have made himself perfect. His very imperfec-
tion is proof of God's perfection.

Descartes' God guarantees cosmic and human order. He is
not capable of any error. "God, I say, who, being supremely
perfect, cannot be the cause of any error."[11] From where then
is error born if God is perfect and would neither want to hurt
nor mislead man? It is born from God's gift to man: free will.
Freedom permits man to choose the right path or the wrong
one. Righteousness is always placed within man's reach. When
man uses his thinking faculty improperly, he is prone to error,
but this fallibility does not stem from God.

> For, in truth, it is not an imperfection in God, that he has
> given the freedom to give my judgment, or to withold it, con-
> cerning things of which he has not put a clear and distinct
> knowledge into my understanding; but undoubtedly it is an
> imperfection in me that I do not use it well, and give my judg-
> ment rashly on things which I perceive only obscurely and
> confusedly.[12]

Descartes frequently brings up the subject of evil, or the *Malin Génie* (evil genius). According to Descartes, evil serves a methodological function. It has no metaphysical value, no substance, no reality. It is a creation of the intellect, stimulating the thinking process. It forces man to doubt, to question. Once man has solved the problem of the moment, evil (error or the *Malin Génie*) vanishes since its *raison d'être* has disappeared.[13]

Descartes' concept of evil is similar to the one enunciated by St. Augustine. Only good exists in the Christian Godhead according to the fourth century saint. God is therefore not the originator of evil. Evil is denied existence in a God-created world. It is not given substance and is looked upon as a *privatio boni*. In his *Argument Against the Manicheans and Marcionites*, St. Augustine writes: "EVIL THEREFORE IS NOTHING BUT THE PRIVATION OF GOOD. And thus it can have no existence anywhere except in some good thing... So there can be things which are good without any evil in them, such as God himself, and the higher celestial beings; but there can be no evil things without good." Evil is thus relegated to a "defect in good things" or to the figure of the Antichrist.[14] Descartes reinterpreted the opening passages of Genesis to suit Augustinian dicta.[15] When God separated light from darkness, Descartes wrote, "he separated the good from the bad angels: for one cannot separate a *privatio* from a real property... God is pure intelligence."[16]

In his *Treatise on the Passions of the Soul* he affirms that the soul and body, though separate entities, are linked via the pineal gland located at the base of the neck. This gland is very sensitive and can easily be swayed in favor of man's soul or animal nature. When Descartes refers to the soul, he implies the "thinking" (or reasoning) faculty since all that is outside of consciousness rests on the irrational and is therefore illusion.

Passions *per se* are neither good nor bad. Man must avoid excesses and divergences and can do so by calling upon his reason, like the Stoics, to direct his will. If the will is guided by reason, a higher morality will come into being and virtue will prevail.

...it suffices to judge well in order to act well, and to judge to

> the best of one's ability in order also to do one's best, that is to
> say, in order to acquire all the virtues and with them all the
> other goods one is capable of acquiring, and when one is sure
> that this situation exists, one cannot fail to be happy.[17]

If reason is faulty, instinct will prevail and lead directly to vice.

> ...the will being much more ample and extended than the
> understanding, I do not contain it within the same limits,
> but extend it also to things I do not understand, and the will
> being of itself indifferent to such things, very easily goes astray
> and chooses the bad instead of good, or the false instead of
> the true, which results in my falling into error or sinning.[18]

Passions revolve around the notion of free will. It is man's obligation to acquire power over them—through reason. Reason, the
product of consciousness, has moral force. It is interesting to
note that the French word *conscience* implies not only the
rational function (consciousness) but morality as well (conscience). In English, conversely, there are two words to express a
sense of morality as distinct from consciousness.

Descartes advocated the use of reason in dealing with all
aspects of life. The rational function, which is God-given, is the
only valid answer to the insurmountable question man confronts
during his terrestrial existence. By perfecting the mind, Descartes believed, man would be able to expand his knowledge,
eventually solving the riddles of nature and thereby conquering
it. Such were Descartes' optimistic views with regard to man's
abilities.

2. *The Dreams*

Descartes' original rendition of his dreams have been lost.
What is extant is their narration by his first biographer, the Abbé
Adrien Baillet, as published in *Olympica*. Many interpretations
of Descartes' dreams have been offered. Among them those of
Dr. Marie Louise von Franz, Dr. Bertram Lewin, Jacques Maritain, Georges Poulet, and Descartes' own explanations. Sigmund
Freud's brief statement on Descartes' dreams is to be found in a
letter he wrote in answer to Maxime Leroy's questionnaire on
the subject. The following interpretation, though drawn from

the views of the above-mentioned writers and psychiatrists, will be based mostly on the ideations of Dr. von Franz, who in the view of this author offers the most profound and complex analysis.

Descartes viewed his first two dreams as rather "menacing," as warnings aimed at his past activities which "though seemingly innocent before man were not so before God." The third dream he considered premonitory, dealing with his future that would be "very sweet and pleasant."[19]

Baillet describes Descartes' mental state before retiring on the night of November 10 as overwrought and extremely excited because on that very day he had discovered "the foundations of a marvelous science."[20] Baillet had even wondered whether Descartes had imbibed too much wine that evening since it was Martinmas, when the custom called for celebration. Descartes assured him that he had not had any wine for three months and "that the Genius which had excited his enthusiasm, to such an extent that he felt his own brain inflamed for several days, and predicted these dreams before he went to bed, and that the mind had played no part in them."[21]

Descartes' three dreams point to the fact that he was going through a psychological and/or intellectual crisis at the time which enabled him to experience in a most potent form the intuition of an *idée vitale* that led directly to his philosophical reforms.[22]

According to Georges Poulet, Descartes' "agitation" was so pronounced prior and throughout his dreams that Poulet labeled them prodromal: an indication of cyclothymia or a manic-depressive psychosis. Descartes, it seems, was prone to antithetical states: elation and depression which usually followed in rapid cycles.[23] The fact that Descartes was living in a foreign land at the time, as a virtual exile and far from his friends, had made him feel his solitude and his introversion that much more acutely.

Dr. Bertram Lewin likewise believes Descartes' dreams to be prodromal, the outcome or "psychic equivalent of a disturbance of the brain such as usually produces migrainous or convulsive symptoms."[24] He bases his assumption on the following ideas: the agitation and acute anxiety Descartes himself noted the days preceding the dream; the unusual "sensory and motor images that appeared in the dream," such as "his one-sided paralysis, his spinning around three or four times on his left foot, the feeling of staggering and being bent over...the sparkling light...inaugurated by the thunderclap."[25] The many sensations experienced, Lewin states, and the turmoil and anxiety inherent in the dream frequently accompnay creative efforts; the discovery of the new entails the destruction of conventional and established traditions.

Freud, although he felt that the dreamer's associations should be known for a valid and fruitful analysis to be given, nevertheless stated that the body in Descartes' dreams represented the phallus, that Descartes' "struggle," in Lewin's words, "to stand up straight symbolized an effort to overcome impotence, that the violent wind was a castration threat, and that the retreat to the college church signified a flight to a protective mother."[26] In his letter to Maxime Leroy, Freud wrote:

> Our philosopher's dreams are what are known as "dreams from above" (*Traüme von oben*). That is to say, they are formulations of ideas which could have been created just as well in a waking state as during the state of sleep, and which have derived their content only in certain parts from mental states at a comparatively deep level. That is why these dreams offer for the most part a content which has an abstract, poetic, or symbolic form.[27]

a. *The First Dream*

...he imagined himself walking in the *street*. He was terrified by the sight of *ghosts* to such an extent that he felt himself forced to bend over on his *left side* to reach his destination; he felt so weak on his *right side* that he could not hold himself up. He was *ashamed* of the manner in which he was walking and so made an effort to stand *erect*. As he did so, he felt seized by a violent *wind*, like a *whirlwind*, and began spinning around *three* or *four* times on his *left foot*. This, however, was not the most frightening part of the dream. He had difficulty dragging himself along and had the impression he was going to *fall* with each step. He noticed a college *courtyard* (with open

gates). He entered and found a retreat, a remedy to his distress.
He tried to reach the *church* and his first thought was to *pray*.
He realized he had just passed a *man* he had once known but
had not greeted. He wanted to turn back and remedy his *dis-
courtesy*. He was pushed back by the violence of the *wind*
which was blowing against the *church*. At this moment he saw
another man in the middle of the college courtyard who called
him by his name and spoke in a civil and cordial manner. He
said that if he were going to look for *Mr. N.* that he had something to give him. Mr. Descartes imagined it was a *melon* that
had been brought from some foreign land. What surprised him
even more was the fact that the other people in the courtyard,
who had gathered around this man to talk, *stood erect* and
firmly on their feet while he, though the wind which he had
thought strong enough to throw him over several times had
greatly diminished, was still bent over and walking unsteadily.
He awakened and felt a *pain* which made him fear that the evil
genius (spirit) was at work and wanted to seduce him. He
immediately turned on his right side (because he had fallen
asleep on his left side when he had the dream) so as to spare him
the misfortunes which might threaten him, punishing him for
his sins. He recognized these as being serious enough to attract
all the thunder from heaven onto his head; though until this
time he had, in the eyes of men, led an almost irreproachable
life. After cogitating on diverse questions concerning problems
of good and evil in life, he fell asleep again.

Descartes "imagined himself walking in the *street*." The
street represents the outside world, the collective. Introverted
and sedentary by nature, Descartes enjoyed spending his time
meditating in his room, probing his thoughts. Secretive and
solitary in his ways, this *chambriste,* now a stranger in a foreign
land, saw himself on the street compelled to deal with the world
of reality, with concrete and not theoretical values. It is no
wonder that he felt frightened and unprotected on the street—a
prey to all unknown forces.

The *ghosts* which terrified Descartes are, according to Dr.
von Franz, the "primordial form of the 'spirit,' an embodiment,
in other words of the autonomous image-creating activity of the
unconscious."[28] Just as primitive man is incapable of thinking
in abstract terms and experiences such notions as ghosts or
spirits, so the human psyche does at its most primitive level.

Civilized man prides himself on his ability to control frightening images or thoughts in his conscious life (in his daily existence), but not so in his unconscious sphere. He is, therefore, frequently tormented by them in his dreams. In that Descartes was so cerebrally inclined and forever identified with his "thinking function," his one-sided attitude was reflected in the compensatory imagery in his unconscious. Ghosts haunted Descartes because he could not interpret the exegesis of such forces which appeared and disappeared within his oneirosphere—nor could he control the emergence of such autonomous images, making matters much worse.

Ghosts are also frequently associated with the dead. Descartes' mother had died when he was an infant. The lack of maternal attention, the deprivation of the warmth and love so necessary to a growing child in addition to his father's remarriage, and his aloofness toward his son, may have been instrumental in stunting the feeling principle within Descartes. The sciences and the church were to replace the void within the young man and act as substitutes for the absent mother and the disinterested father. Descartes' letters to Father Mersenne at the time of Galileo's trial state categorically that "nevertheless, I would not for anything in the world support them against the Church's authority."[29] In his *Cogitationes Privatae*, Descartes writes: "Science is like a woman who is honored if she is humble and remains with her husband, but is vilified if she gives herself to many."[30]

The fright and insecurity Descartes may have been experiencing at this time in the existential domain may have conjured up these visions of ghosts. The Thirty Years' War (1618-1648) was raging and many feared it was going to lead to the demise of European civilization. The conflict between Protestants and Catholics was at the root of the dissension and must have created psychological equivalents within Descartes. War and conflagration are chaotic factors capable of destroying the logic of the well-ordered mechanistic universe Descartes had envisaged. Was his unconscious attempting to erode his belief in an all-supreme and stable God whose function it was to maintain the regularity of all physical laws of motion?[31]

Just as God acts in a stable and continuously logical manner, Descartes believed, so man, if his mind is properly equipped and his will guided by his reason, must likewise follow a well-defined pattern with regard to his life's course. But how then can one account for war? conflict? instability?—the unforseen? The ghosts which appear in his dream spontaneously may be looked upon as autonomous and acausal forces, and thereby capable of creating a disturbing imbalance within him, thus upsetting what he had heretofore considered an orderly and mechanistic scheme of things. It is no wonder that Descartes was terrified. Anything that was out of the ordinary, that appeared and disappeared without rhyme or reason, presented both a psychological and intellectual problem to him, shattering, to some extent, the very foundations of his beliefs. To avoid future disturbances, Descartes rejected in 1644 the premise of methodical doubt which he had advocated in 1637. In a letter to the translator of his *Principes* he wrote "Others should not doubt...they could in but a short time gather everything I have done, and introduce incertitude and doubt into my system of philosophy, from which I carefully tried to banish it."[32] Evidently, Descartes could not cope with the unpredictable, with chance, with conflict, and so he banished it from his system.

The image of the ghosts may be considered as symptoms of Descartes' own fears: the fact that life may not be a cause-and-effect situation, that the universe may not be continuously well regulated, and that man will not be able to dominate nature even though his mind may become that extraordinary tool envisaged by this seventeenth-century optimist. Chaos exists within the cosmos and within the human being—as does the unforseen, the unpredictable, and the acausal.

Descartes found himself "forced to *bend* over on his *left side*," and in so doing "felt so weak on his *right side* that he could not hold himself up." The *left side,* according to C. G. Jung, has been associated with the feeling principle, the unconscious, the heart, and therefore the feminine side.[33] Certain rabbinical commentaries suggest that Adam was man on his right side and woman on his left.[34] Because the irrational domain has been equated with the evil, dark forces of nature, the material side of life, it becomes *sinister* (sinistra). In the Middle Ages the left side was always equated with hell. For Descartes, everything which is not rational or cannot be explained logically presented a problem and, consequently became fearsom and embarrassing—perhaps frightening. The fact that Descartes felt himself swaying or bending over on his left side indicated a need on his part to come to grips with the irrational, the unknown and particularly the underdeveloped feminine and feeling side of his nature. His attitude toward women, discounting his relationship with the Dutch maidservant and the "squint-eyed" girl he had met when quite young, was cerebral, as attested to by Elisabeth Princess of Bohemia and Queen Christina of Sweden.

The *right side* represents the rational, the conscious, the spiritual sphere. Consequently, it is associated with the masculine and solar forces, with light, with everything that functions logically, and is directed by the thinking faculty. Why then should Descartes have felt such weakness on his right side? The unconscious seemed to be pulling him back to the irrational domain, to the acausal sphere, forcing him to pay attention to what had been cut off within him.[35]

The interplay of opposites in the imagery (left and right, light and dark, matter and spirit, the rational and instinctual, masculine and feminine) indicate an inner struggle being waged. The problem of dualism, that is, the reconciliation of apparently conflicting forces (body and mind, man and nature, God and man) with the Cartesian system, not only haunted Descartes but also posed some philosophical difficulties for him, his contemporaries, and his followers: Geulincz, Malebranche, Spinoza, Hobbes, etc. "Our perceptions are also of two sorts, the one caused by the soul [consciousness today], the other by the body."[36]

Descartes felt *ashamed* because he could not stand up straight. According to Maritain, Descartes' shame was a punishment for his hubris. He needed to be deflated. Descartes was convinced he had experienced the *idée vitale* of philosophical reform in a single intuition. To have been filled with such an inflated attitude at the age of twenty-three led to an overly secure and optimistic view of man's importance in the universe. Maritain does concede the fact that Descartes had been endowed with extraordinary "strength of intellectual concentration," with a "passion for truth," and "an uncommonly energetic will, an intrepid pride, coupled with a hyperbolic disdain for the past," which, he concluded, explained in part the "outrageous dogmatism which characterizes and compromises...modern metaphysics."[37] To believe that man is capable of discovering the secrets of the universe, to reduce the infinite to the finite would have unleashed the wrath of a Jupiter, a Zeus, or a Thor—any god. Descartes' sin was the sin of pride.

The violent *wind* that carried Descartes away "like a *whirlwind*" forced him to spin "around *three* or *four* times on his *left foot*." Descartes interpreted this wind as a manifestation of the "evil genius," or "evil spirit," that was pushing him forcefully where he wanted to go. As expressed in Genesis, Isaiah, St. Matthew, St. Paul, and other books in the Bible, wind or whirlwind represents the "divine spirit" which now threatened by its very force to throw Descartes to the ground. It is from the wind that Adam was given a soul; that Isaiah, Paul, and other prophets and disciples experienced the Godhead. The wind, *ruah* meaning breath or spirit in Hebrew, *pneuma* in Greek—represents a creative force, the uniting of the four elements (earth, air, fire, water), able to fecundate and generate what had been arid and divided prior to its coming.[38] Whirlwinds are frequently present in Creation myths. They announce the new, the conscious image about to emanate from the chaotic unconscious domain. The creation of an idea or of a theory may be so disturbing at times that the equilibrium of an individual may be upset, even that of a well-balanced person. Just as the ghosts in the first image represented an autonomous, uncontrollable force that terrified him, the whirlwind likewise stands for an upsurge of some new attitude or feeling within him.

Dr. Lewin sees the image of the whirlwind as a prefiguration of Descartes' concept of vortices. Let us recall that Descartes believed that matter filled space, and matter was made up of infinitely divisible particles; one particle could not move without forcing the others into motion. "This matter formed whirlpools in the skies, and it was because the planets were caught each in its own whirlpool that they were carried around like pieces of straw... Gravity itself was the result of these whirlpools of invisible matter, which had the effect of sucking things down toward their own center."[39]

Descartes was so upset (physically speaking) by the wind, so lacking in control over himself that he could not remain rooted to the ground, fixed, or stable. He felt he would fall at any moment. So intense were the sensations aroused by this image that Descartes may have used these very words from his

Discourse on Method: "But, like a man who walks alone, and in the dark, I resolved to go slowly, and to use such caution in all things that even if I went forward only very little, I would at least avoid falling."[40] The fear of falling may indicate a fear of contacting the earth, the physical or feminine world. It may also symbolize a present or oncoming illness as Poulet and Dr. Lewin believe, an indication or "psychic equivalent of a convulsive or migrainous attack."[41]

Descartes' unconscious seems to have grasped the problem of which his conscious mind was not yet aware. The wind, or spirit, was forcing him into another direction, outside the stable and well-worn path. The wind whirled him around, forcing him to look about. The force of this spirit could, however, eventually overwhelm him by its scope, vigor, and depth, that is, psychologically the onslaught of unconscious images and their concomitant sensations and energy might disorient him. Poulet points to a similar image with regard to changing one's course in *The Discourse on Method.*

> ...imitating in this travellers, who, finding themselves astray in some forest, must not wander, turning now this way now that, and even less stop in one place, but must walk always as straight as they can in a given direction, and not change direction for weak reasons.[42]

The fact that Descartes spins around on his left foot *three* or *four* times is also significant. Three, an odd number, is associated with an active, dynamic, masculine, and incomplete force. Three is the number of the Trinity, indicating a spiritual and religious attitude. In mathematics, three denotes a triangle, the solution of an opposing duality. In mystical terms it represents the manifestation and balancing out of conflicting forces. It is an important factor in medieval syllogistic reasoning indicating the three propositions (major, minor, conclusion) involved. The number four is complete, inactive, whole, and symbolizes the feminine, material, and terrestrial sphere. It is the number associated with the mandala, the four cardinal points, the four Evangelists, the four elements, and for the mystic the tetramorphs. Descartes' inability to distinguish between the numbers three and four may indicate, according to Dr. von Franz, another way of revealing a conflict between the spiritual and physical forces, the thinking and feeling functions within him.

Descartes saw the *college,* entered the open *courtyard,* and looked upon it as a *retreat,* a "remedy to his distress." He tried to make his way toward the *church* "and his first thought was to *pray."* The college may be assoicated with the Jesuit college of La Flèche where Descartes had spent his early years (1606-14) under the protection and guidance of Father Dinet and Father Charlet—his surrogate fathers. The college therefore represents the security and regularity of a God-protected universe. Conversely, this kind of order and conventional way, although they lend feelings of protection to individuals living in such an atmosphere, also spell rigidity. Dr. von Franz points to the fact that the storm is "blowing against the church", so it cannot be the wind that once "filled the early Church." The storm, then, did not begin within the church but rather outside of it.[43]   The Reformation and the storm of anger and bloodshed that had led to the Thirty Years' War and a sudden change in the Zeitgeist were likewise fomenting in Descartes' psyche.

The *church* in Descartes' dream is an ambivalent image. It may be looked upon either as a protective force (security, conventional ideology) or as an obstacle to the birth of new ideas emerging with the Reformation. Etienne Gilson is of the opinion that though Descartes respected and feared the Church, he was "much less interested in defending it than preoccupied with defending himself against it; he tried above everything else to conciliate himself with it...he never devoted himself to anything else except to its own cause."[44]   Descartes attributed the wind to the "evil genius" that was pushing him where he wanted to go willingly, that is, toward God, toward the originator of all movement in the universe. Dr. von Franz notes great confusion in the dream at this point: Is Descartes experiencing the creative force of God, since he wants to go toward Him, or is he referring to the evil spirit of the devil?   In that Descartes was thrust toward the church by the "evil genius" as well as "the spirit of God," the presence of both factors is herein indicated.[45]

Because Descartes could not accept the notion of evil as existing in substance in a God-created world, he was reducing God's infinitude to his own finite-rational realm. In a totality (or the uncreated, the unconscious) moral divisions such as between good and evil simply do not exist. A *complexio oppositorum* lives inchoate in the complete. Once the amorphous or the uncreated takes form, as in an idea, it enters the finite

world and man attaches a sense of morality to it. The problem
then of good and evil, as posited by St. Augustine, had not yet
been accepted by Descartes on an unconscious level.

He may have felt great uncertainty in trying to make a
tabula rasa of all previous knowledge and reduce everything
to his methodical doubt, as related in *The Discourse on Method.*
To overthrow the conventional metaphysical and scientific views
of the day, those taught him by the Jesuit fathers most particularly, could lead to his own incarceration and to emotional
penury. Descartes must have been in a quandary at this juncture:
he is prevented from reaching the church in the dream and,
therefore, in really dealing with the problem. A similar situation
was to occur later on in life in his existential world. Because of
Galileo's condemnation (1633) before the Inquisition for furthering the Copernican view that the earth revolved around the sun
and was not a stationary object and because he held similar
views, he stopped working on his major scientific work, *The
Treatise of the World.* In a letter to Father Mersenne he declared: "...I wanted to completely suppress the treatise I had
written, and lose nearly four years' work, to render complete
obeisance to the Church in its defense of the idea concerning
the movement of the earth."[46]   Although he withheld the
publication of his monumental work, three essays did emerge
from the *Treatise,* one of which was to become Descartes'
famous *Discourse on Method.*

As Descartes made his way toward the church, he noticed
a *man, Mr. N.* whom he used to know and whom he did not
greet. He felt he had acted in a discourteous manner and wanted
to turn back and greet him, but the violent wind prevented him
from doing so. *Another man* now appeared in the school courtyard. He knew Descartes and spoke to him in an obliging and
civil manner. He informed him that if he wanted to find Mr. N.
he had something for him. Descartes felt regret and remorse,
an acute sense of guilt at not having greeted Mr. N. Descartes
gives the reader no associations concerning Mr. N. and so no
identification is possible with either friend or acquaintance. This
man may represent the spirit of reform, something outside of
the Church and outside of the school, a person linked to Descartes' past and with whom he had maintained some kind (if not
cordial) relationship. He may, according to Dr. von Franz, represent an undeveloped aspect of Descartes' unconscious (his feeling

function).[47] The second man standing within the college quadrangle represents that aspect of Descartes which follows the conventional ways and the Catholic credo. The fact that he wants
Descartes to take something to Mr. N. indicates a desire to link
old and new, outer and inner together.

The *melon* image is complex. Descartes thought it "had
been brought from some foreign land." It stands, therefore, for
something emanating from a distant, perhaps exotic country.
He further describes it as representing "the charms of solitude,
but represented by purely human solicitations." Dr. Lewin
looks upon the melon as "sexual material."[48] Poulet considers it "a symbol within which a completely sensual and even
sexual reality is hidden... It represents natural enjoyment or
delight, the physical side of nature, the feminine, erotic, and
instinctual elements in life.[49] Dr. von Franz sees the melon
in a more spiritual light. An ancient fruit, the melon dates
back to biblical times, she writes. During the Exodus the Hebrews who lived in the desert for forty years longed for the
melon they had once eaten in Egypt. In the desert they would
be denied the pleasures of terrestrial existence.

> We remember the fish, which we did eat in Egypt freely; the
> cucumbers, and the melons, and the leeks, and the onions,
> and the garlic: (Numbers 11:5)

> But now our soul *is* dried away: *there* is nothing at all, beside
> this manna, *before* our eyes. (Numbers 11:6)

To forge ahead and to pave the way with new ideas requires suffering and deprivation.

Since melons are a watery fruit, they may be associated
with the primeval or uterine liquid, with the unconscious; with
the alchemist's *aqua permanens;* the *fons et origo* of all things.
A constantly changing, nonstable force before it acquires form
and rigidity, water is the element in which the uncreated resides.
It is a world *in potentia* awaiting form and concretization in the
creative act.

The seeds in the center of the melon imply the mystic
center, that area occupied by the Creator, who has become
manifest in the form of the seed. It is from the center that *all*

originates, the place from which every thought, every branch of the "tree of the world" or of "knowledge" is born and grows. Perhaps one of the most important associations made by Dr. von Franz is that of the melon used as ritual food by the electi in Manichaeism.[50] The Gnostic sect called Manichaeism was founded in the third century A.D. by a Persian, Mani. He was compelled by the Zoroastrians to leave his homeland and several years after his return was flayed to death. Mani adopted the dualism of Zoroastrianism (the force of light, Ahura Mazda, representing Good; that of Darkness, Ahriman, standing for Evil) and transformed it into a struggle between God, "Father of Greatness," and Light and Spirit as against Evil, "King of Darkness," Flesh and Matter. The Manichaeans borrowed their eschatological concepts from Christianity. Jesus became the god of revelation and represented light "mixed into matter," making him the primal man. It was He who compelled Adam to eat the apple. For this last concept, the Gnostics were accused by the Christians of putting Jesus on a par with the snake in paradise. The ethics of the Manichaeans were born from Buddhism. The *electi* (or perfect) were ascetics and adhered to the rules of celibacy and austerity, after which they were certain to know peace following their demise. The lower ranks, the *auditors* (or hearers) were given permission to marry but were asked to limit their sensual pleasures so they might hope to be reborn among the elect. Though Manichaeism died out as a faith around 500 A.D., it was reborn in certain sects: the Paulicians, the Bogomils, the Cathari, and Albigenses.[51]

The goal of Manichaeism was to prevent darkness from invading the world. The *electi*, therefore, were always concerned with saving and spreading "the germs of light" imprisoned in darkness. Such a view was also adopted by the Hebrew mystics of the sixteenth century. The great Cabalist Isaac Luria considered Adam Kadmon the primordial light, primordial man. The light flowing forth from his eyes after God created him was so great that it shattered the vessels in which he was contained, thereby liberating the light throughout the world. Much of this original light was lost in matter. Life's goal, then, was to redeem these sparks of light, return them to the Godhead, thereby retrieving all of His potentialities. The burden of restoration rested on man.

The Manichaeans considered plants, cucumbers, and melons

as containing large amounts of germs of light and the *electi* con-
sumed and stored within them as much light as possible. To eat
meat would be to hurt light in its manifested form and so the
Manichaeans were vegetarians.[52]   St. Augustine, whose works
Descartes knew well, had been a Manichaean early in his life.
When converted, however, he became their enemy since this
Gnostic sect, so popular at the time, became a serious threat
to the new religion.[53]   In *De Genesi Contra Manichaeos,* St.
Augustine mentions the melon as resembling the apple in paradise, which enabled man to have the choice of opting for good
or evil.   In this sense, Dr. von Franz points out, the melon
would represent "the cognitive experience of God."   It would
support Descartes' view that man must use his rational function
to choose between good and evil.   It also enables man to act
positively in storing up such good seeds as to win happiness in
this world and the next.

Dr. von Franz also underscores the fact that the melon
seed boiled in milk was used in medieval times to cure tuberculosis.   Descartes, who suffered from weak lungs throughout
his life and was to die from pneumonia, as his mother had of a
lung infection, might have been concerned about his own health
at this juncture.   The melon may also have stood for a kind of
microcosm, a "psychic totality," a compensating force for the
macrocosm that had fascinated Descartes for so many years and
that had come to fruition in his volume *The World,* which was
to remain unpubished.

That the man standing in the college quadrangle wanted
Descartes to take the melon to Mr. N. indicated a desire on his
part to unite what had been opposed: the Catholic (conventional, secure, rigid ways) with the spirit of reform and creativity,
and other opposing polarities within Descartes himself: spirit
and flesh, thinking and feeling. Thus the melon may be looked
upon as a *mediatrix* bringing together what had been severed.

When Descartes awakened, he felt weighted down, burdened
with pain, and suffering from the bad effects of the dream. He
prayed to God to protect him from punishment for his sins
despite the fact that he felt his life had been irreproachable at
least from the human point of view.

His sense of guilt and the physical pain the dream brought

on is known to heroes who bring forth the new, who break with tradition. Original thinkers when becoming conscious of their acts are not *sine peccato*. The notion of original sin, fundamental to Catholic doctrine and in which Descartes believed implicitly, added to his feelings of guilt. If he were to pursue his scientific work, he might be forced to alienate those trusted and loyal friends he had known throughout his life; the very ones who had brought him comfort during his early years at La Flèche. Or, perhaps he could reconcile the old—and the new? Descartes was at the crossroads.

b. *The Second Dream*

> He thought he heard a shrill and deafening noise which he took to be a clap of *thunder*. He was so terrified that he awakened. He opened his eyes and noticed *fiery sparks* throughout the room. He had experienced this phenomenon frequently in earlier days. It was not really extraordinary for him to awaken in the middle of the night and see the objects closest to him with clarity. But in this last experience he wanted to understand the philosophical reasons for what was occurring and by *opening and closing* his eyes alternately, he was able to observe the nature of the objects surrounding him and drew favorable and convincing conclusions. His fear then vanished and he fell back to sleep.

The shrill noise which Descartes identified as a *thunderclap* had so frightened him that he awakened. He interpreted the thunder as a manifestation of the "spirit of truth descending upon him" and possessing him. Thunder, the weapon of Zeus (Jupiter), Thor, the Hebrew and the Christian God, has immense power and dynamism. It is a violent and creative force.

The *fiery sparks* of light which Descartes saw in his room is a numinous image. Lightning an illuminating force, is an expression of cognition. It is a celestial indication of God's presence. When Moses was on Mt. Sinai, God made his presence known to him via thunder and lightning. In Revelation we read:

> And out of the throne proceeded lightning and thunderings and voice: and there were seven lamps of fire burning before the throne, which are the seven Spirits of God. (Rev: 4, 5)

Paul's conversion to Christianity was accompanied by "the impression of a dazzling light..." (Acts 9:3-5) Many saints claimed they saw light that they equated with God. For St. Hildegard, God was light: "...my soul has always beheld this light," she wrote in her *Revelations*. Jan van Ruysbroeck, the Flemish mystic, made a distinction between "Everlasting Light" that enabled man to see God and a sudden light "blazing down as it were a lightning flash from the Face of Divine Love."[54]

The image of light in Descartes' second dream may be likened to the melon seed in the first: the former representing a germ of light, the latter the eruption of a new idea. Fiery sparks, as Dr. von Franz points out, may be compared to Paracelsus' "idea of the *scintillae* or *oculi piscium* (fishes' eyes) when consciousness is as yet not a unity." These fiery sparks are to be considered "archetypes of the collective unconscious which must accordingly possess a certain inherent luminosity or autonomous latent element of consciousness."[55] Since light is energy, the impact of these sparks may be powerful as they were in the case of Descartes.

What is of great import with regard to the fire image is the fact that Descartes opened and closed his eyes. He was now intent upon observing "the nature of the objects" closest to him. Where fear once prevailed, light, in a mitigated form, dissipated his anguish. He used his dream—his eyes or the cognitive experience—to prevent himself from being blinded by the light. His rational approach to such phenomena would, hopefully, acclimate him to his new obligations and fresh concepts and attitude he must pursue. If he did not approach his problem from a rational point of view (in keeping with his personality), the strain and chaotic conditions within him would be too great and would overwhelm him. By opening and shutting his eyes, Descartes permitted the unconscious content revealed to him in the archetypal images (lightning, thunder, etc.) to sift into consciousness and thus enabled him to slowly integrate the knowledge he had experienced in his mind's eye.

The emergence of a new attitude or new idea is a powerful and terrifying experience, which Descartes felt most acutely in his unconscious. One must be heroic to fight convention and the *status quo,* and bring forth the unknown. Plato fought the Sophists, Kant the Sceptics and Empiricists, Comte the Subjectivists, Bergson the Objectivists, Kierkegaard fought Hegel, and Nietzsche fought the world. Descartes was to fight Fermat's theory of probabilities, Harvey and his concept of the heart as a pump, Pascal's statements concerning the void, Hobbes, Arnauld, and Gassendi.[56]

c. *The Third Dream*

A moment later he had a third dream which was not as frightful as the first two. In this last dream he found a *book* on the table but did not know who had placed it there. He opend it and realized it was a *dictionary*. He was delighted and hoped it would be of great use to him. Another book appeared right under his hand at this very moment, and just as unknown to him; nor did he know where it came from. It was an *Anthology* of Poems by different authors entitled *Corpus Poetarum,* etc. He was curious enough to want to read something in it and his eyes fell on the line *"Quod vitae sectabor iter?"* And this same moment he noticed a man he did not know but who presented him with a poem beginning *"Est et Non"* and told him it was an excellent work. Mr. D. said that he knew it and it was included in the *Idylls of Ausonius* in the large volume of poems on the table. He wanted to show it to this man and began to leaf through the volume, bragging that he knew the *order and arrangement* of everything in it. While he was looking for the poem, the man asked him where he had acquired the book. Mr. D. answered he could not tell him how he had gotten it but that a while back he had had yet another volume in his hand which had just disappeared, also without knowing who had brought it to him and who had taken it back. No sooner had he finished his statement than the book *reappeared* at the other end of the table. He realized now, however, that the dictionary was no longer complete, as it had been the first time he saw it. Nevertheless, he came to the poems of Ausonius in the Anthology of Poems which he had been leafing through but was unable to find the very beginning "Est et Non." He told the man that he knew another one by the same author which was even more beautiful and which began "Quod vitae sectabor iter? The person asked him to show it to him and Mr. D. began to look for it when he came upon some small *portraits engraved in copper,* which made him say that this book was very beautiful, but that the edition was different from the one he

knew. He reached this point when the book and the man
disappeared from his mind's eye without, nevertheless, awakening him.

The *dictionary* which appears on the table in a mysterious
way, Descartes claimed, represents the "summation of all knowledge."   It therefore symbolizes a cerebral, compartmentalized
accumulation of knowledge; it lists words and information in a
cold and objective manner. Descartes viewed the second volume,
the anthology of poems, *Corpus Poetarum,* as "philosophy and
wisdom joned together." In the prefatory letter to the translator
of his *Principia,* he defined philosophy as "the study of wisdom."[57]   The anthology represents what Plato himself had
banned in his *Republic:* the feeling function, always undervalued
in Descartes' case. Poetry (or the arts in general) stimulates and
arouses man's imagination, emotions, feelings, sensations, and
irrational world--also the divine aspect within. The soul lies
embedded in poetry. Descartes, so cerebral, so rational, looked
upon this anthology with "enthusiasm" and as a kind of "revelation."[58] The volume of poems points to the fact that one must
not shut the door to enthusiasm or to emotion, otherwise life
becomes a dry and arid series of days.

Dr. von Franz relates the strange appearance and disappearance of the dictionary and the anthology of poems to the ghost
image of the first dream. It is the emergence, she contends,
of some autonomous complex within Descartes' unconscious,
underscoring his need to relegate all in the universe to the rational function, to grasp everything intellectually. The unconscious
points to the impossibility of such a goal. The appearance and
disappearance of the two volumes is like a feat of magic. The
emphasis, therefore, is placed on the inexplicable, the acausal.
The opposition within Descartes is brought out admirably in
the polarity of images: thinking (dictionary) and feeling (poems).
His basic dualistic concepts could possibly be solved by the stress
he placed on God as the primal cause of everything rejecting evil
as a reality: the originator of an orderly universe, the creator
of innate ideas within man, enabling him to be a thinking object
conscious of himself.[59]

The mysterious appearance and disappearance of the
volumes opens up the question of illusion and reality for Descartes. In *The Discourse on Method* he is still uncertain as to

how to distinguish the two. In his analysis of his dream he is convinced of its authenticity and believes most fervently that it was godsent and therefore a reality. In *Cogitationes Privatae,* however, he considers the dream as having been sent by an "evil spirit" which he labels as a positive force since it prodded him to think more acutely, and since evil has no substance or reality, but a *privatio boni,* no harm can be done.[60]

"Quod vitae sectabor iter?" ("What will my path be in life?") is the name of the first "Idyll" written by the Gallic poet Ausonius, a fourth-century skeptic who had been converted to Christianity not for any lofty reasons but in a pedestrian manner. This "Idyll" deals with a man who is not only tired of the frustrations, anxieties, disappointments, and pain life has brought him, but who is also an exile in his own land and sees the world crumbling before him, destruction and evil raging. Ausonius, tired of the turmoil, is opposed to life and longs for death.

The tumult and anxiety inherent in the poem are perhaps those very feelings Descartes experienced in mitigated form at this time. Let us recall that he was far from home, that a war was raging which threatened to upset the *status quo* in Europe, that his creative genius was breaking through and "descending" upon him. It is no wonder that thought of Ausonius' poem, "What will my path be in life?", came to Descartes in his dream. He was asking himself this very question, arousing doubt, fear, and insecurity within himself. It is simpler to follow the well-worn path than to forge one's own. The choice Descartes would be forced to make might be associated to the two men of the first dream: Mr. N. and the other man standing in the school quadrangle. Which of the two *ways* would Descartes choose? Or would he reconcile the conflict in forces via the melon to be given to Mr. N. by the second man?

Descartes then tells us that he noticed a man he did not know who handed him a poem beginning "Est et Non," praising its excellence. Descartes interprets it in the Pythagorean manner: the distinction to be made between "truth and error in human knowledge and in the profane sciences." "Yes" and "No," words used since the beginning of history, are divisive; they force a choice upon man; they are the source of war and conflict of both a personal and collective nature. Man's life revolves

around these two words. Some prefer to remain silent and not
venture an opinion because if they do, it will give rise to opposing statements, suscitating discussion, and conflict. Descartes informed the man that "Est et Non" was included in
Corpus Poetarum in the Idylls of Ausonius. Descartes wanted to
show it to him and began leafing through the volume, bragging
about his perfect knowledge of the "order and arrangement"
of the book, but he could not find the poem. The man asked
him where the book came from; Descartes did not know.

The stranger (similar to the two men of the first dream)
raises questions and ushers in a mood of uncertainty. He is
doubt. Like Satan, he attempts to force Descartes to decide, to
take a stand. When he asks Descartes where the book came
from and the answer is not forthcoming, he is in effect trying
to shake the scientist's faith in the validity and power of man's
knowledge. He is opening the way for the acausal element to
function. "Est et Non" implies the duality of all that is manifest.
Without light there is no darkness, without good no evil, without
truth no error, without reality no illusion, without the created
no uncreated, etc. If duality does not exist, there is no totality
(in God), and the universe becomes a lopsided entity.

To attempt to affirm everything positively (rationally)
when all is given to flux, is to suffer from the sin of pride. Descartes, who believed that if reason prevailed, man's knowledge
and therefore his power over nature would increase indefinitely,
seemed to imply that man eventually would be God. He de-
plored theologicans who derogated others because of their
views, who aroused divisiveness and controversies, engendering
heresies in this manner. With regard to the concept of good and
evil, he settled that once and for all for himself by denying the
reality of evil, thus troubling Catholic theologians throughout
the centuries. Descartes sought harmony and not conflict.
"Est et Non" ends in silence rather than in divisiveness. He
avoided struggle in the existential domain as a result of the insecurity he had experienced as a child by the absence of a mother
and the coldness of a father.

Telling the stranger that he knows "the order and arrangement" in the volume of poems but is unable to find the poem in
question is another example of Descartes overevaluation of the
rational domain. The unconscious is the stranger spreading

doubt and uncertainty. The dictionary which now reappears is incomplete; the mystery of the volume's origin points to the gap in human knowledge. Nothing is clearcut or simple in the cosmos. Nothing but the infinite controls life and nature. Chance works into everything. There are no definitive answers only approximations. All is theoretical, relative. Man in his finiteness cannot hope to equate himself with the infinite. To do so is to fall victim to an inflated ego.

Unable to find "Quod vitae sectabor iter?" Descartes comes upon some beautiful "*portraits* engraved in copper." These represent personal visualizations and no longer abstract notions. Portraits, like poems, are the work of artists, the product of the feeling function, imagination, sensitivity, and inspiration. He attributes the image of the portraits to the visit of an Italian painter he was expecting the following day.

There is, then, a marked shift from unity in the first dream to plurality in the second and third as attested to by the sparks and the portraits.[61] Choice or conflict, therefore, indicates a bursting of what had once been whole, at least in the unconscious domain. The Christian thesis of "the unity of consciousness and will," Dr. von Franz writes, adhered to by the Jesuits, is no longer a reality for Descartes on the unconscious level.[62] But he did not take to heart the split revealed to him by his unconscious in the form of a plurality of images; he opted for the easier way out—the one-sided rational function.

3. *The Overevaluation of the Rational Function*

Descartes' influence brought about an intellectual and spiritual revolution. He established a method by which objective analysis, synthesis, deductive reasoning, and intuition would be able to extend man's knowledge and make vast complexes of relationships comprehensible. He stimulated in man a desire for truth, inquiry, stability, and progress. Rejecting tradition and authority (except in the domain of faith), Descartes was convinced that reason would one day control all things and the ideal would become real; science would control nature. Many greats to follow echoed Cartesian dicta: for example, Turgot furthered the idea that the "whole human race moves slowly forward";[63] Condorcet suggested that knowledge was the answer to happiness and virtue and ultimately man would experience a state of perfection on earth. The march of Reason and Science was on; they became man's new religion.

As in centuries earlier with Plato, reason was again looked upon as the divine part of man. Instinct, on the other hand, the animal within man, was considered a separate entity that should be controlled, minimized, repudiated if possible.[64] The very duality Descartes had sought to obliterate in his philosophical and scientific credo he served to foment. The split between reason and the irrational in man grew, leading to the painful dichotomy so apparent in the twentieth-century world. As Arthur Koestler writes:

> As modern physics started with the Newtonian revolution, so modern philosophy starts with what one might call the Cartesian Catastrophe. The catastrophe consisted in the splitting up of the world into the realms of matter and mind, and the identification of "mind" with conscious thinking. The result of this identification was the shallow rationalism of *l'esprit cartésian,* and an impoverishment of psychology which it took three centuries to remedy even in part.[65]

Descartes' dreams pointed up the positive aspects of his philosophy as well as its inadequacies and contradictions, namely its complete emphasis on the rational function and its denigration of instinctuality. Man thus became a thinking process and his body is of little or no importance, a mechanism which must be controlled, a kind of automation or robut.

When Nietzsche wrote that Descartes "was the father of rationalism" and consequently the ("Father of the Revolution"),[66] he saw into Descartes' problem and the dangers confronting contemporary society. Cartesianism taught control over passion and desire, detachment from the external world. Emotions, though not evil, always had to be directed into proper channels by cognitive means (logos); progress (ethical, scientific, etc.) was a matter of reason and knowledge; virtue and morality were questions of will. What are the psychological ramifications of such a view? Cartesianism, so ego-centered, is based on the pride of knowledge, on man's cognitive process—on man's perpetual aggrandisement over the rest of nature. It is an abstract system that goes contrary to nature in that it disregards human frailties. The cognitive view of life advocated by Descartes does not take into account man's instinctual world, which is part of the *whole* of man. As the dream clearly demonstrates, Descartes' attempt to suppress his feelings (which he considered inferior), to starve them out, resulted in the emergence of the irrational within him: the appearance and disappearance of the autonomous and thus fearsome forces: ghosts, thunder, lightning, etc. What could not be understood reasonably, injected uncertainity and chaos in his heart. What he did not take into consideration was the fact that when the arcane realm is properly tended to (understood, illuminated and accepted), it acts in harmony with man's cognitive side. When kept in the dark or unattended, it craves for what rightfully belongs to it and may become virulent and destructive. To suppress what has been called the animal in the human being is tantamount to starving him. As a result, the animal within him rages, hungers and loses control, destroying all balance within his personality and, on a collective level, in his land and even in the world.

Descartes' audacity in furthering the power of reason, his desire to do away with "uncertainty" and "disorder",[67] two factors that are antithetical to his nature—aroused in man a quest for the impossible: the perfection of the cognitive process that would eventually lead man to dominate nature. Maritain suggested that for Descartes reason had become a kind of Demiurge;[68] for Koyré, Descartes' ideology prefigured the concept of "man master of the world."[69]

Today, however, with two world wars under his belt, man has, hopefully, become a little more humble. No longer can he iterate Wagner's credo as stated in Goethe's *Faust:* "Though I know much, I seek to know all!"

NOTES

[1]Henri Poincaré, *The Foundations of Science,* p. 389.

[2]New York *Times,* September 9, 1973.

[3]Henri Gouhier, *Descartes,* p. 254.

[4]Charles Adam, *Vie et oeuvres de Descartes* (Paris: J. Vrin XII, 1957) p. 20. Descartes was born in La Haye (Touraine) on March 31, 1596. His father, Joachim des Cartes, was councilor at the *parlement* of Rennes. His mother, physically weak and plagued with a cough, died shortly after giving birth to her fifth child. Only three of the five children survived. Descartes was brought up by his maternal grandmother. His father remarried when Descartes was approximately four years old. They had little in common and the relationship was never a close one. In 1606 Descartes was sent to the well-known Jesuit College of La Flèche in Anjou. He had inherited his mother's pulmonary weakness and was perpetually ailing; therefore, he spent many hours of the day in bed. In fact, he was called le *chambriste* by his schoolmates. Father Etienne Charlet, who was "like a second father to him," and Father Dinet allowed Descartes to indulge his meditative and solitary bent. After completing his studies at La Flèche (1614, an approximate date), Descartes spent two years studying law and passed his exams at Poitiers, earning a degree in civil and canon law. He then went to Paris; traveled to Holland, attracted to that land as were many young Frenchmen at the time, impressed with the military glory of Maurice de Nassau who, though Protestant, had become France's ally against the Spanish domination of the area. It was during the siege of Breda (1618) that Descartes met the well-known thirty-year-old doctor, physicist, and mathematician Sir Isask Beeckmann, later to become head of the College of Dordrecht. They held stimulating conversations together revolving around the sciences and physics which, according to Descartes, "awakened him" from his torpor.

Some months later Descartes went to Frankfurt to attend the coronation of Ferdinand II of Austria. He then moved to Ulm where he spent the winter "dans un poêle," (as he described his comfortably warm room room) in the company of his own thoughts. It was here that Descartes experienced his three dreams which led him to discover "the fundamentals of an admirable science," instrumental in the formulation of his future thought. It has been posited that in 1619 Descartes came into contact with Johannes Faulhaber, a Rosicrucian and mathematician who delved into the metaphysics of sacred numbers, including those mentioned in such biblical books as Daniel and the Apocalypse. Faulhaber's approach to science and mathematics must have played an important part in arousing Descartes' own thought processes and in creating within the young Frenchman's mind a state of "intellectual overexcitement" during the days preceding his dreams, suggested Jacques Maritain. Descartes must also have been familiar, writes Dr. von Franz, with the works of the great alchemists: Raimundus Lullus, Agrippa von Nettesheim, and Athanasius Kircher.

In the early 1620's Descartes traveled to Bohemia in northern Germany, Holland, and Switzerland, and went on the pilgrimage to Our Lady of Loretto near Venice. From 1626 to 1628 he spent his time in Paris leading the life of a gentleman, perfecting himself in music, enjoying the excitement of gambling, and even winning a duel in which he spared the life of his enemy. He came into contact with the astronomer-astrologist J-B. Morin and the mathematician Claude Mydorge, among other well-known scientifically oriented people of the time. In 1628 Descartes returned to Dordrecht where he decided to devote his time to philosophy and to "the study of his inner being." In 1632 he had a liaison with a Dutch servant girl and became the father of a daughter, Francine, who died five years later.

Descartes' philosophical ideas created a potentially dangerous situation for him during his stay in Holland. Castigated by Dutch theologians, fearful because of Galileo's condemnation which shook the scientific world, he changed residences rather frequently trying to keep out of the grasp of the law. He wrote to his friend Father Mersenne to keep his whereabouts secret. Descartes was intent upon "living in peace and continuing the life he had begun, taking for his motto: *bene vixit, bene latuit.*"

Jacques Maritain believed that Descartes revealed his timorous nature when he renounced publication of *The Treatise of the World,* his major scientific work. Even Bossuet, Maritain continued, noted Descartes' lack of courage. To Father Charlet, with whom Descartes had retained friendly relations, he wrote: "I know they believed my opinions to be new, and yet one will see that I used no principle which had not been held by Aristotle and by all those who have ever worked in philosophy."

In 1649 Descartes was invited by the twenty-year-old Queen Christina of Sweden, a highly dynamic and forceful young woman, to move to Stockholm. He hesitated at first, then accepted. The queen, rather bizarre in her habits, demanded that the philosopher arrive at her palace to begin his instruction at five in the morning. He contracted pneumonia and died on February 11, 1650.

See Charles Adam and Paul Tannery, *Oeuvres de Descartes.*
See René Descartes, *Oeuvres et lettres.*

[5]René Descartes, *Discourse on Method and the Meditations,* p. 48.

[6]*Ibid.,* p. 41.

[7]*Ibid.,* p. 28.

[8]*Ibid.,* p. 53.
The latter statement is ironic in view of the importance he placed on his dreams.

[9]*Ibid.,* p. 53.

[10]*Ibid.,* p. 55.

[11]*Ibid.,* p. 141.

[12]*Ibid.,* p. 140.

[13]Gouhier, p. 156.

[14]C. G. Jung, *Aion,* pp. 50-51.

[15]The question of nonexistent evil has given rise to the concept of the Antichrist, the powerful nature of the Devil, Satanism, etc. Conversely, the Hebrew Godhead represents a totality: both good and evil reside in Him inchoate. To reduce the infinite, which is God, to the finite concept of good and evil (which exists only in the mind of man and is a relative question) was anathema to the Hebrews. God's attributes are included in Exodus:

> "And the Lord passed by before him, and proclaimed, The Lord God, merciful and gracious, long suffering, and abundant in goodness and truth." (34:6)

> "Keeping mercy for thousands, forgiving iniquity and transgres-

sion and sin, and that will by no means clear the guilty; visiting the iniquity of the fathers upon the children, and upon the children, unto the third and to the fourth generation." (34:7)

[16]Foucher de Careil, *Oeuvres inédites de Descartes* I, p. 15.

[17]*Discourse on Method*, p. 49.

[18]*Ibid.*, p. 57.

[19]Charles Adam and Paul Tannery, *Oeuvres de Descartes X*, p. 185.

[20]*Ibid.*, p. 181.

[21]*Ibid.*, p. 186.

[22]Jacques Maritain, *Le Songe de Descartes*, p. 25.

[23]Georges Poulet, *Etudes sur le temps humain*, p. 18.

[24]Bertram D. Lewin, *Dream and the Uses of Regression*, p. 39.

[25]*Ibid.*, p. 39.

[26]*Ibid.*, p. 27.

[27]Sigmund Freud, *Standard Edition of the Complete Works*, XXI, p. 203.

[28]Marie Louise von Franz, *Timeless Documents of the Soul*, "The Dream of Descartes," p. 79.

[29]René Descartes, *Oeuvres et lettres*, p. 950.

[30]*Oeuvres inédites de Descartes*, p. 5.

[31]See *Méditations* VI and *Principia* II.

[32]*Oeuvres et lettres*, p. 569

[33]C. G. Jung, *Psychology and Alchemy*, p. 121.

[34]*Dictionnaire des symboles*, p. 215.

[35]Franz, p. 89.

[36]Leonora Cohen Rosenfield, *From Beast-Machine to Man-Machine*, p. 18.

[37]Maritain, pp. 25-6.

[38]*Dictionnaire des symboles*, p. 155.

[39]Lewin, p. 51.
   (He is quoting from Herbert Butterfield, *The Origins of Modern Science*)
   (London: G. Bell and Sons.) p. 51.)

[40]*Discourse on Method*, p. 39.

[41]Lewin, p. 40.

[42]*Discourse on Method*, p. 46.

[43]Franz, p. 94.

[44]Maritain, p. 91.

[45]A-T. X, p. 185.

[46]*Oeuvres et lettres*, p. 949 (February 1634).

[47]Franz, p. 95.

[48]Lewin, p. 38.

[49]Poulet, p. 31.

[50]Franz, p. 104.

[51]Hans Jonas, *The Gnostic Religion*, pp. 206-236.

[52]*Ibid.*, p. 231.

[53]Manichaeism as pratised by the Cathars was still considered a threat to
   Catholic power in the Middle Ages. The Catholic Church sent expedi-
   tionary forces to the south of France to exterminate them. In 1209
   Pope Innocent III ordered a crusade against the Albigenses and the well-
   known warrior Simon de Montfort led the crusade, killing, pillaging, and

destroying entire areas.

[54]Evelyn Underhill, *The Mystics of the Church*, p. 76.

[55]Franz, p. 120.

[56]Roger Lefèvre, *La Pensée de Descartes,* pp. 14-17.

[57]*Oeuvres et lettres*, p. 557.

[58]A-T. X, p. 218.

[59]Franz, p. 124.

[60]A-T. X, p. 218.

[61]Poulet, p. 38 and Franz, p. 134.

[62]Franz, p. 133.

[63]Kingsley Martin, *French Liberal Thought in the Eighteenth Century,* p. 285.

[64]William Barret, *Irrational Man*, p. 83.

[65]Arthur Koestler, *The Act of Creation*, p. 148.

[66]Friedrich Nietzsche, *The Philosophy of Nietzsche*, p. 102.

[67]Alexandre Koyré, *Entretiens sur Descartes*, p. 33.

[68]Maritain, p. 137.

[69]Koyré, p. 21.

For further readings on Descartes consult the following works:

Boorsch, Jean, *Etat présent des études sur Descartes* (Paris: Les Belles Lettres, 1937).

Balz, Albert, *Descartes and the Modern Mind* (New Haven: Yale University Press, 1952).

Edelman, Nathan, *The Eye of the Beholder* (Baltimore: The Johns Hopkins University Press, 1974).

Gilson, Etienne, *Etudes sur le rôle de la pensée médiévale dans la formation du système cartésien* (Paris: J. Vrin, 1951).

Keeling, S. V. *Descartes* (Oxford: Oxford University Press, 1968).

Laporte, Jean, *Le Rationalisme de Descartes* (Paris: Presses Universitaires de France, 1945).

Lewis, Geneviève, *Le Probleme de l'inconscient et le cartésianisme* (Paris: Presses Universitaires de France, 1951).

Papon, Maurice, *Vers un nouveau Discours de la Méthode* (Paris: Fayard, 1965).

CHAPTER 2

*Jean Racine—Athaliah: The Premonitory Dream
and the Prophetic Vision*

*Nature loves to hide herself.
(Heraclitus)*

A dream and a prophetic vision are dramatized in Jean Racine's play *Athaliah.*[1] These visual experiences do not emanate strictly speaking from the author's oneirosphere as was the case with Descartes' three dreams. They are, rather, literary devices around which Racine centered his play. Yet, his very choice of the two numinous experiences involved indicates a projection of his own unconscious contents onto the characters he chose to portray.

Three themes are brought into focus in the dream and the prorphetic vision: the dangers involved in a mother-daughter identification situation; the struggle waged between patriarchal and matriarchal forces in a religious and social situation; and the emergence of the child image, a symbol for the growth and evolution of the creative element within a being or group.

1. *Athaliah: Sources and Plot*

Racine's immediate source for *Athaliah* was the Bible: II Kings (11) and II Chronicles (22, 23).[2] Athaliah was the daughter of Ahab and Jezebel and mother of Ahaziah. Jezebel, renowned for her cruelties, deceits, and persecution of the Prophets, had introduced the worship of Baal to the kingdom of Israel and had a temple constructed to his worship in Jerusalem. After her husband's death, Jehu became king of Israel. Although she tried to seduce him, he would not stand for her evil ways and had her thrown out of a window, trampled on by horses, and her carcass eaten by dogs. Athaliah, her daughter, married Joram, king of Judah. She continued the worship of Baal and persuaded her husband to follow in her idolatrous ways. Destiny reserved a severe fate for both: all their children except Ahaziah were killed by the Arabs and Philistines, whereas Joram died of an excruciating malady. After Ahaziah reigned for one year, he decided to visit Jehu and was killed by Jehu's order. When Athaliah learned of the massacre, she usurped Jehu's throne and then had all the progeny (forty-two children) of the

House of David exterminated.

> And when Athaliah the mother of Ahazia saw that her son was dead, she arose and destroyed all the seed royal. (II Kings, 11)

Jehoshebath, Ahaziah's sister, and daughter of Joram by another woman, noticed little Jehoash still breathing. She took him and brought him to her husband, Jehoiada, the High Priest of the Hebrews, who hid him in the Temple where he was brought up in secrecy.

Racine's play begins at this point. It takes place in the Temple in Jerusalem.

Act I. Abner, one of the officers of the kingdom of Judah, comes to see Jehoiada, who deplores the worship of Baal in his land but is confident of God's power. When alone with his wife, Jehoshebath, he tells her that the moment for action has now arrived. The identity of Jehoash, legitimate king of Judah, whom they have brought up in the Temple under the name of Aliacin, must be revealed. Jehoshebath, however, fears for the young lad's life.

Act II. Zachariah, Jehoiada's son, rushes onto the scene terrorized. Athaliah has entered the Temple and has seen Aliacin. She is shocked by this encounter. Athaliah explains the reasons for her consternation to faithful Mattan, Grand Priest of Baal. She has had a dream in which the very child she now sees in the Temple had stabbed her. She insists upon discovering the identity of this boy. She questions him and is touched and moved by his simple and straightforward answers. She asks him to come to the palace and live there, offering him wealth and pleasures. He, however, refuses and Athaliah is angered.

Act III. Mattan, who has prodded Athaliah to demand the child from Jehoiada, arrives at the Temple. He is certain that Jehoiada will refuse to deliver the child, thereby giving Mattan an excuse to destroy the Temple and annihilate the Jews, leaving him spiritual ruler of Judah. Jehoiada is aware of the critical situation. He has the Temple doors closed. Suddenly, the Divine spirit flows into him. He has a prophetic vision in which he sees clearly the fate of the Hebrews, a disastrous future followed by a glorious renaissance.

Act IV. The great ceremony takes place: Jehoash is told of his true identity and is annointed king. Just as Jehoash promises to remain faithful to Hebraic law and tradition, a young Levite announces the arrival of Athaliah and her army. Jehoiada orders resistance. He invites the chorus to prayer.

Act V. Zachariah relates the details of Jehoash's coronation. Athaliah comes to the Temple. She demands both Jehoash and King David's treasure which, it has been said, is hidden in the Temple. Jehoiada feigns compliance. After Athaliah has entered, Jehoiada pulls back the curtains and reveals Jehoash sitting on the throne. Moments later Athaliah finds herself surrounded by an army of Levites. The proclamation of Jehoash as King, we are told, has led to the dispersal of the queen's army and the strangulation of Mattan. Athaliah, powerless, curses Jehoash and is dragged from the Temple and put to death.

2. *A Case in Mother-Daughter Identification*

Athaliah is a *vagina dentata* type: authoritarian, domineering, cruel, amoral, power-hungry. She is a woman who is guided by affects and clearly not by reason. She functions on the most primitive of levels. Uncontrolled, opinionated, unable to discern the meaning of "moral judgment,"[3] she seeks to destroy everything in the way of her path to power. The tension and consequently the fire that is generated by her turmoil and her constant battle with events and people are the heart of the drama.

Athaliah's bloodthirstiness is the outcome of an excruiating pain experienced long before the outset of the drama, the murder of her son Ahaziah. Unable to bear this loss, she went wild with fury, like a maimed animal hurt, she turned to revenge and had David's offsprings murdered. A solitary figure now, she tries to fill the void in her heart through an insatiable power lust. As a consequence, the feeling value or love principle (Eros) within her personality has become so repressed as to be virtually nonexistent. A power-driven female is usually divested of individual "womanly" characteristics and, as a result, is transformed into a collective mythical figure. In Athaliah's case she becomes a tyrannical queen.

In no way does Athaliah resemble the warm, tender, mourning mother bereft of her sons (Andromache, Hecuba); rather, she is the prototype of a raging demoniacal murderess, Medea in a way but more like Lilith, Adam's first wife according to the Talmud, or Lamia, the night spirit or "evil demon" of Greek religion. The Lilith-Lamia types, along with their sisters, the Sphinx, Gaia, Sheba, and Delilah, are all death-dealing, elemental figures and are classified as Terrible Mother archetypes.

Athaliah's crimes are just as blatant and artful as those of her prototypes, perhaps even more dangerous. In addition to her fiercely vicious acts and her homicidal mania, her offenses take on mythic proportions because they are also of a metaphysical or religious nature. Her actions represent, symbolically, a death struggle between two universal principles: Yahweh's patriarchal, monistic, and spiritual religion and Baal's matriarchal, polytheistic, and materialistic view of life. Athaliah in effect continued the worship of Baal that her mother, Jezebel, had first introduced into Israel, sitting up her own priesthood with its "shameful mysteries," defying Yahweh and ever prepared to attack Him and His sanctuary, the Temple. Removed from the personal level, Athaliah's fight assumed cosmic proportions; mystery, fright, and the supernatural pulsated within every area of her activities.

As a mythical figure, Athaliah can be looked upon not only as a negative mother archetype, but also as a positive one. Like Lucifer, the "light bringer," she is an irritating and destructive force introduced into a given situation in order to force a step in human development. In this case she provokes the Hebrews into establishing a patriarchal society and, by the same token, to take stock of themselves. Athaliah is action personified, a catalyzer. The agent of her enormous energy is buried within her unconscious and emerges from this irrational world in the form of a dream. It is the dream that provokes Athaliah to enter the Temple thereby bringing about a head-on collision between the two opposing religious principles as represented by Yahweh and Baal.

The oneiromantic visions thrust up into Athaliah's conscious mind during her dream indicate the urgency of her plight. Athaliah's dream can be divided into two parts: past and present. In the first part she sees her mother coming to her in "deep night" and "arrayed in pomp, as on the day she died."[5] Jezebel speaks to her daughter and warns her of the terrible fate awaiting her unless she kills "the cruel God of the Jews." Then Jezebel's "shadow seems to lean over her bed," but when Athaliah extends her hands to kiss her mother, the form she believes to be touching disintegrates and she finds herself holding onto bones and bruised flesh.

> Yet all I found was but a horrid mush
> Of bones and mangled flesh, dragged in the slush,
> Of bloody strips, and limbs all shameless scarred,
> That bit by bit the wrangling dogs devoured.[6]

In the second half of the dream Athaliah sees a child clothed "in shining raiment"; but just as she is admiring his nobility, he stabs her.

> At sight of him my fainting spirit rose—
> But when, reviving from my fatal fears,
> I praised his sweetness and his modest mien,
> I sudden felt as though the treacherous boy
> Had plunged a murderous knife deep in my breast.[7]

One must recall that when under the sway of dreams, a feeling of oneness with the universe sweeps over the dreamer, resulting in an elemental attachment to the *pleromatic* world.[8] Since the unknown exists in the unconscious either as past, present, or future and reveals itself under certain circumstances in the form of symbols and images, it can be regarded as Janus-faced, "pointing back to a preconscious prehistoric world of instincts," while at the same time it "potentially anticipates the future."[9] What occurred in Athaliah's dream was a resuscitation of her empirical past and a symbolic view of what was to come.

What is the symbolic significance of this dream that its effect should have been so intense and its dominion so extensive? When Athaliah sees Jezebel's shadow leaning over her, she is in effect looking on her own destructive, guilt-ridden nature through projection.[10] Seemingly, Athaliah has identified with her mother to such an extent that she has never been able to grow as an individual; stunted and passive, she lives a "shadow existence" in her actions and beliefs.[11] If her life is to pursue its course, certainly Athaliah will tread in her mother's footsteps.

The fact that Jezebel is "arrayed in pomp," that is, the

clothes she wore when she died, indicates the sensual and earthly nature of her attitude as opposed to that of the moralistic force she called the "cruel Jewish God," the bitter adversary of the ithyphallic Baal. Therefore, the patriarchal and spiritual society Yahweh represented must be destroyed if the Athaliah-Jezebel brand is to survive.

Athaliah reaches out to touch her mother, expressing the harmony she feels while within her fold. Instead, she comes into contact with disintegrated, decayed bones and flesh, trampled on by horses and half-eaten by dogs. Horses usually represent man's instinctual physical nature; in Jezebel's and Athaliah's case this aspect of their personalities has taken possession of them, driving them wild and compelling them to act as destructive beasts. Although bones usually represent life and strength, in this instance they are associated with decay, rotted flesh, and blood, the implication here being that in their present condition they have lost all usefulness. In effect, they have become negative elements and must be eaten, digested, and absorbed, symbolically speaking, by some outside entity in order to be reborn or transformed into something positive. In Athaliah's dream the dog is the aggressive instrument that can effect the change necessary for renewal. The animal, legendary companion of the dead, has now become the mutilator of the Terrible Mother, eater of corpses. Like the jackal-headed Anubis, the dog is first a dismemberer, then a restorer. The negative-destructive attitude, as represented by Jezebel and her shadowy daughter, has met with a violent end.

The second section of the dream does not deal with dismemberment but with the image of the child Jehoash. It tries to make Athaliah aware of the extreme danger to her if her present attitude persists and propels her actions. The child, as opposed to the archetypal image of the old man representing the past, stands for the future, the fresh, the birth of a new point of view. Jehoash has extremely appealing characteristics; he is dressed in dazzling priestly robes and looks "noble," "modest," and "gentle." Strangely enough, this child is also capable of horrendous acts, according to the dream. He is thus a *complexio oppositorum,* for within him cohabit good and evil. We must therefore presume that the extremes in Athaliah's dream (as seen in the image of her mother Jezebel and the child Jehoash) are inchoate elements within her own personality. This is made obvious when Athaliah begins to experience emotions she had thought were non existent within her. She is utterly captivated by Jehoash's sincerity and nobility; she feels gentleness and even love welling up within her. Caught off-balance and unable to adjust to the new emotions, her facade of harshness crumbles. Unwittingly she exposes her Achilles' heel, the feeling principle, that whole area within her personality she has repressed and which has remained undeveloped. The child (or what he stands for) is, in effect, the killer of Athaliah's chthonic aspects (those characteristics belonging to the Terrible Mother archetype ready at all times to destroy the hero if he does not bring about her demise first).[12]

Athaliah's dream, one of the pivotal elements of the drama, immerses her into her own transpersonal realm, her collective unconscious. The emotions and images gushing forth concomitantly are so potent as to remain fixed in her mind. Try as she will, through prayer to Baal, begging him for comfort and calm, the vision gnaws and persecutes her. The dream returns three times in all its gore. Indeed she is engulfed, trapped like a wildcat within her own inner world. Desperate, she declares that a force beyond her control has driven her to the Temple where she seeks "to attack God in his very sanctuary."[13]

Athaliah's nightmare, then, is the catalyzing agent. It compels her to go to the Temple to destroy Yahweh's earthly realm. As she enters the Temple, a territory foreign to her sensual ways, something frightening and outer-worldly jars her, suddenly intrudes upon the picture. Athaliah is paralyzed. Temporary aphasia. She has seen something that has very nearly catapulted her into another realm.

> But all at once her tongue was frozen and dumb
> And all her pride was stricken to the dust.
> Her rolling eyes, in terror, stared at us...[14]

What has Athaliah seen at this moment? The young Jehoash. Why is his presence in the Temple such a horrendous experience? Because the boy in her dreams has now appeared in flesh and blood—an almost parallel scene to that in her vision; she has the same tender feelings now.

> That miracle dismays, distresses me?
> That sweetness of his choice, his childish grace,
> Make it antipathy insensibly...
> Can it be possible that I am moved by pity?[15]

Startled and bewildered, she begins questioning the meaning of the new emotions within her: can she possibly be responsive to pity? As a preventive measure, she quickly reverts to her enticing Jezebel-like façade and tries to lure Jehoash to her palace, promising glory, wealth, and material possessions. When he rejects the "matter" (mother, earth, the matriarchal) and opts for the patriarchal and spiritual Yahweh, Athaliah reacts still more harshly, attempting to suppress her newborn feelings of tenderness. A conflict ensues of which Athaliah is not aware, tenderness and humanity versus rigidity and bestiality.

Even Mattan notices a drastic change in Athaliah's demeanor. No longer is she the powerful queen figure, a woman capable of rising beyond her personal existence into the collective; rather, she has become a timid woman, filled with remorse, fear, guilt, and hesitation.

> For two days now, I do not know her, friend.
> She is no more that bold, clear-sighted Queen,
> Raised high above the weakness of her sex...
> She founders, hesitates, just like a woman.[16]

Mattan's assessment of Athaliah's character is indeed incisive. He notes well that outward manifestations of inner changes. Indeed, she has become "human." No longer the symbolical mother goddess, the atemporal, archetypal figure, Athaliah now begins to experience weakness, emotions, and pain known to a real mother. The heartless, defiant woman who swore vengeance has now been superseded by another whose anger is "wavering...uncertain." Athaliah now becomes vulnerable.

Mattan, until then subservient to Athaliah, now tries to destroy her. As her power diminishes, so his increases. Unsettled, lacking in self-confidence, no more relying on her own judgment, she listens to Mattan instead of evaluating her situation and achieving a new level of consciousness that would have saved her. She resists the help offered by her unconscious (in the form of a dream) and lets herself be guided by her regressive consort-priest. There remains no possibility of a positive conclusion. Insidiously, and to serve his own ends, Mattan urges Athaliah to demand that Jehoash be delivered to the palace.

When Athaliah enters the Temple, an area she should have fled had she followed the warning in her dream, the atmosphere tingles. She strides forward and demands the child and treasure but is nearly blinded by the sight of the "royal child." In a desperate attempt to destroy the prophecy as revealed in her dream, she calls upon soldiers to kill the child king. It is all in vain.

3. *Matriarchal versus Patriarchal Views*

The eternal conflict between matriarchal and patriarchal concepts, which plagued Racine deeply on a personal sphere, was played out and solved to a great extent in *Athaliah.*

Mattan, the priest of Baal, under the dominion of the Great Mother, Athaliah, may be looked upon as her male consort, a representation of matriarchal consciousness. The Canaanites considered Baal as the "husband" of the land. He was the fertilizer of "mother earth" and as a reward demanded the first fruits that emerged. Taking this ritual literally, the firstborn were sacrificed to Baal. When archaeologists began excavating Gezer, they found small bones placed in jars that dated from 1100 B.C. The Canaanite religion was neither ethical nor moral. It focused on the orgiastic, sensual, luxury-loving aspects of "mother" nature. The fertility and magic rites of Baalism were anathema to the Hebrews. When Jezebel married King Ahab of Israel (847 B.C.), it is said she brought with her four hundred and fifty of Baal's sensual and ecstatic prophets.[17] Athaliah continued this ithyphallic worship.

Mattan, always subservient to Athaliah, wants more than anything to assert himself and prove his worth. He feels he can do so only by annihilating Jahweh and his ministers. But each time he attempts to do so, he gives the impression of being a castrated figure whose every effort leads to blunder upon blunder.

Mattan first comes on the stage in response to Athaliah's summoning (II, v). He listens patiently as she relates her dream (as do the confidants in other Racinian dramas), then suggests that the child be killed and the Temple razed. Although a weakly structured being, Mattan has one important feature: he is extraordinarily perceptive. He guesses the illustrious ancestry of the "child king"; he is convinced that some "monster" is being nurtured in the Temple; he senses the change that has occurred in Athaliah's personality.

Mattan is a solitary figure, an apostate without a family, an unbeliever. Power is the only instinct that can fill the void in his being. Therefore, if he is to survive, he must destroy all obstacles in his path: Jehoiada and the Temple. But what Mattan is trying to destroy in effect is not so much Jehoiada and the Temple, but rather those forces he projects upon them: his growing feelings of remorse and guilt that are concomitant with apostasy, unmanliness, and indecisiveness. To divert these emotions from their natural course, he supersedes feelings of hate and violence. Such activity (or over activity) is one of the best ways to prevent reflection. Repose, on the contrary, encourages thought.

When Mattan confronts Jehoiada, his hatred flares. His rational order of consciousness is so upset by the upsurge of his affective world that he thrusts aside logos. His actions will be totally dominated by his instincts. What irritates him so when he sees Jehoiada, a person devoid of deceit and treachery, clear in outlook, a pillar of strength? Mattan sees his counterpart and cannot stand viewing his own weakness, which becomes all the more blatant when placed in apposition to Jehoiada.

Mattan has neither positive nor negative traits. First and foremost, he is a function of his queen. Unable to cope with his own inadequacies, he is a man who never comes into his own and is never enlightened. Although he has insight, the new feelings that arise from his perception do not represent an act of cognition because the new contents are never assimilated or understood in terms of his own life. He is, therefore, like a dead leaf, pushed here and there by someone or by his own instincts. Mattan inspires neither pity nor fear. He exemplifies a disintegrating matriarchal society.

Jehoiada represents the well-integrated man living out his role in a matriarchal society. He is a man who has experienced the *numinosum,* who lives and loves for and with his God. That he has a wife, a son, and a daughter, indicates that he has experienced earthly as well as heavenly love. The fact that his family numbers four, the quaternity symbolizing "wholeness" and "completeness," is another indication of the balance that reigns within the psyche of the head of this family unit. Jehoiada in this respect is unique in Racinian drama. He is endowed with spirit and with flesh. Such relatedness, *hieros gamos,* between the spiritual and the earthly permits him to become a prophet, a mediator between God and his people, a symbol of God's fruitful union with the earth.[18]

The prophetic vision Jehoiada experiences (III, vii) guides his actions and gives him the strenth to carry them out. The scene of the prophecy is one of the most moving of all Racinian theater. The swell and breadth of divinity not only takes possession of Jehoiada, but overflows, impregnating everybody exposed to the scene with supernatural, atemporal feelings. As Jehoiada speaks, his words seem to grow in intensity, to reach a crescendo of emotion and become very nearly unbearable, like a strident note held for minutes on end. Then suddenly the flux ceases, as if the tonal modulations have come to a violent end at the edge of a precipice. It would be almost impossible to have written such feelings into Jehoiada's verses, to express such poignancy of tone so reminiscent of Isaiah, Jeremiah, and Josea's outpourings, had not the author himself experienced such an inflow of Divinity at one time or another during his life.

From the very outset of the drama, we note that Jehoiada has a highly charged and powerful personality. Indeed, it casts a spell on all those surrounding him. It is almost present in his speech, in the images he uses. When, for example, mention is made of the "bloody" Athaliah who attacks the Hebrew God, Jehoiada counters with an image reflecting Yahweh's power, the drying up of the Red Sea.

> He who can sudden tame the raging waves,
> Can well confound the plots of evil man.[19]

That force of will, which is God's in this instance, is also infused into Jehoiada's being, compelling him to live energetically and dynamically. The miracle of the holy flame is another example Jehoiada gives to indicate divinity's omniscience and immanence: "With fire from Heaven descending on the Altar."[20]

Although Jehoiada is a visionary, he is not immune to the reality of his people's plight. Rather than being blinded, over- whelmed, and subjugated by his vision, such anamnesis as he ex- periences, enlarges it. Therefore, activity not passivity, results. How deeply religious can one be, he questions, if action does not follow?

Once Jehoiada has made his decision—that deceit (hiding the child) is no longer in order—the battle of Yahweh (Jehoiada and his family, Jehoash) must be fought against Baal (Athaliah, Mattan). Like the Zealots who fought so valiantly against the Romans at Massada, so Jehoiada will take his stand: righteous- ness, morality, ethics, against hypocrisy and deception. Jehoshe- bath, his wife, is fearful of the outcome. She realizes that the balance of power weighs heavily against them. They have no soldiers and no armaments, but the enemy has everything. Not everything, Jehoiada counters, because God is not on their side.

> And God on our side count you not all?
> God, Who for innocent orphans deigns to fight
> And founds upon the weak His shining might;[21]

Jehoiada is now being propelled by a catalyst within his very being. Intense, he speaks as though in the very center of a whirlwind. Jehoiada feels degraded when such an apostate as this votary of Baal comes into his presence. He orders the doors to the Temple shut. The climactic moment has arrived. To his terror-stricken wife he offers the consolation that comes with love and faith in divinity. As Jehoiada speaks, his words swell in intensity, reaching a powerful crescendo, until they become very nearly unbearable, like protracted hammer sounds. Sudden- ly, the tonal nuances end abruptly and something seems to possess him. He begins to tremble. An intangible, amorphous entity encapsulates him. His eyes open wide.

> Is it God's spirit taking hold of me?
> It is. It warms. It speaks. My eyes are opened,
> And the dim centuries revealed to me.
> O Levites, let me have harmonious music

To aid the transports of the holy spirit.[22]

The Divine is speaking through him, announcing the eschatological events.

Under the spell of God's presence, rational order dissolves. The emotions Jehoiada now experiences are the product of autonomous contents emanating from an unknown subliminal source within his own being. His conscious mind succumbs to his intuition, which is dependent upon the unconscious process.[23] To inject the import of Jehoiada's prophecy, Racine infuses the entire scene with a counterpoint of speech and choral singing to the accompaniment of musical instruments. Images and metaphors pierce the atmosphere like flames as the prophet reveals the terrifying knowledge of the destruction of the Temple and the scorching of the land, describes the anguished cries and lamentations emanating from the Wailing Wall, and the painful birth of a new Jerusalem as it emerges from the desert, raising its head once again and paving the way for renewed light.

> Sinners, be consumed: the Lord is awake...
> Jerusalem, object of my pain.[24]

Jehoiada's vision, like Ezekiel's or Isaiah's, is a primordial experience that affects his future course of action. It gives him strength with God's help, it paves the way for him to follow, it teaches him to inure Jehoash to the hardships ahead.

> Of God's great plans for you and for His people.
> Be brave, my son, and of a shining faith.
> Now is the time to show that zest and zeal
> That deep within your heart my care has planned.[25]

In experiencing divinity within, Jehoiada has come face to face with the Self. Such a union between inner and outer man is not merely an unconscious or escapist departure into an artificially constructed paradise; rather, this glimpse of oneness is an act of cognition. For prophecy to be truly valid, it must be a catalyst and be experienced consciously. One of the best-known examples of this type of consciousness was experienced by Moses when he saw "God face to face and by day."[26] What Jehoiada has been living through is a *coniunctio* between the collective unconscious as revealed through archetypal imagery, intuitively perceived, and the incisive vision of the conscious personal mind. Such insight into the subliminal workings of the world reveals information concerning, past, present, and future activities.[27]

Jehoiada is one of the most powerful father figures in Racine's theatre. He is in reality the final destroyer of the *vagina dentata* type (in the form of Athaliah here). It is he who also encourages the maternal, gentle, understanding female figure to reign in conjunction with the family. The importance accorded to such a figure as Jehoiada in Racine's theatre denotes what such an *imago Dei* played in his own world. It was the guiding principle that afforded him the equilibrium (his family life) he now enjoyed; the conscious realization of his own worth, his obligations, his piety. Racine's portrayal of the Hebraic seer-prophet type also marked the affinity he felt with the Hebrew psyche at this particular time in his life, the preservation and intensification of consciousness within himself because of his understanding of them.[27] No longer a victim of his instincts, Racine now adhered to a world of moral commandment, not artificially self-described but rather emerging as a result of his own understanding and acceptance of his shadow personality.

Jehoshebath is the prototype of the ideal mother: kind, gentle, pious, submissive, yet endowed with extraordinary heroism. She personifies the positive characteristics of the Great Mother archetype. She suffers no moral conflicts. She knows clearly the differences between right and wrong. She is human and filled with compassion. She reacts in horror at the sight of evil, when Athaliah puts so many children to death, and is always compelled to do what is honorable. Jehoshebath who saved Jehoash, the King, is comparable to the pharaoh's daughter who saved Moses; to the gardner who rescued King Sargon, who had been set afloat down the Euphrates in a basket by his mother; to Christ who was nurtured by shepherds according to Saint Luke.

Although Jehoshebath is a fruitful mother and devoted wife, she is also preoccupied with the spiritual aspects of life. In this respect she had broken the patterns of the Great Mother archetype, the instinctual earth principle that deals only in "matter." Furthermore, Jehoshebath has a free will. Like Rebecca and unlike Sarah, she is to a certain extent mistress of her own destiny. In addition, she can also be looked upon as a redemptive force in that she actively helps save her people by saving Jehoash and by hiding her feelings when it would have been dangerous to reveal them. Jehoshebath, then, is a woman who is always conscious of her actions and her role in life.

However, she is not all-cerebral; on the contrary, she is very feminine, and displays her feelings when she knows it cannot harm. When she does weep, on describing the time she saved Jehoash from his doom, her husband's understanding of these womanly characteristics assures her of the salutary nature of tears: "There's nothing sinful in your tears, dear wife," he says.[29] Emotions must play a role in life; to cut them out is to inflict lameness upon a personality.[30] Thus Jehoshebath represents the female principle integrated into a patriarchal society. Never in danger of losing her femininity, she reacts tenderly, humanely, and with compassion to every situation.

C. *The Child Image: A Symbol for the Creative Element and Wholeness*

Symbolically, the child is both the beginning and end, the *renatus in novam infantiam,* because he lives before man comes of age and exists after man no longer does.[31] The child archetype stands for something new, a force in the process of being formed, and, therefore, represents the future, hope, and progress. As the child moves toward independence, he struggles for recognition; and because he is a growing force, he comes to represent a future state of consciousness.

When a "sacred" or "divine" child is involved (Moses, Hercules, Sargon, Christ), he frequently symbolizes the mystic center, the philosopher's stone many identify with the God within.[32] These "divine children" share certain characteristics: they have been abandoned by their parents for one reason or another, they are frequently in danger, they arise miraculously from unknown places, and, as a result, they are the center usually of some mystery. Jehoash fulfills all of these requirements. He has been brought up in a Temple by relatives, is of some mysterious origin, and is called Aliacin although his real name is Jehoash, further increasing his ambiguity.

For Racine, Jehoash is certainly a Christ figure. He is the divine primordial man, the "treasure," the *imago Dei,* the most powerful force within Racine's unconscious and conscious mind. Thus when Racine created Jehoash he made him beautiful, humble, tender and as perfect as possible, God's living creation before the sins of man sullied him prior to Adam's fall, *sine macula* peccati.[32]   Jehoash's life, consequently, is devoted to God.

When Jehoash appears (II, vii), the simplicity of his speech and righteousness of his thought stuns everyone. It is not until the coronation ceremony, however (IV, iii), that his being is infused with a sacred aura, that the entire atmosphere radiates with divine presence. The implications of this ceremony are so vast, the waves of emotion aroused by it so flamboyant, and the impact of the metaphysical experience so shattering that Racine has the ritual not only enacted onstage, but reported as well afterward in part by Zachariah (V, i).

Seen symbolically, the coronation is a sacrificial religious ritual. As the divine will has made itself manifest in the Temple, speaking through the priest Jehoiada, the young child Jehoash is in the process of undergoing an inner transformation, evolving from the realm of the individual to that of the collective, from the human to the suprahuman, from the egocentric to the self-less, from boyhood to manhood. Now Jehoash must confront the world and its hardships; he must fulfill the image of the new king as bearer of goodness.

It might be interesting to examine a certain intrinsic rhythmic pattern. As Athaliah slips down from her role as the archetypal Terrible Mother figure to the individual human level, Jehoash at the same time ascends from a personal to a suprapersonal being. As the force of divinity descends into the earthly realm, in this case the Temple, the religious community is imbued with the strength necessary to fight the forces of evil and to display the Ark of the Covenant in all of its glory and omnipotence. When danger has reached its peak, Jehoiada tells Jehoash to mount his throne, then closes the curtains. Athaliah enters and demands the child. In one of the most poignantly dramatic moments in the play, Jehoiada draws the curtains and there appears before the Queen the young King in all of his dazzling radiance. Suddenly, the inside of the Temple becomes

visible and armed Levites rush forth from all corners. Athaliah's
soldiers desert her because they too have been overwhelmed
by "The voice of the All-Powerful." A new world is now to
emerge with Jehoash as Leader, ready to devote and sacrifice
himself to and for mankind. The Hebrews had prayed for a
miracle; the miracle of enlightenment has occurred.[34]

The fact that Athaliah takes place in the holy city of Jerusalem, and more specifically in the sacred Temple, indicates a
spiritual intimacy of Racine's with God. He is able to enter
totally into God's sanctuary (his evil aspect projected onto
Athaliah and his good elements onto Jehoiada and Jehoshebath)
and not merely allude to it. It would seem that an integration of
conflicting polarities has happened within his psyche through
projection.

That Racine's "integration" was in the process of taking
place can also be attested to by the central image in this drama,
the child. Archetypal symbol of the Self, the child is the fruit
or the outcome of a welding together of formerly opposing
polarities (conscious and unconscious, passive and active, etc.)
within the personality. The coming together, or the *coniunctio,*
of formerly antagonistic entities paves the way for the creation
of a new attitude, a fresh spiritual point of view. Furthermore,
the product that emerges from this union comes to represent
a symbol of unity and totality. The disparity between Racine's
psychic state when writing Athaliah and when creating his first
play, *The Theban Brothers*, is a symbol of unity and totality.
The disparity between Racine's psychic state when writing
Athaliah and when creating his first play, *The Theban Brothers*
is enormous. The latter featured warring royal twins, the sizygy,
two halves of one egg. The brothers not only killed each other,
but were also the cause of the death of all the other protagonists
in the work. The series of plays that followed bathed for the
most part in Greek and Roman sunlight, fatality, and doom.

With his return to Jansenism and a taste of worldly joys in
the form of family life, Racine experienced a new understanding
of the Scriptures. The Greek and Roman female types, destruc-

tive in the main, still persisted in his group of women (e.g. Athaliah), but to a lesser degree, and they were countered by such womanly beings as Esther and Jehoshebath. A deeper realization of life's forces, as expressed through an assimilation of Jansenist doctrine with its highly moralistic, rigid, stern, and patriarchal bent, opened up a whole new world for Racine. He began feeling an affinity with the Hebrews of the Old Testament; and with such understanding, new springs and sources of inspiration had been tapped; no longer the Greek world, but his own heritage, the Judeo-Christian concepts. This broadened point of view permitted him to envisage existence not in terms of death and despair but rather as a struggle that each being must undergo in order to bring forth fresh entities like the child embedded within each of us, when allowed to develop brings forth self-realization.

NOTES

[1]Jean Racine was baptized on December 22, 1639, in Ferté-Milon. His mother died in 1641, shortly after the birth of his sister, Marie. Jean's father remarried in November 1642 and died three months later. The young Racine went to live with his paternal grandparents, the Desmoulins, who were righteous, kind, and highly moral people. Misfortune was further heaped on him with the death of his grandfather in 1649. His grandmother, perhaps financially unable to keep up the expense of running a private home, retired to the Jansenist convent-monastery at Port-Royal-des-Champs. It was here, befriended by the deeply religious Jansenists, that Racine was to live and be educated.

Officially, the doctrine of Jansenism was created in 1640 with the publication of the *Augustinus* by Cornelius Jansen, called Janesnius, Bishop of Ypres. In this religious work he stated that the ideas of St. Augustine concerning grace had been misinterpreted and that he was now explicating them correctly. Since Adam's fall, Jansen explained, man has never had free will: he is subject either to grace or to concupiscence. If God were to grant him eternal grace, then man would never veer toward sin. Since this is not the case, man is drawn to evil. On the other hand, God endows certain people with what is called "efficacious grace" —when they cannot help but do good. Salvation comes to pass when God grants this special grace. Man's future, under this concept is predetermined and depends wholly upon God and not upon man's deeds or any human intermediary. Conversely, according to both Jesuit thinkers and Papal decree, man is given free will. It is he who choses to do good or evil. Neither grace nor concupisence determines his action or his situation.

The Jansenist doctrine, which preached the all-powerful nature of grace, ran contrary to the Catholic Church and Jesuit dicta, and was thus considered heretical. Louis XIV, his ministers, and most particularly the Sorbonne theologians, made up of a majority of Jesuits, were unfavorably disposed toward the Jansenists and persecuted them ceaselessly. The situation grew steadily more serious. In 1709 the Solitaires, as the Jansenists who lived in the convent of Port-Royal were called, were dispersed. In 1710 the convent buildings were leveled. In 1711 the three thousand buried at Port-Royal were disinterred and removed to other areas so that nevermore would another "heretical" sect arise on that ground.

During the years Racine spent at Port-Royal he lived through monstrous and fabulous days—a time when men fought harshly for ideas and for pinciples, when they expressed in moving and profound terms their belief in the divine. He could not help but respond affectively to such traumatic moments. When the time came, Racine moved to Paris. He decided to become a dramatist but the decision engendered conflict. The Jansenists considered anything connected with the theatre "infamous," "sinful," and "artificial"—evil in all ways. The Solitaires made known their disapproval to the aspiring young dramatist. He, however, was fired with a will to succeed that made him totally impervious to all imprecations leveled at him by the Jansenists. His first play, *The Theban Brothers* (1664), mirrored his desire to become a dramatist and Port-Royal's disapproval of his goal. It dramatized a power struggle between two opposing groups: the aggressively "heroic" and the pacifist elements within man and society. Both are destroyed, sacrificed, or swallowed up in the process because neither, evidently, represented a viable or fecundating viewpoint. *The Theban Brothers* was performed seventeen times and considered a failure. *Alexander the Great* (1665) fared no better. After a series of cruel missives, Racine broke with Port-Royal, accusing the Fathers of being jealous of the worldly successes of others and for this reason condemning poets; he also added that Jansenism was on the decline. The bitterness and pain that spread through Jansenist circles was swift and penetrating.

Andromaque (1667) was Racine's first triumph. He was now master of the art of dramaturgy and success followed success: *Britannicus* (1669), *Bérénice* (1670), *Bajazet* (1672), *Mithridates* (1673), *Iphigenia* (1674), *Phaedra* (1677). *Phaedra* became a turning point in Racine's career. Afther this play he gave up the theatre and its "sinful" life. He became reconciled with the Jansenists and their way became his. When marriage was suggested, he complied. He had seven children, was named adviser to Louis XIV, and, with Boileau, became official court historiographer. After Racine repudiated the theatre and assumed a bourgeois life, his personality seemed to alter. His tempestuous emotions calmed, his world became orderly, and he achieved a sense of harmony and balance. Moreover, the divine now assumed a primary role in his life. God became his frame of reference and everything seemed to emerge from this source.

Racine wrote two more plays, *Esther* (1687) and *Athaliah* (1690), both of which had been ordered by Madame de Maintenon, the wife of Louis XIV, to be performed by the young girls of Saint-Cyr, the school she had founded for young ladies of impoverished noble families.

Racine died peacefully on April 21, 1690, of what some people have since and variously diagnosed as hepatic cancer. and tuberculosis. His body was sent to rest at Port-Royal-des-Champs, as he had requested. But on December 2, 1711, after Port-Royal was razed—the very grave-yard where he had been buried, desecrated—Racine's body was trans-ferred to the Church of Saint-Etienne-du-Mont in Paris. There he was again laid to rest.

[2]II King, 11 and II Chronicles, 22, 23.

[3]C. G. Jung, *Aion*, p. 9.

[4]Moses and Elijah denounced the false God Baal. Baal is a representative of the female matriarchal society as witnessed by Samson's imprison-ment in the Temple of Dagon, a corn god of the Cananites and father of Baal. Such an episode is an example of man's (the hero's) servitude to the Great Mother. Another example occurs when Hercules is forced by Omphale to wear woman's clothes.

Erich Neumann, *The Origins and History of Consciousness*, p. 160.

[5]*The Complete Plays of Jean Racine* (trans. by Samuel Solomon), II, p. 439.

[6]*Ibid.*, p. 400.

[7]*Ibid.*, p. 401.

[8]Neumann, p. 277.

[9]C. G. Jung, *The Archetypes and the Collective Unconscious*, p. 279.

[10]*Ibid.*

[11]*Aion*, p. 266.

[12]*The Archetypes and the Collective Unconscious*, p. 279.

[13]Jean Racine, *Oeuvres complètes* I, p. 878.

[14]*Complete Plays*, p. 397.

[15]*Ibid.,* p. 407

[16]*Ibid.,* p. 418.

[17]Emma Hawkridge, *The Wisdom Tree,* p. 143.

[18]*Aion,* p. 279.

[19]*Complete Plays,* p. 383.

[20]*Ibid.,* p. 385.

[21]*Ibid.,* p. 388.

[22]*Ibid.,* p. 428.

[23]*Aion,* p. 282.

[24]*Complete Plays,* p. 436.

[25]*Ibid.,* p. 436.

[26]C. G. Jung, *Symbols of Transformation,* p. 324.

[27]C. G. Jung, *Psychological Types,* pp. 507-8.

[28]Neumann, p. 380.

[29]*Complete Plays,* p. 390.

[30]*Ibid.,* p. 391.

[31]*The Archetypes and the Collective Unconscious,* p. 178.

[32]*Ibid.,* p. 166.

[33]*Aion,* p. 236.

[34]Since *Athaliah* is a play in which divinity enjoys a primal role, it is enacted in the most sacred of areas, the Temple King David had begun to
build and King Solomon completed. For Racine, the Temple, like the
cathedral, is a sacred area where communion with the divine can be experienced. Never before had Racine openly chosen such a holy locale for

a drama. Never had he struck so deeply into the hearts and minds of people and himself.

For the mystic, the Temple represents the "Center," the core of the cosmos. Indeed, Philo and Josephus both held that King Solomon's Temple was a "figurative representation of the cosmos."
(J. E. Cirlot, *A Dictionary of Symbols,* p. 315.)
Included in the Temple were the seven-branched candelabra, symbolizing the seven heavens and the seven planets, and the Ark of the Covenant, containing the two tablets with the Mosaic law inside the Tabernacle, the holiest of places. The Ark of the Covenant is a "wooden chest... which Moses was commanded by God to construct to contain the two Tablets of the Law. It was lined with gold within and without, and surrounded with a golden mold... This Ark was carried by the Levites throughout Israel's wanderings in the wilderness; when not mobile. it was placed in the Holy of Holies inside the Tabernacle, where it was beheld only by the High Priest on the Day of Atonement."
(*The Encyclopedia of Jewish Religion,* ed. R. J. Zwi Weblowsky and G. Wigoder.)
Since God's living word had been imprinted in these scrolls, they came to represent the spiritual as well as the physical force and energy needed for perpetual rebirth (eternity), and because of their "containing" quality, they are frequently associated with the womb, the heart, and the drinking vessel. Thus they are both energizers and nourishers as well as living entities.

The Temple, therefore, assumes the force of a protagonist living both an exterior and interior existence. On the outside it represents a bold, majestic front; within it is an area replete with secrecy, mystery, fascination, immense activity, and strength.

> As though in the depths of this vast edifice
> God is an avenger armed to punish her.
>   (*Oeuvres complètes,* p. 878.)

It is also a place needful of and offering protection, "O holy Temple," articulate when necessary and silent if imperative. "The holy arch is mute..." Furthermore, within its walls there resides the royal child, Jehoash, that "treasure," whose destiny is the determining factor in this drama. When the Temple closes its doors at the end, it envelops the child's enemy and seals Athaliah's fate, then ejects her from its ironclad grasp to be killed by the tidal flow heaving its crushing power against her.

SECTION II

THE EIGHTEENTH CENTURY

3. *Denis Diderot—D'Alembert's Dream: The Relating of a Myth*

4. *Jacques Cazotte—The Devil in Love: A Dream Initiation*

CHAPTER 3

Denis Diderot—D'Alembert's Dream: The Relating of a Myth

...these atoms move in the infinite void, separate one from the other and differing in shapes, sizes, position and arrangement; overtaking each other they collide, and some are shaken away in any chance direction, while others, becoming intertwined one with another according to the congruity of their shapes, sizes, positions and arrangements, stay together and so effect the coming into being of compound bodies.

(Aristotle, On Democritus.*)*

D'Alembert's Dream is not a dream in the true sense of the word, but rather an ideal formula used by Diderot[1] to express his scientific and philosophical ideas. He also considered the irrational domain as a vehicle capable of circumventing political and governmental restrictions that might be imposed on his written work. In a letter to Sophie Volland (Sept. 22, 1769) he intimated that the unconscious would give him relative liberty of expression.

> There is some skill in having put my ideas into the mouth of a dreaming man; it is often necessary to give wisdom an air of folly in order to procure a hearing. I would rather it be said, "But that is not so absurd as one might think," than to say, "Listen to me; here are some very wise things."[2]

Diderot also employs the dream, perhaps without realizing it, as a device to plumb his own depths to reach the level of the myth within himself. In this respect, *D'Alembert's Dream* may be described as a "global intuition of the universe," a "profession of faith."[3] Whether simulated or not, dreams in general frequently contain mythical material. *D'Alembert's Dream* is no exception. Diderot's myth narrated in dialogue furnishes readers with a cultural reality, a true story, the birth of new concepts, and fresh attitudes not only on a personal but also on a transcendental scale. The concepts under scrutiny therefore mirror the scientific attitudes (Enlightenment) of Diderot's era and also communicate a sense of eternity (when broaching such topics as monism, the notion of universal flux, the meaning of existence, and life and death). The ideations explicated in *D'Alembert's Dream* in a scientific frame of reference thus became the very problems that both tormented and inspired the metaphysically oriented Romantic and Symbolist poets and novelists of the nineteenth century. *D'Alembert's Dream*, then, is Janus-faced: it looks back to the very dawn of history, to the birth of thought, to pre-Socratic philosophers, but it also anticipates the future, man's excoriating solitude, his sense of finitude, and, by the same token, his overpowering arrogance.

1. *The Enlightenment*

D'Alembert's Dream reflects most incisively Diderot's contemporary world—the Enlightenment. This movement was brought about in the main by a group of *philosophes* who, though not philosophers in the strict sense of the word nor founders of any specific school of thought, adopted certain tenets of Cartesian views (his experimental method, his emphasis on clarity and order, his belief in the development of reason as the great factor leading to man's perfectibility) but rejected his physics and metaphysics. The use of Descartes' method led to what the seventeenth-century philosopher would have despised: a rejection of authority on a political, economic, and religious plane. What was not logical, factual, or backed up by evidence the philosophes considered to be invalid. Tradition and the status quo gave way to an independence of spirit that fought dogmatism persistently. Such an atmosphere paved the way for toleration, deism, skepticism, even atheism. Reason had become liberated from the stifling constrictions heaped upon it by the various churches and political institutions.

The philosophes became the great disseminators of science. And this is the spirit in which *D'Alembert's Dream* was written: to make understandable and thus readily accessible scientific reasoning in the heretofore sacrosanct domain of history, geology, botany, chemistry, astronomy, law, and education.

History was no longer a matter of providence for the philosophes. Political, economic, and military events were not a question of God's will being carried out on earth as theologians, such as Bossuet, had claimed. History was strictly a human affair. Wars, treaties, victories, and defeats should be recounted accurately and therefore source material should be used, analyses of facts be required and, insofar as Voltaire was concerned, a moral should be drawn from great historical events, thus helping man to learn from previous mistakes. Warriors can only bring destruction upon their country, implied Voltaire in his *History of Charles XII* (1731), no matter how idealistic their intentions. Before Gibbon's *Decline and Fall of the Roman Empire*, Montesquieu published his *Considerations on the Greatness and Decadence of the Romans* (1734) and based his arguments not on divine intervention but on human ideas and actions. He believed that once a country loses its need or desire for virtue, it disintegrates and is transformed into a decadent, tyrannical force.

Diderot broached the question of evolution, heredity, birth defects, geology, and chemistry in *D'Alembert's Dream*. Although his reasoning was at times faulty, his open and un-dogmatic quest for knowledge gave rise to further discussions and works in these fields. Whereas geological speculation had begun with the ancients (Aristotle, Lucretius), and had con-tinued throughout the centuries (to include Leonardo da Vinci, Descartes, and Leibniz), the modern science of geology was given impetus in eighteenth-century France. In *Periods of Nature* (1779), Count de Buffon had the courage to suggest that the earth antedated the Bible and did not begin with it but rather had gone through a series of geological stages before be-coming what it was. Jean-Jacques Rousseau, fascinated by anatomy and botany, was the author of *Chemical Institutions.* The physician Ferchault de Réaumur, inventor of the ther-mometer, discovered instincts in ants and bees. Abraham Trem-bley studied the regenerative process and demonstrated that polyps when cut in two reform themselves. Antoine Laurent Lavoisier was one of the founders of modern chemistry. The micrographic works accomplished by John Needham, the foun-der of the Belgian Academy of Sciences, were used to prove (erroneously) the theory of spontaneous generation. Sir Isaac Newton's law of universal gravitation was substituted finally for Cartesian vortices.

Diderot and his "liberal" contemporaries, brought a spirit of inquiry into the domain of religion. In *D'Alembert's Dream* Diderot furthers the belief that everything is matter, that man lives in a Godless world, and that organized religion is not only unnatural but dangerous and destructive too. Without the boldness of Pierre Bayle (*Diverse Thoughts on the Comet,* 1682 and *Historical and Critical Dictionary,* 1697), who fought for religious toleration, reviled dogmatism, and used logic, the power of reason, and the examination of source material as his weapons for gaining knowledge, Diderot might not have ventured as far as he had in his own speculations. As a result of Bayle's intellectual heroism and the general spirit of investigation that reigned, a freer religious atmosphere developed in France. Deism, an English import, gained in popularity. The Deists believed in a personal God who had neither become manifest in history nor immanent in nature. Reasons, not revelation, was His source. They accepted the notion of immortality of the soul and the reality of good and evil. In the eyes of the Deists organized religion was superfluous and dangerous, a spreader of bigotry, hatred, and war. In *Promenades of a Skeptic* (1747), Diderot points up his disbelief in religious mysteries and the supernatural, and does not hide his antagonism toward Christianity and its powerful and exploiting clergy. In *Philosophical Thoughts* (1746) he adopts a virtually pantheistic view of divinity: "Enlarge God, see Him every place or no place at all." He goes a step further in *Letter on the Blind* and expresses nearly atheistic views: one cannot believe in God without being able to see him, to touch nature. The beauty of nature is meaningless without sight. One must have concrete evidence. The *Letter on the Blind* was considered such a dangerous document to religious dogma it earned Diderot a stay in the Vincennes prison (1749).

The fact that *D'Alembert's Dream* is written in dialogue form indicates Diderot's fascination with a multitude of subjects and varied viewpoints in his perpetual quest for knowledge. Such dichotomy in man's thought processes and ideations was not merely an intellectual concept for Diderot, but rather a living reality. When broaching questions of religion, politics, economics, and mores, he viewed them in terms of relativity and not dogmatically as was usual in the France of his day. Diderot understood the dangers involved in imposing one's own beliefs on others, thus attempting to annihilate whatever differs from one's own beliefs. Had the Jesuit missionaries Diderot questioned in his *Supplement to Bougainville's Voyage* done the so-called "noble savage" a service in "civilizing" him? in bringing Christianity to the South Seas? What were the results of such activity? What had heretofore been natural became sinful and guilt-ridden; pettiness, deceit, and crime insinuated themselves into these societies; disease was introduced, decimating entire populations. Nor did the philosophes in general, such as Montesquieu (*Persian Letters,* 1721, *The Spirit of Laws,* 1748) and Voltaire (*Philosophical Letters,* 1734) veer to the opposite extreme by idealizing primitive life. What was good for one group, they inferred, was not always favorable for another; all is relative to climate and to the temperament of the people involved.

Diderot reevaluated the entire learning process in *D'Alem-*

bert's Dream. Rather than accepting Descartes' belief in innate ideas, he opted for John Locke's theories that claimed sense perception was the source of knowledge. Many philosophes substituted Descartes' "I think, therefore I am," for "I feel, therefore I am," a thesis propounded by the Abbé de Condillac in his *Treastise on Sensations* (1754). Claude-Adrien Helvetius carried Locke's ideas to the extreme in *Essays on the Mind* (1758), claiming that neither heredity nor innate faculties influenced man's perceptions. Education and legislation—environment—were factors involved in man's development, posited Diderot in *D'Alembert's Dream,* views that have been taken up by modern behaviorists.

One of the century's great achievements, and the credit to a great extent must go to Diderot, was the publication of *The Encyclopedia, Methodical Dictionary of the Sciences, Arts, and Trades.* Diderot set to work on it in 1746 with the well-known mathematician d'Alembert. At first their intention was merely to translate Ephraim Chamber's *Cyclopaedia.* However, finding it too restrictive in content, the two associates decided to include original articles, descriptions of arts, crafts, and industries and also rework the English essays. Diderot worked tirelessly for years and had the fortitude to face up to the Jesuits and their condemnations. Superstition, intolerance, persecution, and religious dogmatism are fought wherever possible, if not overtly, then covertly in a complex series of cross-references.

2. *D'Alembert's Dream: The Myth*

D'Alembert's Dream, a dialogue between Diderot, d'Alembert (who talked in his sleep), Mlle. de Lespinasse (d'Alembert's platonic friend), and the well-known Dr. Bordeu, features a series of contrived dreams and images which contain mythical material. Myths may be defined as a dramatic relating of experiences or a description of qualities or thoughts that are deepest within man. Myths are the outcome of original experiences, not always personal, but rather impersonal or transcendental. In ancient times, for example, people believed that flowers, rocks, water, ice—that is, all of nature's forces—were inhabited by gods. Primitive man did not just watch the sun rise and set and accept it as such. He assimilated this external experience which then became an inner one. For instance, he likened the sun's daily journey through the skies to a hero's fate. He did likewise with everything in nature: rain, thunder, harvest, drought. The fascinating and terrifying images man's unconscious produced as a result of these experiences took the form of dreams, premonitions, and fantasies; they became symbolic expressions of an inner drama he could only cope with by projecting into nature or the environment. These projected dramas, or myths, transcended the individual conscious mind and occurred everywhere, in all of mankind. Every culture has its Creation Myth, God Myth, etc., and these myths, whose origins are in many cases prehistoric, are recorded sooner or later.

D'Alembert's Dream is Diderot's myth, an exploration and narration in terms of both the individual and collective spheres, of questions concerning monism, universal flux, existence, life, and death. Diderot injected into these basic questions the excitement, the drama, the awe with which the ancients approached their world. For Diderot the cosmos is animistic. A stone does feel. The universe throbs, pulsates, and is in a perpetual state of flux. Death as an end does not exist. And Diderot weaves his tale around the concepts of his day as fascinating and tremulous as the mysteries of old.

a. *Monism*

One of the most significant notions broached in *D'Alembert's Dream* is monism. The belief that all phenomena result from one unifying principle or are manifestations of a single substance was derived for the most part from the theories of Heraclitus and the ancient atomists Leucippus and Democritus. For Heraclitus "The all is divisible indivisible, engenders does not engender, is mortal and immortal, it is Logos and eternity, father and son."[4] Leucippus and Democritus believed the universe to be composed of atoms that wandered about in space, forming, severing, and reforming themselves into bodies in an endless process. Atoms were eternal; the structures they formed, however, were mortal. Lucretius explained the notions of the atomists in *De Rerum Naturae* and stated that everything in the universe (including man) lives and functions according to its own laws and not according to supernatural powers. Diderot used the atomic theory to explain the formation of beings as a fusion and reshuffling of atoms.

> First nothing, then a living point... To this living point is applied another, and yet another and thus the result of these successive increments is a being that has unity, for I cannot doubt my own unity... But how did this unity come to be? ... I tell you, philosopher, I can understand an aggregate or tissue of tiny sensitive beings, but not an animal...a whole; a system, an individual, having a consciousness of its unity![5]

Diderot looked upon nature as a great whole; an *All* that continues its existence in a continuously circular pattern; and man is part of it. He explained this concept succinctly and with tongue in cheek in *Discussions Between d'Alembert and Diderot.*

> I confess that a Being who exists somewhere and yet corresponds to no point in space, a Being who, lacking extension, yet occupies space; who is present in his entirety in every part of that space, who is essentially different from matter and yet is one with matter, who follows its motion, and moves it, without himself being in motion, who acts on matter and yet is subject to all its vicissitudes, a Being about whom I can form no idea; a Being of so contradictory a nature, is an hypothesis difficult to accept.[6]

Because Diderot experienced the cosmos as a totality, he considered time as an aspect of it both in terms of the collective and on an individual basis. Eschatological (or linear) time with its artificially conceived notions of past, present, and future did not exist except in the finite world. Cyclical or mythological time, however, he experienced in what philosophers and mystics term an eternal present or actuality, a state longed for desperately by Rousseau and later by the Romantics because in this pleromatic realm one is divested of individuality and temporality and thus existential pain. Diderot expressed the duality of the time concept, that is, man in terms of his ephemerality and his eternality, systematically and via a series of comparisons.

> ...but what is our duration compared with the eternity of time? ...An unbounded series of animalcules in the fermenting atom, the same unbounded series of animalcules in this other atom that ıs called the Earth. Who knows what races of animals will come after ours? Everything changes and everything passes away, only the whole endures. The world is forever beginning

and ending; each instant is its first and its last; it never has had, it never will have, other beginning or end.[7]

The problems of the individual vis-à-vis the collective are also explored in *D'Alembert's Dream:* a perusal of dichotomy and the one. *En vrai philosophe* he accepts the concept of the singular and the plural, that is, man as an individual, as a member of the society in which he lives, and as a part of the cosmic sphere just as he affirms the dual nature of time. Unlike Anaximander, who saw man as a tragic figure traveling along the road from mortality to immortality in the Great All, Diderot, the realist-optimist, considered the interplay of the single and the plural as a positive manifestation of life's universal and dynamic process. A comparison may be made between Diderot's views in this domain and those of Empedocles who saw the one and the impersonal in terms of grammer, as an infinitive representing the one and the many in a sentence: "an uninflected form of the verb expressing existence or action without reference to person, number, or tense."[8] The dichotomy between the single and the multiple was considered by Diderot as a reality, part of the dynamic process that was life and with which man has to cope; it was this very activity that gave him the power to mold his own destiny. For the Romantics and the Symbolists such duality aroused abrasive conflicts within their beings, ushering in feelings of despair and *ennui.* Diderot understood the struggle in nature as well as the unity of cosmic reality and pinpointed in the most rational way what was for some a metaphysical notion.

b. *Flux*

Diderot viewed the eternal flux in nature in a positive and reasonable manner, but also implicit in his ideas was a sense of mystery. If time is cyclical and if "everything in nature is linked," if "there is but a single great individual, the great all,"[9] then how do evolution and progress occur? According to Heraclitus—and Diderot shared this belief—"Combat is the father of all things, the king of all things."[10] Struggle then becomes a cosmic force, a creative one. Everything that comes into being is the consequence of a primordial struggle between the One and the Multiple. The polarities within the cosmos, that is being or what is and the non manifested being or what could or will be are always at odds with each other. There is a force in nature,

Heraclitus
progress
through
contraries

Heraclitus tells us, that compels the One to become Multiple and that reduces the Multiple to Unity. This force is called the *harmony of contraries* and is inherent in all aspects of nature. Therefore, behind apparent harmony lies dissension; behind conflict, serenity. Becoming exists within the harmony of contraries, that is, the spirit of reconciliation and diversity. Consequently, beginning and end are one and the same thing. For this reason, life (and man's existence) must be looked upon as part of a cosmic struggle, one facet of the All in its eternal movement.

For Diderot, as for Heraclitus, nothing was static, whether substance, idea, feeling, or sensation.[11] All was in an eternal process of association and dissociation. This notion of continuous alteration of form Diderot expressed in terms of a molecular image: "In this vast ocean of matter, not one molecule is like another, no molecule is for one moment like itself."[12] Interestingly enough, Diderot's mobile view of the universe not only fitted his philosophical and scientific concepts but his temperament as well. The "pantophile," as Voltaire called him, was forever on the move, observing, suggesting, inquiring, creating. He was flux incarnate.

Since the All moved, everything (matter for Diderot) was a living or sensible entity composed of continuously forming and dividing molecules. Molecules, according to Diderot, are endowed with eternal energy, not an energy that is injected into them from without, but is inherent to their nature, compelling them to fuse into a variety of associations. Diderot's notions concerning energy were in direct opposition to those proposed by Descartes. It was God who set the cosmos in motion, declared Descartes. He was Creator and world architect. The eighteenth-century philosopher was of the opinion that motion and matter were one and the same, that nothing propelled molecules into action from the outside.

Environment and need also play their part in the dynamic process of life. They influence the transformatory dynamism, that energy which alters molecules into animals, insects, humans. Nothing, therefore, is definitive, movement is continuous. Diderot wrote: "Homegenous, it was material; heterogenous, one neither conceives its inertia before development, nor its energy in the developed animal."[13]

If flux is eternal and universal and if everything is material, then what is man for Diderot? A fusion of molecules or atoms that are at once separate and joined together. He used the image of the beehive to make his point: although an individual bee may either die or disappear, the hive as a unit remains because the change in place and form of individual bees within the whole occurs at an infinitely slow rate.

> Would you like to transform the cluster or bees into one single animal? Modify a little the feet by which they cling together; make them contiguous instead of continuous. Between this new condition of the cluster and the former, there is certainly a marked difference; and what can that difference be, if not that now it is a whole, a single animal, whereas before it was a collection of animals?[14]

What distinguishes man from animal? His mind, Diderot asserted, which through his memory enables him to become conscious of his own existence.

c. *Existence*

For Diderot existence was based almost exlusively on man's consciousness of "having been himself, from the very first instant of reflection until the present moment."[15] Existence, therefore, is in great part memory. If memory did not exist, life would be "an uninterrupted series of sensations linked together by nothing."[16] Diderot defined memory as the ability to recognize and identify objects, individuals, messages, and other entities after the acquisition of knowledge. Memory becomes a point of repair that leads to the reconstruction of past and present activities and events perceived originally by the senses. The theory of association, which is related to the notion of sense perception (advocated by Locke, Condillac, Diderot, and other philosophes), affirmed that events which are close in time and space will be associated more readily by individuals than those experienced farther back because of the factor of contiguity. Diderot expressed the theory of association as follows:

> But vibrating strings have yet another property, that of making other strings vibrate; and that is how the first idea recalls a second, the two of them a third, these three a fourth and so on,

so that there is no limit to the ideas awakened and intercon-
nected in the mind of the philosopher, as he meditates and
hearkens to himself in silence and darkness. This instrument
makes surprising leaps, and an idea once aroused may sometimes set vibrating an harmonic at an inconceivable distance.
If this phenomenon may be observed between resonant strings
that are lifeless and separate, why should it not occur between
points that are alive and connected, between fibres that are
continuous and sensitive?[17]

Let us recall that Descartes proved existence with the well-
known apothegm: "I think, therefore I am." Locke, who rejected Descartes' notion of innate ideas, regarded experience as
the source of knowledge, that is, sensation with the help of reflection. Condillac, who adopted Locke's views although he was
not a materialist, claimed that knowledge originated in sense
perception and reflection was merely transformed sensation.
Judgment was the outgrowth of sensations stored in the mind
and reproduced under the proper stimulus by the memory.

According to Diderot, association and interraction of ideas
came into being in forms and tonalities and were organized along
certain spatial and temporal lines. In this respect he could be
considered a precursor of the Gestalt-theory partisans. It was
the visual sense that predominated for him. Rather than resorting to abstract discussions, when he explicated certain concepts,
he had recourse to imagery: the beehive, spider web, monastery,
organ, oscillating cords. This technique, used with felicity from
Plato to Montaigne and into modern times, is also a vehicle implicit in the myth. In that the eye is a sense, that is, part of
man's most primitive domain, it also is a symbol for intellectual
perception, illumination, and enlightenment. Resorting to the
visual sense, Diderot in effect appealed to both parts of man,
spirit and body, thus once again unifying what is disparate.

The mind for Diderot formed images even when the object
was absent from view. These forms, made up of particles or
atoms, were eternally active, appearing and disappearing from
the mind's eye (inner eye). Such a process is attested to during
d'Alembert's so-called dream, where he describes in his sleep
what had been heard or seen during the previous days. Although many people pay little or no attention to visual images
experienced during their waking or sleeping states, Diderot

intimates, the images' impact on the individual are extremely important; they excite the imagination and man's creative instinct. In his novel *The Indiscreet Jewels* Diderot wrote: "Objects which have struck us forcefully during the day occupy our soul at night; the lines they impressed during our waking hours in the fibers of our brain, subsist..."[19] Some individuals are convinced, Diderot continued. they have the power to bring certain images (hallucinations, mirages, nightmares, etc.) into existence at will. Certainly the will of the individual does play a part, as in the case of contrived dreams or controlled reverie. But in the real dream collective forces of spontaneous origin are at work and these would be known to the individual experiencing the autonomous pulsations as fear, affection, joy, or hatred. Such is the mystery into which Diderot plunges his reader— the immense riddle of the unconscious.

d. *Life and Death*

Since the universe is one, then life and death are reverse sides of a whole. Based in part on the concepts of Epicurus and Lucretius, Diderot suggested that everything is matter (atoms, molecules) and that matter, whether inert or not, in sensible; it goes through a continuous process of joining together and separating. Stages in the configuration of atoms are forever being experienced, from inanimate to animate conditions, and this alteration of activity may be looked upon in terms of potential and kinetic energy.

> At first you were nothing at all. You began as an imperceptible speck, formed from still smaller molecules scattered through the blood and lymph of your father and mother; that speck became a loose thread, then a bundle of threads. Up till then, not the slightest trace of your own agreable form; your eyes, those fine eyes, were no more like eyes than the tip of an anemone's feeler is like an anemone. Each of the fibers in the bundle of threads was transformed solely by nutrition and according to its conformation into a particular organ.[20]

The mind and spirit, Diderot further posited, are likewise arrangements of atoms.[21] Organs are formed (either the diaphragm or the mind and take on specific shapes via a nutritive process: passing from the state of inertia to one of sensibility or animation.

To best illustrate the transformatory process, Diderot had recourse to the image of the statue. In *Discussions between D'Alembert and Diderot* he suggests that there is little difference between man and a marble statue. "Flesh can be made from marble, and marble from flesh."[22]   The statue is inanimate; it "has inactive sensitiveness; and man, animals, perhaps even plants, are endowed with active sensitiveness."[23]   The change between one phase of existence and another occurs during the eating process. "I shall make it [the marble] edible," Diderot wrote.[24]   The steps in this process take place as follows: take a marble statue, then hammer and pound it until it is pulverized.

> When the block of marble is reduced to impalpable powder, I mix it with humus or leaf-mould; I knead them well together; I water the mixture, I let it decompose for a year or two or a hundred, time doesn't matter to me. When the whole has turned into a more or less homogeneous substance, into humus, do you know what I do?[25]

Peas, beans, cabbage, or other vegetables are planted in the humus. These grow and are nourished by the soil, blended into the pulverized marble. After several months, when the vegetables are ready, someone picks them, eats them, and in so doing is taking the marble into himself. "I like this passage from marble into humus, from humus to the vegetable kingdom, from the vegetable to the animal kingdom, to flesh."[26]   Diderot's hylozoist theory (nutritive concepts) concerning ingestion is fundamental to his argument: the struggle waged between atoms as they pass from the animate to the inanimate world: "Eat, digest, distill."[27]

"Life is a succession of actions and reactions," Diderot wrote, "Living, I act and react as a mass...dead, I act and react in the form of molecules..." Death then is a dispersion of molecules, thus rendering matter inanimate. "Then I do not die?... No, no doubt, I don't die in that sense, neither I myself nor anything else... Birth, life, decay are merely changes of form... And what does the form matter? Each form has the happiness and misfortune which pertain to it..."[28]   There could be little or no fear or outrageous religious protocol associated with death for Diderot: life and death were part of a universal whole, an element of a continuous dynamic process. And in this connection it is interesting to note that Diderot died in contentment, while dining.

D'Alembert's Dream is Diderot's dream. As such, it encompasses the individual and the collective, the mortal and immortal, the finite and the infinite. It reflects the doctrine of his day—Enlightenment; it sums up certain views of the past—cosmic concepts; it intuits movements that will become popular in the centuries to come—metempsychosis, palingenesis, synesthesia.

Because the dream was contrived and consciously oriented by Diderot, it enabled him to explain his thesis of cosmis functioning both clearly and systematically; in that it stemmed from the domain of the irrational, it included elements of mystery and acausality, plunging him into the most creative of waters— the universal flow of things.

D'Alembert's Dream is clearly a document of the soul in the profoundest sense of the word, and because of the depths it reaches and the universality of the ideations and feelings expressed, it appeals to the rationalist and the mystic alike. As Paul Vernière wrote:

> In *D'Alembert's Dream,* man and the world are alone, face to face; God is not only silent but absent; but by this same token the universe acquires a kind of divinity in which man participates when he knows how to recognize, in life's infinite paths, in the changing modalities of eternal Nature, the new forms of power and beauty with religious fervor.[29]

NOTES

[1]Denis Diderot was born at Langres in 1713. His father, a cutler by trade, was an upright and realistic man. The spirit of law and order prevailed in his home and town. Diderot moved to Paris at the age of fifteen. There he studied philosophy and earned a Master of Art's degree at the Collège d'Harcourt. His father tried to persuade him to study law and he complied for two years, but then abandoned it in favor of mathematics, physics, and the classics. Diderot did not have an all-consuming interest. He was enraptured by very nearly all phases of life. To support himself during his carefree but frequently difficult years of his youth, he gave private lessons in mathematics and translated a *Dictionary of Medicine* and a *History of Greece*. In 1745 he rendered the Earl of Shaftesbury's important *Essay on Merit and Virtue* into French. In 1743 he married Antoinette Champion, the owner of a small lace and linen shop in Paris. They were temperamentally unsuited to each other. Only one child survived from their union, Diderot's beloved Angélique, later known as Mme. Vandeul, the author of her father's *Memoirs*. Diderot's works were varied and many: novels, essays, dialogues, etc. In 1765 Catherine II of Russia bought Diderot's library. Ironically, Diderot, one of the most outspoken antagonists of despotism, was invited and accepted the Czarina's invitation to visit her in St. Petersburg (1773-1774). Diderot's last years were rewarding and serene. He died in 1784.

[2]Otis E. Fellows and Norman L. Torrey, *The Age of Enlightenment*, p. 331.

[3]John Pappas, "Science versus poetry," *Thought*. No. 179. Winter, 1970.

[4]Jean Brun, *Héraclite*, p. 122.

[5]*Diderot Interpreter of Nature*, p. 65.

[6]*Ibid.*, p. 49.

[7]*Ibid.*, p. 72.

[8]*Webster's New World Dictionary.* 1966.

[9]Denis Diderot, *Oeuvres*, p. 899.

[10]*Diderot Interpreter of Nature*, p. 126.

[11]To further stress this point, Diderot had recourse to the fire image in his *Philosophical Principles:* "You who so easily imagine matter in repose, can you imagine fire in repose? Everything in nature has its own different form of action, like this mass of molecules which you call *fire.* In this mass which you call *fire,* each molecule has its own nature its own action."

Ibid., p. 128.

[12]*Ibid.,* p. 72.

[13]*Oeuvres,* p. 881.

[14]*Diderot Interpreter of Nature*, p. 56.

[15]*Oeuvres,* p. 881.

[16]*Diderot Interpreter of Nature*, p. 68.

[17]*Ibid.,* p. 56.

[18]See Diderot's *Letter on the Blind* and his extraordinary *Salons.*

[19]*Oeuvres,* p. 159.

[20]René Pomeau, *Diderot,* pp. 11-36.

[21]*Diderot Interpreter of Nature*, p. 84.

[22]*Ibid.,* p. 49.

[23]*Ibid.,* p. 50.

[24]*Ibid.,* p. 51.

[25]*Ibid.*

[26]*Ibid.*, p. 52.

[27]*Ibid.*, p. 53.

[28]*Ibid.*, p. 79.

[29]Paul Vernière, *Diderot*, p. LXI.

CHAPTER 4

Jacques Cazotte—The Devil in Love:
A Dream Initiation

Each one experiences his individual universe in the dream, whereas in a waking state all men have a common universe.

(Heraclitus)

Jacques Cazotte,[1] an Illuminist, believed the dream was part of an initiatory procedure. His novel *The Devil in Love* (1772) is based on just such a dream, one which instructed him in certain secret rites fundamental to the Martinist Order and which broached specific metaphysical questions. Metaphysically, the cosmic world is brought into focus via the initiatory dream in Cazotte's narrative and permits him to explicate the same question posited by Diderot: the theme of transformation within a monistic cosmos. Whereas Diderot approached this nebulous area in a scientific manner and for the most part according to Cartesian rationalism, Cazotte injected it with mystery and magic. He deals with three other equally important questions, certainly fascinating to him and to moderns alike—the feminine principle, the problem of the *puer aeternus,* and the writer as *vates.*

Unlike the philosophes such as Voltaire, d'Alembert, and Diderot, for whom the exterior world was to a great extent the *fons et origo,* Cazotte experienced the oneirosphere as strongly or perhaps more powerfully than the workaday world. He had a deep sense of the sacred and was convinced that behind the visible world lay hidden a domain filled with living and breathing souls capable of arousing feelings of malaise and ecstasy in those sufficiently sensitive to experience them.

The Illuminists were influenced most deeply by the Swedish scientists, philosopher, and theologian Emanuel Swedenborg. For Swedenborg the invisible world was merely an extension of the visible domain; interplanetary space, therefore, was peopled with angels who lived in a variety of spheres, according to their degree of perfection; the soul was eternal and reincarnated. Swedenborg claimed he had discovered secret correspondences between himself and the universe at large, enabling him to come into contact and record his conversations with divine spirits, and angels as well as his revelations of God.

Martinez de Pasqualis, another Illuminist, founded the Masonic lodge in Montpellier in 1754 and later the Martinist Order. Martinism was a composite of the Kabbalistic rites of the eleventh century, early Gnosticism, and Neoplatonism as prescribed by the Alexandrian spiritual leaders of the ancient world. Pasqualis' *Treatise of the Reintegration of beings into their first properties, spiritual and divine powers and virtues* taught man how to expiate the crime of original sin. Prior to his separation from God, resulting from Adam's and Eve's evil ways, man was devoid of arrogance and corruption. Because of the schism between himself and God, man revealed his desires for infinite knowledge, his intention to become a creator, a Demiurge—God's rival. But despite man's evil ways, Pasqualis affirmed, all was not lost. Man's salvation was possible because of God's infinite goodness. To contact cosmic forces, God, and the dead, who now inhabit other regions, man must go through a rigorous initiatory period. The neophyte must learn to overcome temptation, take an oath of secrecy, learn certain magic formulas and secret words, and prostrate himself on the ground. Only then can he recover his essential dignity and increase his spiritual knowledge. Some members of Pasqualis' sect experienced union with Christ, a reintegration in Him, and thus became part of what Pasqualis called an "elect group."[2]

Claude de Saint-Martin, Pasqualis' disciple, felt that his master had been overly immersed with theurgy and not sufficiently involved with divinity. In *The Unknown Philosopher* Martin stressed a return to biblical texts, the Gospels, and the Book of Revelation in particular. According to Saint-Martin, once man had fallen out of God's favor and was cast out of the Garden of Eden onto earth (or matter), he became subject to misery, disease, and death. Because he had once been part of God, however, he longed to return to this original state of unity. The Martinists believed man capable of elevating himself sufficiently—from matter to spirit—to return to his primordial paradisiac state. In order to succeed in his goal, man must listen to certain "inner signs" and to his "inner voice," God's way of acting through him. Man can hear God's dictates when he descends into himself and practices certain arcane exercises both Pasqualis and Saint-Martin taught the members of their

order. Once a profound withdrawal into self has been experienced by the neophyte, he becomes "reintegrated" into God
or reenters the state of primordial unity. For the Martinists,
intelligence and will are the only active forces in nature capable
of "modifying phenomena." If man masters these agents, he
can descend within, which is tantamount, in mystical terms, to
an ascension toward God and a higher order of things. Man in
complicity with God is capable of carving out his own destiny.

In *The Unknown Philosopher* Saint-Martin suggests that
the true neophyte should rely on both God and his own will to
build himself up—to construct himself, as Solomon's temple had
been built, from individual pieces of stone to a unified solid
monument. Only through a unification of disparate forces
within man can inner growth and illumination occur. The
building process of the inner man may be accomplished through
self-discipline; to achieve this end carnal lust must be annihilated
and terrestrial bonds severed. Initiations based on individual
tests, including those associated with the four elements, could
lead to an individual's rebirth. Saint-Martin quoted from the
Gospel of St. John: "Jesus answered and said unto him, Verily,
verily, I say unto thee, Except a man be born again, he cannot
see the kingdom of God." (3:3)

1. *The Dream and the Initiatory Procedure*

In *The Devil in Love* the reader becomes privy to an initiatory dream that revealed to him, so Cazotte claimed, the secret
rituals of the Martinist Order. When Cazotte wrote his novel,
he was not a member of any occult society. Shortly after the
book's publication a "grave" looking gentleman "draped in a
brown coat" knocked at Cazotte's door and was admitted. The
Stranger began making all sorts of "bizarre" motions with his
hands, those used as signs of recognition by members of secret
societies such as the Martinists and Masons. Cazotte, who did
not understand the esoteric meaning of such antics, grew impatient. When the stranger finally realized that Cazotte was
neither a member of the Martinist nor the Masonic Order, he
was dumbfounded. How could Cazotte have described the secret
rituals so precisely in his novel if he had never been exposed
to them? How could he have depicted gestures known only to
those who had risen to the First Degree? "What!" he asked,

"those evocations amid ruins, the mysteries of the Kabbalah, the occult power over air, the striking theories implicit in the power of numbers, the will, the fatalities of existence—could you have imagined all of these things?"[3]

Cazotte was a religious mystic, clairvoyant, and theosophist who believed in his ability to communicate with living spirits whenever he so desired. When spirits made their presences known to him at various times, they directed his thoughts, he maintained, into certain channels. Just as bodily motion destroys the "column of air which we support," so everything in the universe is alive and moves and is transformed into something else with each breath or thought wave.[4] The void does not exist. Cazotte even distinguished between the opacity of certain souls: those who want to remain earthbound retain a kind of thickness and resemble the living being for a long time; those who want to withdraw into heavenly realms become transparent.[5] What Cazotte sensed and what physicists have proven today is the fact that all living things (plants, animals, humans) possess a type of "energy matrix," that is, they are endowed with a physical body (atoms, molecules) and another corpus made up of energy and referred to as "the biological plasma body." (In physics, plasma is considered "the fourth state of matter—streams of masses of ionized particles.")[6] Cazotte, highly sensitive and introverted, might have felt the flow of his energy or the pulsating of the magnetic fields of which the atmosphere is replete; or he might have entered into another time dimension where past, present, and future no longer exist as separate entities.[7] His initiatory dream therefore expanded his universe.

The Devil in Love relates the adventures of the twenty-five-year-old Alvare, a Spaniard who is serving as captain of the guards to the king of Naples. He spends an evening with some acquaintances and becomes fascinated with certain feats of magic he observes. He too wants to command spirits and become master of his destiny. His host warns him not to be too hasty in undertaking a science for which he is not yet prepared. One needs a long initiation period, he tells the headstrong young man, otherwise spirits can become destructive forces. Alvare, an impetuous youth, refuses to listen to the *magister*. When they next meet, on a Friday, Alvare is given the formulas for evoking spirits. He must say the word *Beelzebub* three times—and he does. Suddenly, a horrible camel's head appears before him and says "Cho vuoi?" Seemingly unruffled, but inwardly terrified, Alvare orders him to transform himself. A white spaniel now gambols about. A lavish repast then appears for Alvare and his friends. Finally, a beautiful page makes her presence known, who later introduces herself as Biondetta. Alvare and Biondetta leave for Venice. She serves him faithfully. He worships her and puts her on a pedestal; but to satisfy his "baser" instincts, he takes the courtesan Olympia as his mistress. Jealous of Biondetta, Olympia has her rival stabbed. Alvare, nearly crazed with anguish, repents his evil ways and nurses Biondetta back to health. After he falls asleep, from exhaustion, he has a dream: he sees his mother and takes her to the ruins of Portici, but she warns him of imminent danger. As the two walk through a narrow passage, with a precipice on one side, he feels a hand he identifies as Biondetta's trying to push him into the precipice. Seconds later he feels another hand, that of his mother, protecting him from the fall. He is grateful to her for never having abandoned him, even in his dreamworld.

The dream preoccupies Alvare. He wants to know whether Biondetta is a real human being. How was she created? Why did she appear to him after certain magic rituals? Biondetta tells him she is a sylph, a spirit made of air, and took on human form to serve him. But after she became manifest, she realized she also possessed a heart and feelings and fell in love with him. Alvare decides to marry her. One day, when walking in the street, he chances into a church. There he sees a tomb with marble figures carved around it that are in mourning. One statue draws his attention. "I believe I am looking at the image of my mother," he says to himself. Is it a warning? He thinks it is a presage of his mother's death and wonders whether his lack of tenderness and the "disorderly nature" of his life led her to her tomb.[8] Alvare decides to return to Spain and to his mother. He writes Biondetta a letter that he will send for her once he has announced their marriage plans to his parents. However, then he sees her in her carriage in tears since she believes he has run away from her. They leave for Spain together. Many unpleasant catastrophes take place: storms, broken carriage axles, and so on. Finally, they arrive near his hometown

where Alvare learns that his mother is dying. He remembers
the vision of the tomb in the church and becomes increasingly
anxious. Meanwhile, however, Biondetta charms him and not
only conquers his heart but his body as well, then finally reveals
her true identity: "I am the Devil, my dear Alvare, I am the
Devil." She extracts the treasured words from him: "My dear
Beelzebub, I adore you..."[9] and now tells him of her powers and
how she used artifice to gain control over him. To prove her
statements she reverts back to the horrible camel's head. Alvare,
beside himself with anguish, throws himself on his bed, where
he sleeps. When he awakes, a servant tells him he has slept for
fourteen hours. Alvare realizes that what happened after his
return to Spain was but a dream. He rises, dresses, and goes to
his mother's home He tells her of his fantasies and she calls
one of the great doctors of Salamanca. The prognosis is good:
the Devil did seduce Alvare but did not corrupt him since the
young man felt great remorse. Alvare would succeed in eventually freeing himself, but only after the inner struggle and torment
that now troubled his mind would cease, indicating the Devil's
departure from him.

What Alvare is unaware of and what his host, the magician,
tries to point out to him are the dangers involved when too much
power is given to the inexperienced. A period of initiation (the
word comes from Latin, meaning "beginning," or more broad-
ly, "entrance") and gestation must precede the gift of power.
Such initiation rituals, which place the neophyte on "the right
road,"[10] are an important phase in human development—a
rite de passage from an inferior to a superior state. The rituals
he must go through act on him deeply and intensely and finally
become part of the human experience that is life. The neophyte
must never divulge the secret; to do so would be meaningless
since one cannot learn experience intellectually, or familiarize
oneself with pain, discipline, death, and fright, or tense one's
will cerebrally. These emotions must be incised in an individual
through a long period of gestation. Experience cannot be communicated from one to another; each individual profits from his
own experience to grow and fulfill his latent or potential possibilities. To accomplish this goal, he must be active, not passive.

Initiation is a confrontation with fear, death, and chaos, and if successfully experienced, it may lead to rebirth, order, and illumination.

Alvare was unwilling to go through the long preparatory ordeal of initiation. He chose to plunge unprepared right into the experience of magic, to conquer, via formulas, forces that were beyond his control. What he was banishing, psychologically, was the confrontation and rejection of ugliness, evil, and unregenerate characteristics. To seek to surmount the human condition is the lot of great heroes. It is a Promethean quest. It is the goal of the trained magician who may accomplish his feats by occult means. For Alvare, who is uninitiated, such feats will not lead to rebirth and illumination.

Initiation may also be looked upon as a desire and means of discovering nature's secrets and, in so doing, the key to its transformatory process. The transforming principle in nature, or the notion of eternal flux, which Heraclitus, Empedocles, Anaximander, and other ancients experienced as a living doctrine, enabled the monistic universe to pursue its course in a never-ending death-rebirth cycle. The concept of monism is based on an energetic process of transformation; all within the cosmos is linked but evolves eternally and is in a perpetual state of transformation from the tiniest pebble upward.

Such a transformatory doctrine confirmed Cazotte's belief in deity. God was revealing Himself perpetually in His infinite manifestations. Everything that exists, then, has a soul since it is God-created. All is linked, although on the surface certain actions, sensations, and thoughts might be considered isolated; they are, nevertheless, dependent upon a universal plan, a cosmic whole—an immense analogy. According to the Illuminists, God's statement *fiat lux* set the entire machinery into motion, transforming chaos (or the unmanifested) into cosmos (the orderly and manifested).

The metaphysical and scientific notion of transformation may be illustrated in *The Devil in Love* in its symbol: water. The main incidents take place in Venice, a city surrounded by canals and waterways that ruled the Mediterranean from the tenth to the fifteenth centuries and was called "queen of the seas." Water is a primal image; it is an element in the creation of the world and a preserver of life. It is immortal, formless, and circulates, therefore may be considered a world *in potentia.* When immersing oneself in water, one experiences, symbolically, a return to a preformal state, the possibility of death and rebirth. Water has also been linked to the unconscious—to that timeless, formless area in which infinite riches are hidden and all is possible. For Cazotte Venice and its water symbolism expressed the grandeur of a bygone world as well as the myriad possibilities life offers in the preformal state. Thus it was the perfect vehicle to describe his mystical and theurgic notions. According to Cazotte, transformation not only existed on a natural and religious plane but also on a magical level, when individuals believe they can gain control of cosmic forces and thus master the world. Cazotte practiced his own brand of magic and was not alone in this field. Magic had been popular since ancient Egyptian times; during that period it was claimed man could constrain the gods to execute orders by performing certain rituals and reciting precise incantations. In Babylonia and Assyria magic ceremonies were held in order to direct and destroy demoniacal forces. In medieval times angels and demons were evoked by spells, pacts, and santanic orgies. And Greek alchemy, Neoplatonism, Arab theology, the Kabbalah, and occultism (Paracelsus, Agrippa von Nettesheim, Jakob Boehme, Robert Fludd, Saint-Martin, etc.) believed in a world soul and in astral souls that could be contacted if so willed. "There is not a part of man which does not correspond to an element, a plant, an intelligence, a measure, a reason in the Archetype."[11]

The magician in *The Devil in Love* concentrates his mystical powers on objects and cosmic forces. His feats in ceremonial magic enable him—so he believes—to divine powerful universal truths, a higher wisdom, and at times even to experience a rapport with God, the Devil, angels, or demons.[12] Alvare asks his mentor the following question: "Do you believe there exists a science which teaches how to transform metals and how to reduce spirits to obey us?"[13] Alvare is immediately convinced of man's Promethean powers by the magician who strikes his pipe three times on the table, then commands a spirit to light it and return it to him. The naive Alvare is dumbfounded by this power, which he terms a "natural religion."[14] His curiosity is peaked. He too wants to partake of the secrets of the universe. He too becomes Faustian in his desires—or gives way to hubris.

Cazotte's interest in magic was pragmatic. He frequently talked with dead friends and relatives to gain information from them as how to confront satanic souls, demons, and elementary spirits that hovered about in the air in order to try to dissipate the power of evil in the world.[15]   Unlike St. Augustine, but similar to the Gnostic, evil was a reality for Cazotte, an entity with which each individual must deal.

When Alvare faces evil in the form of the camel's head, the spaniel, and Biondetta, he is, psychologically, coming into contact with his most archaic, unintegrated, regressive, and fragmentary self—nearly autonomous forces within his psyche. These unformed potentialities are in a chaotic state and therefore cannot be controlled.   They surge forth unannounced and their impact upon Alvare is great.   Their leap into consciousness at times destroys their equilibrium.

It is significant that in *The Devil in Love* evil is brought into existence in the form of a camel.   The camel, an animal associated in the Zohar with the serpent of the Garden of Eden, spells danger.   The serpent had convinced Eve to eat the apple from the Tree of Knowledge, thus bringing about the fall of man into matter or consciousness—that is, life. The same may be said of the camel.   Alvare remarks on his "cold sweat"[16] when this animal's head first appears.   He tries to fight off his fear and succeeds when he orders the camel's metamorphosis into the white spaniel, reminiscent of the black dog in *Faust.*   Since ancient Egyptian times, dogs have been considered man's faithful servants and friends but also companions of the dead as they make their way into the domain of Osiris and Isis.   The dog symbolism is perfectly valid in Alvare's case from both a psychological and metaphysical point of view because the dog will accompany him for a short period during his perilous "night sea journey" into his inner world.

The fact that Alvare rejects the disciplines and ordeals required by the magician in the initiatory process, indicates a refusal to come to grips with the forces of nature and with certain unregenerate aspects inchoate in his psyche.   Although Alvare succeeds in bringing about a change via the ceremonial art of magic, the alterations effected do not lead to an evolution in his personality.   Rather than helping him build a solid structure within himself by struggling with each force with which he came into contact, he yields to them, thereby demonstrating his dependence upon them.

2. *The Feminine Principle:*
Its Positive and Negative Sides

Two important feminine characters are revealed in Alvare's dream: his mother and Biondetta. They may be looked upon as *anima* figures or man's inner attitude toward a woman. Anima figures have appeared in dreams, myths, and literary works of all types and are usually repositories for the unconscious feelings and states of those who project onto such beings. These forces remain unconscious because no conscious relationship with such types has yet been forthcoming.

Alvare's mother represents a celestial being for him: merciful, kind, tender, nutritive, understanding; a world soul, the Virgin Mary, Isis, Sophia. He considers her a positive force in his life. And yet, one may wonder if this is so.

Biondetta is a chthonic demon, a thanatotic force, like the Greek Lamia, harpy, and Erinyes or the Arabic jinn. She is instinctual, demoniacal, seductive, devouring entagling. She arouses lust, torment, and corrupts, enticing man toward base ends. She emerges from the most primitive strata of life and frequently leads either to the destruction of others or to her own.

It is not strange that women have been linked to the forces of evil. Eve seduces Adam, leading to the fall; Dalilah cut Samson's hair, an act of symbolic castration. The woman represents Intellect (*Binah*) in the Kabbalah, thus she arouses curiosity and dissatisfaction, whereas the man stands for Wisdom (*Hokmah*), the ordering factor of divinity. It is, then, the woman who compels man to lose sight of the spirit, to become disoriented and estranged, or to neglect the God within. The evil woman, nevertheless, has her positive side. She creates duality, binary opposition, thus generating action and thereby making growth a possibility. Biondetta assumes such a role in *The Devil in Love*.

Biondetta enters into the story by a feat of magic. She identifies herself as a sylph who first acquires the body of a woman and then a heart. Sylphs are air spirits. One of the elements, air symbolizes for the mystic an aspect of the life process in dematerialized form: *pneuma, ruach,* the creative principle. In Genesis it is stated that God "breathed into Adam's nostrils the breath of life; and man became a living soul." (2:7) Such a postulation would also fit the definition of compressed or concentrated air: it causes fire, energy, activity, passion, the heat of creativity, novelty, and, finally, the birth of new attitudes. As Mephistopheles for Faust, so Biondetta becomes an irritant, an impediment, a hindrance forcing Alvare to act and rise from his lethargy, to perhaps struggle—to emerge, symbolically, from the paradise state of adolescence to that of maturity where conflict must be met and dealt with. Without the appearance of Biondetta, Alvare would not have had the urge to strive for anything; he would have lived as a child under the "kind" dominion of his mother.

Biondetta may also be regarded as a succubus, a woman who is neither human nor divine but has the power to unite with man, usually during his slumber. The notion of such unions existed since ancient times: for example, Zeus fathering Alcmene's son Hercules, in the story of Eros and Psyche, in the divine birth of Dionysus and Christ. Relations between man and the gods or God, the unnatural union between the human and the spiritual world is referred to in the Bible: "the sons of God saw the daughters of men that they were fair; and they took them wives of all which they chose." (Genesis 6:2) The Talmud's and the Zohar's approach to the succubus (and incubus) is tolerant: sexual relations with demons were not considered sinful since men experienced these unwittingly during their sleep. The Catholic Church, however, frowned upon such unions. Individuals were punished and frequently put on trial by the Inquisition.[17] Such an approach led to witch-hunts and similar ordeals and punishments.

Biondetta, as the devil's appendage, appears as an impediment, a force with which Alvare will have to deal, a bridge he will have to cross. It is at these very junctures—each time Alvare has a problem—that the kind, gentle, positive, *possessive* mother will make her presence known in a dream or a hallucination, thus preventing what she sees as the destruction of her son.[18]

The first dream occurs after Biondetta has been stabbed by

the courtesan Olympia. Alvare feels guilty toward Biondetta
and responsible for the incident. "I see only an adored woman,"
he says about her, "victim of ridiculous bias, sacrificed by my
vain and extravagant confidence, and overburdened by me with
the most cruel abuses." The fact that Alvare experiences guilt
indicates that the problem he is having with Biondetta (as representative of the seductress) is coming into consciousness, thus
preventing him from coasting along in life and living a peripheral
existence. His relationship with her now requires sounding out,
a confrontation, a struggle if it is to be meaningful. In the dream
Alvare sees his mother and tells her his adventure; then he decides to take her to the ruins of Portici.

> Let us not go there, my son, you are in obvious danger. As we
> were passing through a narrow passageway...a hand suddenly
> pushes me toward a precipice; I recognize it as Biondetta's.
> I was about to fall when another hand pulls me back, and I
> find myself in my mother's arms. I awaken, still gasping from
> fear. "Tender mother!" I cried out, "you do not abandon me,
> even in the dream."[19]

Though Alvare's mother permitted him to leave home and
country, according to the custom of the time, she possessed him
so completely on an unconscious level that she had made him
entirely dependent upon her. Psychologically, he is still living
in her womb. And so, the dream indicates, this saintly mother,
the symbol of tender love, a positive principle to her son, is in
fact a destructive force in his life. It was she, as a result of her
protracted solicitude, who forced him to remain enclosed in
the paradisial or undifferentiated state of security. She denied
him the struggle of life, the plunge into diversity.

That the dream takes place near the Portici ruins denotes
that Alvare is coming into contact with a "dead" or "decayed"
past. His mother is associated with a regressive era, a spiritual
desolation. Alvare is linked with a frame of existence that is no
longer meaningful to him and from which life has been extinguished, although the outer core still persists.

Biondetta, on the other hand, risks everything she loves
when attempting to push him into the precipice, or the pitfalls
of life, consequently to point up the hazards, struggles, and
battles of daily existence. The hand, according to ancient

Egyptian doctrine, was looked upon as a powerful instrument, a kind of pillar (the palm is at the center and the fingers radiate outward). It is supportive, holds together, and acts. Alvare, then, almost falls into life—as Adam and Eve fell into matter—that is, into consciousness—thus experiencing their own identity, living out their own lives, and struggling through a variety of entaglements during their terrestrial state. Alvare's mother, however, holds her son back, preventing his fall and possible death, but by the same token rejecting the possibility of any kind of development on his part. Only through danger and the struggle of polarities can life be experienced and strength gained.

Although the real struggle never came to pass, Alvare does become curious about his dream, compelling him to ask Biondetta about her origins. Why did she come into his life as an ugly camel's head, then as a white spaniel? He must know the answer, he exclaims, and also confesses that his heart belongs to her. When she informs him that she is a sylph and was created in order to serve him, she acts as a ploy. The reverse is actually true: he is dominated by her. As a sylph, she represents an inferior or primitive stratum of life. It is this kind of woman who lures and torments man, who seeks to unite with him. Such a bond, if it were realized, would lead only to self-destruction since sylphs are not humans and neither their bodies nor psyches can satisfy man's desire.

The second dream—waking this time—occurs in a church. Alvare sees a black marble tomb at the end of the chapel surrounded by mourning white figures. A strange light illuminates the area. Alvare stares at one of the statues, which looks just like his mother; he considers the image a premonition of his mother's death: "Oh the most worthy of women; as misguided as he is, your Alvare gives you all the rights of his heart. He would rather die a thousand times than stray from the obeissance he owes you..." He is devoured by an insurmountable passion and asks his mother's help to overcome it. "Come, then," he says, "let us [editorial us] open my heart to my mother, and let us once again place ourselves under her dear shelter."[20]

The church, similar to the underground recesses of the first dream, is an enclosed female symbol; like a walled city or castle, a place of containment or redemption, it indicates an unconscious desire of the dreamer to experience security, structure, and the peace of childhood and adolescence. The weeping statue in its whiteness, beauty, and purity beside the black marble tomb stands for the dual elements involved: the spiritual and the earthly. Both, however, are associated with weeping and death. The image clearly indicates that if Alvare is to remain in this cloistered atmosphere, dependent and thus stifled by Mother, it would surely lead to the tomb: from the *womb* to the *tomb,* as the saying goes. In hermetic tradition a return to the mother means dying.

That Alvare interprets his mother's presence in this vision as a sign of her impending death due to his vagaries and decides to return home as quickly as possible is a completion in the existential domain of the prognostications inherent in both dreams. By a return to the *womb* he is preparing his own *tomb—* a regression to the infantile way; another indication of his inability to pursue the ordeal of the initiatory practices suggested by the magician at the outset of the novel. Rather than assuming the fight for life and the fear and pain this entails, thus making him independent and fulfilled, he succumbs to the pressure and remains a *puer aeternus.*

3. *Puer Aeternus*

The *puer aeternus,* the eternal boy or adolescent, never discovers his identity and is forever subject to the domination of his mother, or of a female figure who symbolizes or is associated in some way with her. The *puer aeternus* is so subjectively linked to his mother that he can love no one beside her. He is therefore incapable of carving out his own existence and thus leads a provisional life, perpetually dissatisfied. Examples of such types are Endymion, Attis, Narcissus.

Alvare lives in his mother's circumscribed world: her homeland, sense of values, and her religious scruples. Interestingly enough and in keeping with the *puer aeternus* theme, the father image (save for the fleeting magician) in the story is nonexistent, fortifying in this sense the parasitic mother-son relationship. Alvare is incapable of breaking away from his childhood and the perfect mother *image:* home and church. The fate of the *puer aeternus* lies just in this impasse: in the avoidance of the conflict imposed upon by life. He lives through the dictates and experiences of others rather than knowing them himself. Opposition does not exist in his world; therefore he is not compelled to act or undergo pain and is a blocked individual. Alvare, in essence, withdraws from life, from what his mother considers the corruptible world. By not facing Biondetta, or what she represents (sensuality, irrational domain), no conflict is engendered. He never overcomes his identification with his mother or the original wholeness of the paradisial state. Under such circumstances Alvare cannot develop what lies *in potentia* within his unconscious. He should have struggled with fear and death; he should have discovered his own corruptibility, his own fragmentation. His mother prevented him from participating in the human condition; by the same token she castrated him psychologically. He never took part in the "primordial struggle"; neither polarities of the feminine psyche were integrated into his being.[21]

4. *The Writer as Vates*

Cazotte claimed that he wrote *The Devil in Love* as a result of a dream. His oneirosphere thus opened the doors to certain arcane rites and clarified specific metaphysical questions. But Cazotte was not alone in experiencing the pleromatic world. Dreams and clairvoyance have always been part of the poet's domain: in Latin, *vates* is the word for "poet" and means "visionary" or "prophet." In ancient times the creative artist was looked upon as a seer: a being who observed life beyond the world of appearances and saw its eternal aspect; therefore could envision life as a unit, not merely in its ephemoral or differentiated phases. For many, however, prophetic dreams, coincidences, and mantic procedures have usually been relegated to the domain of superstition, ignorance, nonsense, or magic. Albertus Magnus, the great medieval magician felt that coincidences and supernatural happenings, which he described in his *Mirabilis Mundi* (1485), belonged to the realm of magic and were an attempt by man to capture outer forces in order to understand and cope with them. The Bible, the Koran, the Book of the Dead, and the I Ching also include atemporal happenings and present them as manifestations of divinity. Goethe, attempting to pin a scientific label on supernatural happenings, declared in his *Conversations with Eckermann*, "We all have certain electric and magnetic powers within us and ourselves exercise an attractive and repelling force, according as we come in touch with something like or unlike."[22]

There was little difference for Cazotte between the material, or realistic, world and the nonmaterial or nontemporal realm. He could hop through centuries, wander into outer space, commune with souls and demons, cover spatial areas, and transcend the differentiated world. What did such an ability mean for the psyche? Did the powers given to him in his initiatory and precognitive dreams imply that the psychic function exists outside the "spatio-temporal law of causality?"[23] Ever since Newton established his theory of causality, man has been led to believe that everything within the universe has a causal explanation. If Newton's law were valid, then it might be postulated that chance itself would be the result of a causality that has not yet come into existence. Then how could one know about something that has not yet taken place? How could one explain telepathy? coincidence? synchronicity? Swedenborg's vision of Stockholm burning at the very instant the fire was raging did not take spacial distances into account. His vision and the event occured at the same time.[24]

Causality is a philosophical principle that came into existence as a result of natural law. Modern physicists, whose conclusions are based on statistical truths, consider the acausal principle to be relative to factors that are unfamiliar to man. An acausal event is virtually impossible to imagine. Since it is unthinkable to belive in anything that is not based on what we already know, we must conclude that acausal events do not appear in nature. Although the world of chance (or of coincidence, precognitive dreams, telepathy) may seem frequently to be causally connected, in reality it is not: you buy a theater ticket with the same number printed on it as your house or telephone number; you dream of receiving a letter and it arrives the following day. Coincidences sometimes run in series such as the cycles of the gambler with his good and bad days. Einstein, impressed with Paul Kammerer's experiments along these lines described in *Das Gesetz der Serie,* did not relegate synchronistic events to the realm of superstition or magic.

Initiatory or precognitive dreams or telepathy cannot be explained by the time and space factor since each breaches distances. The psyche travels in "a variable space-time concept" or in another dimension governed by laws and an order foreign to

us.   One may posit the belief that acausal phenomena (as in
ESP) is an energy relationship.[25]   But if the event has not yet
occurred, how can energy apply?   Man's rational space-time concept is an abstract intellectual notion, a hypothesis, as is his belief in causality.[26]   The psyche functions in another dimension
and according to laws of its own.   Certain "patterns of behavior"
may be deduced or "archetypal patterns" from the psyche, each
giving off affects or a "specific charge,"[27] but they cannot yet
be explained.   When someone dreams or experiences certain
coincidences (synchronistic events), emotional aftermaths occur;
one is affected by certain "unconscious instinctual impulses and
contents."   When the unconscious flows into consciousness it
brings certain subliminal intuitions or perceptions, "forgotten
memory images."   The images that emerge may be acausal; that
is, the person experiencing them cannot think of any connection
between what happened in reality and the occurrence in the
dream.   Therefore the images that came into consciousness have
no rational or causal relationship with the objective situation the
person has just experienced—at least, not as far as he knows.

Some mantic or prophetic processes, according to Jung,
may be explained in terms of emotions.   By arousing someone's
fears or hopes (or interests), one stimulates some content within
the unconscious that then manifests itself in one or another
archetypal dream motif.   Such a situation might have been the
case with Cazotte's initiatory dreams.   The archetypal images
that came to him, which he either transferred into poetical
images in his writings or expressed vocally to his friends throughout his life, emerged from his collective unconscious (in a nontemporal frame of reference).   Many archetypal dreams nourished in the collective unconscious include a collective past and
present, implying an abolition of what rational man alludes to
as time and space.   Jung describes such happenings in the following manner:

> The deeper "layers" of the psyche lose their individual unique-
> ness as they retreat farther and farther into darkness "lower
> down," that is to say, as they approach the autonomous func-
> tional systems, they become increasingly collective until they
> are universalized and extinguished in the body's materiality,
> i.e., in chemical and substance.   The body's carbon is simply
> carbon.   Hence "at bottom" the psyche is simply "world."[28]

This "bottom level" lives within each of us. By tapping such resources or lowering the threshold of consciousness (which comes automatically with *un abaissement du niveau mental*), a person may experience the effects that open the door to "absolute knowledge." As far as one knows, no mechanistic laws exist that relate causal to acausal processes. Acausal phenomena are "the precondition of law, the chance substrate on which law is based."[29]

How else except thorugh the acausal-factor theory, which permits the unconscious to exist and live beyond the physical space-time delineations, can one explain Cazotte's vision of his own death, that he saw his head cut off thirty years before the event? that he described the death of others (if this is the fact, although some deny its veracity) as they also occurred in his vision? Jung posits:

> ...the meaningful coincidence or equivalence of a psychic and physical state or event which have no causal relationship to one another. Such synchronistic phenomena occur, for instance, when an inwardly perceived event (dream, vision, premonition, etc.) is seen to have correspondence in external reality: the inner image of premonition has "come true," similar or identical thoughts, dreams, etc. occuring at the same time in different places. Neither the one nor the other coincidence can be explained by causality, but seems to be connected primarily with activated archetypal processes in the unconscious.[30]

The creative act, like the dream, draws upon unknown factors and therefore belongs to the field of acausal phenomena. The artist or the visionary extracts "the contingent partly as a universal factor existing from all eternity, and partly as the sum of countless individual acts of creation occurring in time" and reduces this material to his own frame of reference.[31] Wagner, Mozart, and Rachmaninoff described inspiration as a burst or an upsurge of productivity. Rachmaninoff said that when he walked in the country, his head seemed to burst into music and all the notes flowed into existence right before him. "All the voices at once. Not a bit here, a bit there. The whole grows. When it comes, how it began, how can I say? It came up within me, was entertained, written down."[32] Certainly something within the unconscious has been triggered off by some unknown acausal factor. The more scientists investigate the "extra-temporal" or what has been alluded to today as the "sub-atomic" and the "super-galactic" spheres, the more they become aware of nature's diversity and man's longing to understand and regain a sense of its primordial unity—and the more *"science parallels mysticism."*[33] Kepler in his *Stella Nova* affirmed that one must go beyond the world of appearances to experience reality.

> Nothing exists nor happens in the visible sky that is not sensed in some hidden manner by the faculties of Earth and Nature: these faculties of the spirit here on earth are as much affected as the sky itself... The natural soul of man is not larger in size than a single point, and on this point the form and character of the sky is potentially engraved, as if it were a hundred times larger.[34]

Leibniz believed in the monad, the smallest entity of all. As science advanced, certain "elementary particles" (electrons, protons, neutrons, etc.) made up of matter were discovered to be making their way around space, imposing their force in what looks like a series of pathlike "rows of tiny bubbles in a liquid."[35] Because of the energy aroused by these particles, physicists are able to examine "the transformation of mass into energy and of energy into mass."[36]

More and more, quantum physicists are drawn to a realm that had previously only interested the mystic—that of acausal phenomena. That such a working rapport may become even more popular in the near future is not unthinkable. Let us recall that in 1956 the Atomic Energy Commission succeeded in isolating neutrinos, "the most ghost-like or elementary particles." They were alluded to as "ghost-like" because they have "no physical properties: no mass, no electric charge, and no magnetic field."[37] Yet, they exist.

Equally fascinating is Adrian Dobb's theory, which postulates "a second time dimension in which the objective probabilities of future outcome are contained as compresent dispositional factors, which incline or predispose the future to occur in certain specific ways."[38] According to his theory, a physical explanation for telepathy and precognitive dreams and hallucinations could be forwarded. Dobbs employs the word "pre-cast" rather than "precognitive",[39] indicating certain factors that could be perceived and would predispose a happening "toward a given future state." But such "pre-casts" are not merely haphazard, nor do they follow any known rational system. Man can discover something about these factors only through "hypothetical messengers," which Dobbs labels "psitrons" and which function in a second time dimension. The psitrons have "imaginary mass (in the mathematical sense) and thus, according to the theory of relativity, can travel faster than light and indefinitely, without loss of (imaginary) momentum." Professor Margenau of Yale expressed his ideas concerning imaginary mass as follows:

> At the forefront of current physical research, we find it necessary to invoke the existence of "virtual processes" confined to short durations. For a very short time, every physical process can proceed in ways which defy the laws of nature known today, always hiding itself under the cloak of the principle of uncertainty. When any physical process first starts, it sends out "feelers" in all directions, feelers in which time may be reversed, normal rules are violated, and unexpected things may happen. These virtual processes then die out and after a certain time matters settle down again.[40]

Other theories concerning "will influence" and "mind influence" were posited by Sir John Eccles, who believed that certain entities or substances act upon neirons in the brain and frequently influence brain activity in a startling manner.[41] Certain factors within the brain may increase or decrease its awareness and expand its consciousness, thereby making telepathy, clairvoyance, and other acausal situations possible.[42] The manner in which energy is transformed into consciousness remains a mystery. That such questions have invaded the scientist's world is particularly revealing of the course of today's research.

Artists, perhaps more sensitive than the average person, sense their way into other dimensions, magnetic fields that remain shut to the "normal" individual. When Cazotte and other visionaries described their dreams and hallucinations, the scientists and rationalists of that time for the most part scoffed and ridiculed them. Creative writers, such as Nodier, Nerval, Gautier, Balzac among others, took them seriously. As *vates,* they sensed the validity of the acausal-factor theory long before physicists began to concentrate their efforts on these matters.

NOTES

[1]Jacques Cazotte was born in Dijon on Oct. 7, 1719. The son of a town
clerk, his father saw to it that he received a fine education. Cazotte
studied at Jesuit schools in his native city and by 1740 had earned a
bachelor of law degree. He continued his studies in Paris, hoping to
obtain a secure government post in the navy department. He worked
diligently in his legal capacity while, at the same time, discovering in
himself a love and talent for literature. He indulged his bent and wrote
two tales: *La Patte du Chat* (1741) and *Les Mille et une Fadaises* (1742).
By 1743 he was named "writer ordinary" for the navy, and four years
later "principal writer." Cazotte was appointed controller to Iles-sous-
le-Vent and left for Martinique in 1747. Despite difficult material conditions he remained there until 1752. He wrote two ballads (*Les Prouesses
inimitables d'Ollivier, Marquis d'Edesse and La Veillée de La Bonne
Femme ou le Réveil d'Enguerrand*) which earned him a *succes d'estime*:
he was also the author of articles on music. In 1759 Cazotte returned
to France. He married in 1761 and moved to Pierry, an estate he inherited from his brother. He had three children. The publication of
The Devil in Love brought him the material resources he needed to
emerge from what seemed to be continuous financial difficulties. With
the passage of years, Cazotte, steeped in mysticism, took a spiritual
helpmate, the Marquis de la Croix. He was forever predicting events
that would occur. One evening in 1778, La Harpe reports, Cazotte
was at a dinner party and prophesied that Condorcet would take poison;
Chamfort would commit suicide by cutting his veins with a razor; Louis
XVI would be guillotined; thousands would die in a similar manner;
and that women as well as men would be brought to their death in
open carts. As for himself, he had described his end thirty years before
the French Revoltuion, in a long poem entitled "Ollivier": "I saw my
head lined up on the tiers, next to 800 other heads of both sexes, of all
ages and color." The predictions all came true. Letters to his friend
Pouteau were found in which Cazotte revealed his counterrevolutionary
plans. Accused of treason, Cazotte was guillotined on Sept. 25, 1792, on
the Place du Carrousel at 7 o'clock in the evening, after a trial that lasted
twenty-seven hours. When the time came for his end, he stared at his

prosecutor, his eyes never expressing a trace of anxiety or concern. He spoke gently and firmly to his wife and daughter, then looked toward heaven, lowered his eyes to express his thanks to the people who had imposed his death sentence on him, then shouted to the multitude: "I die as I have lived, faithful to my God and to my King."

See Edward Pease Shaw, *Jacques Cazotte*, p. 73.

[2]Gérard de Nerval, *Oeuvres* II, p. 1138.

[3]*Ibid.*, p. 1136.

[4]*Ibid.*, p. 1154.

[5]*Ibid.*

[6]Sheila Ostrander and Lynn Schroeder, *Psychic Discoveries Behind the Iron Curtain*, p. 213.

[7]The Oriental considers such divisions artificial, intellectual concepts, devoid of meaning.

[8]*Romanciers du XVIII siècle*, p. 352.

[9]*Ibid.*, p. 370.

[10]Serge Hutin, *Les Sociétés*, p. 7.

[11]Joshua Trachtenberg, *Jewish Magic and Superstition*, pp. 115-131.

[12]Jérome-Antoine Rony, *La Magie*, p. 25.

[13]*Romanciers*, p. 315.

[14]*Ibid.*, p. 317.

[15]Nerval, p. 1138.

According to the Kabbalists, air, water, fire, breath, as well as the ten spheres (Sefiroth) that make up the cosmos, are emanations of the All Being (En-Sof). After the creation of man (when man fell into matter), the divine aspects within him had been contaminated and therefore, had to be rehabilitated. They could be purified by means of certain disciplines: prayer, fasting, theurgical practices. In this way the Devil (Evil) could be extracted from man; his material nature reintegrated into the All-Being for the Kabbalist and into Christ for the Gnostic. The Fall, it must be recalled did not only affect man, but the entire hierarchy of spirits that resided at various levels within the cosmos— between man and God.

[16]*Romanciers*, p. 319.

[17]Trachtenberg, p. 51.

[18]*Romanciers*, p. 343.

[19]*Ibid.*, p. 344.

[20]*Ibid.*, p. 352.

[21]Erich Neumann, *The Origins and History of Consciousness*, p. 131.

[22]C. G. Jung, *The Structure and Dynamics of the Psyche*, p. 449.

[23]C. G. Jung, *Memories, Dreams, Reflections*, p. 304.

[24]*Structure*, p. 480.

[25]*Ibid.*, p. 434.

[26]*Ibid.*, p. 436.

[27]*Ibid.*

[28]*Memories*, p. 390.

[29]*Structures*, p. 515.

[30]*Dreams*, p. 388.

[31]*Structure*, p. 519.

[32]Ostrander and Schroeder, p. 154.

[33]Arthur Koestler, *The Roots of Coincidence*, p. 50.

[34]*Ibid.*, p. 106.

[35]*Ibid.*, p. 61.

[36]*Ibid.*,

[37]*Ibid.*, p. 62.

[38]*Ibid.*, p. 70.

[39]*Ibid.*

[40]*Ibid.*, p. 71.

[41]*Ibid.*, p. 74.

[42]*Ibid.*, p. 77.

SECTION III

THE NINETEENTH CENTURY

5. *Charles Nodier—The Crumb Fairy: A Hieros Gamos or A Sacred Marriage of Sun and Moon*

6. *Gérard de Nerval—Soliman, Sheba, Adoniram, and the Occult*

7. *Honoré de Balzac—Louis Lambert: The Legend of the Thinking Man*

8. *Théophile Gautier—Arria Marcella: The Greek Versus the Christian Way*

9. *Charles Baudelaire—"Parisian Dream": The Drama of the Poetic Process*

10. *Victor Hugo—"What the Mouth of Darkness Says": The Dark Night of the Soul*

11. *Joris-Karl Huysmans—Down There: Satanism and the Male Psyche—The Black Mass and the Female Principle*

12. *Arthur Rimbaud—"After the Flood": From Chaos to Cosmos*

13. *Stéphane Mallarmé—Igitur or Elbehnon's Folly: The Depersonalization Process and the Creative Encounter*

CHAPTER 5

Charles Nodier—The Crumb Fairy

A Hieros Gamos or A Sacred Marriage
of Sun and Moon

A union even in death—is a marriage—which gives
us a companion for the night. It is in death that
love is the sweetest; for he who loves, death is a
wedding night,—the secret of most tender mysteries.
(Novalis. Hymns to the Night.)

In "About Some Phenomena of Sleep" Charles Nodier[1] wrote, "The first perception which emerges from the inexplicable vagueness of the dream is as limpid as is the sun's first ray when dissipating a cloud... It is in this region that the immortal conception of artists and poets bursts forth." For Nodier the dream world was not gratuitous. It had incized itself into his life and acted upon all aspects of it. The dream was a link between waking and sleeping states; a transformer of reality into illusion; a *rite de passage* that enabled him to communicate with other species, the dead, and past civilizations, as well as to anticipate future events. The dream was the very lifeblood of his creative effort. Even during his sleeping hours, he claimed, thought made its inroads into his unconscious, taking on its most lucid and powerful form and developing illusions, perceptions, and insights.[2]

Nodier's short story *The Crumb Fairy* is an example of the powerful role played by his oneirosphere in stimulating the creative forces within him. It is a prolonged reverie, a series of irrational images linked together in a relatively comprehensible pattern. Nodier was not alone in choosing the short story as a vehicle to express his phantasms. There were many, among them Byron (Dr. Polidori), Shelley, Walpole, Radcliffe, Lewis, and Hoffmann. Nodier had a particular penchant for the fantastic tales of Ernst Theodor Hoffmann. He praised *The Devil's Elixir* (1861) and *Night-Pieces* (1817) among others in his essay "The Fantastic in Literature." To Nodier he was a visionary; the world of magnetism and of the occult Hoffmann brought to life ushered in moods of nostalgia and malaise. He seemed to be endowed with a sixth sense that enabled him to understand man and nature, obscure relationships, and phenomena that escaped scientific explanation.[3]

Hoffman's influence is clearly discernible in *The Crumb Fairy* with its atmosphere of disenchantment and gloom as well as its quest for the supernatural. But scientific and metaphysical credos are also integrated into the fabric of the plot and the souls of the *dramatis personae.* Questions broached by Diderot in *D'Alembert's Dream* (monism) and by Cazotte in *The Devil in Love* (metempsychosis) are posited in Nodier's tale but are expanded upon. Although under the guise of specific individuals and events, it is the collective domain that is at issue in *The Crumb Fairy:* two cosmic principles, the universal male and female forces as they participate, symbolically, in a *hieros gamos,* the alchemical formula for the sacred marriage of sun and moon.

Nodier was not a realist and found it difficult to adapt to the workaday world. He could not face the ugliness of the burgeoning industrial civilization rising about him and longed to transcend the realm of appearances to withdraw into his own inner domain, so rich was it in spirits and in anima figures of all types. Like the German Romantics Novalis, Schelling, the two Schlegel brothers, and Tieck, Nodier was convinced that man could not know happiness on earth because his soul was living in exile and longed to return to the heavenly spheres from which it had come. Man, then, was a being divided. To assuage the sorrow of his fate on earth, he looked toward the past and the future, to nature, and to the cosmic spheres for salvation. In these vast expanses—whether abstract or concrete—he could experience God or the eternal and thereby was divested of his finitude and his identity, thus earning a sense of wellbeing.

These aesthetic metaphysicians believed nature to be a living organism and not a mechanism capable of being reduced to its various components or elements. They established what has been called an "autocracy of the imagination." In opposition to the eighteenth-century philosophes and ideologues, they distrusted the world of appearances and longed to commune with a profounder realm in which God would make His presence manifest. They believed that man's fall from paradise as related in the Bible, which had led to earthly existence, was tantamount to a separation from God. Because man was no longer *one* with divinity, he had become divided and so belonged to two spheres: the world of matter (the earth) and that of spirit (the divine realm). For the metaphysicians life on earth became a long search to find a way to experience that primordial unity with God or the existence man had known before the Fall, before his birth. To be united with divinity could be experienced, they suggested, during certain moments in life: in periods of dream, esctasy, or illumination, when the individual is divested

of his identity and flows into the All, or Universal Force.[4] Man's
earthly existence, therefore, consisted of an unending deisre for
oneness with God or with the Cosmic Soul. Life (the birth of
man) was looked upon as a separation from God; and so death,
in this context, became a return to Him. From such a vantage
point, death was not to be feared or treated as something ugly;
it was merely a *rite de passage,* an initiatory process into another
frame of existence.[5]

Nodier felt very acutely the conflict of opposition and
longed for the serene state of unity. His protagonist in *The
Crumb Fairy* achieves this condition and lives in a world where
duality is banished. But Nodier knew only too well that the
paradisiac fate of his hero is incompatible with life on earth, and
therefore he labeled him insane, a "lunatic." Questions concerning insanity were popular in the nineteenth century; inquiries and
studies abounded. In fact, the idea for Nodier's tale came to
him, it has been affirmed, after he read a letter in *La Revue de
Paris* (May 1829) from the Duke de Levis to a Dr. A. concerning
new treatments used in Scottish mental institutions.

The Crumb Fairy opens as the carpenter Michel, interned
in the Glasgow "lunatic" asylum narrates the events of his life.
Orphaned at an early age, he is brought up by his uncle, a carpenter, at Granville in Normandy. A solitary lad, he makes
friends with a tiny old lady whom the children of the district
call the Crumb Fairy because she lives on the crumbs given her.
She claims to be a descendant of Belkiss (another name for the
Queen of Sheba) and her goal in life is to settle in Greenock
where she owns a house. Michel gives her enough money to pay
for her trip. After his uncle's departure for the sea, Michel's
life-style changes. The money he earns as a carpenter he gives
away to the needy. He becomes destitute; but miraculously, he
finds seven louis his uncle has sewn into the buttons of his jacket
and these save him from starvation. Out of gratitude he goes
on a pilgrimage to Mont Saint-Michel. On his way he saved
someone from sinking into quicksand whom he later discovers
is the Crumb Fairy. They become engaged. Since she has lost
all of her possessions he gives her his louis. He then hears that his

uncle who is now considered insane, claims to be the superintendent of Princess Belkiss' palace. Michel goes in search of him and leaves on the ship *The Queen of Sheba;* but the ship sinks. Once again Michel saves the Crumb Fairy who has followed him secretly. In return she gives him a diamond-studded medallion with a portrait of the Queen of Sheba who, she asserts, is really herself when young and beautiful. Michel eventually lands on the Scottish coast and meets the charming Folly Girl-free. Since no rooms are available at the inn, he must share one with the bailiff. That night he has a nightmare and in the morning is found with the bailiff's wallet in one hand, a dagger in the other, and the dead bailiff beside him. He is arrested. His lawyer pleads insanity, but Michel is found guilty and sentenced to death. A letter arrives: Michel must choose between the portrait on the medallion and the diamond frame. He chooses the portrait and the judge receives the frame. However, unless a girl consents to marry him, Michel must die. Folly offers herself, but Michel refuses because he is already affianced and wants to keep his vow to the Crumb Fairy. He prefers to die, Michel maintains, rather than break his engagement. Then the Crumb Fairy arrives and releases him from it. Michel is found innocent and the bailiff is found very much alive.

The story now switches to Greenock. Michel and the Crumb Fairy are living together in blissful contentment: by day she is a wizened old woman and by night she comes to him as the beautiful Belkiss. Their union is complete. Only one cloud emerges on the horizon: unless her husband finds the mandrake, the miraculous plant that will return her youth to her, the Crumb Fairy will die within a year. Michel leaves in search of the mandrake and finds it at a herbalist's shop in Glasgow. It is at this point that he is interned in the "lunatic" asylum. In an epilogue Michel returns to Belkiss and they live happily every after.

That Nodier chose the fairy tale as the vehicle for his narrative is not surprising. The fantasies and obsessions described therein released him from the pain and emptiness he felt after his daughter's marriage. "Until my death, which can come at any time," he wrote in a letter (January 3, 1830), "I only want to write 'Fairy Tales'." For the psychologist the fairy tale is an invaluable source for study. As Dr. von Franz writes:

> Fairy tales are the purest and simplest expression of collective unconscious psychic processes. Therefore their value for the scientific investigation of the unconscious exceeds that of all other material. They represent the archetypes in their simplest, barest, and most concise form, the archetypal images afford us the best clues to the understanding of the process going on in the collective psyche. In myths or legends, or any other more elaborate mythological material, we get at the basic patterns of the human psyche through an overlay of cultural material and therefore they mirror the basic patterns of the psyche more clearly.[6]

Archetypal images of all sorts are brought into focus in fantasies, dreams, and hallucinations in *The Crumb Fairy*. There is, however, one dream in particular that sums up in a most incisive manner the entire gist of the tale: Michel's nightmare at the inn. Although this dream is said to have been inspired by a similar one recounted in Balzac's *The Red Inn* (1831), in which a murder had been perpetrated by a man in a semisleeping state, the fact that Nodier chose to narrate such an incident in *The Crumb Fairy* indicates the depth of his projection upon it. Michel's dream is a reenactment, in symbolic form, of an unconscious struggle between the male and female principles in an attempt to reach a state of serene unity.

The dream begins as Michel hears all sorts of noises: creaking hinges, howling winds, and whispering voices, followed by harrowing visions. Four heads emerge as if from one body: the head of a grimacing savage cat, of a dog with bristling hair and oozing blood from its jaw, of a horse's head "half calcinated by the sun," and behind them the head of a monstrous-looking being.[7] A hand suddenly juts forth and pushes the bailiff's body, which now looks like a cadaver, next to Michel. The hand then touches Michel around the neck; it feels cold, like ice. It now grabs the bailiff's money and Michel rushes forward with his dagger striking out in all directions. He sinks the dagger into the monster, the cat, the dog, and the horse. Other animals—owls, serpents, salamanders—suddenly invade the room. He grabs the wallet and returns to his bed "triumphant." The following morning the bailiff is found dead and the wallet is in Michel's hand along with the knife.[8]

Scholars have commented on the cruelty of Michel's dream: the knifings and the gore. Such activity, however, is understandable in view of the fact that Nodier had witnessed a series of guillotinings at Besancon during the Revolution. These beheadings had had a traumatic effect upon him and haunted him ever since. It is no wonder that visions of terror, horror, and mutilation are included in most of his works. It was his way of expelling some of his fears and aggressions, of reaching the primitive elements and impulses within his own psyche.

The bailiff is described by Michel as having "the magnificent head of a Danish dog." He communicated with Michel by barking at him and the young lad was astounded "at the precision of his language and the exquisite delicacy of his judgments."[9] Michel, needless to say, is the only one who sees the bailiff in this manner, and one must confess that their strange relationship transcends the norm. In that the bailiff carries a wallet filled with the receipts collected from the Isle of Man, he represents society with its social structure and its materialism. Yet, there is something odd about him. According to Platonic belief, the head of man symbolizes his highest spiritual attributes, his divine intelligence; the body is his animal side. Nodier, however, devaluates this age-old way of thinking. The head is the animal; the body is man. The rational function, therefore, is not man's highest sphere for Nodier. The head is limited in intelligence; it cannot articulate except in a series of barks. Nodier's image indicates a desire to break out of the constricting pattern imposed upon man in his conventional relationships.

That the bailiff has a dog's head is significant in other respects. In ancient Egypt the dog accompanied the dead to the domain of Osiris and Isis. In Greek mythology Cerberus stood guard outside Hades, thus preventing the shades from leaving their abode. In the Bailiff's case the dog might also be associated with death. It is a premonitory symbol, announcing the bailiff's murder, at least with regard to Michel's unconscious. The animal-man's murder and the stealing of the receipts indicates Michel's destructive attitude toward the materialistic and hierarchical ways of society.

The four terrifying images (savage cat, bristly dog, calcinated horse's head, monstrous face) are important in themselves and also for the symbolic meaning of the number involved. Numbers have numerous qualities: they are transforming agents in that they change chaos to order and they are compensatory forces.[10]   The number four represents a totality, completeness, and rational organization. The four then is inimicable to Michel since it stands for a world from which he seeks to escape and which he will either annihilate or transcend.

The cat, according to ancient Egyptian lore, is a moon figure. It was sacred to both Isis and Bast, the "guardian of marriage." Frequently, the cat is associated with woman because of its sensuality and its enigmatic and mysterious ways. Because of its inner world, its secretive and unpredictable actions and thoughts, the cat is also considered evil and dangerous. Michel's cat is wild: it represents the viscious, destructive forces within the female, which he seeks to destroy. His cat is a projection of his own feminine nature, that powerful, unconscious, and annihilating element which seethes within hin.

The dog with the bristling hair also represents a bestial force within the narrator. Because its hair rises, it is in an angry, aggressive mode; it is ready to bare its bloody fangs and kill whatever comes within its reach. The horse and the monster represent unregenerate instincts.

The dagger used by Michel to perpetrate the murders may be likened to sword symbolism. Heroes such as Roland, Siegfried, and King Arthur destroyed their enemies and became the protectors of virtues, hence giving birth to new attitudes. The sword in the hands of such monstrous beings as Morholt, Goliath, and Grendel served to destroy man's well-being and to disrupt the serene social atmosphere. For Michel the sword serves to cut his ties with the world of instinct (the forces he projects onto the animals in his vision) and with society in form of the bailiff and the materialistic social order he represents.

The brutality of the dream indicates a state of ebullition within the oneirosphere. Michel cannot seem to face the archaic forms within him, as symbolized by the animals, nor the workaday world in which he lives, as represented by the bailiff. He therefore seeks to destroy them and does so in his dream but not in his "real" world of fantasy, or "lunacy" as adumbrated in *The Crumb Fairy.*

1. *The Hieros Gamos:*
The Sacred Marriage of Sun and Moon

It is within the framework of insanity that Nodier broaches the cosmic problem of the warring male-female principles and the *hieros gamos,* or marriage, of sun and moon. In conventional alchemical practice the sun is considered the male principle and represents spirit, order, and illumination, the purest and highest thinking processes known to man. The moon, on the other hand, is viewed as feminine, fickle, dark, and enigmatic, and therefore frequently dangerous. In *The Crumb Fairy,* interestingly enough, the situation is reversed. The sun becomes the feminine force, a composite of two anima figures: the ancient and wizened Crumb Fairy who represents wisdom in its most active form; and the passive Belkiss, who emerges at night and stands for passion. They are the regulators of Michel's life.

Michel is the moon figure, the "lunatic" (*lune* in French means "Moon"), who not only incorporates certain aspects of the feminine personality (purity, tenderness, gentleness) but also is under its dominion. He functions only as a reflection, not an instigator of the two anima figures, and has no identity of his own; he is what psychologists term a "medium" personality, that is, he is influenced by outside events, by feelings and sensations generated by others. Physically he is male, psychologically, he is female. As a composite of male and female characteristics, he may be referred to as androgynous, one of the most archaic archetypal images known—a being that existed according to Platonic and Kabbalistic belief, before the two sexes came into being.

Androgynism is also found in the symbol of the mandrake, the plant Michel cultivates in the lunatic asylum and which is mentioned at the beginning and end of *The Crumb Fairy.* The mandrake, an age-old plant, is associated with both poisonous and healing properties. Theophrastus saw it as half man and half woman because its roots resembled human form and it was self-reproductive. It was also likened to the human being because it was said to scream when uprooted from the ground. The metaphysician Eliphas Lévi was convinced that the first men on earth to walk were "giant mandrakes." Joan of Arc, it was said, traveled with a mandrake hidden under her breats, and that it was this plant that gave her the power to foretell the future and command armies.[11] The mandrake image in *The Crumb Fairy* symbolizes what alchemists would call the philosophers' stone—the elixir of life or the *élan vital*. The philosophers' stone was supposed to bring about the spiritual re-creation of man; psychologically, a rebirth within the psyche. To achieve such a goal, the alchemists had to transform the imperfect (imbalanced) into the perfect (harmonious)—a reblending of nature, a reforming of matter, a reshuffling of inner contents. The mandrake, as the philosophers' stone, belongs to the world of absolutes; therefore, it is inimicable to life, the very antithesis of its energetic process that is based on opposition and acausality. To conceive of the reality of the mandrake or the philosophers' stone is an attempt to shy away from the workaday world, to escape into an Edenlike atmosphere, or to regress into an infantile state.

The mandrake, given narcotic values—by Hippocrates among others—was capable of prolonging Michel's beautiful fantasy world. Hence it was fitting that he should cultivate the plant in the lunatic asylum, the implication here being that only in the protected atmosphere of the asylum, where people live out their illusions, can the mandrake—the symbol of utopia and perfection—flourish.

As an androgyne, Michel, serving to illustrate an inability to identify completely with either sex, is an in-between. He is the antithesis of the masculine hero type (Roland, Bayard, David) and resembles more fully the effeminate Romantic figures (René, Adolphe, Obermann) peopling the literary scene in nineteenth-century Europe. Michel's lack of sexual identity is apparent in the moon-and-sun imagery, which is the heart of the tale. In archaic times these astral bodies were personified and each took on the personality traits and sexual configuration of gods and goddesses.

Before the moon came to be identified with woman (after the advent of patriarchal societies, such as the Egyptian), the sun was female and was known to the ancient Sabbaean worshipers in Yemen as the goddess Shams. She was the all-powerful force that regulated cosmic activity. With the advent of patriarchal civilizations, however, the woman yielded her power to the man and became associated with the moon, whereas male qualities were attributed to the sun. Psychologically, such a change in religious power mirrored a concomitant trend within the human psyche: while the male figures were in the ascendancy and becoming identified with the sun (the most powerful force on earth), female forms were relegated to what was considered a lesser sphere, the moon. But the female element was still a potent force. Counting, for example, was based on the rhythmic life of the moon. This astral body also stood for love and fertility. It caused rain, storms, floods, and tidal waves, and therefore influenced nature's growth power. Moon goddesses of antiquity (Ishtar, Hathor, Artemis) were regulators of life on earth and were instrumental in the continuation of the great death-rebirth cycles by playing the prime role in the dismemberment mysteries (Zagreus, Pentheus, Orpheus, Osiris).

Neither political, economic, social, nor psychological conditions remain fixed. Just as flux exists in the universe, so it is present in all phases of life; in the sexual sphere the power struggle between the male and female principles pursued its course throughout the ages. At one period in time, one force dominates while the other sturggles for recognition; at another, the reverse is true. In nineteenth-century France the rigid patriarchal system was giving way to matriarchal forces. This change of emphasis is translated in *The Crumb Fairy* on the sun and moon imagery, and in the protagonists with which each of these astral bodies is identified.

The moon has been endowed with many characteristics. Said to be responsible for outer disturbances (e.g. storms and tidal waves), it also supposedly includes chaos within the mind, arousing turmoil, generating overactivity, and causing many people to go insane.[11] It is the moon that radiates an eerie light in darkness, that dulls illumination, thus becoming the instigator of vision. The ancient moon goddesses Cybele and Hecate were named *Antea*, defined as "The Sender of Nocturnal Visions." Museos, the Muse-Man, Hecate's son, was also called "The Son of the Moon."[12] The moon has also inspired magic, understanding, ecstasy, and intuitive insights; those forces emanating from the darkest and most archaic regions within man.

In alchemy, silver is associated with the moon. Although a pure and high metal within the hierarchy of metals and chemicals, it is not as dazzling nor as perfect as gold (associated with the sun) and thus illuminates only partially. Fantasy, fear, and the dream are born in such penumbra. It is here too, in the silvery aspcets of the moon, that intuitive forces reside within man: that which shines at night in darkness. Hence the moon is identified with poets. It is subdued, enigmatic, it arouses the ineffable and intangible entity—the creative element in man.

Michel is such a "moon man." He is not a thinking power and functions solely in the realm of feeling and intuition. Fantasies and strange ideas are forever aroused within him and always in opposition to the orderly, logical, and rational domain lauded by society. Nodier describes him as having compassion and love, both physically and spiritually and in terms of the moon. Michel is "pale," his eyes have the "transparency" and liquid "gaze" of a person from whom the fire of "an astral body" has been "eclipsed"; his world is bathed in darkness; it is ambiguous, "lost in the illusions of the imaginary world."[13] Like the moon, Michel stands solitary in the vast expanse of blackness surrounding him.

To become a moon man requires a long period of gestation. According to alchemical tradition, and Nodier believed in this concept, a *rite de passage* has to be endured before a higher spiritual state of consciousness can come into being. Unlike the eighteenth-century rationalists, who believed reason to be the supreme form of consciousness, Nodier, in accord with the alchemists, was convinced that the realm of logic alone could not lead to greater knowledge. Higher consciousness was to be found in "obscure movements," in the variety of impulses buried within man's being, in his intuitions. It is no wonder that the Gnostics associated the moon with the divine Sophia who symbolized "the fallible aspects of God."[14] In ancient days moon people were considered the spokesmen of the gods, the possessors of some divine power. One listened to their statements and prognostications with awe and fear. Moon-thinking, it was believed, opened new insights and fresh orientations.

Michel is capable of divining and understanding more deeply than the so-called rational or normal person: "I believe that lunatics occupy a higher rung on the ladder which separates our world from its satelite." It is from this superior vantage point that they are able to communicate with supreme intelligences, those that remain incomprehensible and unknown to the normal human being. "It is absurd to conclude that their ideas lack meaning and lucidity just because they belong to an order of sensations and reasoning which is completely inaccessible to our education and habits."[15] The insane are free from the constrictive time-space limitations imposed upon the ordinary individual and are therefore capable of embedding their thoughts into cosmic spheres of influence, thereby gaining greater wisdom from their peregrinations. "And what will prevent this indefinable state of mind, which ignorance labels folly, to lead in time to the supreme form of wisdom via a path unknown to us..."[16]

A price must be paid for divining cosmic secrets. The collective sphere in which the lunatic lives divests him of all identiy. Solitude and an inability to communicate with others result. Michel, for example, could not fall in love with a flesh-and-blood woman. He lived exclusively in a world of fantasy; as he himself confessed, his entire life was "nothing but dreams and caprices ever since the Crumb Fairy became involved in it."[17]

Michel, the moon man, functioned relatively well in the everyday world as a carpenter. It was his attitude toward women that was out of the ordinary. His mother having died shortly after his birth, he had been deprived of maternal warmth and had never learned to relate to the female principle. Hence he could never consider the woman as an individual and friend but saw her instead as a transpersonal, mythological, or spiritual creature to whom he could turn for solace and comfort. In this respect Michel was a true lunatic; under the influence of the moon he lived in a perpetual dream, acquiring insights and perceptions in this vast and, according to Nodier, superior world. The profound knowledge he acquired, however, was not compatible with conventional social order. Michel was attuned only to the cosmic field—to transcendental values—to the All.

The sun principle is incarnated in the Crumb Fairy and Belkiss, or Michel's unconscious inner attitude toward women.

The ancient Crumb Fairy is a supraterrestrial, spiritual power. She stands for what Michel had lacked in his life: the positive mother figure, the wise, understanding, gentle, loving, and tender being. "My affection for you," she says to Michel, "is greater than a mother's affection, and it has its chasteness."[18] Due to the Crumb Fairy, Michel experiences love and security. Since he was twelve years old, she had inspired feelings of "tender veneration and almost religious submission which tended toward another order of sentiment."[19] She was Michel's "guardian angel" during his school years and helped him and his friends with their studies.[20] She is a miracle worker, in other words, the helping mother type; and this role she plays throughout life, or at least as long as he needs her. "I had the joy of advising you, of helping...and you have not reached the point of being able to get alone without me."[21] No matter how kind or solicitous a mother may be, such a helping attitude, if prolonged for too long, becomes destructive. It prevents growth, which results from a confrontation with the realities of the world. Examples of possessive mothers have existed since antiquity: Cybele and Attis, Ishtar and Tammuz, each of these young men died after an unsuccessful attempt to win independence from his overwhelming mother-influence.

A price must be paid for everything in life—even for kindness. The Crumb Fairy extracts her pound of flesh: the golden louis to return to her home in Greenock; a second gift in gold when she claims to have been divested of all she owned; a choice she forces on Michel during his trial (the portrait of Belkiss on the medallion or the diamond frame). These tests are all part of the initiation ritual required of Michel to become a moon man. He passes the tests which means, in psychological terms that he will remain under the dominion of the Crumb Fairy, that is, his relationship with her must lead to a condition of stasis. Michel's withdrawal from the existential world and submission to the dictates of the Crumb Fairy is a regression into an archaic and infantile realm: the serenity and security of a paradisiac state. The Crumb Fairy undermined the very foundations of Michel's personality, or he permitted such a disintegration of his ego because of his own fallibility. The ego, defined as the center of consciousness, stands as a mediating force between the inner and outer worlds. Its function is to adapt to both. In Michel's case the ego had lost its power and gradually found itself incapable of acting outside of the fantasy world. Why should he battle out his existence on an external level when all was taken care of so beautifully in his inner domain?

The loss of his ego make him helpless and childlike; thus, he had to be forever cared for and guided. It is significant that, at the end of the story, the Crumb Fairy's home is compared to a doll's house.[22] He lives protected and content in all ways. "Happiness means to have nothing to reproach oneself."[23] Conflicts are gone, as are feelings of guilt, rebellion, and chaos— all of those irritating, frustrating, yet growth-provoking qualities. Michel will never ascend to superior knowledge (either spiritual or terrestrial) because he is caught in a vise: he is prisoner of his inner domain, not master of it. A world in which the dynamic quality of opposition and energy—those life-giving forces, is absent—is a dead one.

Belkiss (the beautiful, sparkling, and youthful side of the Crumb Fairy, the Queen of Sheba) is also a symbolic representation of an archaic sun figure. She appears only after Michel passes the first stage of the initiation process: from son-mother motif to son-lover. In Arab legends, many of which Nodier had read, Sheba is known under the name Nilqis or Balqis (Balkis). Sheba came from the sun-drenched land of Yemen and followed the oldest religion known to man: the Sabbaean cult that adored the supreme cosmic force—the sun. Michel describes the "divine Belkiss" in terms of the solar disk and calls her "the Princess of the South."[24] For Michel she is pure sunlight.[25] When Michel's passion is aroused, Belkiss is transformed into fire: "moved, agitated, palpitating, ready to bound forth, to join her lips to mine... I felt that the warmth of her kiss poured torrents of flames into my veins."[26] When she appeared to Michel at night, she was radiant light, a celstial illumination around whom "all the torches were lit at the same time,"[27] a diamond "sovereign of all the unknown realms of the Orient and the South, inheritor of Solomon's ring, scepter and crow."[28] Since Belkiss is transformed into a fire figure, she radiates sparks as powerful as the solar conflagration and becomes a dangerous force. Like Circe, she has the power to entice, hypnotize, mesmerize, and eventually to destroy. Michel will become the passive instrument, victimized by her sway. Men who have difficulty relating to women on certain levels frequently succumb to them; Venus, for example, destroyed those who did not fall under her dominion. Michel rejected the flesh-and-blood woman, the charming Folly Girlfree, and became progressively engulfed in Belkiss' image, and eventually he drowned in it. Like the novitiate who loses himself in prayer, the mystic in contemplation, and the artist in his creative endeavor, so Michel, suggested Nodier, became united with his sublime collective figure—Belkiss, or the Queen of Sheba,[29] who took on the traits of the Virgin Mary—the woman in front of whose image he knelt, whose "mysterious voice" spoke to his soul.[30] Like Dante's Beatrice, Belkiss was Michel's spiritual bride; as Mary became the Bride of God and the Queen of Heaven.[31]

By day Michel conversed with the wise Crumb Fairy, his nights were devoted to Belkiss; his existence revolved around these formidable powers—the Eternal Feminine as symbolized in the Solar principle. The *hieros gamos* between Michel and the dual anima figures brought about a symbolic union between sun and moon; hence Michel may be looked upon as a "Heavenly Lover," the "Bridegroom of the Soul."

The third force, earth (or matter), which would have solidified the union between the solar and lunar principles is missing. Michel rejected the terrestrial sphere in the form of Folly Girlfree. Although he liked her and found her kind and gentle, she did not "live in the same region" that he did, he told her. His bond with her could never have been "sacred." Moreover his heart could know "no love for any earthly creature."[32] Eventhough the *hieros gamos* between sun and moon as personified by the protagonists occurred, only a duality emerged. The third force, manifestation, which would have given balance to the union, had been rejected.[33] The *hieros gamos* as experienced in The Crumb Fairy is therefore one-sided. It describes a cosmic union that could never, by its very limitations, lead to spiritual regeneration. Because the earth principle is lacking, a conflict of opposites, generating the growth process, has been dissipated. Michel's rejection of the existential domain led to vegetation and incarceration in the insane asylum. No rebirth was possible under such circumstances, only a prolonged condition of stasis.

What is of utmost interest in *The Crumb Fairy* is the exigency felt by Nodier to unify what was divided in the *hieros gamos*. That an androgynous figure such as Michel pervaded the literary scene answered a need among the people—to rectify an imbalance on the contemporary social structure—to reshuffle the system. The society which both Nodier and his protagonist rejected was based on rigid patriarchal tradition, a system in which reason, logic, and rational attitudes prevailed; characteristics personified by the masculine sun principle. The world of feeling, tenderness, understanding, and Eros had been neglected: qualities embodied in the female moon principle. For sensitive people such as Nodier and the German and French Romantics, the dichotomy between these two ways of life grew until it became a gaping wound. The soul, or anima got lost amid the stiff, unbending clarity of consciousness.

The imbalance felt so acutely by the poets and artists of this period was the natural outgrowth of the patriarchal aspects of Christianity, emphasized by St. Paul. He had done his best to unseat matriarchal worship, as witnessed by his attitude toward Diana in Acts (19:24-28). As a result of the suppression of matriarchal deities, some strange Christian sects arose during the early centuries. The Collyridians in the fourth and fifth centuries worshipped the Virgin Mary in the same manner as the ancient Egyptians and Greeks had adored Isis and Diana. In early Christianity the cult of the Virgin had not yet been strongly integrated into church doctrine, and the miracles of the Virgin in medieval times and later history (e.g., Lourdes, Fatima) were individual expressions of an immense need among the people. The scant details offered in Biblical texts with regard to women were elaborated upon by monks and religious people during the Middle Ages ostensibly for propaganda purposes. The many cathedrals and sanctuaries built during that period could thrive only if pilgrims or parishioners filled their halls, thus legends and tales grew around these places of worship, many of which were devoted to the Virgin. The cult of the Virgin had become very popular in France during the twelfth and thirteenth centuries. This new focus resulted from the Crusades and the concomitant influence of Middle Eastern and

Oriental religions in which the female figure played a powerful role. The Feast of the Immaculate Conception, for example, took three centuries to travel from East to West.

So great was the need to experience the positive female principle in the form of mother, bride, and sister in the nineteenth century that the Catholic church, heretofore unwilling to consider Mary a heavenly being, was to yield to this demand a century later and change its dogma with the doctrine of *Assumptio Mariae:* "Mary as the bride is united with the son in the heavenly bridal chamber, and, as Sophie, with the Godhead."[34] Mary, who rose bodily to heaven, became the Bride of God and the Queen of Heaven, thereby enabling all men to project onto this "celestial" and "perfect" figure, finding peace and comfort in such a notion.

The Crumb Fairy delineated in symbolic terms the necessity of rehabilitating certain aspects of the female principle—those long-neglected characteristics of warmth, tenderness, and compassion.

NOTES

[1]Charles Nodier was born out of wedlock in 1780 at Besançon and was not legitimized until 1791. His father, a rather dogmatic man, presided for a short period over the criminal tribunal of that city during the Reign of Terror. Nodier recalled years later with horror some of the particularly excoriating spectacles he had witnessed as a child and inserted some of these terrifying episodes in his short stories: rolling heads, pathetic cries, blood flowing into gutters. Such traumatic experiences might have accounted in part for the hypertension he later developed. But there were other reasons, too. Ever since he could remember his family life had been unpleasant. His mother, whom he never mentioned in his writings, was a housemaid. She was brusque, ignorant, unfeeling, and Nodier disliked her. From his mother he inherited Addison's disease and also suffered from other ills: insomnia and periodic fevers, which were not to abate with the passing of years. The opium he took every now and then seemed to aggravate his condition.

Although a devout Catholic, Nodier did not find salvation in a conventional approach to worship; his needs were more complex. The writings of mystics such as Jakob Boehme, Emanuel Swedenborg, Claude de Saint-Martin, Martinez de Pasqualis, and Jacques Cazotte stimulated his imagination and helped him develop his own conforting credo.

Nodier married in 1808 and had several children, but only one, Marie, survived. She was beautiful and charming and was the focal point of her father's life.

Nodier's knowledge was vast and he worked hard. He wrote on a variety of subjects: natural history (*Dissertation on the use of Antennae Insects*, 1789), philology (*Dictionary of French Onomatopoeias*, 1808; the *Army's Secret Societies*, 1815), and fantastic tales (*Smarra*, 1821; *Trilby*, 1822; and more). Nodier was appointed librarian of the Bibliothèque de l'Arsenal in 1824 and received the most creative people of his day at Sunday night gatherings: Gautier, Nerval, Balzac, Hugo, Sainte-Beuve, Lamartine, Dumas, and others. He was a story teller in his own right and used to regale his guests with stories by Scott, Hoffmann, or his own. He spoke in a clear and elegant manner, gesticulating from time to time, his long slender hands enacting the dramatic events he recounted, while his face mirrored a sense of excitement or serene melancholy.

The years passed. After the marriage of his beloved daughter (1830), Nodier suffered a type of depression. He felt he had lost the main attraction for his *Salon*. More important, he could no longer see his daughter daily and the void gnawed at him. He became more introverted. His dreamworld intruded persistently upon his real life and brought with it the necessary joys for survival.

Nodier died at the Arsenal, perhaps because of diminishing élan vital, on January 27, 1844.

For further information on Nodier see:

Pierre-George Castex, *Le Conte fantastique en France*. Paris: José Corti, 1952.

Alexandre Dumas, *Mes Mémoires*. V. Paris: Pierre Seghers, 1970.

Hubert Juin, *Charles Nodier*. Paris: Seghers, 1970.

Michel Salomon, *Nodier et le groupe romantique*. Paris: Perrin Co, 1908.

Auguste Viatte, *Les Sources occultes du romantisme*. II. Paris: Honoré Champion, 1969.

[2]Charles Nodier, *Contes*, p. 152.

[3]George René Humphrey, *L'Esthétique de la poésie de Gérard de Nerval*, p. 52.

[4]Una Birch, *The Disciples at Sais*, p. 70.

[5]Albert Béguin, *L'Ame romantique et le rêve*.

[6]Marie Louis von Franz, *Interpretation of Fairy Tales*, I.

[7]Nodier, p. 248.

[8]*Ibid.*, p. 249.

[9]*Ibid.*, p. 245.

[10]C. G. Jung, *The Structure and Dynamics of the Psyche*, p. 456.

[11]*Ibid.*

[12]Esther Harding, *Woman's Mysteries*, p. 109.

[13]Nodier, p. 180-1.

> Gustavo Le Rouge, in his *La Mandragore Magique*, wrote that according to Laurens Catelan (1568-1647), this root was "virile sperm." Rabbinic tradition claimed the mandrake grew in the Garden of Eden at the foot of the Tree of Knowledge. Shakespeare speaks of this plant in *Antony and Cleopatra:* "Give me to drink mandragora." That the plant shrieked when touched is referred to in *Romeo and Juliet:* "And shrieks like mandrake torn out of the earth, that living mortals, hearing them, run mad." Machiavelli's *The Mandragora* tells of the plant's erotic powers that aroused men to sexual heights.

[14]Hans Jonas, *The Gnostic Religion*, p. 176.

[15]Nodier, p. 179.

[16]*Ibid.*, p. 310.

[17]*Ibid.*, p. 231.

[18]*Ibid.*, p. 280.

[19]*Ibid.*, p. 193.

[20]*Ibid.*, p. 275.

[21]*Ibid.*, p. 201.

[22]*Ibid.*, p. 279.

[23]*Ibid.*, p. 291.

[24]*Ibid.*, p. 213.

[25]*Ibid.*, p. 226.

[26]*Ibid.*, p. 234.

[27]*Ibid.*, p. 306.

[28]*Ibid.*, p. 239.

[29]*Ibid.*, p. 226.

[30]*Ibid.*, p. 231.

[31]*Ibid.*, p. 296.

[32]*Ibid.*, p. 54.

[33]As there are three forces in the universe (God, nature, man) in alchemical tradition, which are manifested in three chemicals (Sulfur, salt, mercury), so man is divided into spirit, body, and soul. Michel's relationships could also have consisted of a triumvirate, each an analogy of the other, had the third force been acceptable to him.

[34]C. G. Jung, *Psychology and Religion: West and East*, p. 170.

CHAPTER 6

Gérard de Nerval—Soliman, Sheba, Adoniram, and the Occult

The ruins of Time build mansions in Eternity.
(William Blake, Letter to William Haley.)

Like Cazotte and Nodier, Nerval[1] used the dream visions
arising from his unconscious and transposed these into the
written word. Unlike his predecessors, he consciously cultivated
them until they became the main source for his creative work.
The images embedded in Nerval's version of the Queen of Sheba
legend, published in *Voyage in the Orient,* are archetypal: that
is, they emanate from his most primitive depths, the collective
unconscious, and, as such, are endowed with universal and
eternal significance. Because Nerval was a student of alchemy,
the Kabbalah, Orphism, and Illuminism, his preoccupations with
mystical matters are expressed in a variety of ways in the dream
motifs making up his interpretation of the Sheba legend. He
interwove entire philosophical and cosmogonous systems and
rituals (Masonic, alchemical, psychological) into the framework
of his tale.

1. The *Dramatis personnae*
and the Dream *Visions*

The Queen of Sheba, as woman and legend, had fascinated
Nerval as well as Nodier. Whereas Nodier's interest in this ancient queen was limited to a figure in *The Crumb Fairy,* she became a passion and an obsession for Nerval. He first wrote about
her in 1835 in the form of a libertto for Meyerbeer. Although
the project remained unrealized, the haunting vision of this regal
figure grew in intensity with the passage of years. In 1843, when
traveling in the Middle East, Nerval investigated the metaphysical
aspects of the myth and the role played by ancient occult societies to which the Near East gave birth.

For Nerval, whose interpretation of the ancient myth differs from biblical tradition as related in II Chronicles and I Kings,
the two most important figures are the Queen of Sheba (whom
he also refers to as Balkis), and Adoniram, a character he created,
the master builder of the palace and the temple (perhaps based
on Hiram).[2] Solomon, alluded to as Soliman in Nerval's tale,

is no longer the wise monarch of antiquity, a type of *anthropos* figure or semidivine personage who understood the language of the birds, but a materialistic, deceitful, greedy, and lustful monarch.[3]

Soliman is denigrated by Nerval. His face is marked with "perpetual serenity" and though he is old, there are no wrinkles; he wears only an expression of "the immutable peace of ineffable quietude." Everything he dons is of gold: his clothes, shoes, and crown, as well as this throne. He looks like "a golden statue, with ivory hands and mask."[4]

To further lower the image of Soliman, Sheba comments on the sumptuousness of his palace, the riches it contains, and expresses in subtle terms her disdain for his excessive use of gold, the heaviness of the ornamental detail. Most shocking of all is the fact that it took him seven years to build the temple and thirteen for the palace. She has praise only for the architect genius who built these monuments, whom she does not know.

Sheba criticizes not only Soliman's excessive materialism but also his attitude toward women, as expressed in Ecclesiastes: "And I find more bitter than death the woman, whose heart is snares and nets, and her hands as bands: who so pleaseth God shall escape from her; but the sinner shall be taken by her" (7:26). As for Soliman's poetry in The Song of Songs, it is contrived, cerebral, obscure, and filled with sophisms and contradictions. Poetry, she maintains, must come from the heart. According to the Bible, the Queen of Sheba asks Solomon certain questions that are intended to test his wisdom. In Nerval's version her three questions are answered only after the high priest, Sadoc, tells his monarch the answers he had bribed one of Sheba's followers to reveal.

Despite her distaste for Soliman, Sheba decides to entertain him by showing off her magical powers. With her ring she calls her birds and has them cluster over their heads like a canopy, sheltering them from the brilliance of the sun. As the thousands of birds fly above them (scarlet, black, all hues of blue) Soliman in awe of Sheba's power kneels before her. She is worthy, he tells her, of commanding both kings and the elements. She gives him her precious ring as a gift.

Nerval's rendition of the bird incident is in sharp contrast to the biblical account. In the Bible Solomon understands not only the language of the birds and of other animals, but also rules over a whole group of demons with whose help, it is said, he built the temple (I Kings 4:29-34). Because God was satisfied with the temple Solomon had built in His honor, the Midrash Bereshith Rabba says that "The power over the animal world, lost by Adam through his sin, was regained by Solomon." In the Talmud it is stated that "Solomon before his fall was lord over all the terrestrials and celestials." According to certain Arab legends, Solomon's birth was so grandiose an event as to recall that of a Messiah: "The child Solomon is born with a radiance of light in his face, Iblis (e.g., Satan) and his hosts melt as lead of iron melts in fire, the angels come down on earth to assist at birth, the earth is laughing in joy, the wild animals bow toward him and the tame ones come near."[5]

In Nerval's version not only is Sheba invested with magical powers, but she also has an augural bird, the Hud-Hud, or Hoopoe. This bird has been described as having a long slender bill and "an erectile tuft of feathers on his head."[6] Arabic and Persian lore claim that the Hoopoe bird can perform stunts of magic and foretell the future.[7] The Koran (Sourate 27) gives this account:

> Solomon succeeded David. He said: "Know my people, that we have been taught the tongue of birds and endowed with all good things. Surely this is a signal favor."
>
> Solomon marshalled his forces of djinn and men and birds, and sent them in battle array...
>
> He inspected his birds and said: "Where is the lapwing? I cannot see him here. If he does not give a good excuse, I shall sternly punish him or even slay him."

Sheba's Hoopoe bird has a black beak, red cheeks, gray eyes, and plumes of gold. It is faithful to its mistress and good to all whom it loves. Whenever the Queen is faced with grave problems, she consults her bird. It was said that if the bird should ever alight on a man's hand, Sheba would know that he would be her love.

Sheba—"The Queen of Noon, the Queen of the South, the

Queen of the Morning," or "The Divine Balkis"—is creative and mysterious.   She arrives in Soliman's kingdom from Yemen (known in ancient times as Sheba) with sixty elephants, camels, Abyssinians, Ethiopians, and with caravans filled with incense, perfumes, gold, precious stones, ivory, ebony, and costly garments (Jer. 6:20) (Ezek. 27:15, 20, 22).[8]   A Sabbaean star worshiper, she regulates her life according to the movements of the sun and the planet Venus and refuses to continue her journey at night when her deity is absent.   With the first rays of the sun Sheba enters Jerusalem, the city of gold, and greets the divine body—the sun.

Although Sheba is always mistress of herself, she is also complex: active, calm, volatile, reserved, naive, clever, cerebral, emotional, cruel, and tender.   Her eyes are mysterious and revealing; her face is "ardent and clear like newly molten brass." She represents all that is pure and exciting and takes on "the mystical face of the goddess Isis."   Dressed in white, in a diaphanous gauze gown, she appears like a cloud," a lily lost in a cluster of jonquils."   She represents a new order as contrasted with Soliman's traditional beliefs and reactionary doctrines.[9]

Adoniram, the artist-creator (Adonai-Lord or Adon-man, or a combination of both), is of unknown origin and in this respect is unlike the biblical Hiram.   He has a "strange and fascinating beauty" and godlike qualities.   He is withdrawn, introverted, rebellious, perpetually dissatisfied with his artistic endeavors, and searches for some superior force that will enable him to create the greatest masterpiece of all time.   The artist-creator, whose mind "boiled like a furnace," lives in a world of his own and dreams of gigantic artistic structures—of the impossible.[10]

Adoniram is the prototype of the romantic artistic creator: suffering, somber, mysterious, misanthropic, secretive, and audacious.   He is misunderstood by the populace, upon which he looks with "disdain," considering its concept limited and its vision superficial.   He "participated in the spirit of light and the genius of darkness" and belongs to a world where imagination is fomented by the perpetually turbulent waters of the unconscious.   Indifferent to women, they in turn try to avoid the fire in his eyes.   His one thought, his one passion is creation.   His sole companion, Benoni, is a child artist who came from a Phoenician family.[11]

Adoniram's thoughts forever revolve around the past—prebiblical and even preadamite times—when the world was ruled by a series of great kings.[12] After the destruction of these preadamite monarchs the world started to degenerate: diversity, contradiction, and lack of discipline led to laziness and a withering of the creative faculties. When Adoniram, who worked night and day preparing his sculptures and monuments, saw his workers feasting at Soliman's reception in honor of the Queen of Sheba's arrival, he turned aside in disgust. People, he thought, should not indulge in this manner; they should not feel satisfied with past accomplishments—in this instance, the construction of the palace and the temple, symbols of Soliman's vanity. These monuments are ephemeral; a spark can reduce them to cinders; conquering armies can raze them. Only Cain's descendants, Adoniram believed, were worthy of admiration.

According to certain Kabbalistic, Masonic, and Rosicrucian traditions, Cain, together with his sisters, withdrew to the south after he had killed his brother Abel. There he founded a city Enochia, which he named after Enoch, his firstborn. Alchemists have likened Enoch to the Hermes of the Greeks and the Mercury of the Romans. Cain's daughters, according to the Kabbala, were loved by the angels Aza and Azael. Because of such an infranction of the rules, the angels were cast down from heaven, "imprisoned" in matter, and their divine natures covered by earthly bodies.[13] Their union with mortals engendered a race of giants, the "mighty men of old," the "men of renown" mentioned in Genesis: "There were giants in the earth in those days; and also after that, when the sons of God came in unto the daughters of men, they bare children to them, the same became mighty men which were of old, men of renown (6:4). As for Cain, he toiled, searched, dug into the earth, and finally came upon fabulous metal mines. After discovering the secret of welding metals, be bequeathed his knowledge to Tubal-Cain and his descendants.

Cain's descendants, Adoniram felt, had created such extraordinary works in metal that the forms they molded were unnamable—so remarkable in fact, they frightened God, who caused the earth to tremble when he looked at them. The extraordinary city of Babylon, Adoniram maintained, with its wondrous Hanging Gardens, had been built from cast-off materials used by the artisans of Enochia. The pyramids themselves, he declared, had been fashioned by Cain's descendants, and for this reason would last for all eternity. Adoniram himself dreamed of building a sphinx so incredible that it would make Jehovah turn pale.

Adoniram's contemporaries were mediocre artists. A true artist does not copy nature, he claimed, he searches for "unknown forms, unnamed beings, incarnations in front of which man steps back...faces capable of instilling respect, gaiety, stupefaction, and terror." The Egyptians and Assyrians, both closer in time to Cain's descendants, were audacious artists who wrenched their creations out of the rock. Their minds leaped forward; their imaginations were undaunted. The Hebrews, on the other hand, were controlled by matter; they were "servile" imitators of nature and therefore art had been lost to them.[14]

When Sheba meets Adoniram, it is as if two worlds have blended into one, as if frictions has ceased to exist. Adoniram's voice takes on strange tonalities as he speaks to her. Since she knows nothing about him other than that he had built the palace and the temple, she cannot understand the intensity of his reaction to her nor hers to him.

Adoniram tells Sheba that he has learned the art of sculpture by hammering, cutting, and incising rocks right out of mountains, forcing his scissors into the earth's crust. One day, as he was walking about, he tells her, the earth seemed to open up before him. Rock upon rock just fell away. He investigated the gaping maw and discovered a cave, a buried city with vaults and arcades, a forest of stone that had, seemingly, remained in the same state for thousands of years. Colossal figures, a series of "giants," seemed to emerge from the darkness, like those that had disappeared from the earth centuries before. Animals could also be delineated in the inner city and looked like nothing he had ever seen, terrifying specters carved out of man's wildest imagination. Adoniram remained in this dead city, observing these phantoms of bygone kingdoms, and learned from them the *tradition* of his art.

When alone with Sheba, Adoniram advises her openly that to marry Soliman would be like blending the blood of a racially

pure person with that of a slave. Does a lion lie with a domesti-
cated dog? he questions. Soliman's race is impure, he has inter-
married with all peoples; his Hebrews, once courageous, creative
and warlike have been reduced to a shadow of themselves; they
are effete, lazy, and unimaginative. Once peace had settled
on the land, it brought luxury and sensuality—and a preference
for gold rather than iron. Whereas Sheba (whom he sometimes
calls Balkis) is the daughter of a patriarch and therefore should
not sully herself by such a marriage.

Adoniram stands with Sheba and Soliman before the
thousands of people of Jerusalem. Sheba testing his power asks
him to call his workers together. Undaunted by what seems an
amazing request, he makes the *Tau* sign (a Masonic symbol)
and within seconds a "human sea" swarms toward him, men
from distant valleys and planes, subdivided like armies into three
columns of 100,000 artists, 30,000 iron workers, 80,000 stone-
cutters and masons, 70,000 transporters of materials, and 3,300
intendants. The Queen is perplexed. How can Adoniram call so
many workers to him with such speed? Did he have some extraordinary power at his disposal? She humbles herself before his
"sublime" and "occult" ways and gives him a necklace of precious stones.

Soliman, displeased by Sheba's admiration is jealous of the
artist's youth, beauty, and vitality, but mostly of his creative
powers. He strikes back at Adoniram by condemning everything he had previously praised: he calls Enochia, built by
Cain, a "criminal city" (Gen. 4:17); the art of molting metals,
discovered by Cain and carried on in the darkness of the earth
by Tubal-Cain, an imperious art. Then Soliman praises his own
ideas and accomplishments: the simple, pure, and orderly
lines of his temple and unity of its plan; it is the antithesis
to Adoniram's night realm with its horrendous monsters and
idols.

In a play of wills and in an attempt to right a wrong, Sheba
dwells on the topic of idolatry. One can idolize routine: for
example, Soliman's traditional ways that had once brought
order out of chaos but now have become destructive and offen-
sive forces. As for Soliman's artistic endeavors, whether in
poetry or the sculptures he ordered his artists to make during
his reign, they are staid hieratic figures borrowed from the

Egyptians, but without the spark, the lifeblood, the creative élan that the originators of this art had possessed.

The dichotomy between Soliman's old, routine ways and the Sheba-Adoniram creative force becomes accentuated in a series of events, for example, when Soliman feasts the Queen of Sheba at Mello. From his villa, situated on the top of a hill—an "aerial" domain—one is able to observe green and fertile valleys interspersed with palm and pine trees as well as a series of white tombs, symbolizing most dramatically the differences between the two ways of life. Mello at the top of the hill stands for the spirit; the valley of Josephat represents fertility, life, and death—the cycle of existence. During the course of this meeting Sheba reveals the story of her ancestors. She comes from the formerly arid and sterile land of Yemen, but her people transformed it into one of the richest kingdoms in the world. For two centuries they dug rivers, elevated mountains of granite higher even than the pyramids, dug "cyclopean vaults under which entire armies could march, built aqueducts, canals, industries, prairies, and planted forests.[15]

Soliman stops her with a counterargument. One should not attempt to reverse the order of nature by creating artificial civilizations, by bringing industry and commerce to a land unable to support such additions. Judea, he declares, was arid and should not be encouraged to include more inhabitants within its boundaries than it can feed. If all of Yemen's artificial lakes were to dry up, Soliman asserts, Sheba's people would be burned by the sun. "One must not tempt God nor correct his works. What he does is good."[16]

Sheba, who stands for the new, active, aggressive, and creative principle, believes that Soliman's doctrines would force society to remain in swaddling clothes; his doctrines would hold mankind down and prevent independence of thought. Man is a builder of palaces and towns; he can work in copper, gold, and metals of all types. God gave his creatures the "genius of activity" and this should be developed and used to benefit both body and spirit.

The "molten sea" episode is perhaps the most extraordinary in Nerval's narrative. Adoniram had dreamed of building a molten sea—an immense brass vase—a feat, if it could be realized, that would verge on the miraculous. The time is now ripe to test his work before the Queen, Soliman, and the populace. Adoniram dons the white apron of the architect and commands his workers to carry out his carefully laid plans. As the activity begins, Sheba declares that he looks like a divinity of fire commanding a cataclysmic event to begin. The boiling metals start "breathing," the open furnaces groan, the massive brick towers are like flames reaching out into the atmosphere; the world about them takes on a variety of colors—reds, purples, blues, oranges, white—the flowing brass flashes through the darkness of the night as a creation that defies spacial limitations comes into being.

Suddenly, Adoniram's helper, Benoni, discovers three workmen standing where no man should have been. He realizes they have betrayed his master. Benoni runs to Soliman and informs him of the treachery, but it is too late. As the mass of burning metal pours forth with volcanic speed, torrents of brilliant colors sweep over the area—blood red to gold. The populace is immobile, stunned. Silence clothes the city. Adoniram sees a shadowlike figure cross the bed of molten metal, and convinced it is a saboteur plunges the iron hook he is holding deep into the intruder's chest, then hurls the body with superhuman force all the way to the city's ramparts. It was Benoni he killed by mistake.

Adoniram's experiment is under way and the entire area is liquid fire. Frenzy and excitement abate when the mold, into which the metal had run, suddenly cracks. The experiment fails. With this realization Adoniram lets out an inhuman scream —a wail that rends the earth—the pain only an artist-creator knows when unable to realize his dreams. Adoniram attempts to combat the flow of the liquid metal, to war with the elements—fire and water—but to no avail. Detonations are heard like a series of "furious volcanoes," reminiscent of that terrible night when Sodom and Gomorrha had been destroyed. Dishonor has been heaped upon Adoniram. He leaves the multitude and withdraws into his own working area. There is a strange figure that seems to be moving about. Adoniram hears his name pronounced three times; an apparition then comes into view, a huge human form rises and walks toward him. The person is carrying a hammer. He leans toward Adoniram and speaks: "Awaken your soul, arise, my son. Come, follow me. I have seen the evils which have befallen my race, and I have taken pity on it."[17]

It is here that Adoniram's descent into the abyss begins: the world of the past, or psychologically that of the collective unconscious. Adoniram listens to Tubal-Cain, the "instructor of every artificer in brass and iron" (Gen. 4:22), as he speaks of his ancestors and his own suffering. Adoniram feels himself advancing into a deep area of silence and night, into some infinite space—and he experiences a strange affinity with this mysterious man who is guiding him through these unknown, cold, damp regions. He hears the dull, regular beat of the earth's heart and begins to see a white point in the distance, a world of people living in the shadows of these immense inner realms. Cain had lived here. The emerald stone, which marks the center of Mount Kaf, Adam's burial place, gleams before him. In Mount Kaf's gallery hang the pictures of seventy emperors who had reigned for seventy thousand years before the creation of man, when the earth was inhabited by four giant races, which, according to the Koran, had been formed into "noble, subtle, and luminous matter" from a very hot fire and were called Dives, Jinns, Afrites, and Paris. These original races had warred with each other for twelve thousand years. Then, tired of observing their brutal ways, God fashioned man, a race blended from spirit and matter, which the Koran defined more precisely as lime and sandy earth. Tubal-Cain and his ancestors were descendants of the fire people and not of God's second creation, man. Adonai's tyranny, Tubal-Cain explained, ends in these regions. The fire people living under the earth are fed from the fruits of the Tree of Science.[18]

No sooner does Adoniram hear this statement than he feels life breaking through all about him. The heart in this central region of the earth is the normal temperature for these souls made from the element of fire. Although the people are deprived of the sun, warmth is given them by fire, infusing them with life. They are walled up within the earth by God who has become envious of their power and has forbidden them to communicate with man, fearing they might teach them the meaning of eternal happiness. But those who live on earth, Tubal-Cain states, are made out of mud, have limited mental faculties, and are subject to death.

Adoniram's stay in the underworld, as described by Nerval, takes on the grandeur of an illusion—of an apocalyptic vision. The gigantic people in these cavernous realms, who had lived on the earth in the early days of creation, converse with Adoniram. He studies their art: the fluid vegetation made out of metals, like "arborescent" trees, plants, and flowers, forever giving off a variety of aromas; the winged lions, griffons, sphinxes, androgynes; the infinite number of creatures standing about mysteriously as though animated by some arcane force.

Adoniram meets Cain, the "tiller of the ground" (Gen. 4:2), the vagabond whom God would not destroy nor have destroyed. His beauty, Adoniram judges, is "superhuman"; his eyes are sad, his lips pale, his forehead wears the expression of concern, and upon his brow is outlined the form of a coiled golden serpent. He speaks to Adoniram and reveals the secret of his origin, of his pain. He is a descendant of the fire people, an industrious yet oppressed race. Because of him Adoniram suffers. All of Cain's progeny are doomed to pain as a result of his murder of Abel. Cain justifies his acts as he talks to Adoniram: he had been unjustly treated by God; he was the one who had sacrificed and worked hard to bring agriculture to the world; he was the one who taught man how to plant wheat, to turn the arid land into arable and fertile fields. His brother Abel had merely kept the cattle; had rested under a tree. Moreover, Adam and Eve and God Himself had loved Abel more than him. Cain introduced murder into the world to rectify an injustice—only after ingratitude had caused him to suffer bitterness. Those who work hard in the world, he continues, are not rewarded but oppressed. After the murder, Cain experienced guilt; to make up for his crime, he helped Adam's children by teaching them the superior arts: industry and science. But God, angered with him, never forgave him for revealing certain secrets of man.

Adam's voice calls forth to Cain. "What did you do with your brother Abel?" And Cain's heartbeat, the weight of his act, forces him to sink to the ground. Cain's son Enoch now speaks to Adoniram, enumerating the things he has done for man: namely, that he had taught him the art of stonecutting, of building houses, and of grouping these into citylike formation. He "revealed" to them the manner in which societies are built. Man was but a brutish beast before nations began constructing cities based on Enochia.

Tubal-Cain resumes his narration. While man was being destroyed by the Flood, the descendants of the fire people still living on earth were saved. Tubal-Cain and his ancestors sent flames to cut the rock in two and dug long galleries beneath the earth where man could hide; they built the plain of Gizeh and the pyramids. After the Flood, when Tubal-Cain walked upon the earth, he saw the change that had been wrought: the people were small and thin and the climate was cold. Thus he withdrew to the inner domain, the lands of his fathers. And the wife of Noah's second son, Ham, found Tubal-Cain's son handsomer than any earth man. From their union, Nimrod's father, Cush, was born. He taught his brothers the art of the hunt, founded Babylon, and undertook the building of the tower of Babel. When God realized that Cain's blood was the cause of such marvels, He dispersed his people.

Adoniram is unable to see the soul of Tubal-Cain's son. He had died after the Flood and belonged to the earth, as did his descendants; they all remained invisible to the fire people. But Adoniram hears him say that in a moment of despair God had appeared to him and said:

> —Hope...
>   Without any experience, isolated in a world
>   unknown to me, I answered timidly.
>   I am afraid, Lord...
>   He resumed:—This fear will be your salvation.[19]

Then God informed Tubal-Cain's son that his name would remain unknown, as would his great deeds; that from him weaker beings would be born and would die; only their souls would remain eternal, thereby retaining that "precious spark" that made for both their suffering and their genius. His descendants would be superior people, but honored only after their death. They must accept their fate: their earthly existence where they are doomed to suffer, where they will be rejected and know poverty and despair. Adoniram realizes that as the heir of these fire people, he too will have to submit to his destiny.

Adoniram returns to earth as mysteriously as he entered its depths. With the knowledge he has gained, he makes his molten sea and astounds the multitude, the ten thousand workers, Soliman, and the Queen of Sheba. As he wins his acclaim,

Sheba's bird, Hud-Hud, recognizes his master and alights on Adoniram's hand. Sheba knows then that Adoniram is to be her lord. He recognizes her as the Spirit of Light and realizes that she too is made of fire and that she is of the same lineage as he, a descendant of Tubal-Cain and in direct line with Nimrod's brother, Saba. But this secret, he informs her, must be kept from man. Sheba becomes Adoniram's bride and carries his son within her. They decide to leave Jerusalem separately, as this would be the wiser course.

The three companions who betrayed Adoniram the first time he attempted to create his sea of molten metal find him in the temple. They try to extract the secret of his art from him—that of the master artist—which may be learned through a password only he knows. When Adoniram refuses, one of the men takes his scissors and plunges them into Adnoram's thigh, the other takes the point of his compass and digs it into Adoniram's heart. Then they bury him and plant a young acacia branch on the grave. When Adoniram is no longer seen in Jerusalem, rumors of his death flood the city. The people demand retribution, and Soliman orders nine masters to find the artist's body. When they come upon a freshly planted acacia branch on top of which a strange bird has lit, they dig into the ground. They decide that the first word anyone of them is to utter when they discover Adoniram's body is to be the password: *Makbenach,* meaning, "The flesh is leaving the body." Soliman and the people are informed of Adoniram's demise.

After Sheba's departure Soliman tries to find solace in other womens' arms but is unable to do so. He builds a temple to Moloch and has another castle constructed for himself on Mt. Kaf. There he casts his spell: he commands all the animals, elements, and substances to remain immobile—not even to decompose; then he mounts his throne and dies. But Soliman has forgotten to include the little worm in his spell, and after two thousand years it has eaten away the pillars that supported the throne. When the throne falls, the spell is broken and the world is released from its immobility. Life begins anew, according to the Koran (Sourate 34):

> And when he had decreed his death, they did not know that
> he was dead until they saw a worm eating away his staff. And
> when his corpse fell down, the djinn realized that had they had

knowledge of what was hidden, they would not have continued in their abject servitude.

2. *Soliman-Sheba-Adoniram and Masonic Symbolism*

Nerval's version of the Soliman-Sheba-Adoniram myth had special significance for the Masons. In fact, every detail and every event depicted is replete with Masonic symbolism.

Adoniram (or Hiram for the Mason) is a seminal force, a master builder, a generative power. He is a doer, an actor. His strength lies in the consciousness of his creative instinct and the desire to make his labor manifest. His great work consists in building a soul—in transmuting himself, a creature of matter, into a purer, higher, and more spiritually oriented being. His trials and turmoils are a series of *initiations:* the word initiation comes from the Latin *in ire,* meaning "to go within" or to reconstruct one's knowledge of life. For the Mason the real world is the inner one; the exterior realm is merely a facade, a mask. When Socrates said "Know thyself," he meant discover the inner man, the real being. To gain such knowledge requires probing, a sounding out of the force within.[20]

Adoniram had to discover his spiritual self—that is, the fire that burned in him or his own creative element. To search out the "spark" he had to shed all "base metals," all superficial forms of material existence—the world of appearance—and the impurities in which he was embedded. Adoniram's ordeal has become the essential part of the ceremony of reception to the Grade of Master in the Masonic Order. Each initiate is compelled to go through the test of the four elements—earth, fire, water, and air—in order to find the inner core, the focal point from which all creative spirit emerges. Man's task in life also centers upon finding his core, bringing forth and developing the "celestial" force that lives within him. For the Mason, Christ offered himself as the supreme symbol of such work.[21]

In the Masonic initiation ceremony, as in the ancient mysteries, the acolyte experiences the "death" of the profane self and the "birth" of the new spiritual being. The object of the initiation is to lead the neophyte into the experience of an inner illumination—the transcendental light or the center of self.   Since Masonic initiation is most intuitive, it proceeds through universal symbols, signs, and analogies, which bring the neophyte into closer contact with the invisible and infinite world, creating unity out of diversity.

Because the inner experience the initiate undergoes cannot be expressed verbally (an emotion cannot be articulated), it must of necessity remain secret.   As the neophyte proceeds, he may at some point know what is termed "efficacious grace," or the divine state preceding man's fall.   According to some eighteenth-century Masons, namely Martinez Pasqualis, the initiation is supposed to help man reintegrate into the universal pleroma.   When this occurs, the neophyte is imbued with a type of "nostalgic desire for a rhythmic Light and Harmony," which he had once known and which he longs to experience again.[22]

Solomon's temple is also an important symbol for the Masons.   It represents the rebuilt human body, the one which the neophyte has reworked after his successful initiation—a body renewed is the most perfect of all possible earthly bodies.[23]   According to the religious philosopher and Mason Claude de Saint-Martin, the Temple stands for the mind, the abode of the spirit and divine essence.   Since man is God's priest, it is his duty to spread His word by enlarging the godly area, by seeking to enlighten His living corpus within man.

At the outset of Nerval's tale, Adoniram had already built the temple, and therefore had completed a certain stage in his initiation.   He had revealed both his power and wisdom when making the Tau sign, thus calling his thousands of workers together in seconds.   According to Masonic belief, the Tau sign indicates "rectitude in action"; the square in the Tau sign implies that all lines are put in "right relation to each other and are united with each other."[24]   But Adoniram's power was evidently not complete since he was a victim of treachery, the implication being that he had not yet sufficiently sounded out his own depths.   The deceit meted out to him by three workers was a manifestation of his own weakness, perhaps his vanity, his inability to see himself in the proper perspective. He had not yet mastered his own creative impulses.   More tests were needed; greater depth had to be known.

Adoniram's stay in Cain's realm may be looked upon as a

withdrawal from the outside world into man's inner domain. It permitted him further reflection and increased knowledge, a period of meditation that is indispensable if truth and reality are to be experienced. The Buddhist, for example, has made meditation central to his religion. The Mason is also intent upon the in-dwelling process so that all facets of external reality may be examined from within in greater harmony. *"Visita Interior terrae, rectificandoque, invenies occultum"* is the Masonic credo.

Adoniram's inner probings permit him to come into contact with the divine spark that lives within him: the creative principle that permits him to perform his miracle of the molten sea. In the arcane realm of his ancestors, Adoniram takes stock of himself; he converses with Cain, Tubal-Cain, and Adam— the forces they represent within him as experienced through projection. They had been dormant until stimulated or provoked into action during Adoniram's inner meanderings. The in-dwelling, the meditation paved the way for his discovery that he was the descendant of fire people. Once he has contacted these elements, once he has dipped into the realm of the infinite, he returns to the upper world resurrected or reborn. Now he can become the creator of immortal works that had lived only *in potentia* within his fantasy world. Had Adoniram not experienced the first great failure and pain, he might not have felt impelled to meditate, to turn inward, to communicate with those transcendental forces within him. He would not have labored to express what lived within him, and so would not have achieved his monumental work.

When Adoniram left the inner world of contemplation, Tubal-Cain told him he needed a hammer (or malet) for his work. This instrument, basic to the Masonic cult, represents the will needed to accomplish one's work and to achieve one's goal. It is an instrument used to transform crude matter into perfect shapes—a tool capable of building a temple (body-mind). Before performing the miracle of the molten sea, Adoniram dons his white wool apron, which symbolizes constant toil for the Mason. Then, by an incredible tension of the will, he begins his task.

Adoniram is slain by workmen for not revealing the secret word, which stands for the creative process, the secret that Masons even today are not supposed to disclose. So he is stricken first with scissors, which according to Masonic tradition indicate "discernment in investigation," then with a compass, symbolizing "moderation in the search," passion controlled and measured by reason.[25]   A clap of thunder was heard when Adoniram died. Such cosmic manifestations always occur when traumatic events take place: Christ's death, Charlemagne's battle with the Saracens, Moses' reception of the Ten Commandments on Mt. Sinai.

In terms of ancient solar beliefs, the acacia branch the assassins had placed on Adoniram's grave indicates new vegetation that comes into being as a result of the sun's force: a visualization of Adoniram's own creative powers. In this respect, Adoniram has been compared to Osiris, who was dismembered and whose wife-sister, Isis, rebuilt him, after which he withdrew into the underworld. According to Egyptian mythology, when the sun descended into Osiris' tomb, he was reborn into a new phase of existence. Then his widow, Isis, gave birth to their son Horus, just as Sheba gave birth to her son after Adoniram's demise. Masons are called the "Children of the Widow"; but with the birth or reappearance of the god—understood as a purification of the self—the Masons take on the name of "Children of Light."[26]

The fact that Adoniram found his final resting place under the alter in the temple he had himself constructed indicates that he succeeded in his endeavors: his body had been rebuilt and rested on the holiest of central points.[27]   Adoniram's resurrection in the son Sheba bore him made him eternal—able to participate in cosmic life, in divine knowledge. The reborn Adoniram is considered omnipresent in each initiate. Only his flesh had left his bones—*Makbenach;* his soul had attained immortality.

3. *The Alchemical Significance*

Nerval's Soliman-Sheba-Adoniram legend is also an alchemical document. Alchemists believe the world is one, a vast organism that is alive and animated and, thereby, possesses a soul. All is linked within the universe, like the rungs of a ladder, from the tiniest particle of sand up to God.[28]

From primordial unity there arises duality: woman and man, solid and liquid, life and death. To assure some semblance of balance within the universe a third force, manifestation, comes into being. These three forces are present in the cosmos (God, nature, man) and are manifested in three principles: sulfur, salt, and mercury. In the human being they are referred to as spirit, body, and soul. Everything contained in this trinity becomes an analogy of the other since all in the universe is, as we have stated, linked. The star of Solomon (David), for example—which is not only a Jewish but also a Masonic and alchemical symbol—is composed of two interlocking triangles indicating the union of duality.

The alchemist's scientific goal of extracting the "gold," or "philosophers' stone," from base metals requires seven stages of purification: separation, calcination, sublimation, dissolution, distillation, coagulation, and coction, also expressed as black, white, yellow, red. The alchemist cooks the various elements he seeks to transmute in what has been called a type of "philosophical egg," a receptacle like a uterus. In this receptacle the elements are blended by means of fire and pass from chaos to purity. Such a mixing process has an inner philosophical meaning. In Adoniram's case the mixture had been faulty the first time he attempted to create his molten sea. Therefore, the substance in the philosophical egg had not yet been sufficiently purified. Only after his visit to the inner world and his confrontation with all the substances within the earth could he reach the state of purity necessary to create his gold or, symbolically, his great work.

In the underworld Adoniram saw the base metals in a state of ebulition: both solid and liquid as they poured out of each other. And he exposed his "naked human spirit"[29] to these elements in the raw: earth, air, water, and fire, thus gaining the secret of how he must proceed in the various stages of distillation, or the creation of his molten sea. Adoniram actually had to experience, physically, the turmoil and the chaos necessary to undergo the distillation, coagulation, and coction that would lead him to the perfect creation.

Nerval details Adoniram's evolution in terms of color. Black (chaos) represents putrefaction, the chaotic period when Adoniram had failed in his mission and had been instrumental in causing Benoni's death along with the hundreds who were burned and drowned during the uncontrollable flow of molten metal. Blackness, for the alchemist, symbolizes the demise of the profane, the uninitiated human being, the one who lacks vision, maturity, and thus discernment. As the cooking process is pursued, the black is transformed into white, which represents the resurrection of the elements: a change in attitude, form, and substance. When she first meets Adoniram, Sheba is dressed in a white gauzelike garment. Although Adoniram has failed in his molten sea experiment, Sheba does not repudiate him; she is perplexed. She does not know what course to follow. She marvels that he had been able to control thousands of workmen but is still unaware that Adoniram is to become her god of fire, that he will attain enlightenment.

In the underworld Adoniram is exposed to intense heat: red is the most important tonality. Here he is transformed into a young king and relives spiritual and physical suffering (he dies insofar as the earth people are concerned) and is reborn as the *spiritus mundi,* aware of his powers and his art. The miracle of the molten sea is performed, but it was within the bowels of the earth that he learned the secret of creativity or how to make the "philosophers' stone," which the alchemist Paracelsus had described as being a composite of opposites: fluid, liquid, like mercury able to penetrate hard bodies, transforming them all into gold.

In the last phase—that of rubido or redness—fire became the most important of all principles or vehicles of transformation. It is the first sign of divine emanation, a fecundating entity able to engender all beings, a vital force that makes for the very composition of the universe itself.[30]   Fire is fluid, it gives light and warmth, electricity, movement, and energy; it illuminates and permits vegetation to grow (man, animal, vegetable, mineral); it also destroys as it did during Adoniram's first attempt at the molten sea. He was blind and unaware of his betrayal because he was too interested in his own aggrandizement to be a true master. His perspective was so limited that he unwittingly sacrificed the child, Benoni, his only friend and helper, concluding unwisely that Benoni had betrayed him.

Creation occurs only when power (fire) is transformed into the act in a channeled and orderly manner; when the various possibilities in life are reduced to one. Adoniram had not yet reached this stage.

For the alchemist, as we have said, there are three forces present in the cosmos (God, nature, man) and are manifested in three principles: sulfur, salt, and mercury.[31]

Because Adoniram is the energetic, creative element in the drama, he may be associated with sulfur. Astrologists have likened sulfur to the sun principle, which may also be used to define Adoniram's role in this tale. He stands as does the sun, for life, creativity, a power-driven force, and universal strength and form. Since all astral bodies are endowed with sexes in alchemy, he would be identified with the father principle. Insofar as he is likened with sulfur, he would represent the masculine, active element, hot and powerful enough to attack other metals. Because he is so powerful a principle, he is also a complex of opposites; and when considered in terms of sulfur, he is unchangeable, fixed in his intentions, with only one goal in mind—creating.[32]

The alchemist classifies sulfur, mercury, and salt in terms of four elements—earth, water, fire, air. In his visible and solid state (sulfur-sun), Adoniram would represent the earth principle —that is, the fecundating force, the physical, strong, masculine type whom Sheba calls a "real" man. In that he is also a fire principle (sun), as the descendant of Cain and Tubal-Cain, he stands for passion and creativity. Like the sun, Adoniram disappears from view and pursues his existence in an occult or subtle state. His withdrawal is proof of his ability to live in two realms: that of sunlight or reality and that of the hidden underworld, the domain of occult and subliminal forces.

Metals are considered living entities by the alchemists, endowed with souls. So the molten sea, which is made of brass, is also equipped with body and soul. The soul is the vaporous element that emanates from metals as they are being distilled. The body, or matter, is the part of the metal that remains visible. When metal is heated and flows, both body and soul are united into one. Adoniram's initial failure shows that his initiation or the work in progress had not yet been perfected. He had not been able to fuse body and spirit into a harmonious whole.[33]

Sheba alchemically is associated with mercury and astrologically with the moon. As the moon, she reflects the sun's strength—that is, she is fertilized by the sun and cannot act or function independently. Her moods also vacilate. Nerval refers to her as the "Morning Star," and in this respect she possesses some of the sun's characteristics and is frequently mistress of herself; her thinking function predominates under certain circumstances (rather uncommon in most women). When she talks with Soliman about poetry and artistic creativity, and argues in favor of her God and her people, she is always opposed to him. Her manner of discourse is reasonable and rational—hence male-oriented—though she argues in favor of the heart and accuses Soliman of being overly cerebral in poetry and too materialistic. To add to her conflicting nature, the caravans she brought with her to Jerusalem are piled high with matter: precious stones, ivories, myrrh, aromatic perfumes, those very things she claims to detest.[34] Because she represents mercury and the moon, as well as the sun principle, her attitude is ambiguous and enigmatic.

When likened to mercury, she may be considered passive, cold, and, at the same time, volatile. Like mercury, she is malleable and changes as each new situation arises; she acts and reacts accordingly and not to a set pattern. She can "fuse" as does mercury, also sparkle and burst forth as she does when meeting Adoniram for the first time. Here she may be compared to a liquid because of her ability to insinuate herself into various events. Like mercury she is an occult force with magic power and an ability to rule over the bird world.

Adoniram, according to alchemical tradition, is considered the active principle; Sheba, by definition, would be the relatively passive element: each is constantly attracted by the other. During their earthly life they are separated from one another (man and woman); they combine under the influence of fire (passion). By means of the alchemical fire, Sheba is able to know Adoniram. Her feelings guide her, not her cold, rational mind. Through these feelings—where neither the eye nor the body can penetrate—the inner fire causes her to seek her mate.[35]

Soliman stands for the alchemist's salt and the astrologer's ether. He is a mediating element, a modality or state of matter that brings things together. By contrasting Soliman's materialism, Sheba learns to appreciate creativity and spirituality. Soliman's sage and "passionless" brow enables her to become interested in Adoniram's youth, beauty, and energy. Soliman's wisdom (or, in Nerval's rendition, his senility) makes Adoniram's creative force stand out all the more compellingly; Soliman's hypocrisy, dishonesty, jealousy, and pettiness underscore Adoniram's sincerity, honesty, and originality. As associated with salt, it is Soliman who makes the union of Sheba and Adoniram possible; without this presence or blending power, without his intervention, they might never have met. In this respect, Soliman is comparable to the "vital spirit" of the alchemist, which makes for unity and brings matter of all types and forms together.

In order for the three elements (mercury, sulfur, salt) to operate, activity must occur, thus enabling an alteration in their consistency. Adoniram's molten-metal experience, or the alchemist's heat, enabled him to create his great work. The meaning of this miracle has been compared to the great creation myths in the world religions.

The union of Sheba and Adoniram, or the discovery of the "philosopher's stone," paves the way for ecstasy or the soul's liberation from the body, the birth of the child (the artistic creation), and the immortality of man. The original substance from which the new and creative elements are born must, of necessity, die—or the hero becomes incorporated into the status quo. The alchemist believes, however, that he or what he represents lives on in his child (his creation) and, as such, will regenerate once again in nature's cyclical process: · darkness of night, whiteness of dawn, redness of the resplendent days.

The three assassins of Adoniram represent the forces of nature: spirit, soul, and body. They were, alchemically, responsible for bringing out Adoniram's dissolution, putrefaction, and rebirth. Once union had taken place between Sheba and Adoniram (mercury and sulfur), a condition of stasis would have developed had the murder not taken place. Since all in nature is in a perpetual state of flux, it follows that the metamorphosis would take place and with it renewal, reassessment, and reevaluation. The child born of Sheba and Adoniram would, it is presumed, go through his own initiation and life process, seek his own purity and potential, and evolve in his own way.

The Ars Magna of alchemy is the science that permits man to reconstruct the very processes of life and earth in his laboratory, to purify the substances with which he is working by ridding them of all base elements; this allows absolute beauty, truth, and goodness to emerge. Nature's processes are eternal. Gold is a state of mind and it too is subject to change, evolution, and spiritualization.

4. *The Psychological Implications*

The Soliman-Sheba-Adoniram drama as conceived by Nerval is equally fascinating from a psychological point of view. It demonstrates perhaps more readily than any other of his works the need to overthrow the old, repressive, and conventional attitude that the author held and to fructify his personality with the addition of that foreign element.

Sheba represents the Eternal Feminine. The fact that she came from a sun-drenched land and adored the solar disk indicates her need for illumination (consciousness) and her longing for the spiritual or wise attitude she thought Soliman would bring to her. She came with gifts from the distant land of Yemen. She spoke of the fecundity of her native country, the riches her earth yielded now that it had been brought under cultivation. Sheba, therefore, brings certain values to Soliman: beauty and work, also aggressiveness and pride. In Nerval's tale she is an independent figure, a composite of masculine (sun) and feminine (moon) traits: passionate and cerebral, active and passive.

The riddles she poses to Soliman activate her masculine side—that is, the thinking principle witin her—and not her affective tendencies. Since the word *question* may be translated from the Hebrew as "test" or "tempt," her questioning becomes comparable to the Sphinx's riddle in the Oedipus myth and may signify a test for power. Will Sheba's way predominate or Soliman's? That is, will the patriarchal or matriarchal society win out? Since Soliman's patriarchal society had already regressed to a luxury-loving, sensual, and almost pagan community, it is only a matter of time until it disintegrates completely. Everything is corruption in this court. He even answers the riddles deceitfully. No tension, no struggle, no heroism exists

Blake

any longer. When a land (or personality) is in a regressive situation, it no longer experiences the strain or sacrifice necessary to build and evolve. Nothing, therefore, can readily come from Sheba's relationship with Soliman. It is based on artifice and mistrust. We know from the outset that another hero will and must be found, another force able to fructify, to bring about that renewal so necessary to pave the way for rebirth.[36]

Sheba is Adoniram's anima figure: goddess, queen, mother, sister, and wife. She is a positive force in his life just as she is destructive for Soliman. She is not only seductive in that she seeks to attract Adoniram, but as a goddess, a sybil of sorts, she also wields magic powers. She is subtle when resorting to deceit (giving Soliman a sleeping potion when he tries to make advances toward her); strong when she must maintain her independence, sacrificing her magic ring and yielding her power over birds.

In Nerval's tale, the Hoopoe bird belongs to Sheba; in the Biblical legend it is Soliman's. The bird is frequently looked upon as "an intuitive thought" because it is believed to have the power of experiencing inner feelings before it emerges into consciousness. Moreover, the bird has spiritual attributes. It acts as a guide for Sheba's own feelings, points the way, and more important, confirms externally what she feels inwardly; her love for Adoniram. Through the bird she is led to fulfillment, and her gentle, feminine, loving aspects come into being. She experiences Eros (relatedness) with Adoniram who, in this story, represents not only the artist-creator, but a higher form of spirituality.[37]

Soliman, the father image, the patriarch, stands for the old order. He lacks initiative and spirituality and is carried along by the court's corruption. To maintain his power he resorts to trickery, bribery, and lies. Captivated by the beautiful, winsome Sheba, he would offer her anything in his kingdom, his entire being if need be, to win her affections. She remains uninterested because he lacks the one element she longs for, the masculine or higher spirituality. Her rejection of this monarch is another example of the ritual slaying of the old kings: the ruling attitude has become sterile and must die.

Adoniram, although a fire principle as is Sheba, differs

from her considerably. He is a rebellious and creative spirit of mysterious origin. He represents a personality unaware of its potential unfulfilled, untried, unredeemed. His imagination, his desire to create, and his dissatisfaction with himself compel him to experience inner torment. The failure of his molten sea or of his external attitude leads to profound introversion. He withdraws from the world, afraid of life, and concentrates on his inner development. He is living, therefore, a one-sided existence. Unwittingly, he had sacrificed his only friend, Benoni, really a projection of himself: the child artist who has not yet developed the strength necessary to perform a heroic work. The child in Adoniram had to be sacrificed in order to bring about inner development. Isolation had to be complete to pave the way for knowledge.

Adoniram then withdraws into his inner world, a cleft in the mountain. Mountains have always been placed where gods dwelt (Olympus, Parnassus), where their words were heard (Mt. Sinai), where punishment was experienced (Prometheus immolated on Mt. Caucasus), as ethereal areas (Christ on the hill of Calvary), and as sanctuaries for mysteries (Holy Grail on Mt. Salvatch in the Pyrenées). Mountains may be regarded as vehicles for mystical or spiritaul ascension, for psychological growth.[38]

During his underworld visit Adoniram confronts his collective unconscious and experiences its riches. Tubal-Cain, Cain, Adam, and the superhuman metallic forms or phantoms that he sees in this realm permit him to bring these aspects of his personality into consciousness. Each being and each figure represents an inner quality: fear, guilt, suffering, nobility, obsessions of various sorts, phobias, longings, hatreds. His rejection at the hands of society has been transformed into feelings of hatred for Soliman and his God. Adoniram seeks to destroy these negative father images as represented by the patriarchal society in which he grew up. Along with his ancestors—Adam, Cain and the rest—he is willing to sin by destroying the values these negative father images stand for and, in so doing, bring into the world the unnameable, the unimaginable.

To consider oneself the harbinger of extraordinary ideas or fresh approaches to art or life in general is to suffer from *hybris*, or an inflated ego. Such an imbalance does not go unchecked. The first time Adoniram felt himself capable of great things, he was betrayed by his workmen, as Christ and Osiris had been in their time. Such an outcome indicates that no man or God has the answer to life, that the cosmos, always subject to perpetual changes and upheavals, is forever evolving. Answers, at best, may be only temporary. The new element Adoniram introduced into Soliman's empire—the molten-sea experiment—was the product of his life experience and not that of another. The secret it contained could not be divulged to another.

Man cannot rest on his laurels, nor can he state his artistic mastership in a given work. Just as the cosmos lives and breathes, alters in form and shape, so the personality responds in a variety of ways to each new event and fresh coincidence. It is the individual who must learn to cope with the ever-changing forces and progress accordingly.

For Nerval the urge for the new—through an alliance with the positive aspects of the Great Mother archetype, which Sheba represented, and with Adoniram, a projection of himself as the suffering artist-creator—was a necessity for his wellbeing and for his evolution as an artist.

NOTES

[1]Gérard de Nerval was born in 1808. The son of a doctor who had served in Napoleon's Grande Armée and of a mother he did not remember, who died from a fever contracted when traveling with her husband on a military mission in Germany, he felt an aching void from his earliest days. Until the age of seven he lived with his maternal grand-uncle, Antoine Boucher, a pantheist, at Mortefontaine, in the Valois region. After his father's return in 1814 to civilian life, he moved to Paris. Subject to a highly disciplined army type routine, the young lad found life difficult. More important, he could not communicate with his father who was determined to have his son become a physician. Nerval wanted a literary career. He yielded to his father's wishes and went to medical school, but since it was not to his liking he dropped out after two years.

Nerval made his entrée into literature with a translation of Goethe's *Faust* I (1827) which was well received. He frequented the Nodier Cénacle and became friendly with Balzac, Gautier, and Hugo, among others. The year 1834 was momentous for him. Nerval attended a production at the Variétés Théâtre and saw what he considered to be the most exquisite, most perfect actress of them all: Jenny Colon. He fell hopelessly in love with her, and his feelings were not reciprocated. Despite the rejection, Nerval spent the rest of his life adoring her. He sought her image in others, he created protagonists, such as the Queen of Sheba, modeled on her. She was a *femme inspiratrice*. As the years passed, Nerval's behavior became increasingly quixotic. His malady was diagnosed as schizophrenia. In 1841 he was interned in Dr. Esprit Blanche's clinic—the first of seven internments. In 1843 he left for Egypt and the Near East. His writings at this period, published in volume form in *Voyage in the Orient,* delve into the ancient Egyptian mysteries and the secrets of the Pyramids. Nerval's sonnets, *Les Chimères,* are examples of some of the most extraordinary poetry in the French language. The *Daughters of Fire* and *Aurélia* bring to life certain aspects of the Great Mother archetype: the understanding, compassionate, idealized woman as well as the deceitful, egotistical types.

There is a sense of urgency and of desperation implicit in all of Nerval's writings. One actually feels the cry of despair, the haunting and recurring tonalities of sorrow and even the panic. Nerval's inability to relate to people on a solid footing, the rejection he experienced by those he most loved, and society's indifference to his plight, encouraged him to seek solace in his dreamworld. There he felt safe. He could not be rejected. He would never experience alienation. Such a course had devastating side effects. External reality atrophied. Suicide, by hanging, followed in 1855.

[2]Robert H. Pfeiffer, *Introduction to the Old Testament*, p. 38.

[3]For further information on the Biblical legend and a variety of interpretations see the following:

Salo W. Baron, *A Social and Religious History of the Jews*, I (Philadelphia: Jewish Publication Society, 1952).

Heinrich Graetz, *History of the Jews*, I (Philadelphia: Jewish Publication Society, 1974), (reprinted from 1891-98 edition).

Rivakah Schärf Kluger, *Psyche and the Bible* (Zürich: Spring Publications, 1974).

Héberlot de Molainville, *Bibliothèque Orientale*.

André Chastel, "La Légende de la Reine de Saba," *Revue de l'histoire des religions*, tom 120-124, juillet-août, 1939-1941.

[4]Gérard de Nerval, *Oeuvres complètes*, II (Paris: Pléiade, 1961), p. 514.

[5]Kluger, p. 93.

[6]*Ibid.*, p. 109.

[7]Merdowski, *The Epic of the Kings Shab-Namka the National Epic of Persia*, pp. 1-17.

[8]*Oeuvres*, p. 511.

[9]*Ibid.*, p. 517, 514.

[10]*Ibid.*, p. 506.

[11]*Ibid.*

It is interesting to note that Rachel called her son Benoni, "son of my suffering," because her labor pains were so great. After she died, her husband Jacob, called their son Benjamin. (Gen. 35:18)

[12]According to certain Kabbalistic and Talmudic scholars the world was ruled by a series of great kings. Isaac de la Peyrière in his volume *The Pre-adamites* (1655) gives an account of these kings, their powers and their downfall.

[13]A. E. Waite, *The Holy Kabbalah*, p. 274.

[14]*Oeuvres*, p. 509.

[15]*Ibid.*, p. 556.

[16]*Ibid.*, p. 537.

[17]*Ibid.*, p. 552.

[18]*Ibid.*, p. 687, 553.

[19]*Ibid.*, p. 562.

[20]W. L. Wilmhurst, *The Masonic Initiation*, p. 78.

[21]Paul Naudon, *La Franc-Maçonnerie*, pp. 84-95.

[22]*Ibid.*

[23]Harold W. Percival, *Masonry and its Symbols*, p. 7-15.

[24]*Ibid.*, p. 10.

[25]Naudon, p. 86.

[26]Serge Hutin, *Les Sociétés secrètes*, p. 72.

[27]Percival, x.

[28]Serge Hutin, *L'alchimie*, p. 45.

[29]Wilmhurst, p. 146.

[30]Hutin, *L'Alchimie*, p. 65.

[31]*Ibid.*, p. 61.

[32]*Ibid.*, p. 75.

[33]Chastel, p. 164.

[34]Gaston Bachelard, *La Psychanalyse de feu*, p. 34.

[35]Kluger, p. 89.

[36]*Ibid.*, p. 94-98.

[37]Emma Jung and Marie Louise von Franz, *The Grail Legend*, p. 192.

[38]Wilmhurst, p. 110.

For further references on Gérard de Nerval in general and the Queen of Sheba myth in particular see:

Gershom G. Scholem, *Kabbalah* (New York: Quadrangle, 1974).

Mellor, Alec, *Dictionnaire de la Franc-Maçonnerie et des Franc-Maçons* (Paris: Pierre Belfond, 1971).

Viatte, Auguste, *Les Sources occultes du Romantisme* I et II (Paris: Honoré Champion, 1969).

St. Martin, Claude de, *The Unknown Philosopher* (New York: Rudolf Steiner Publications, 1970).

Richer, Jean, *Nerval expérience et création* (Paris: Hachette, 1970).

CHAPTER 7

Honoré de Balzac—Louis Lambert:
The Legend of the Thinking Man

*For I have seen and I have known the essence
of all beings, depths and nothingness.*
                                    (*Jakob Boehme,* Confessions*)*

Honoré de Balzac's[1] novel *Louis Lambert* (1832) narrates
the legend of the thinking man: a being who has so overde-
veloped his intellect that he can only survive in the rarefied
atmosphere of abstraction. Cut off from the world of reality—
or a conscious frame of reference—he is finally overwhelmed by
the forces of the unconscious; he withers and dies. A *vates*,
Balzac intuited in *Louis Lambert* what was to become an acute
problem for contemporary society: alienation on a personal
and collective scale. The roots of this dichotomy and the over
evaluation of the intellect (or the Apollonian side of man)
with a concomitant devaluation of instinct (the Dionysian spirit)
are to a great extent to be found in Platonic, Christian, and
Cartesian thought. To aim for too lofty a goal is to create imbalance. As Nietzsche warned: "O Zarathustra, stone of wisdom! High thou flingest thyself, but every stone that is flung
must fall!"[2]

An analogy between Louis Lambert and an image in the
Zohar may be drawn to illustrate the destruction that can occur
to a human being when too much emphasis is placed on *thought
power*. It has been stated that before the advent of the biblical
Adam, God had created the "perfect Original Man," the "Primordial Man," Adam Kadman. He was an emanation of "the
'fullness' of divine light" to be understood as spirit or divine
intelligence. Before flowing into "primeval space...like a beam,"
he was unmanifested, therefore undifferentiated, uncontained,
and free. Once he took on form (developing eyes, ears, mouth,
nose), he required an envelope of matter and was enclosed in a
vessel. The energy necessary for this transformation activated
the fire of ideas or the radiance of divine light and led to the
"shattering of the vessel." The *scintillas* scattered everywhere
on earth, thus blending spirit (light) with earth (physis) and
paving the way for the creation of mankind. This image of
the "breaking of the vessel," and Adam Kadman's end may be
considered as both a cosmological and psychological drama.[3]
It is the enactment of the creation and the life process: from
unity to differentiation, from spirit or divine intelligence to

human mind power. It is a visualization of man's "fall" on to earth or his birth into the differentiated realm and with it the realization that all aspects of life must be lived in order to be able to experience existence as a whole. To know the mind alone shatters the body and, therefore, the mind as well. Such was Louis' harrowing course.

Louis Lambert is the story of an extraordinarily brilliant country lad who lives exclusively in the domain of the intellect: thought is the *sine qua non* of his existence. At the age of fifteen he writes a "treatise on Will" in which he attempts to explain the substance of thought and will, their mechanism and their relationship. Thought, he affirms, is material and is projected everywhere (outwardly and inwardly) into animate and inanimate objects. Whether manifested or unmanifested, it follows a hierarchical order: from differentiated phenomena on a lower level to the One in God. As time goes on, Louis neglects the things of the earth and so they atrophy. The great god Pan has died for Louis. His prodigious intellectual expansion results in the creation of a one-sided being and leads to a progressive withdrawal from reality. Louis meets Pauline who represents the ideal for him—the real *ange-femme*: gentle, spiritual, all love. They become engaged and the wedding date is set. However, the day before the ceremony is to take place Louis falls into a catatonic state. Pauline takes him to her home and cares for him. While society pronounces him insane, she states that she can reach him and that he is one of those beings who has been divinely endowed and whose destiny it is to experience higher, more spiritual spheres. Louis dies at the age of twenty-eight.

1. *Thought becomes an instrument of destruction*

Thought killed Louis Lambert, Balzac affirmed. Thought "is more powerful than the body; it eats it, absorbs it, and destroys it."[4] Louis succumbed to the fate of the man who lives only amid conceptualizations and abstractions. He symbolizes the overly rational being whose feelings are undeveloped. Balzac used scientific and philosophical arguments to uphold his posi-

tion concerning thought power. Along with the atomists Democritus and Leucippus and mystics such as Boehme, Saint-
Martin, and Swedenborg, everything in the universe, Balzac
contended, was material and in a perpetual state of flux. As
such, thought is material. It is a force, like fluid, that can travel
throughout the cosmos. For Balzac the power of thought also
had psychosomatic and psychogenic effects: an idea can harm
or sicken, bring joy or health, or kill. In *Ignored Martyrs* Balzac
wrote:

> An idea is then the product of nervous fluid, part of an inner
> circulatory system, similar to the circulation of the blood, for
> blood engenders nervous fluid in the same way as nervous
> fluid engenders thought. One or the other can be misused.
> When the misuse effects the blood, it is called *sickness;* when
> it effects *thought*, it is called insanity.[5]

Mesmer whose experiments had aroused Balzac's interest, also
spoke of a "universal fluid" that exercised a "mutual influence
on celestial bodies, earth, and animated bodies." This force is
likewise capable of communicating impressions and activity of
all types within the human being, thus rehabilitating the imbalance within the body and healing the individual.[6]

Because thought became such a potent factor in Louis'
existence, it took precedence over all else. Most important
perhaps was the fact that it severed him from the earthly realm,
that is, from the nutritive elements which furnish man with the
food necessary to expend his creative effort. Without the body
the mind cannot evolve. In Louis's case, intellectual sterility
was followed by death. He never experienced the *complexio
oppositorum.* Like Adam Kadman, he was enclosed in his own
unconscious, his own "radiant" realm or the *interior homo
noster* (the Primordial Man in each being), opting for the "pneu-
matic higher man" or the life of thought.[7] He became all brain
and no brawn.

One may wonder what factors were at work throughout
history to bring a creature such as Louis Lambert to life.

Plato perhaps more than any other philosopher may be
labeled the instigator of the divinization of *Reason* (*Logos*).
In his celebrated image in *Phaedrus* he depicted a charioteer

who symbolizes Reason driving two horses: a black one representing instinct and wantonness, who got out of hand and had to be whipped, "tamed and humbled";[8] and a white horse, a "lover of honor and modesty and temperance," who did not need to be brutalized but was "guided by word and admonition only."[9] Reason, according to Plato, was godliness; instinct was considered animal like and therefore was deprecated. Aristotle reaffirmed Plato's position: reason and the rational way were the *sine qua non* of the wise man. Seneca (in Letters 74 to Lucilius) encouraged the Stoics in this way: "Love then reason. Its love will arm you against the hardest of events."[10]

The Christian ethic adopted the Platonic credo: the spiritualization of reason. Instinct, considered the lowest and basest part of man, was repressed. The goal of the Christian was to annihilate the flesh; to reject basically what was part of the human condition. Such a credo led to self-abnegation, flagelation, asceticism, and other disciplines capable of destroying man's physical side or reducing it to a state of virtual impotence. This repression of instinct also led to blockage and built up tension within the psyche, resulting in obsessional preoccupations with opposite views. It is no wonder that St. Anthony and St. Theresa, among many, experienced unbelievably erotic fantasies. Unlike these saints who fought the battle of the opposites and were thereby strengthened in the process, Lambert circumvented the conflict, escaping directly into the mental (heavenly) spheres.[11]

Louis was the natural outcome of such philosophical and ideological concepts. Balzac, a literary man above all, in his descriptions of Louis, sought to express physically this overly intellectual side in accordance with the theories of Jean Lavater and Franz Joseph Gall, to which he subscribed.[12] These phrenologists believed that the outer man revealed the inner being. To express Louis' cerebral frame of reference and the progressive aridity that resulted, Balzac described him as "pale" and "white," a lad who "avoided the shadow and was always running toward the sun."[13] Balzac equated the solar force with the intellect: the light-giving brain, the world of conceptualizations and abstractions. Every word, gesture, and sensation as delineated by Balzac was designed to exteriorize Louis' life of the mind: his judgments and perceptions. So filled was his head that it became "too heavy" and his movement overly measured

and controlled, in perfect accord with his introverted, meditative, and feelingless existence. "I perfer thought to action, an
idea to work, contemplation to movement."[14] It was as though
Louis were intent upon economizing his energy, bottling it up,
channeling it directly toward his mind. Only in thought would
he expend his *puissance vitale* (vital fluid).

An adherent of vitalism, Balzac believed that man is born
with a certain amount of *puissance vitale* that determines his
longevity. If he reduced his activity (both intellectual and
physical), he conserves his vital fluid and may, therefore, live a
longer time. Father Grandet, for example, lived to an old age
because he walked slowly and spent little money, thus retaining
the vital power within him rather than expending it. In this
respect he dictated his own destiny. Unlike Grandet, Louis was
overwhelmed and then victimized by his mind.

Even as a young lad, Louis concentrated his efforts on
improving his mind. His mother noted the fact that when he
returned from the lycée for vacations, he either remained in the
house reading or took his books into the woods and there, deeply
entranced (not in nature but in the intellectual experience),
fed himself on endless amounts of information: history, physics,
philosophy—"a kind of hunger that nothing could satisfy, he
devoured all types of books."[15]

Louis' attitude toward learning, interestingly enough,
differed considerably from that of his peers. They read books
not only for the information to be gained, but also to learn
how to cope with life's joys and sorrows, and to help them
battle with events in the existential domain. Louis, who had
total recall, absorbed volume upon volume but became acquainted only with facts, principles, and concepts, a world unrelated
to the telluric domain. For him a word permitted a leap back
into history so as to restore "the abysses of the past"—knowledge of Greece and Rome. He even enjoyed reading dictionaries,
analyzing words he looked upon as concrete objects, each possessing a physiognomy and history of its own.[16] Louis' reading
capacities were so finely developed that he could scan seven
or eight lines at a time. More important was the fact that his
mind understood the meaning of the word as rapidly as his
eyes visualized it. The energy needed for such instantaneous
comprehension (visual and cerebral) was extraordinary.

At fourteen Louis understood the how and why of the transition between sensation to thought to the written word or from idea to form, from the abstract to the concrete. Such image-making activity, defined as "a general movement from the unconscious to consciousness"[17] (or the release of unconscious contents into the conscious mind) is creative. His brand of image-making activity led him, he claimed, to experience various "layers of thought" and even "the disposition of his soul at distant periods." He seemed capable of retracing "the progress and the entire life of his mind, from the most anciently acquired idea to the last one emerging; from the most confused to the most lucid."[18]   Like a geologist, he burrowed vertically into his intellect and the energy provoked by such activity aroused all types of visualizations he then fixed on images. Such a dynamic process, Balzac suggested, gave Louis second sight and enabled him to conceive of things, peoples, and place-scapes as though they existed in actuality when they were "merely" figments of his imagination.

Louis' intellectual preoccupations were then twofold: passing from the abstract to the concrete. Abstract thinking processes are habitually associated with the "higher center of the brain, with the cerebrum," whereas the imaginative faculty "corresponds to the lower unconscious, the 'magical' domain."[19] The implication here is that at this early period in his life Louis was using both parts of his brain, the higher and the lower; the separation between upper and lower spheres (inner and outer worlds) had not yet taken place. He therefore could still function relatively well in both domains.

Balzac recorded one of Louis' mental experiences when both parts of his brain were still functioning. One day, as the young student was reading a tract on the Battle of Austerlitz, he suddenly felt himself *carried away into the event.* He *heard* the cries of the soliders, the cannons firing; he *smelled* the powder, the horses, and the men. He was so deeply entrenched by his thoughts that he "lost consciousness in some way of his physical existence,"[20] as though he had become detached from reality and was living in the abyss of his own mind. He found this state enriching and thereafter "abandoned himself with love to the torrent of his thoughts."[21] So intrigued was Louis with the riches he discovered during this experience, he sought to study the multitude of sensations they aroused in him. He concluded he had contacted some collective force and was therefore capable of transcending rational time-space concepts. It is significant that Louis should have focused on the Battle of Austerlitz (1805), a struggle in which Napoleon came out the victor over the emperors of Austria and Russia.

Louis identified with Napoleon as so many young people of his era had. Like the emperor, Louis saw himself as a conqueror: a usurper of power in the intellectual field. Napoleon had used his will to rise from obscurity to political heights, so Louis would also accomplish this feat. "I feel I'm strong, energetic and will be able to become a power; I feel within me such a luminous life, one that could animate a world."[22] Both men had electrifying spirits. The cult of energy, of fire—the Promethean way—possessed Louis as it had Napoleon. And Balzac described Louis in terms of electricity: his head was "charged with thought as a Leyden jar with electricity."[23] Unlike Napoleon, however, whose energy flowed outward, whose visions were concretized in acts, Louis fought to control his inner scapes, soaring deeply within the remotest of areas, thus removing himself more and more from reality.

"To think is to see."[24] To deduce cerebrally, Louis felt, was to visualize. In his "Treatise on Will" he defined the will as that area where thought evolves; volition as "the act by which man uses his will"; thought as the quintessential product of will; the idea as the act by which man uses his thought.[25] The will, he affirmed, "is like the circulation of nervous fluid, it responds to thought," setting up an infinite amount of positive and negative reactions within the individual that do not take spatial areas or eras into account. Therefore, past and future may be integrated into the present. When Louis sank into himself, as he had while reading about the Battle of Austerlitz, he came into contact with the universal in man or, in psychological terms, the collective unconscious. In this timeless and spaceless area time concepts were no longer valid for him: another dimension had been activated where premonitory experiences, transmission of thought, the *déjà vu,* and other parapsychological phenomena occurred. Balzac lists some of these events to substantiate his argument: in Rome Apollonius of Tayana related the horrendous facts surrounding the death of a tyrant living in Asia, miles away, at the very moment it had occurred; martyrs and saints spoke of having experienced the stigmata, Christ, and the Virgin Mary. Swedenborg, when in London, described the huge fire taking place in Stockholm as it was raging. Swedenborg was also convinced that he had traveled into heavenly spheres and had conversed with angels. "I was there, I saw them with my own eyes, I speak from experience."[26] Like Swedenborg, who believed in the perfectibility of matter, Louis too had transcended what he considered the sphere of gross matter and entered the rarefied atmosphere of the collective spirit.

Thought being material, it is motivated in relationship with the energy with which it is endowed: it can be either an active or a passive force. Swedenborg wrote of two creatures inhabiting man: the inner (thought is the essence of this entity) and the outer being. It is the former that must be cultivated. To build from within is to perfect the "angel" inhabiting these recesses. Too much energy has been wasted in developing the "exterior sense," thus permitting the atrophying of those sublime forces inherent in man.

Once Louis had acknowledged the dual nature of man, he went further than the mystics because he sought to separate or to depersonalize the inner being. In psychological terms he was working toward the loss of identity, the obliteration of the ego, the dispersion of the individual into the collective domain. Orientals experience the depersonalization of the ego during their mystical trances. To achieve such a state has been the goal of many of their practises and disciplines, which for them are healthy because they are implicit in an age-old religious philosophy. As such, they are authentic experiences. For the Occidental, however, whose focus has been traditionally extroverted, who has worked toward strengthening and solidifying his ego, such attempts at its annihilation may have disastrous effects. A progressive depersonalization of the ego with a concomitant loss of contact with the workaday world makes for a schizophrenic state. While at the lycée Louis sometimes practices what could be termed as depersonalization exercise: a severance of the *homo duplex*. Whereas such endeavors are normal when experienced in dream sequences, to attempt to carry them out in the existential world may lead eventually to an inability to relate to it.

Louis recounted in this context an extraordinary premonitory dream that eventually led to the separation of his inner and outer being (thought and body). The lycée had planned a school outing to the Rochambeau manor. Louis had never been there before; yet, when he arrived at the location, he was dumbfounded because what he had dreamed the night before was to the last detail what he saw on that day: clusters of trees, the color of the water, the towers of the castle.[27]

This ectopsychic (beyond the psyche) event led, he believed, to a breakthrough for him. He decided now to go a step further: to transcend time and space not only in sleep, but in his waking hours and as a conscious endeavor. To achieve such a separation at will would enable him to experience a closer rapport with God (the transcendental force), to ascend the hierarchical spheres within the heavens until he would become part of the new Jerusalem as described in the Apocalypse, after which he would be reintegrated into the Godhead. "The universe, then, is variety in Unity. Movement is the means, the Number is the result. The end is the return of all things to Unity, which is God."[28] Boehme, Swedenborg, and de Saint-Martin adumbrated similar views.[29] What Louis was accomplishing from a psychological point of view was a progressive depersonalization, a withdrawal from reality or regression into the transpersonal state. The nondifferentiated world of the One or of God, the total rejection of the conflict of opposites—so vital a factor in the life process—indicates not only a rejection of telluric existence but an attempt at self-destruction.

As Louis' inner trajectory (both actual and metaphysical) increased in depth, cutting him off progressively from the earth principle, he became steadily "whiter" and "paler." The sun, associated with the mind, intellect, the radiance of thought, is the Apollonian spirit in man, was likewise dimming. "His eyes, once so fiery, now resembled a glass pane from which the sun had suddenly withdrawn its illumination."[30] In the beginning Louis had used his mind as a catalyst for spiritual transformation, as an instrument for refining his thought. With his rejection of the earth, or nutritive sphere, his natural life force (instinct) was stifled. Thus the finely tuned instrument that was his brain had become a mechanism for destruction. His intended marriage, or symbolically his descent into matter (the physical world), to use the Kabbalistic image, led to the "breaking of the vessel," that is, the permanent separation between inner and outer world.

The very thought of activating the physical side of his being (if the marriage ceremony were to be completed) was too great a demand; it meant sacrificing the spirit. The collective forces protected him from this fate and a catatonic state of schizophrenia ensued. Pauline, the *ange-femme*, interpreted his withdrawal from the world as expanded consciousness—as a reintegration into divinity.

By denying earth and flesh, Louis had succeeded, theosophically, in experiencing a transfiguration: from earthly gross matter to celestial purity. In Platonic terms: "Evil is the vulgar lover who loves the body rather than the soul, and who is inconstant because he is a lover of the inconstant, and, therefore, when the bloom of youth which he was desiring is over, he takes wings and flies away, in spite of all his words and promises; whereas the love of the noble mind, which is in union with the unchangeable, is everlasting."[31] To have married Pauline would have been a step backward in his reintegration into the pleromatic world—or his transfiguration. It was, therefore, anathema to him.

1. *Pauline: the Ange-Femme*

The only rapport Louis had ever had with women was in a religious context, and he approached Pauline as a parishioner his God. He idealized her and endowed her with the characteristics of an *ange-femme*. Comparable to the Virgin Mary or to the Gnostic Sophia, she encompassed perfection. Like Sheba for Nerval, she exhibited compensatory characteristics, those lacking in Louis' conscious orientation. Pauline was all-feeling and had a strong ego and she related well to others despite the fact that she lived a relatively secluded existence.

Louis had many illustrious predecessors who raised woman to the highest possible degree; but in so doing they cut her off from nature and thus from fertility. Dante, for example, described his Béatrice as follows:

> More lovely, more sublime than any creature...
> Thou hast so ennobled the nature of man... (Canto xxxiii)

For Louis and Dante the woman becomes a container, an

object, the reflection of man's love. She is not an initiator of
activity, but the recipient of his aspirations—an empty shell, a
figure devoid of desire, of her own. Insofar as Pauline is concerned, she is an appendage of Louis.[32] In that she belongs
to a higher sphere than normal woman, his joy resides in the
contemplation of her beauty, in her ethereal nature. It is as
though Louis were reenacting Plato's image in *Phaedrus:* "he
sees her and falls back in adoration," or he "receives the ef-
fluence of beauty through her eyes."[33] Louis was in such awe
of what he considered to be Pauline's divine nature that he
wanted to live with her alone, away from other human beings.
He would no allow another "creature with a human face to enter
the sanctuary where you will be mine."[34] Pauline was completely dehumanized in Louis' mind's eye.

As an *ange-femme*, Pauline functioned as a spiritual principle. It is written in Genesis (6:2) that angels came down to
earth and married the daughters of men, thereby injecting
divine characteristics into earthly creatures. In the New Testament angels remained exclusively messengers, either positive or
negative. As personifications of divine attributes, angels attained
cosmic proportions but were always mediating forces without a
will of their own, bearers of command. Ibn Daud and Maimonides, interestingly enough, looked upon angels rationally as
"pure intellect." Such a definition would coincide perfectly
with Louis' evaluation.

To increase the mystery surrounding Pauline, Balzac described her as having a Jewish grandfather, thus making her more
remote, more sacred. She had that "Jewish beauty," that "biblical innocence," lending her an element of historicity. Her skin,
like Louis', was "unpolished white,"—which Balzac compared
to the dress of the ancient Levites. Her silent and meditative
ways enabled one to feel the living essence of "the angel under
this form."

As Louis' love took on dimension, he no longer saw his
existence as strictly his own but as linked to hers. Although
only a reflection of his radiance, an illusion, a vaporous entity,
she was, paradoxically, a psychopomp; she led him to his ex-
tinction. Her presence forced the issue: Louis was confronted
with the physical (marriage) side of life. Pauline was the catalyst
who brought his state of worship, longing, sublimation, and

inertia to an abrupt end. Unable to accept the telluric side of existence and the sensual demands that would have been made upon him in a marital situation, his mind broke.

Louis' relationship with Pauline may be compared to the vision of the Homunculus in Goethe's *Faust*. Let us recall that Faust's assistant had created an all-thinking, all-spiritual being— suggesting in this sense enlightenment—imprisoned in an alchemical vessel. When "beauty" in the form of Galatea appeared on the scene, this dry, arid Homunculus was stirred beyond control. Unaccustomed to beauty (the feminine principle), the Homunculus was not prepared to cope with the force that arose within him, that is, to integrate his feelings; he overreacted. Something within him had ignited and was too powerful to contain. The fire blazed so frenetically that the glass shattered.

The two images from the Kabbalah and from *Faust* are visualizations of the Lenged of the Thinking Man. Because Louis had rejected nature, or Pan, he had never penetrated the "entire world of the living."[35] Therefore, he was unable to cope with certain forces within himself—and these destroyed him. Some great religious leaders realized that when both sides of the *homo duplex* are developed, the *whole* of man comes into existence, thus endowing him with greater insights into the workings of the cosmos—God. Buddha, for example, had been married and had had a child; he had lived in the flesh before withdrawing. Moses, likewise, had been married and had had children; he had grown in stature from the conflict of opposites. The concept of life's experience is affirmed in Ecclesiastes:

> I applied mine heart to know, and to search, and to seek out wisdom, and the reason *of things*, and to know the wickedness of folly, even of foolishness *and* madness. (7:25)

The overevaluation of the spiritual in man, resulting from Platonic doctrine as incorporated in the Christian ethic and further developed by Cartesian rationalism, led to a repression of the Dionysian in man. The outcome was the creation of a top-heavy creature, an unnatural being. Man's natural urge, so important a factor in giving birth to the creative element, was driven underground. Jung wrote:

> I prefer to designate the creative impulse as a psychic factor similar in nature to instinct, having indeed a very close connection with the instincts, but without being identical with anyone of them.[36]

Thought when defined as "an internal condition of cognition," as a natural dynamic process, and as a blend of instinct and spirit is creative. Louis, whose life consisted of the rational sphere alone, was arid. He was no longer a three-dimensional human being but had become "flat and without substance." To live in the sphere of thought alone, in a domain considered by so many to be heroically sublime, but in actuality leads to alienation from society and from self—is to seek thanatos or death.

NOTES

[1]Honoré de Balzac was born in Tours on May 20, 1799. He went to the College run by the Oratorians at Vendôme and continued his studies in Paris. Although his parents wanted him to prepare for a law degree, he was drawn to literature. Balzac's early literary endeavors, *Cromwell* (1822) and *The Inheritor of Birague,* were poor quality. His financial situation was precarious and would be for the rest of his life; his business ventures nearly always failed despite his extreme enthusiasm.

By 1829 Balzac began winning praise from the critics: *The Last of the Chouans, The Wild Ass' Skin* (1831), *The Curé of Tours* (1832), *Louis Lambert* (1832), *Eugénie Grandet* (1832), *Father Goriot* (1834), and so on. Sometimes Balzac devoted as many as eighteen hours a day to his work without respite. *The Country Doctor* was written in seventy-two hours.

Balzac, intensely energetic and imaginative, regarded himself as the Napoleon of literature: "What Napoleon did not achieve with the sword I will accomplish with the pen." And he did in his gigantic project *La Comédie Humaine* (1842-1846).

Balzac was a believer in the doctrines of the Illumists, particularly those of Swedenborg. Equally fascinating to him were the scientific ideas of Lavater, Gall, Geoffroy Saint-Hilaire, Cuvier, and Mesmer.

In 1832 Balzac began corresponding with the Polish Countess Hanska. As the years passed, she became his confidante, his great love. Because his work was so demanding and activity of all types so taxing, Balzac's health began to deteriorate. By 1849 his heart was so weak that he could hardly walk without gasping for breath. Almost yearly he suffered from bronchitis. His one desire, however, was to go to St. Petersburg and to marry Countess Hanska. His wish was granted on March 14, 1850; but by the time the couple returned to Paris, Balzac was dangerously ill. He sunk into a coma and died on August 18, 1850. So deeply involved had he been throughout his life with his characters that, it has been reported, he mentioned one of them shortly before dying: "Only Brianchon could save me."

[2]C. G. Jung, *Two Essays on Analytical Psychology,* p. 38.

[3]Gershom Scholem, *Major Trends in Jewish Mysticism*, pp. 265-6.

[4]Honoré de Balzac, *La Comédie Humaine* VI, p. 426.

[5]*Ibid.*, p. 423.

Anton Mesmer (1734-1815), whose works revolved around hysterical patients and their cure through hypnotism, enjoyed great success. In his much-talked-about Parisian clinic (founded in 1778) Mesmer stressed the fact that magnetic power which flowed through the cosmos was by his command concentrated on him. His influence during the Revolutionary period in France, the Empire, and the Restauration, despite the interdict replaced upon him in 1783 by the Royal Commission, was enormous. Both scientists and the deeply religious were hostile to his theories. Balzac, however, was very impressed and himself practiced the art of healing with his hands. He had his mother consult the famous Saint-Amour when she was ill; he also suggested to Mme Hanska that she have "iron magnets" put on her during moments of stress.

[6]Henri Evans, *Louis Lambert*.

[7]C. G. Jung, *Mysterium Coniunctionis*, p. 429.

[8]B. Jowett, *The Works of Plato*, p. 415.

[9]William Barrett, *Irrational Man*, pp. 73-76.

[10]*Les Stoiciens* (Paris: Pléiade, 1962), p. 796.

[11]The Platonic and Aristotelian systems and their worship of reason and the rational function in man continued their course throughout the centuries. The Middle Ages responded with great antagonism toward the body. Although François Villon expressed the ironies in bitter and humorous terms, implicit in man's desire to reject earthly joys, he was imbued with such a credo. The notion of asceticism, the power of the rational principle as adumbrated in scholastic and religious tracts of the time, were evidenced in the allegorical *Romance of the Rose*, the mysteries revolving around the theme of the *Holy Grail*—examples of spiritualization of terrestrial delights. Other facts were also present: a longing for life and the body as attested to in the sensual *Tristan and Isolde* and the *Lays* of Mary de France. The Renaissance attempted to cast off the cloak of restrictions imposed upon telluric existence. Life was not supposed to be a veil of tears. Poets, such as Ronsard, opted for joy and

earthly poetry. Louise Labé wrote of her passionate love; the celebrated Diane de Poitiers was painted partially in the nude, as were other nymphs who frolicked around in pools and gardens. A spirit of rebellion and a lust of life manifested itself and found its most outspoken partisan in François Rabelais who believed in man's basic goodness—in man as a whole—the physical and spiritual as one. The classical seventeenth century put a sudden halt to the ebullience manifested in the works of Renaissance poets and painters, imposing the mask of reason upon the creative element: the rational, the intellect—the Cartesian spirit took hold.   Reason alone should dictate man's acts.   Only through reason could man progress, evolve, and conquer nature.

[12]The ideas posited by the Swiss phrenologist Jean Lavater were also incorporated into Balzac's creative works.   Lavater stated in *The Art of Studying Physiognomy* (1722) and in *Physiognomical Fragments for the Promotion of Knowledge and Love of Man* (1775) in which Goethe collaborated, that it was not the structure of the head that was of import in discovering the traits of the inner man, but the play of facial expressions and characteristics.   There was a correspondence between the physical traits of a being, his clothes, and his environment—each depending upon and influencing the other.

Balzac was equally drawn to the theories of Franz Joseph Gall and his science of physiognomy as expressed in Anatomy and *Physiology of the Nervous System in General* (1810-1819) in which Gall studied the relationships existing between facial characteristics and specific character traits.   Gall was one of the instigators of theories revolving around modern neurology when he stated that the brain "was a heterogenous organ, a confederation of small distinct systems, endowed with specific functions and susceptible of being altered, isolated, by lesions."

For additional information see Jacques Borel, Seraphita (Paris: José Corti, 1967).

[13]Honoré de Balzac, *Louis Lambert*, p. 93.

[14]*Ibid.*, p. 110.

[15]*Ibid.*, p. 111.

[16]*Ibid.*, p. 27.

[17]Edward S. Casey, "Toward an Achetypal Imagination," *Spring*, 1974, p. 3.

18*Louis Lambert*, p. 31-32.

19Michael Fordham, "Jungian Views of the Body-Mind Relationship," *Spring*, 1974, p. 168.

20*Louis Lambert*, p. 32.

21*Ibid.*, p. 57.

22*Ibid.*, p. 122.

23*Ibid.*, p. 59.

24*Ibid.*, p. 63.

25*Ibid.*, p. 79.

26Borel, p. 153.

27*Louis Lambert*, p. 71-73.

28*Ibid.*, p. 176.

29For a fine study on Boehme see:
Alexandre Koyré, *La Philosophie de Jacob Boehme* (Paris: J. Vrin, 1929).

For a study on Calude de Saint-Martin see:
Arthur E. Waite, *The Unknown Philosopher* (New York: Rudolph Steiner, 1970).

30*Louis Lambert*, p. 49.

31Plato, p. 308 (*The Symposium*).

32James Hillman, "Anima," *Spring*, 1973, pp. 103-115.

33Plato, p. 410, 414 (*Phaedrus*).

34*Louis Lambert*, p. 127-141.

35Erich Neumann, *Depth Psychology and a New Ethic*, p. 116.

36 C. G. Jung, *The Structure and Dynamics of the Psyche*, p. 118.

CHAPTER 8

Théophile Gautier—Arria Marcella: The Greek Versus the Christian Way

Surely I dreamt to-day, or did I see The winged Psyche with awakened eyes?
                    (John Keats, Ode *to Psyche)*

CHAPTER 8

Théophile Gautier—Arria Marcella:
The Greek Versus the Christian Way

Surely I dreamt to-day, or did I see The winged Psyche with awakened eyes?
                    (*John Keats,* **Ode** to Psyche*)*

The parapsychological experience as related in Théophile Gautier's[1] short story *Arria Marcella,* which was published in *la Revue de Paris* in 1852, reveals a fundamental conflict between the notion of the ancient Greeks and Romans and the attitude of the Christians. "Do not burden me in the name of that morose religion which was never mine; as for me, I believe in our ancient gods who loved life, youth, beauty, and pleasure; do not force me into that pale nothingness," said Arria Marcella, the Pompeian beauty, to the austere and negative Nazarene who castigated her for what he considered her earthly and evil ways. Paganism for Gautier and for the burgeoning group of polytheistic mystics in France, emphasized terrestrial joys and the beauty of the human body; Christianity, on the other hand, stressed ascetic attitudes, earthly suffering, repentance for sin, subjugation of natural instinct so as to win paradise in after life.

Let us recall that around the middle of the nineteenth century there emerged a whole movement of sensibility and of thought that yearned for a return to Paganism and that evinced a profound and generalized disaffection from modern western civilization and from Christianity. Gérard de Nerval's poems "Myrtho" and "Delfica" delineated the realm of beauty and harmony known to the ancient Greeks. The "mystical pagan" Louis Ménard who reinterpreted Greek legends in the light of contemporary society, believed Polytheism to be the instigator of the republican form of government and Catholicism that of absolute monarchy. In *Poèmes antiques* and *Hymnes orphiques,* Leconte de Lisle sought to recreate in his images the perfection the Greeks had achieved in their sculptures and temples. In so far as religious ideations were concerned, he contrasted polytheism, as incarnated in Hypatia, the beautiful philosopher-martyr, with the ignorant, superstitious, and ugly masses as represented by Christianity. Théophile Gautier likewise longed for a return to the Greek way and to a society whose goal was aesthetic and not utilitarian; to a religion based on beauty and not repression.

Gautier was a man who found it difficult to adapt to his century; to the ugliness of the newly created industrial cities and to a utilitarian world. He could find happiness, however, in an atmosphere of dazzling beauty, guiltlessness and serenity in love. He experienced such ineffable feelings in the theatre and ballet; in the pictorial arts; and in the creative process. During these privileged moments, he transcended the restricted confines of his existential domain and succeeded in relieving—at least momentarily—his gnawing sense of solitude.

Illuminism, Buddhism, and alchemy were popular panaceas the nineteenth century offered to those who were unable to accept the contemporary world. Gautier was haunted by a sense of mystery, awe for the occult, and fear of the unknown. He believed in universal correspondences and in transmission of thought, also in mesmerism, vampirism, sympathetic magic, and the *déjà vu*. According to his son-in-law, Emile Bergerat, Gautier was extremely superstitious. Indeed, he seemed to be superstition incarnate and believed in divination, premonitory dreams, signs, omens, and magic. His daughter, Judith, added that he was convinced that occult forces dictate his destiny and that he could influence them in certain ways.

Gautier was not alone in his attempt to seek evasion from what he considered to be an overwhelmingly mundane world. Charles Nodier had dramatized arcane realms in his stories *Smarra, The Crumb Fairy*, and *Infernalia;* Gérard de Nerval had concretized esoteric happenings in *The Enchanted Hand, The Green Monster*, and *The Devil's Portrait;* Balzac had dealt with the unknown in *The Red Inn* and *The Unknown Masterpiece.* Gothic tales were in vogue in Paris: Horace Walpole's *The Castle of Otranto*, Ann Radcliffe's *The Haunted Chamber*, Mathew Lewis' *The Monk*, Dr. John Polidori's (or Byron's) *The Vampire*, and Mary Shelley's *The Dream.* These works and others sent chills coursing through the spines of people who opted for a world of phantasmagoria. E. T. Hoffmann's supernatural narrations *The Devil's Elixir, The Educated Cat*, and *The Violin of Cremona*—were even more popular in France than the Gothic tales. These stories revealed Hoffmann's preoccupation with animal magnetism, astrology, and all types of occult forces. Science likewise aroused the imagination of a vulnerable populace. Studies in somnambulism, witchcraft, satanism, and lycanthropy had been published by eminent medical men such as Dr. Alexander Betrans.   The invisible world had inspired musical works as well: Weber's *Der Frei-schütz*, Berlioz' *Fantastic Symphony*, Tartini's *The Devil's Trill*, Liszt's *Mephisto Waltz*.   Delacroix had painted a "Dante and Virgil."   Hugo had long since written *Our Lady of Paris* in which grotesque monsters of all sorts were brought to life. The list is long.

          The plot of *Arria Marcella* is simple.   The tale begins at the Studii museum in Naples in the nineteenth century.   Octavien and two of his friends are busily studying the archaeological finds of Pompeii.   Octavien's attention is drawn to a large seg-ment of petrified lava depicting a woman's bust and side.   The three young men later take the train to Pompeii.   They visit the dead city, including what had once been the home of Arrius Diomedes.   In the vaulted corridors they see seventeen skeletons, which are the remains of those people who had fled for protec-tion during the eruption of Mt. Vesuvius in 79 A.D.   One of the skeletons resembled the woman whose petrified form Octavien had seen at the museum in Naples.   Octavien is gripped by the vision of this Pompeian beauty.   After dinner, he decides to stroll about in the old city alone.   Octavien walks aimlessly about as if in a somnambulistic state.   The city seems to take on a new dimension for him.   It comes to life: the roads are filled with people, the markets and the amphitheaters are bustling with life.   Octavien decides to go to the theatre and sees a beautiful young woman in the gallery.   He is convinced that she is the living incarnation of the figure in the petrified lava.   After the performance, the woman sends her servant to Octavien to invite him to her home.   He accepts and enters a magnificent abode. There he sees her on a divan.   She is beauty incarnate.   Later, as they are about to consummate their union a sinister old man enters the room.   Clothed in black, he is wearing a cross and represents the new Christian sect.   He begins deprecating the woman's ways and angrily admonishes her for carnal sin, ex-plaining sacrifice, guilt, and the idea of a heavenly existence after death.   Arria Marcella rebels against the Nazarene's oppressive attitude, a world of perpetual sorrow, punishment and ugliness which he describes.   Octavien listens to the dialogue in horror.

Then the vision suddenly vanishes. The following day Octavien's friends find him unconscious. Although he never understands what had happened to him, Octavien knows that the vision of beauty he had experienced was a living reality. Even after he marries, Arria Marcella remains his secret love. No mortal woman of his day could compare to the Pompeian beauty whose presence he had experienced so intensely during that one night of splendor and near perfect joy.

1. *An Alchemical drama*

It has been posited by psychologists and metaphysicians, in accordance with alchemical tradition, that just as metals buried deep within the earth go through a physical process of change from base metals (lead) to purer and more noble forms (silver, gold), so the human personality experiences a concomitant evolution: from a state of unconsciousness, immaturity, and irresponsibility to consciousness, maturity, and responsibility.

Just as the alchemist projects on the metallic substances with which he deals, so there is a corresponding rapport between the writer and the character he creates. The alchemist, moreover, expresses the three phases of the transformatory process that he conducts in terms of color: *nigredo, albedo,* and *rubedo.* Gautier does likewise, revealing in this manner an inner climate that varies from anxiety, sorrow, joy, serenity, and near-ecstasy. Goethe, who wrote On the *Theory of Colors* (1810), indicated that tints and hues not only disclose inner moods, but also act on man's outer world: they excite, calm, vitalize, or subdue him. The same may be said in the case of *Arria Marcella.*

Octavien's descent into an anterior existence, then, will be looked upon as a psychological and metaphysical transformatory process; an initiation via color into his inner world.

1. *Nigredo.* The first alchemical phase, or blackening process, has been called variously the "primal darkness" of the Gnostics and is comparable to chaos, to the *massa confusa* before the separation of the elements; a state in which matter is reduced to a liquid condition or "a quality of the *prima materia*."[2] A catalyzing agent—fire—is then used to attack the base metals. It burns and dissolves them, reducing their component parts to

different forms. With the alterations of their chemistry, a re-arrangement or reassembling of their material state occurs—an attempt on the alchemist's part, so to speak, "to correct nature."

Octavien experienced the *nigredo* phase in the Studii museum in Naples. His attention was drawn to "a piece of coagulated black cinder bearing a hollow imprint; one would have thought it to be the cast of a statue, broken in the founding process."[3] The image of a beautiful young woman immediately sprang to his mind. What had once been alive and vibrant, spreading joy and contentment, he mused, had now become ossified and fixed.

The fire used by the alchemist as an energizing force capable of dissolving the components of the metals in question is ex-pressed in Octavien's case by the combustion aroused when he first sees the hardened lava in the museum. The passion which the stone-hard material evoked in him (like an inflammable object) gave rise to a chaotic, affective situation. It blotted out lucidity; it blurred any rational outlook. Octavien's tumultuous reactions permitted the unconscious domain to invade his con-scious outlook or, in other terms, the conscious attitude had been driven into subliminal, shadowy, or black areas. Later, when he visited the house of Arrius Diomedes and was shown the seventeen remaining skeletons buried in its corridors, he saw among them the imprint of the lady whose image had been impressed in hardened lava in Naples. Since his friends were with him, he attempted to restrain his emotions. Yet, he was visibly moved.[4]

The imagery in the first phase of Octavien's journey into his inner world is black. "Day had fallen and night had come"; yet, like the alchemist's *massa confusa,* other tonalities also penetrate this mixture, those associated with a dying sun, the end of the rational and male-oriented world. It is at this junc-ture, interestingly enough, that Gautier mentions Faust's meeting with Helen in the Realm of the Mothers—that is, in psychological terms, the collective unconscious, where the imagery is likewise *nigredo,* and during which time the transformatory drama takes place. As Octavien's agitation increases, time elapses. Night has blackened; consciousness has retreated and the advent of the moon as the symbol of the feminine world, the unconscious, makes its dominion known.

2. *Albedo.* The second alchemical phase, or the washing of the elements (ablution, baptism), has been called by the alchemist the "silver" or "moon" condition that occurs when the chemicals are balanced and their component parts sorted out. It is a return from disorder to order, from darkness to an inner light, a kind of reshuffling of metals and chemical agents—of emotions.

Psychologically, the albedo phase may be experienced as a silent, inactive period that comes over the individual after the preceding stormy incidens, permitting the energies within the unconscious to recede, thereby paving the way for a broader, clearer vision or a new attitude. In Gautier's words:

> The moon illuminated the pale houses with its white rays, dividing the streets into two slices of light, silvery and bluish shadow. This nocturnal day, with its gentle hues, dissimulated the gradations of the edifices.

Octavien saw fleeting human forms and shadowlike entities in this half-lit area; he heard a kind of whispering about him, which sent chills up his spine. Solitude and mystery invaded the scene. He felt as if he were part of a dream.[6]

Suddenly, the colors altered, the vision became clearer, and time seemed to have regressed as the past intruded into the present. Octavien had overcome the time barrier and had penetrated into the fourth dimension. The entire ancient city had taken on life. It resembled a diorama, a spectacular three-dimensional picture whose dynamic color effects result from a play of lights. The temple of Isis, the fountain of Plenty, the sculptor's workshop, and the theater now came into focus. Octavien entered the theater and there his vision was concretized before him: Arria Marcella was seated in the gallery. He was shocked by the experience and felt as though "electric" sparks had shot through him, as though scintillas gushed from his very insides.[7] He was "magnetically" troubled, and as time rolled back for him, he believed himself to be confronting his dream.[8]

3. *Rubedo.* In the last phase of the alchemical process there is a predominance of red. It is either as a primary color or as a secondary one with violets, roses, and oranges set against contrasting tones such as white and yellow, thus aggravating the

harshness of the hues. It is during this phase that the alchemist's
fire rises to its most powerful intensity, when all the elements
turn red and impurities have been extracted from them. The
philosophers' stone, it is said, now comes into being. For some,
this precious stone contains the elixir of life; for others, it is
gold or the *prima materia* out of which this metal can be produced. According to Paracelsus, the philosophers' stone was
capable of all things: of healing the sick, of transforming negative into positive faculties, of unifying what was divided, of relating man to God.

Arria's courtyard was adorned with Greek marble columns
and was a medley of flamboyant colors: red, blues, and pinks.
Arria Marcella, reclining on a bed at the end of a large room,
looked "voluptuous and serene." Her cheeks, white for centuries, had begun taking on the pink hues of joy; her lips redden-
ed. She lifted up a goblet filled with deep-red wine "like congealed blood."[9] Her earrings were described in terms of infinite
scintillas. They were shaped in the form of golden scales, and, as
she moved, they sparkled, reflecting the light in the room. Her
necklace of gold beads shone even more brightly and sparks
seemed to emanate from the golden snake bracelet she wore,
encrusted with precious stones for eyes. Arria confirmed her
restoration to life when she said:

> One is truly dead only when one is no longer loved, your
> desire restored my life, your heart's powerful evocation did
> away with the distances that separated us.[10]

When Faust and Helen were seated side by side in the Realm
of the Mothers, they were figured as King and Queen (or the alchemical symbol of Sol and Luna). A *coniunctio* took place:
opposites were united in a mystical coitus; instinctive energy (the
sexuality they both had known in the past) was transformed into
a spiritualized one. The ritual of marriage (the Sacred Marriage
the alchemists celebrated in terms of their chemicals and the
Greeks relived at Eleusis in "silence, darkness, and perfect
chastity") took place. In Gautier's tale the *hieros gamos* does
not occur. Life and death do not merge, nor do male and female
or spirit and body. The desire, therefore, is ever present. The
ability to created the philosophers' stone—the distillation process
that makes all things possible—which ushers in a *renovatio,* or
birth of a new attitude, is aborted by the introduction of a

negative father image.

Gautier's alchemical drama ends unresolved. Octavien had not integrated the female principle, as represented by Arria Marcella, into his psyche. He therefore could not experience a union with her that would have enabled him to bring to consciousness the anima image (or differentiate what was unconscious). Unfulfilled in this respect, he remained with a sense of longing, nostalgia, and malaise. He would never be able to love a *real* woman completely; the one envisioned in his fantasy world would always gain precedence: "I would only be able to love outside of time and space."[11]

2. *A Parapsychological Happening*

Whether Octavien's vision is termed a hallucination or a somnambulistic escapade, the experience was of a psychological nature. According to C. G. Jung, "the human capacity for extrasensory perception is conditioned by a psychological factor."[12] Octavien was a lad given to fantasy and to depression. He could not adapt to the workaday world and preferred escaping into a fabulous era, where the *imago mundi* represented joy and beauty. Such a *regressus ad uterum* toward some mythic or supernatural time enabled him to reintegrate into a past where life was new and fresh and all things became possible.

The concept of time, then, is an important factor in this tale. Such emphasis is attested to by the protagonist's name, Octavien, which comes from the Latin *octavus,* meaning eighth. According to numerologists, the number eight symbolizes eternal time. Octavien, in this respect, sought to return to a cyclical or timeless era, the *eternal present* of Plato, Aristotle, Empedocles, and Pythagoras.

Historical time, commonly alluded to as eschatological time (as opposed to cyclical time), arose with consciousness and with so-called "civilization." Primordial time (or primitive time) was measured in terms of cyclical events. The primitive looked upon each day as a conquest over night, as a cycle, or circle, to be understood and experienced by him. There was no beginning and no end. The concept of past, present, and future was nonexistent. Since the primitive lived close to nature, he became one with the cosmos and placed himself within the endless series of cycles. Therefore, no split existed between him and nature, no consciousness of himself as a separate entity from the forces surrounding him and from the world of phenomena. For the primitive death was part of organic phenomena or of seasonal changes. It was not seen as a separation or as an end and thus fear did not enter into the picture.

With the advent of Judaism and Christianity, eschatological consciousness was born. Past, present, and future became distinct phases of existence and the belief in "temporal consciousness" altered man's status in relation to the cosmos and so with himself. He emerged as a separate entity from nature. With such a cleavage, death became a fearful experience, a problem or something inflicting pain, a separation or end.

"Temporal consciousness" came into being when the concept of creation *ex nihilo* was adopted by the Hebrews in the Old Testament. In Genesis, for example, it is stated that the world was created out of chaos or nothingness and in six days. The world, therefore, had a beginning and as such an end. The notion of *aeternitas* or *aeon* gave way to the belief in *sempiternitas*.[13] The greater man's consciousness became of his identity and individuality, the more fragmented became his existence. Divisions into centuries, decades, years, days, hours, minutes, and seconds followed.

Time became linear or eschatological. The belief in an end after death was inherent in early Judaism. However, with the passage of years, as man severed himself more and more from nature, without its strength, support, and eternal qualities, man found himself alone. He could no longer face the idea of death as a void, as an end in itself, as a cutting off from life; nor could he accept the idea of an eternal God and a mortal man born from dust and returning to it.

The more intolerable the belief in death (or the more intolerable the idea of life on earth) had become, the greater was man's longing for a world hereafter. Another realm was created by the Hebrews, by Plato (the realm of essences and perfection), and by the Christians (heaven, hell, limbo, and resurrection).

With the advent of science, technology, and the worship of reason there arose another stumbling block. Man began discarding his old beliefs, that is, the precepts offered by organized religion. The notion of the resurrection of Christ and the belief in transcendence, paradise, and hell were rejected by many in the modern world. Once again man became entrapped by time. Time was considered synonymous with death—and death was a finale. What remained for these people who had divested themselves of religion as an aid and a buffer in facing death as an end to life? Means and ways of coping with death, to be sure, had come into being throughout the centuries. The Stoic was convinced that man must think about death at all times in order not to fear it. The nihilist was determined to accept the meaninglessness and the futility of life. The atheist became his own god, the molder of his destiny and responsible for all of his acts in terms of himself and society.

Certainly such attitudes were reasonable. But man is not a creature of reason. His irrational forces are powerful. Some people—and Gautier was one of them—experienced life at certain times in anguish and as alienated human beings. A spirit of malaise permeated Gautier's work periodically. It was no wonder that he (and many Romantics) rebelled against eschatological or linear time and sought to become reintegrated into cyclical or mythical eras. In such climes he could feed on the Platonic belief of metempsychosis and the Far Eastern doctrine known as the Akasic Record. Both concepts brought him solace.

When Gautier wrote in *Arria Marcella* "nothing dies, all exists always; no force can annihilate what once was,"[14] he was reiterating the Platonic doctrine. Human beings live on eternally in an endless variety of forms implicit in the transformatory process in nature. Plato expressed this same notion with regard to memory. He made the distinction between two types of memories: *anamnesis,* a recollection of events experienced in the existential world based on rational recall, comparable to eschatological time, and *mneme,* or "primordial memory," which recalls anterior existences and is the sign of true wisdom, comparable to cyclical time.

The parapsychological experience that Octavien related may be looked upon as an example of Platonic recollection of some anterior existence. Empedocles also believed in the continuity of life. In *Purifications* he declared: "I once was a boy, a girl, a bush and a bird, a mute fish in the sea." Pythagoras was described as "an extraordinary man of science," because "he saw with ease what he had been ten and twenty human existences back."[15]   Closer to Gautier was Goethe's statement included in a letter to I. Falk: "I am certain that I have been here as I am now a thousand times before, and I hope to return a thousand times."

Gautier found even greater support for his belief in reincarnation and in the capacity to return to anterior existences in the Akasic Record, the Far Eastern and Greek doctrine that had also influenced Goethe. It affirmed that everything that happened on earth and within man's mind had been indelibly recorded on the Akasa, a type of *ether* believed to encircle the world. According to sixteenth century visionaries, if man disciplines himself in the practice of clairvoyance for many years, he will be equipped to perceive through Astral Light certain signs within the Akasic Record.[16]   Dutoit-Membrini, in his *Divine Philosophy,* defined Astral Light as a kind of sensorial experience, like a third eye of knowledge that emanates from sidereal influences and permits an individual to experience divine illumination.   Just as the body originates from the "powder of the earth," he suggested, so the soul is made up of starry substances. The stars act strongly upon each person, and each must try to understand and determine the outcome of these influences.[17] Hermes Trismegistus, the founder of alchemy, wrote in his *Poimandres* that all planetary power, either in the form of parts or of elements of the planet, is present in the soul before it even comes into being. Because of this "link" there is a connection between man on earth and his "astral sources" in the cosmos. The planets and the stars affect man's very existence—his cosmic fate or heimarmene.[18]

To believe in the Akasic Record is to conquer death and by extension old age. This philosophy and its sister mystic faiths— to which Gautier also adhered—did away with the concept of death as an end. It is no wonder, then, that Gautier entered the fourth dimension and there succeeded in resurrecting, via certain images and symbols, the hetaera female—that eternally appealing, eternally fascinating woman.

Pompeii was a city known for its visual beauty, works of

art, amphitheaters, temples, public baths, mansions, beautiful walks, marble and bronze sculptures, mosaics and ornamental paintings in both private and public houses. One of Pompeii's most striking artistic compositions was "the Battle of Alexander" mosaic; however, most of its frescoes were of an erotic, even pornographic nature: there were many depictions of the ithyphallic god Priapus who was the offspring of Dionysus and Aphrodite.

Cities in general are associated with women since they are enclosed in a protected area, sheltering their inhabitants from the dangers of the outside world. In the Old Testament, Jerusalem, Babylon, and Tyre are all referred to in the feminine. That Pompeii had been destroyed, the city with which Octavien identified so powerfully, might imply that the beauty and carefree existence exemplified by Arria Marcella had also been obliterated within his conscious outlook but had been resurrected, along with the ancient city, in his unconscious. Its rebirth, then, filled a need in Octavien: a longing for the effervescence and irresponsibility associated with youth, beauty, and sensuality. In this respect, Gautier's tale may be viewed as the creation of a compensatory situation; one which would help fill a void in his existential world.

It is through the museum, another enclosed and protective uterus-like area, that Octavien's unconscious had been aroused, thus opening a pathway leading back to a former sphere of existence, to a world in which he longed to participate. The museum, according to André Malraux, is an interesting phenomenon. Its creation in the Occidental world stemmed from man's desire to halt the march of time; his need to create limits, categories, to make order out of disorder, to fix the fluid and to transform the ephemeral into something eternal. By "containing" fleeting and disparate factors in worldly existence, man feels more secure and less isolated. The museum's function is to arrest time via the work of art. When Octavien saw the stone-like lava in the museum which had retained a female form for more than two thousand years, past and present had been fused.

The museum for Octavien succeeded in renewing a bond; in enabling him to plunge back into a period of mankind's history to which he related. The piece of lava in question assumed, therefore, extraordinary importance for him. It had become a

hierophany, paving the way for his inner trajectory. Like Mallarmé's hero, Igitur, who descended "the steps of the human
mind...to the beginning of things."[19] Octavien also entered into
the limitless world of the collective unconscious.

The psychic energy aroused by Octavien's confrontation
with the lava hierophany created a kind of "magnetic field,"
or "center of energy," within him, comparable in certain respects
to a volcano.[20] The somnolent feelings the petrified lava stirred
in Octavien's psyche put him in contact with the collective unconscious, a primordial sphere devoid of past, present, and
future. During the period of hallucination we see two factors
coming into play: Octavien becomes more perceptive as he
merges with the universal pleroma, that is, his senses grow
more acute and his intuition becomes more finely attuned; at
the same time he experiences *un abaissement du niveau mental.*
The parapsychological experience narrated by Octavien is not to
be considered a "supra normal" happening, but rather an example of what can occur when one is "pre-disposed" to certain situations or when one is in a "psychologically receptive
state."[21] The resurrection of this Pompeian beauty was for
Octavien a compensation for the void he felt in his daily life.

3. *The Pagan Versus the Christian Outlook*

The hetaera who floated into Octavien's life was of the
courtesan type: beautiful, entertaining, and charming. This
type of woman used to be associated with Aphrodite worship
and was introduced into Greek society by ordinance of Solon.
Her function was to see to the pleasures of unmarried men,
thereby preventing any threat to the structure of marriage.
Many hetaerae were well known for their refined and exquisite
ways and attracted men of renown. Aspasia of Miletus drew to
her the most extraordinary men of her day, including Socrates
and Pericles; the latter abandoned his legal wife to marry her.
There were other hetaera types: such as Semiramis, Cleopatra,
Diane de Poitiers, and Jeanne d'Aragon.

The hetaera is a collective figure: the source of pleasure,
energy, and life. She has come to encompass an ideal because
it is by her charms that man indulges in the sexual and creative
act, that he feels forever young and is eternally reborn. She has

positive attributes in that she may act as a man's companion on an intellectual, spiritual, and sexual level. Frequently, she is looked upon as a *femme inspiratrice.* But she may be a destructive force in a man's life when playing the role of seductress, thus attracting him away from his true destiny and his realistic frame of reference.

Arria Marcella filled a void in Octavien's life. She enabled him to come into contact with his instinctual world. His symbolic Orphic descent into the past, or the womb, the "darkness of night," or the Realm of the Mothers, to use Goethe's imagery, permitted him to confront the earth principle or anima image— what he most lacked in his conscious life. His confrontation with Arria Marcella was accomplished in three steps: the museum, the city, and the hetaera's house. In the last phase she became the source of his life and power. Her darkened room, or cave, enabled Octavien's feelings to burgeon and his unconscious to unfold its secrets. No longer would he have to sacrifice his instinct to obligation, his joy to sorrow, nature to spirit, earthly existence to an illusory heavenly domain.

What Octavien was reentering when lying on Arria's bed was a *mystery:* that nocturnal experience which enables a hierophant to return to his origins, to the very *principia vitae.* From such a union with the hetaera type the earth becomes fruitful once again, inspiration is aroused and excitement bubbles. The cult of sexuality and beauty Octavien conjured up revealed the aridity of his own existence—that is, he had been cut off from nature and from the harmony of what Michelet called the healthy Greek religion.

It was a Nazarene, a disciples of Jesus Christ, "an unfortunate person,"[22] who put an end to Octavien's joys in lovemaking. This negative father image symbolized for him a powerful factor in Christianity: the painful, guilt-ridden attitude. At opposite ends was the Greek way: representing beauty of form and balance of personality.

> ...Arria Marcella in a voluptuous and serene pose brought to
> mind Phidias's reclining woman on the Parthenon's pediment:
> her shoes, embroidered with pearls, were lying at the end of
> the bed, her beautiful naked foot, purer and whiter than marble,
> was extended to the edge of a light blanket...[23]

For the Greeks, body and mind were not antagonistic but rather worked together: soma and psyche were blended into a harmonious whole. Nature rejoiced at happiness; trees and flowers offered their most exquisite colors to the human eye. Silent documents were infused with life, becoming living monuments of the present.

For the Greeks, and for Octavien as well, but to a lesser extent since he had been brought up in a Christian-oriented society, the universe was peopled with gods and goddesses, heroes and traitors—figures of all types. They were concretizations of the people's inner world, reflections of their *état d'âme*. Far from perfect entities, they incorporated human qualities and defects. The fact that they were immortal made them stand out as examples to be followed or avoided: combinations of carnal and sacred forces within man and his universe.

Some Greek heroes suffered negative fates as the playthings of destiny or as punishments for their transgressions. Their journey through life with tasks to be fulfilled or dangers to be avoided enabled them either to confront or to be engulfed by outerworldly or inner forces. Courage, strength, and heroism were virtues lauded by the ancients.

With the birth of Christianity an alteration of focus occurred. Power, strength, and courage were no longer valid virtues. In their place "weakness, suffering, poverty, and failure are given special dignity."[24] Such an ideation resulted from Christ's credo and was "given supreme representation in the crucifixion itself where God is degradingly scourged and dies the shameful death of the criminal on the cross."[25] There is then a conflict with regard to values: those set forth by the Greeks and Romans pitted against the goals sought for by the Christians.

The intrusion, therefore, of a negative father image at the climax of Gautier's story is not surprising. This figure destroyed the eruption of natural joy and created a mood of confusion, fear, and "horror." He dispensed pain and malaise.[26] The Nazarene, a representative of a patriarchal religion, spread the doctrine of sin, guilt, and an "austere" way. He spewed forth reproach upon the couple, calling their love infamous. Asceticism was his way, self-flagellation and punishment for any earthly happiness.[27]

Arria retorted courageously. She called the negative old man the harbinger of a "morose religion" that had never been hers. The ancient gods, she further declared, "loved life, youth, beauty, and pleasure,"[28] and she refused to be submerged by this credo of "pale nothingness" that he was flaunting. The disciple of Christ then addressed Octavien. He told him to abandon this "larva." The atmosphere tingled with bitterness and anger. Individuals seemed to vanish. The struggle between two cosmic principles—the Greek way and the Christian attitude—began.

The fight between paganism and Christianity with regard to telluric existence is most intense in *Arria Marcella*. Certainly Gautier was influenced by his *Zeitgeist* and suffered the torment (unconsciously) of sin and guilt implicit in a religion based on the symbol of "the crucified Christ pierced by the lance."[29] For the Christian, human pain results not from outside forces, but rather from within, and can only be overcome by one's "own sacrificial knife."[30] To such an excoriating attitude is added the implication of the Christian sacrificial credo, which "is symbolized by the death of a human being and demands a surrender of the whole man—not merely a taming of his animal instincts, but a total renunciation of them and a disciplining of his specifically human, spiritual functions for the sake of a spiritual goal beyond this world. This ideal is a hard school which cannot help alienating man from his own nature and, to a large degree, from nature in general."[31]

Gautier succeeded in restoring order to his chaotic inner world and affecting harmony between antagonistic principles within him only through sublimation in the work of art. In *Arria Marcella*, therefore, he created a world of beauty and fantasy where his hero—the author by extension—succeeded in bringing his ephemeral dream to life in an eternal form.

NOTES

[1]Théophile Gautier was born at Tarbes in 1811. His family moved to Paris three years later. There, the young southerner started his schooling. At the Lycée Charlemagne he met the future poet, essayist, and short-story writer Gérard de Nerval who was to become his lifelong friend.

Gautier's literary career began officially with the publication of a slim volume of *Poems* in 1830. His contribution did not create a stir, nor did his publications that followed: *Albertus* (1832), a theological legend, *Les Jeunes-France* (1833), and a volume of short stories. *Mlle de Maupin* (1835), a novel satirizing virtue, journalism, and the bourgeois in general, won the attention of many. At first, perhaps, because of its outspoken credo. Gautier stated that art should be divested of all morality. In Gautier's credo for "Art for Art's Sake" he declared: everything that is useful is ugly. Beauty alone is worth enduring: plastic beauty of form, contour, harmony of lines, and color tones. Everything that is useful is ugly.

In Gautier's most celebrated poetic work, *Enamels and Cameos* (1852-1872), he blends literary with metaphysical notions. He looked upon the poem as a sculptor considers his tone, as a goldsmith labors over precious metals. The word, like a hard object, must be hammered, chiseled, and melted down to suit the artist's vision. To create a work of art is difficult, both physically and emotionally, particularly for someone like Gautier who was perpetually haunted by an ideal, by perfection—by beauty.

Gautier died in 1872.

[2]C. G. Jung, *Psychology and Alchemy*, p. 220.

[3]Théophile Gautier, *Contes fantastiques*, p. 215.

[4]*Ibid.*, p. 224.

[5]*Ibid.*, p. 229.

[6]*Ibid.*, p. 232.

[7]*Ibid.*, p. 240.

[8]*Ibid.*, p. 241.

[9]*Ibid.*, p. 244.

[10]*Ibid.*

[11]*Ibid.*, p. 246.

[12]C. G. Jung, "A Letter on Parapsychology and Synchronicity," *Spring*, 1960, p. 203.

[13]Helmuth Plessner, "On the Relationship of Time to Death," *Eranos Yearbooks*, III, p. 233.

[14]*Ibid.*, pp. 239-40.

[15]Jean Brun, *Empédocle*, p. 187.

[16]Alice Raphael, *Goethe and the Philosophers' Stone*, p. 123.

[17]Auguste Viatte, *Les Sources occultes du romantisme* II, pp. 58-70.

[18]Hans Jonas, *The Gnostic Religion*, p. 157.

[19]Stéphane Mallarmé, *Oeuvres complètes*, p. 434.

[20]C. G. Jung, *Symbols of Transformation*, p. 232.

[21]Jung, *Spring*, p. 205.

[22]Gautier, p. 247.

[23]*Ibid.*, p. 244.

[24]Edward Edinger, *Ego and Archetype*, p. 153.

[25]*Ibid.*

[26]Gautier, p. 247.

[27]*Ibid.*

[28]*Ibid.*, p. 248.

[29]J. G. Jung, *Symbols of Transformation*, p. 290.

[30]*Ibid.*, p. 291.

[31]*Ibid.*, p. 435.

It is interesting to note that in 1903 W. Jensen wrote a novel, *Gradiva*, based on an episode similar to the one related in *Arria Marcella:* a re-entry into the past as experienced by a cerebral archaeologist. Freud interpreted the dreams that a bas-relief of a woman found in Rome had aroused in the hero. In the young archaeologist's dream the woman, whom he called Gradiva, came alive; but when he awakened, the image disappeared and he wept as though he had lost a very dear friend. Freud suggested that the hero had had no female relations (except with those in bronze) and since he was an introverted thinking type, he found it impossible to relate to women in real life. Thus he projected the love he had repressed in early manhood on Gradiva. But the erotic feelings the bas-relief had aroused within him had freed him from the constrictions. The conflict in his unconscious was lived out at the end of the novel and he found a flesh-and-blood woman, thereby liberating himself from his fantasy existence.

CHAPTER 9

Charles Baudelaire—"Parisian Dream":
The Drama of the Poetic Process

Man cannot long endure the state of awareness or
consciousness. He must ever again escape into the
unconscious, for there live his roots.
                    (Goethe, Reflections and Maxims)

The dream became a way of life for Baudelaire.[1] It offered him a momentary means of healing a ferocious inner schism. The ideal, the ordered, the perfect, the beautiful, and God were the spheres he sought and reached during the poetic process. At other times, he found himself submerged in the real, the sordid, the satanic, and *spleen* took hold. A living incarnation of the Dioscuri, Baudelaire was torn by the antagonistic forces that lived within him and so viewed life as a protracted mutilation and dismemberment.[2] He never made Heraclitus' dictum concerning the harmony of contraries his own: "that which is in opposition to itself is at the same time in harmony with itself."[3]

"Parisian Dream" (1860), from *The Flowers of Evil*, is a poem comprising two parts and fifteen stanzas. It is a diary, the recounting of an authentic journey, an Orphic descent into the most primitive and celestial regions of the soul. A theft of fire and a flagellation occur during this adventure. The poet concretizes the forces and undulations he encounters—from the most exquisitely sublime to the most excoriatingly—sordid—and incorporates them in his cosmic vision.

"Parisian Dream" was dedicated to the painter Constantin Guys whose dandyish qualities Baudelaire admired and described in terms of modernity and elegance: "Modernity means the transitory, the fugitive, the contingent—half of art; the other half being eternal and immutable."[4] Realism and naturalism, which Baudelaire considered prosaic and vulgar, were banished by Guys. Instead, the painter captured the fragile poetry of a mood, the infinite flow of crowds in fluid images and incorporated these into the collective view. For Baudelaire, Guys' cold and objective canvases were a living manifestation of the *complexio oppositorum*, the blending of the individual antagonistic forces into the harmonious composite picture. Baudelaire achieved such balance during his moments of extreme creativity. However, once the poetic vision subsided, he fell back into the profane world—the domain of chaotic multiplicity—and longed more desperately than ever to plunge back into his oneirosphere.

Stanza 1

De ce terrible paysage,	The image of this terrifying landscape,
Tel que jamais mortel n'en vit,	Such as no mortal has ever seen,
Ce matin encore l'image,	This morning still,
Vague et lointaine, me ravit.	Vague and distant, ravishes me.

The poet looks out upon the city of Paris with its stone monuments and houses, its winding roads, its greenery and the ever-flowing Seine. The day is coming to a close. The curtains on the windows are being drawn. Gaslights will soon be lit in the streets; candles and oil lamps in the homes.

A "terrifying landscape" unfolds before the poet on three different levels: the concrete, as he gazes onto the city of Paris; the creative, as he views Guys' painting before him (or his own poetic vision); and the human, in his subjective and objective relationship to the other two forces, or objects. Such a triad (poet as the creative agent; city and painting as expressions of the creative act), according to Pythagorean numerology, of which Baudelaire was an adept, "constitutes life."[5] Three, or the triangle, is an active number. It is superimposed as a balancing factor on an ever-conflicting duality; it also represents the cosmic, natural, and divine spheres.

The landscape envisaged by the poet is "terrifying." The word *terrible* in French not only implies something extraordinary and marvelous, but also affinities exist between it and the Latin word included in the body of the adjective: *terrere* ("terrifying"), *ter* ("three times"), and *terra* ("earth"). All these forces are at work in Baudelaire's poetic image, further emphasizing the state of chaos within the creative artist. Overcome by the weight of guilt and remorse implicit in a world of contingency, the poet knows that lamentations are of no avail, that only via the creative act can he experience liberation. Therefore, he yields to his dream and escapes into dimensionless realms. Gone is the need for confrontation with one's vices and shameful nature. Also obliterated is the feeling of imprisonment in a cumulative and "irremediable" past with its ever-thickening density.

As the day dims, so the poet's oneirosphere increases in power.   Images leap forth, creating mysterious and marvelous scapes.   "Such as no mortal has ever seen."   Inner and outer worlds fuse and the poet slips into the dream—space dilates. Powerful sensations pour into his psyche, disorienting and frightening yet also delighting him.   Feelings of giddiness accompany his departure from his past and from the telluric domain.   Ecstasy and terror grip him.

The poet's vision is unique.   No mortal has experienced what he now knows.   He oscillates and vibrates as ambivalent sensations multiply, generating renewed excitement, energizing his very being, and arousing within him feelings of plenitude. As his flight heightens, so his sense of liberation intensifies. References to earthbound existence follow; these increase the dichotomy of the image, hence its dynamism.   "This morning still" intrudes and jars him.   The pronoun "this" fills him with arid impressions of entrapment, as though he were abruptly pulled back to the temporal domain.   Eschatological time takes hold.   "This morning" situates the poet's vision not only in terms of the specific day, but with regard to the city of Paris and the canvas before him (the reality of his own poem).   "Morning," by its very complexity, injects feelings of temporality, specificality, and also of renewal.   The birth of cyclical or mythical time is taking place.   The emergence of a new day, a fresh beginning, discharges the poet from his oppressive impotence. "Still" introduces the notions of duration, endlessness, and permanence to the mood as multiple possibilities unfold before the poet. Hope floods the scene.

With the juxtaposition of "this morning" and "still," two types of Platonic memory are evoked: *anamnesis* (voluntary recall), equated with eschatological time, that is, life considered as a fleeting or passing moment and, therefore, arousing feelings of nostalgia, and *mneme* (involuntary recall), a force ushering in the remembrance of an archaic past, anterior existences—Baudelaire's mythical domain.   This dual notion of time permits the poet to experience both "vague and distant" images; the submersion of the individual into the collective or the eternal— into the city of Paris or the work of art.

The city dims as night encroaches.   Details are smudged and delineations on both the canvas and the city grow unclear as individual existences and the world of multiplicity recede into the oneness of the cosmic perception. But the poet's identity has not yet been diffused. He still experiences himself as subject of the activity taking place, the "me" of "ravishes." The word *ravish* brings into focus sensations, feelings, and ideas. Implicit in this word is the brutal and aggressive act of rape. The poet must experience a kind of "rape" or "ravishment" in order to transcend the existential domain. Just as Persephone was ravished by Pluto and led into his fertile underground world (*plutos* in Greek means "plenty"), so the poet must now set forth on his journey into his subliminal spheres. It is from these blackened regions that his dream will take root (the poet), that the *renovatio* will come to pass.

Stanza 2

Le sommeil est plein de miracles!	Sleep is filled with miracles!
Par un caprice singulier	A strange caprice urged me to
J'avais banni de ces spectacles	Banish from these spectacles
Le végétal irrégulier	The irregular vegetal

"Sleep" numbs the poet's senses as memory, in the shape of the dream, takes on color, weight, and form. Access to another world, an ancestral past that has lain follow for centuries, is being gained.

For the ancient Egyptians, Hebrews, and Greeks slumber had both mantic and healing powers and was considered such an important factor that it became part of initiation rituals. The world *initiation* (which means "beginning" or "entrance") affords individuals entry into new spheres; a real inner journey or *katabasis*. Plutarch described initiation ceremonies as a descent into "a marvelous light" during which the neophyte passes into "pure realms and prairies resound with voices and dances, with sacred words, and divine apparitions inspire religious respect."[6]

For Baudelaire sleep and dream were part of a ritual capable of provoking the sacred, that is of provoking the creative process, which is "filled with miracles." A "miracle" is a religious frame of reference is a manifestation of a supernatural event, an apparent contradiction of scientific law. It is, then, the eruption of the irrational, the irregular, or the acausal factor in what is considered to be the orderly, regular realm. When such an unexpected experience occurs, the poet is able to contact consecrated elements within the cosmos. The "strange caprice" urges him to reject the continuous, symmetrical, and rational existence to which he has grown accustomed. This "strange caprice," in itself an acausal factor, carries the spirit of contradiction inherent in the poet's psyche with it. It is this "miracle," or this "caprice," that paves the way for intuition.

The "miracle" of sleep implies the emergence of a mysterious and divine realm where object and subject are fused; the dual is unified. Like the ancient alchemists who were the depositors of tradition, the poet likewise enters this new world alone and becomes the guardian of his own secret, his art. The initiation process, therefore, must not and cannot be revealed to anyone. It can be effective only for the person experiencing its ardors. As Roger Bacon wrote: "By revealing the written secret, *Opus terium*, one diminishes its power. The masses understand none of it; they would use it for vulgar purposes and would thus remove all of its value."[7]   Hence, the poet must withhold his secrets from others who would only distort his message and his vision must be revealed through emblems (symbols) only to those with a discerning eye. Like the alchemist, the poet prepares his chemicals, ovens, and coctions, and then enters into active relationship with them. Once the fire of his discovery has been introduced into the components, the process begins. The poet's rational sphere diminishes in scope; the "strange," or the irrational world, takes hold, the "miracle" grows bolder; his fantasy roams and he plunges into the void.

Limitations are now nonexistent. But the poet, aware of the intrusion of a counterforce (his antagonistic self), willfully "banishes" the activation of whatever is "irregular" in nature (the acausal factor in the world of contingency). However, to do away with the "irregular" is to divest oneself of the "miracle" or that intuitive faculty indispensable to the poet's creative power. To opt for regularity, even in the dream (the nontemporal realm), is to call upon the rational, Cartesian, clocklike system—or nature's symmetrical aspects as opposed to the unconscious and limitless spheres. There are antagonistic forces at work within the poet, and so he seeks to do away with the capricious element in nature, thus trying to conform to the rules and the customary pulsations of the universe as these proceed in their ordered course.[8] The conflict between the poet's need for order in diversity, stability in motion, and chance in the continuous, points to an inner dismemberment occurring within his psyche. It also makes comprehensible the emphasis placed on certain images in the verse: combinations of circles, spheres, and straight lines, as in the thyrsus and the caduceus,[9] all bathed in the event-transforming water image. Such a variety of visualizations indicate the fact that only via opposites can the world be experienced and the work of art come into being.

For the poet the word *vegetal* takes on a plethora of meanings. It includes such plants as the opium poppy and hashish thus opening the way for cosmic knowledge and immortality. In *Artificial Paradises* Baudelaire wrote that under the influence of these two plants he transcended the human condition and experienced synesthesia: "The eyes pierce infinity. Sounds take on color, colors take on musicality."[10] Grapes are likewise "vegetal." Wine (or spirits) contains a "mysterious God" capable of diffusing remorse, annihilating pain, and annulling time; wine also arouses gayety and excites courage.[11] But opium, hashish, and wine have their destructive sides. The drugs attack the will, which to Baudelaire is "the most precious of organs,"[12] and wine unleashes maenadism or Dionysian frenzy, giving only illusory satisfaction. To Baudelaire fulfillment is the result of a concerted act of the *will*, which ushers in the Apollonian, or thinking, factor—man's capacity to discern and to order. The miraculous or acausal element must also participate in the creative process, thus enabling the poet to gain access into the intuitive realm. Without nature or the vegetal world no sustenance can be gained. If fertility or the energy able to set the triad in motion were denied, the birth of the poem would be impossible.

Stanza 3

Et peintre fier de mon génie,	And, painter proud of my genius,
Je savourais dans mon tableau	I savoured in my painting
L'enivrante monotonie	The intoxicating monotony
Du métal, du marbre et de l'eau.	Of metal, marble and water.

The painter (who is poet, Demiurge, Great Artificer)—the "genius" now passively enjoys his creative effort. He observes the unique qualities he projected onto his work of art: images "no mortal has ever seen," a creation born of "miracles." His genius distinguishes him from others; he is, as is his work, the product of the "irregular" factor in the universe. Audacious and intrepid, he feels himself endowed with supernatural and perhaps even divine faculties. A feeling of voluptuousness overcomes him while he "savours" his painting: visceral elements are trapped in the absorption of the forms he views. The word *savor* indicates an activation of his taste buds. He is mesmerized as he literally drinks in his vision, thus incorporating the "vegetal" element he had rejected in stanza 2. Extremes grow less abrasive as *un abaissement du niveau mental* imposes itself upon him.

Nothing satisfies the poet for long as "The intoxicating monotony" of a relatively uniform state takes hold. Paradoxically, ambivalent feelings intrude upon the serenity he now knows. Drunkenness enables the poet to annihilate the rational world of constriction and pain; drowning the culpa-burdened impressions. Such loss of consciousness obliterates duality, and with it excitement. Feelings of exaltation and seduction, associated heretofore with the "miracle," are now infused with monotony and *ennui*. Sluggishly, the absence of multiplicity fills the creative genius with a renewed sense of disgust and longing; melancholia, interspersed with growing impressions of powerlessness, benumbs him.

"Metal, marble and water" refer to the Paris before him as well as to the artist's transcription of this city on canvas (or in the poem). Giant masses of metal and marble structures come into focus. The alliteration of *m*etal and *m*arble reinforces the notion of the collective image; by using the individual words, their separate identities are singled out, thus emphasizing the fundamental binary opposition also implicit in the vision. Furthermore, the juxtaposition of metal and marble in terms of texture, density, and color, together with the serpentine Seine, (the third factor), intersperses the picture with staccatolike tremors and undulations, thus replenishing the tableau with fresh tonalities. The composite view reveals complex forces at work: liquids confronting solid objects and ideas attacking sensations—like acids biting into metals in rhythmic cadences as in a Dürer engraving.[13]   The mutliple blendings created from the one to the many in a series of affective visualizations may be defined in Baudelaire's terms as an example of eurythmy: an interplay of words, images, and sensations.

Metal may be associated with the alchemical and therefore with the creative process.   Since metals were created when the earth first came into being and evolved in geological strata and in cosmological transformations—in accordance with the heat of the fires to which they were exposed and the acids and oxygen content with which they came into contact—a mythological time scheme is here implied.

Marbles, like metals, range from the most exquisite and precious to the most vulgar and coarse, and are valued for their color, texture, and availability.   Artists fix their visions in marble. They hack out forms with hammers mallets, and saws; then they polish these forms until they radiate and their satany sheen emerges.   Gautier wrote in his poem "Art" that the sculptor's work is arduous as he confronts the cold, harsh and impassable stone and imposes his stamp on it for eternity.

In accordance with Baudelaire's monistic beliefs, water is associated both with metal and marble: when metal is melted down, it becomes fluid; when marble is crushed, it is transformed into water.   According to Thales, the principle of all things resides in water, which stands for a world *in potentia*.   Liquid, as opposed to solid metal and marble, insinuates itself everywhere, circulates throughout nature, and makes for growth, fertility, and greenness.   Thus it stands for virtuality and change, perpetual motion.   Like fire, water is a transitional element, a mediator between life and death—the poet and his creation.   A water surface can take on a mirrorlike sheen as do polished marble and metal. A lake for example, can reflect celestial bodies bodies, thereby unifying heaven and earth.   Larger expanses of water have hypnotic qualities about them, their perpetual motion mesmerizes and stupefies.   When water is aroused, it may grow into a cataclysmic force, as in floods; but once its flow subsides, new permutations and fresh attitudes come into being. In that water changes the destiny of man, it has a sacred and purifying quality.   To some, holy water is capable of miracles; to others, baptism absolves from original sin; to the mystics, initiations permit access to new cosmic realms.   Psychologically, water has been linked to the unconscious and accordingly to the feminine principle. Within this undifferentiated body inhabited by the uncreated, live innumerable riches inchoate: a *complexio oppositorum.* Under proper stimulus, water gives birth to creativity, but it may also destroy: literally, and also when the unconscious overpowers consciousness leading to the dissolution of the ego. In Ophelia's case, for example, first came the mental collapse, then the physical.

Water permitted Baudelaire to immerse himself in the *fons et origio* and return to a pre-formal state: to a new beginning and the possibility of altering his destiny.[14] The poet is mesmerized by the rhythmic patterns of the water he views, thus aiding him in his meditation that finally brings him to a trance-like state, first lulling, then liberating him. To inhabit this undifferentiated realm for any length of time leads to a reintegration into a prexisting state. As Bachelard wrote: "The person vowed to water is a person in vertigo. He dies at every instance."[15] And, indeed, this is so. There were moments when Baudelaire, in despair, longed to be submerged in water, thus to put an end to his worldly turmoil. In "The Voyage," for example, he wrote: "O Death, old captain, it is time! Let us raise the anchor!" But even tumult diminishes in this world subject to perpetual flux. As in Genesis, the waters recede for the poet and land takes on its solid configurations. The rational principle imposes itself, the irrational retreats. The artist-poet, now master of his method, is prepared to record his adventure.

Stanza 4

Babel d'escaliers et d'arcades,	Of Babel stairways and arcades
C'était un palais infini,	Was an infinite palace,
Plein de bassins et de cascades	Filled with basins and cascades
Tombant dans l'or mat ou bruni;	Falling into dull or burnished gold;

The poet's vision expands. Three spheres are now activated: heaven, earth, and the infernal domain.

Babel with its stairways and arcades sweeps into view, as

does a sense of verticality and extreme dynamism in multiplicity. The sons of Noah had built the Tower of Babel in order to commune with deity and seeking to annihilate the dichotomy between the finite and the infinite realms. By marching through the "Door to God" (which Bab-el means), they experienced a veritable cosmological drama, an example of *enantiodromia* (when fear of being buried by flood waters led them to opt for the opposite extreme—the building of a tower that would set them above others). When man arrogates God to himself (or, in psychological terms, when he identifies with the self or inner divinity), he loses perspective and becomes alienated from the world and from himself. Breughel the Elder's painting of Babel represents creatures inflated with their own egos and capabilities and suffering the confusion of languages. It is not uncommon for a creative individual to depict mountains or towers in his work, thus denoting certain unconscious states of hubris. Baudelaire's Tower of Babel enables the poet (himself), a priviledged human being, to experience the transcendental universe. Vision seems unlimited. Baudelaire felt capable of breaking out of the universe of sensible forms and becoming a mediating force between heaven, earth, and hell. In his poem "Correspondence," for example, one has the feeling that from these heights he understood the "confused words" he heard and that he considered himself able to communicate with all things and beings—both animate and inanimate. Unity is experienced by the poet through multiplicity and through the hidden via the visible. The poet-visionary is also a psychopomp who searches out the uncreated in order to endow it with form.

The "stairway" in the Tower of Babel (or ziggurat) is usually spiral or circular in shape. Such undulating movements are associated with the serpent and give the impression of something evolving, growing, and rotating as well as of a primitive dance. The coiled positions of serpents frequently resemble the involutions and convolutions of the brain, making an analogy with wisdom possible. Like water, the spirals and circles of the "infinite palace" and their vertical configurations (like the up and down of a ladder) imply perpetual and regular activity. The energy thus generated from this archetypal image permits the poet to escape from the material world.

Baudelaire's palace with its inner rhythms and mazelike spacial areas is reminiscent of Coleridge's "Kubla Kahn" (1797), a poem written on awakening from a dream-filled sleep.

> In Xanadu did Kubla Kahn
> A stately pleasure dome decree:
> Where Alph, the sacred river, ran
> Through caverns measureless to man
>   Down to a sunless sea.

The "infinite palace" is likewise reminiscent of the "inner palace" referred to by mystics and defined as the Kabbalistic center, the "unmoved mover" or *complexio oppositorum*. In this enclosed yet "infinite" area the poet feels linked to his past and exposed to his ancestral memories, and so is engulfed with feelings of plenitude and loss, fulfillment and diminution, form and formlessness, fall and redemption. By experiencing the most primitive elements within him in the remotest and most isolated of areas, he contacts his own depths, his abyss, the void which preceded the cosmological creation: "And the earth was without form, and void; and darkness was upon the face of the deep." (Genesis 1:2)

Such an "infinite palace," by its very limitlessness, is also a source of danger. Like the labyrinth in Crete that housed the Minotaur, the endless configurations of this mazelike area can lead to confusion and death by its very complexity. When disoriented, the poet loses consciousness of his situation and so may merely float about, bounded by nothing. Only when aware of opposition, when a certain amount of constriction is present, can the energy needed to realize the unrealized be aroused. The unlimited may frequently remain an expression of potential states.

The palace housed many "basins." These containers, both circular and concave, were filled with a vital fluid—water. But if perpetually imprisoned (or protected) within the basins and not properly stimulated, passivity, sterility, and stagnation may ensue. Conversely, the "cascades" are dynamic, cleansing, purifying forces. They uproot inertia, passivity, and stagnation. The pulsations from these cascades, therefore, revive the ripples and dissonances and set the law of attraction and repulsion to work again. New combinations of waters rushing down cause perpetual rebirth. "One cannot twice bathe in the same waters," wrote Heraclitus,[16] for everything is in a state of flux. The alchemist Marie the Jewess, who invented the *Balneum Mariae* (the double boiler), regulated the fusions and distillations of liquids with water and heat; so the poet's inner content is likewise reshuffled by the catalyzing agent of the cascading waters.

"Falling into dull or burnished gold" is another example of the tension involved in Baudelaire's use of verticality: from the heights of Babel, in the first line, to the depths within the earth where gold is mined. Within this darkened, chthonic realm (the grotto or cave) the seed of creation is implanted. Associated with the female (the womb), the embryo is nurtured and grows. But by the same token the embryo must die; eventually it must become totally exiled from the manifest world and alter in form and consistency for renewal to occur. According to the Gospel of Saint John, Christ said: "Verily, verily, I say unto you, Except a corn of wheat fall into the ground and die, it abideth alone: but if it die, it bringeth forth much fruit." (12:24)

Hence the poet must experience a "fall" into matter as Adam had; as occurred in Egyptian and Greek myths with the sun's daily demise. Only after the fall can the creative life process continue. Psychologically, such a fall, or regression, into self must take place so that the poet will be exposed to the gold, or treasure, hidden beneath. The poet-creator, therefore, must sink into sorrow, divest himself of illusions, and exile himself in his abyss—all of which is part of the Orphic descent.

The "gold," upon which the cascading water falls, may be likened to the alchemist's gold (the philosophers' stone) or the supreme illumination. In Hebrew the word *gold* (*aor*) means "light"; in Latin *aurum* is equated with "intuition." The Kabbalists believed that within the earth there exists a godly light that was lost after "the breaking of the vessels" and the dispersion of Adam Kadman, the primordial man. Within matter, then, there resides both light and heat. Embedded in the *prima materia* the poet experiences the infinite, and from this unlimited area he must select these essences or amorphous entities that will be necessary to his work of art; then he polishes them and sets them into gemlike form in his poem. But gold may be either "dull" or "polished" (which is also true for the poem). When extracted from the ground, the rivers and sands in which the precious metal is found are not a thing of beauty. Like an undeveloped idea, an unchanneled emotion, so artisans must transform the collective element into the individual work of art.

Paris grows visible once again. The poet sees its golden domes and monuments reflected countless times by the dull and brilliant street lights, their interplay creating new and lustrous configurations. As night descends, clusters of crystal chandeliers and lamplights inject a pointillistic mood onto the scene; a world of diversity and dynamism does away with the last vestiges of repose.

Stanza 5

Et des cataractes pesantes,	And weighty cataracts,
Comme des rideaux de cristal,	Like crystal curtains,
Se suspendaient, éblouissantes,	Hung, dazzling,
A des murailles de métal.	From metal walls.

The "cascades" of stanza 4 have now been transformed into "cataracts." Cataracts, which usually fall from high places, are turbulent and frequently opaque in texture. Their downpour, so ferocious at times, may be compared psychologically to the eruption of an affect or an instinct into a harmonious situation: the breaking through of the Dionysian principle in an Apollonian frame of reference. Cataracts are "weighty" because they are unleashed with force; their presence is terrifying and painful as is an electric charge (or the power of an emotion). Such a deluge (of instinct) may drown or mutilate; it may also regenerate and purify. The opacity of the waters is like a curtain, severing the individual from the world at large. In ancient Egypt the great cataracts divided the known from the unknown world. Cataracts also denote the opacity that leads to blindness when they refer to the growth of a membrane over the eye. When compared to "crystal curtains," they reinforce the divisive effect. In Baudelaire's view cataracts therefore represent duality in the sense world.

Crystals also play a double role. They come from water and are transported by water. They are creators of light as well as preventers of vision. The fact that crystals are associated with curtains in this stanza brings to mind the city of Paris and the opening image in the poem: the candlelight seems to effect many crystals, veiled and hidden behind the drawn window curtains. "But night has descended. The bizarre and doubtful hours come into being when the curtains of the heavens close, when cities become illuminated," Baudelaire wrote in *Painter of Modern Life*. As night shields the lights within the houses, so the poet's inner world is likewise masked. The brilliant crystals, like stars shining in dotted landscapes, are clues to riches hidden within the blackness.[17]

As an object of contemplation, crystals, like water, have a hypnotic effect depending upon the regularity, the motility, and the depth of the rays of light shining upon them. In this respect, crystals are things of beauty that draw individuals to them; by the same token, they are cold bodies. The Greek word *crystal* is derived from "ice" or "frozen water." It was thought in ancient times that stones produced crystals only in extreme cold, in the high altitudes of the alps. Pliny in his *Natural History* (Book xxxii) wrote that no art can equal the beauty of rock crystals with their icelike purity and their stonelike transparency. The alchemist and magician Albertus Magnus believed that in the highest mountain tops ice was so dry that it congealed into crystals. In Job crystals are compared to wisdom, although unequal to it (28:17). The terrifying vision in Revelation is embedded in crystal.

> And before the throne there was a sea of glass like unto crystal: and in the midst of the throne, and round about the throne, were four beasts full of eyes before and behind (4:6).

The fact that crystals are suspended like curtains in Baudelaire's poem indicates the necessity of a barrier between the poet and his vision. These partitions, like congealed stalactites, stop the flow of light, interrupt the onrushing rhythm of the "weighty cataracts," and block emotion. This containment increases both dynamism and productivity.

The "metal walls," from which these "dazzling" crystal curtains hang, imply an even stronger separation. Walls were protective devices in the Middle Ages, preventing invasions from enemy armies. In biblical times they were used to encircle cities, thus assuring the safety of citizens.

> And I will make thee unto this people a fenced brason wall: and they shall fight against thee, but they shall not prevail

against thee: for I am with thee to save thee and to deliver
thee, saith the Lord (Jeremiah 15:20)

Walls were stormed during several periods in history. In the
Epistle of Paul to the Hebrews we read: "By faith the walls
of Jericho fell down, after they were compassed about seven
days" (II:30).

Walls are to a certain degree beneficial for the artist, as are
all barriers. The true poet-creator is compelled to surmount the
difficulties facing him. And if he succeeds, he may extract the
profoundest and most superb elements within himself. The
wall, being a containing factor, is usually considered a mother
symbol, a nutritive, fertile force: a soul. The Shulamite in the
Song of Solomon refers to herself as wall (8:10). When experiencing the wall, the poet feels his soul.

With the juxtaposition of metal and wall, Pythagorean and
astrological correspondences also come into view. Earthly metal
becomes linked to the metal with which each of the seven astral
bodies is associated: Sun is gold, Moon is silver, Venus is copper,
Mercury (the same metal), Mars is iron, Jupiter is tin, Saturn is
lead. Metal, as a representative of cosmic energy (psychic energy
or libido), has emotional value and also takes on specific character traits. The baser metals, such as lead, represent flesh, lust,
and the animal in man. Gold symbolizes the highest intellectual
and spiritual faculties within the human species. To extract the
quintessence of these metals, to transmute them from lower to
higher forms, is equivalent to liberating the poet's creative energy
from constriction in the sense world and causing the birth of the
poem.

Baudelaire's vision of sparkling metals and crystals engulf
yet separates, accelerates and halts, captures and ejects, submerg-
es and saves, suspends and falls, collectivizes and individualizes.
This kind of cosmic sweep Baudelaire expressed in *Salon 1846.*

> Let us imagine a beautiful expanse of nature where all is ver-
> dant, red, powdered, and glistens in complete liberty; where
> all things, diversely colored and according to their molecular
> make-up, change from second to second in accordance with
> the displacement of light and shadow and the inner travail of
> the heat; everything is in a state of perpetual vibration, com-

pelling the lines to tremble, thus completing the eternal and universal law of motion.[18]

Stanza 6

Non d'arbres, mais de colonnades	Not trees, but colonnades
Les étangs dormants s'entouraient,	Surrounded the slumbering ponds,
Où de gigantesques naïades,	Where gigantesque naïads,
Comme des femmes, se miraient.	Like women, gazed at themselves.

Trees and colonnades have affinities. Both point upward and both are embedded in the ground; both symbolize man's relationship with the cosmos. But since the tree is a natural phenomenon, it holds a superior place to the pillar in the hierarchy of being. The tree was sacred: the oak to the Celts, the fig to the Hindus, the pine to the Greeks, the cedar to the Egyptians, and the Tree of Knowledge to the Hebrews. Colonnades, on the other hand, are man-made. Used in construction of temples, monasteries, and palaces, they adorn the outside of buildings, such as the colonnade in Rome and the Louvre in Paris. Baudelaire's colonnades stand for stability, solidity, and strength. They represent to a great degree man's power over nature since he is the artisan who fashions them to suit his purposes. In that columns are set at regular intervals to form a colonnade, an illusion of infinity is injected into the image, recalling the "infinite palace" of stanza 4. The circular pattern created by the colonnades surrounding the "slumbering ponds" are restatements of the thyrsus and caduceus images enveloping the poet with feelings of wholeness and peace.

The relaxed and sensual atmosphere of tropical climates is further enhanced by the image of "gigantesque naïads" sculpted into the columns. Languidly, the female figures look down upon the immobile waters below, reflecting and meditating upon their powerful beauty in Narcissus-like manner. Baudelaire is not referring to the usual delicately charming water nymphs who gambol about in streams and rivers. Here the "gigantesque naïads" represent fructifying elemental figures. In Greek mythology some nymphs were guardian goddesses of marriage; sculptures also often represented them in the act of nursing, and some brought up the children of the gods (e.g. Zeus and Dionysus). Because of the healing and inspirational power of many springs in which these naïads bathed, these women were said to have been endowed with mantic powers and therefore were capable of stimulating man's creative factor, enabling prophetic and poetic images to emerge. As the naïads gaze deeply into the waters, they absorb their images, as reflected in the "slumbering ponds," in one gigantic cosmic correspondence. The poet too observes the analogy in the infinite mirror reflections given off by these bodies of water: trees, heavens, draped female figures holding up infinite columns are all delineated in this microcosmic reproduction of the macrocosm.

Stanza 7

Des nappes d'eau s'épanchaient, bleues,	Blue sheets of water poured out
Entre des quais roses et verts,	Between rose and green quays,
Pendant des millions de lieues,	For millions of leagues,
Vers les confins de l'univers;	To the ends of the universe;

"Sheets of water" (like the "crystal curtains" of stanza 5) act as natural separations, dulling the poet's vision and hiding the multiple secrets within the manifest world. An alchemical mixture is occurring: solvents are being added to the saline solutions, forming and reforming the coloration of the vision.

The blue of the water reflects the tones of heaven, thus creating universal correspondences between celestial and earthly spheres. By the same token, verticality imposes itself on horizontality, adding depth and nuance to the image. Blue is of particular interest to Baudelaire in that it represents spiritual spheres: a multiplicity of shadings as with white puffs of cottony clouds interacting upon one another within the unified expanse of sky. Roses and greens are interspersed amid the elevated quays and act as steppingstones to the unfolding of the dream. Quays are elevated constructions set into water: foreign ships approach them and trade takes place near them. Like colors, quays are passageways, melting places between one's nation and the world at large—the finite to the infinite. The rose visible in Baudelaire's tableau denotes emotions; not the passion of red, but a more subdued, mystical, and reversed relationship. In the medieval allegorical poem "The Novel of the Rose," this flower was associated with the mystic center, the point of creation. It also refers to the rose-shaped stained-glass window of Notre Dame, thus bringing to mind the kaleidoscopic tonalities that bathe this medieval monument and adding a religious flavor to Baudelaire's image. The rose, a flower with myriad petals, offers its sweet-smelling odor to all who surround it; but thorns to the one who plucks it. Green, a fertile color depicts growth, hope, perpetual summer—the *renovatio.* "Trees are green, lawns are green, mosses are green; green runs serpentlike around tree trunks; the unripe stems are green; green is fundamental to nature because green easily blends into all other tonalities," suggested Baudelaire in *Salon 1846.*[19] Because colors play such a singular role in Baudelaire's metaphysics, they incorporate "harmony, melody, and counterpoint."[20] As colors blend into the immensity of the cosmos, reaching out into the confines of the earth—as does water—so the poet, like the thaumaturge, captures the infinite correspondences and analogies within the framework of his work of art.

Stanza 8

C'étaient des pierres inouïes	There were incredible stones
Et des flots magiques; c'étaient	And enchanted undulations; there were
D'immense glaces éblouies	Immense mirrors dazzled
Par tout ce qu'elle reflétaient!	By all they reflected!

The stones that now come into view are "incredible," that is, prodigious, strange, and extraordinary. Like the philosopher's stone they make everything possible—a cohesion of disparate elements or, psychologically, a reconciliation with self. Stones are durable and hard. Some stones, however, are made of softer matter and can splinter, disintegrate, or turn into sand, dust, or crystals. When stones shatter, they dismember; they can cut, bruise, blind, maime, and kill. Stones are hierophanies: the Kaaba in Mecca, the dolmens and menhirs in Brittany and Cornwall; the Greek omphalos, a conical-shaped stone, representing the naval or center of the earth and venerated at Delphi. In Genesis it is written: "And this stone, which I have set for a pillar, shall be God's house" (28:22). For Baudelaire stones are part of an evertransforming universe; as their form and consistency perpetually alters, so their meaning does—gliding from the profane to the sacred.

The "enchanted undulations" of these stones evoke a supernatural quality—even the presence of divinity. The word *enchanted* as associated with the stones ushers in an outer-worldly moon. Magic, as an art, was practiced since Egyptian, Assyrian, Chaldean, and Hebraic times, enabling the thaumaturge not only to penetrate the very mystery of heaven and earth, but to control the vital rhythms of the universe as well. The sorcerer transcends the normal. Like the poet, he understands esoteric languages, arcane symbols, and experiences, thereby having a symbiotic relationship with the cosmos. The magician holds mysterious powers that grant him the ability to call on celestial spheres as well as on underworld shades. Libod Drusus, the Roman magician mentioned by Tacitus in his *Annals,* used to read incantatory poems in order to contact the departed. And Lucian described certain magicians, precursors to Faust, who signed pacts with the King of Hell.[21] The poet, through the wizardry of his imagination, becomes a *magister,* a thaumaturge, capable of transmuting the physical ugliness embedded in the world of phenomenon into "music of the spheres."

The feat of magic is accomplished by tapping certain undulations and airwaves as they circulate throughout the atmosphere. Water is transformed into clusters of "immense mirrors" capable of conjuring up dazzling forms and sensations (glass, cutting, freezing, hardness, blinding, terror, blue, rose), each acting upon the other. Mirrors or bodies of water are like magic wands; they concretize what is essentially amorphous and fluid. In that they reflect the phenomenological world, they have been associated with the poet's imaginative faculty and with consciousness as well. Mirrors, however, often falsify reality by absorbing the image placed before it and also abolish distances and dimensionality. The mirror is passive and unable to initiate activity; it is a receiver and reflector like the moon. Dazzled by the multiplicity of these reverberations that seem to absorb their own incandescence, the mirror and the images stir what has been stilled, exteriorize the hidden and concretize a world *in potentia.*

Stanza 9

Insouciants et taciturnes,	Unconcerned and taciturn,
Des Ganges, dans le firmament,	The Ganges in the firmament,
Versaient le trésor de leurs urnes	Poured the treasures from their urns
Dans des gouffres de diamant.	Into diamond abysses.

The flamboyant mood aroused by the infinite cosmic correspondences, which the poet seeks to encapsulate in his creation, suddenly alters. The poet begins to abstract himself from the marvels about him; he remains unruffled by the magnificence of his vision. Taciturn, he interiorizes the images (the urn in taci*turn* of line 3) as he takes in the outer world, distilling their contents into an urnlike object. The poetic vision swells.

The Ganges, incizes in the firmament, discharges its treasures in liquid forms, recalling the azure blue and water images of stanzas 6 and 7. The poet is not only referring to the river in India, which rises from a glacier in the Himalayas, but to all similar bodies of water—which are looked upon by him as prototypes of the *one* in India. The Ganges runs through Benares into the Bay of Bengal and absorbs vast areas in its 1,560 mile course. The Hindus believe the Ganges fell from heaven and would have divided the earth in two had not Civa, the ambivalent god (creator-destroyer) caught it in the matted locks of his tangled hair[22] (the Himalayan hills). The river is endowed with treasures and with death. It is sacred to the pilgrims who bathe and purify themselves in its waters. Pilgrims also attribute miracles to this holy water (as they do at Lourdes) and take bottles full of it home with them. But in the delta area the Ganges is swampy. Although it is good for the rice plantations the river spells death from cholera for countless humans. Thus when the miraculous waters of the Ganges pour down from their urns (alchemical vessels), they become a concoction that can be either productive or destructive, as do the blendings operating within the poet's being.

Treasures are not easily accessible. They must be sought and fought for whether found in caves (Gilgamesh, Thor, Indra) protected by snakes or dragons, in sanctuaries (saints' relics as those of St. Jacques of Compostelle) guarded by priests or monks

in fields of wheat (Ceres), or as grapes (Bacchus) prized by
farmers. Treasures exist for those who believe in them and come
to those who have the will to seek them. Great sacrifices must
frequently be made to obtain them. The treasures stored in the
urns are poured into "diamond abysses." Embedded in their
native habitat, diamonds in the raw are crude and gross. They
shine and take on depth and texture only during the refining
process.

The poet regresses from the existential world and blends
into the earth, the "diamond abysses," that feminine and nourishing principle, in order to come into contact with the treasure
in its unrefined state. He is experiencing his Orphic descent—
the great death-and-resurrection mystery that is part of every
poet's initiation into the creative sphere. Let us recall that
Orpheus, considered the greatest poet and musician of all time,
the possessor of the seven-stringed lyre capable of mesmerizing
people, animals, and rocks, had gone to Hades to recapture
his wife Eurydice who had died as a result of a serpent's bite.
Because he could not obey the strict proviso set down by Persephone as the condition for his wife's safe return, Orpheus lost
her forever. Once he returned to earth, he became an ascetic.
Orphic rites, which Pythagoras spread throughout the ancient
world, were based on the purification of human nature: an attempt to transform what is brute and crude in man's terrestrial
being (the elements imprisoned in his "titanic body") into its
divine form. To transcend man's earthly and limited state
through ascetic practices (purification rituals, prayers, expiation)
facilitated his liberation from flesh and the innumerable transformations—his heimarmene. According to the Orphic initiatory
process, each neophyte must pass into the land of the dead for
seven nights and seven days. He remains in the dark, cavelike
area to experience both physically and emotionally the terror
connected with death. In this manner he identifies with the
death and resurrection of Dionysus-Zagreus (Orpheus or Christ).
For the poet such a descent into Self means coming into contact
with the most archaic spheres of the unconscious, the collective
and mythical past, the "inner firmament" where diamonds become visible in all of their resplendence.[23]

Food prevails in the abysses; the seed is nurtured (the
word-idea seansation) and germination takes place. There is
valid reason for the Greeks to have named their god of the

underworld *Pluto* (meaning "plenty"). It is within the poet's depths that he experiences his own transformation; that he encapsulates, limits, and stifles the infinite sensations living inchoate within his oneirosphere. It is likewise within this region that he imbibes the waters of Mnemosine (to the right), enabling him to recall anterior existences (thus the meaning of life and death); or drinks from the River Lethe (to the left), offering him forgetfulness or oblivion. Once the poet has experienced his depths, he must call upon his conscious mind to sift, differentiate, and decide what to bring to light and compress into the poem.[24]

Stanza 10

Architecte de mes féeries,	Architect of my fantasies,
Je faisais, à ma volonté,	I caused
Sous un tunnel de pierreries	A tame ocean to pass
Passer un océan dompté;	Under a tunnel of precious stones;

Architecture is based on correspondences of patterns and organizations of space, form, color, and material; an interplay of abstract and concrete relationships. The word *architect* implies a fashioner of monuments such as pyramids, ziggurats, cathedrals, temples—buildings that inhabit cyclical time schemes, thus integrating past into present and future eras. Architect, therefore, evokes a sense of nostalgia and continuity for Baudelaire; from the ancient Egyptian and Greek temples to modern Paris.

Like the poet, the architect is a mathematician, philosopher, and inventor. He is unique. Daedalus, the great forger, sculptor, and architect of the labyrinth was also a fine mathematician. He was imprisoned in his own creation by Minos as punishment for having aided Theseus and Ariadne to escape, thereby going against the monarch's will. But Daedalus constructed wings for himself and Icarus, his son, and they flew away from Crete. Icarus arrogantly used the power he did not understand and flew too close to the sun. His wings melted and he drowned in the sea. Daedalus, however, more conservative and realistic in his needs and more scientific in his attitude, escaped to safety. His wings, or flying machine, that had saved him he dedicated to

Apollo, the God of light and wisdom.

An architect, then, is one who brings order out of disorder; who fixes the unpredictable; who works with space and numbers. Numbers have a numinous quality about them and appear frequently in works of art when a person suffers from some psychic disorder. They symbolize a need to compensate for some chaotic inner state.[25]   Numbers are not invented by the conscious mind but emerge from the unconscious spontaneously, as archetypal images, when the need arises.   The Pythagoreans based their philosophical and metaphysical arguments on astronomical, geometrical, and numerical calculations.   They proved that stars and planets existed on different planes—that the sphere was the perfect geometric figure.   In their "theocentric universe" they believed that astral movement was circular and eternal and therefore divine (eternity is an attribute of divinity).   They juxtaposed the "intelligent," rational, circular, and uniform movements of the heavenly bodies with the "irrational," eratic, and disorderly paths of terrestrial entities.   Terrestrial motion, they further observed, was rectilinear and therefore limited (the object moves, rises, falls, and then remains immobile).   Because heavenly bodies function in a closed orbit, their course is immutable and eternal. Stars and planets, according to Pythagoreans, move in harmony with a heavenly plan in perfect order and are endowed with souls and intelligences.   That part of the universe which stands between the sphere of the moon and the earth is dominated by chance and is mortal and perishable, as opposed to divine planets, which are immortal.   The duality between the celestial and terrestrial domains creates binarism in substance: celestial bodies are simple in formation, consisting of fire and ether; earthly bodies are complex, unstable, and impure since they are a mixture of the four elements.   Duality in man is an extension of this same division in earthly elements.   The divine spark in the body is part of the World-Soul and therefore is eternal, mobile, rational, and pure.   Because it is imprisoned in the body, it is subject to material and sensual influences which it must fight off through ascetic practices.

For Baudelaire the poet is the architect, Daedalus, Pythagoras—the one person to stabilize chance.   Amid the fantasies and scattered ideas that leap into his mind, he uses his will to mold and fashion his work of art, bringing it that inner light, that aspect of the World-Soul that lives within him, those very elements Baudelaire had used to describe Wagner's music: "will, desire, concentration, nervous intensity, explosion." The post-architect orders chance; he decides over the destiny of sensations, harmonies, images, words, and colors that appear and reappear within his being. The will "is the most precious of organs," Baudelaire wrote in *Artificial Paradises.*[26]

The poet must pass alone "under a tunnel of precious stones," or jewels, like the alchemist who experiences his initiation in solitude: *Visit the Interior of the Earth, via Adjustments you will Find the Hidden Stone.*[27] Once the eyes become accustomed to the darkness, delineations and nuances appear; giant phantoms and forms spread their incandescent light amid the pure rock formations and precious stone (stanza 8). The poet begins to find his way about in this subliminal realm. The inner illumination he experiences is not the harsh, blinding light of the sun, but rather the soft, reflective rays offered by the moon. Armed with his will, the product of his rational mind, the poet passes through the oceanic forces living within him. Those perpetual currents of energy buried in his oneirosphere, which surge forth every now and then in the form of archetypal images, are tamed by the artisan of words. Master of space and time, he controls the free-flowing tides (the eruption of the creative element within him) and is not victimized by the winds, quicksand, and other acausal phenomena. "He captures the transitory," and forms the formless, "Dreaming his own dream and asleep in his own reality." The poet is no longer a "fugitive in a contingent" world.[28]

Stanza 11

Et tout, même la couleur noire,	And everything, even the black color
Semblait fourbi, clair, irisé;	Seemed polished, bright, iridescent;
Le liquide enchâssait sa gloire	Liquid enshrined its glory
Dans le rayon cristallisé	In the crystallized ray.

According to Baudelaire color is based on harmonies, that is "chemical affinities" embedded in every fiber of nature. "Form and color are one."[29] Color is the product of a relationship in time and space. "Melody is unity in color, or general color."[30] That everything, even black, seemed "polished, bright, irridescent" to Baudelaire, becomes understandable since color was implicit in his metaphysical system and black includes all other colors; hence it is, like the ocean, a *complexio oppositorum.* "Black," wrote Baudelaire, is "zero solitary and insignificant."[31]   The number zero represents nonbeing or unity in disparity because it is circular and because it stands for eternity. Although blackness pervades the poet's vision, the polish, brightness, and irridescence emerge in brilliant hues, as previously (stanza 10) diamonds and crystals became visible during the poet's Orphic descent.

The "irridescent" quality of the image, as it stands out from the blackness of the atmosphere, takes on the pastel tones of a rainbow and becomes a link between heaven and earth. In biblical terms it is a manifestation of God's covenant with Noah after the Deluge, thus symbolizing a *hieros gamos.* The poet views these brilliant forms in their disparate state and the infinite possibilities offered him. His poem, therefore, utilizes these harmonies and cacophonies and become fluid yet solid, irridescent while embedded in blackness, and amorphous yet concrete. The ideal type of execution, Baudelaire wrote in "The Painter of Modern Life," should become "as unconscious, as *flowing* as digestion for the mind of the healthy man who has just dined." The poet, master of his technique, will know how to "enshrine" his vision in the purest, highest form possible and in so doing will have completed the last phase of the alchemical process.

Stanza 12

Nul astre d'ailleurs, nuls vestiges	There was no astral body, no vestiges
De soleil, même au bas du ciel,	Of the sun, even in the lower skies
Pour illuminer ces prodiges,	To illuminate these prodigies,
Qui brillaient d'un feu personnel!	Which blazed with a personal fire!

The repetition of the word *no* (*nul* in french also means "zero"), which Baudelaire equated with black, not only implies a strong negative feeling (or the presence of a void) but also a kind of melancholia. But the darkening atmosphere of twilight has its positive side too insofar as Baudelaire is concerned. This midway hour ushers in the dream he wrote in "Twilight Evening" (1855).

> Twilight has always been for me the signal of an inner feast and likewise the liberation from anguish. Whether in the woods or in the streets of a great city, the darkening day and the dotting of stars or lanterns illuminate my mind.[32]

The colors that emerge during the twilight hours, similar to those that become visible in caverns or during the poet's Orphic descent, reflect the day's turmoil; they are subdued, like memory, and resurrect past states. But then a conflict emerges within the poet at this juncture between his conscious memory (his desire to see everything) and his unconscious power of recall (the absorption of segments of past events).

The sun has vanished (or man's ability to discern and differentiate) and the poet, a prey to the countless marvels of his own prodigious visions that radiate against the blackness of Parisian skies, is now enclosed in night. He identifies with Guys' canvas once again, the work of a master at blending the particular (his own personal vision) with the collective (people as a group). "The crowd is his domain as air is that of the bird, as water is for the fish. His passion and his profession is that of *espousing the crowd*."[33] The personal and ephemeral now become fused with the eternal and impersonal and the poet creates his own myth: "Human relations are almost completely divested of their conventional and intelligible form before abstract reason; they show the really human side of life, the eternally comprehensible, and reveal it in a concrete form, exclusive of all imitation, which gives all true myths their individual character and makes them recognizable at first glance."[34]

Stanza 13

Et sur ces mouvantes merveilles	And on these mobile marvels
Planait (terrible nouveauté!	Hovered (frightening newness!
Tout pour l'oeil, rien pour les oreilles!)	All for the eye, nothing for the ears!)

Un silence d'éternité.   The silence of eternity.

    Captivated by his dream, the poet hovers about in abstract and concrete dimensions; he glides like a bird whose soul merges with the vast expanses. But the very novelty of his vision becomes an excoriating experience. The "terrifying landscape" he encountered at the outset of his quest (stanza 1) has now been transformed into the very heart of a mystery, disorienting the poet who lives in a chance-ridden universe. The alliteration of "*m*obile" and "*m*arvels" underscores the musicality of the poetic experience, giving the impression of his release from the "weighty bonds of earth."[35] As the poet soars through the air, he encounters the essence of beauty—that midway place between what Pythagoras calls the eternal realm and the world of congingency: "Beauty is inevitably made up of the dual, though the impression it produces is one of unity."[36] The poet experiences the play of opposites as well as continuity in eternity during his oneiric excursion. Baudelaire described this process in "The Voyage."

> To plunge to the depths of the abyss, Hell or
> Heaven, what difference?
> To the depths of the Unknown to find the new!

    "All for the eye" because it alone, wrote Baudelaire, leads directly to the soul, it possesses "the window which opens onto infinity," the ability to "surpass nature."[37] The eye is man's sun. Like the eye of God, it sees all. In Proverbs we read:

> The eyes of the Lord are in every place, beholding the evil
> and the good (15:3).

Eyes enable light to filter into the darkness of the body; they permit intellect or reason to illuminate instinct. When alluding to the divine eye, the Egyptians featured a circle, the iris, surrounded by the pupil, the center of which they called the "sun in the mouth" or the "creative Word." Because Baudelaire speaks of the eye in the singular, he is referring to the divine eye, the eye of intelligence, the eye located on the forehead of Shiva (Creator-Destroyer).

    In the phrase "nothing for the ears" Baudelaire refers to the fact that although endowed with two ears, mortal man cannot hear the "music of the spheres." Eternity speaks to the poet in silence; it manifests its presence in myths, legends, and poems. Nonidentity has now come into being: the alchemical blend has been completed, each factor canceling the other out. "Thus the lover of universal life enters into the crowd as electricity into an immense reservoir... It is an *I* insatiable for the *not-I,* which at each instant renders and expresses it in eternal and fleeting images more alive than life itself."[58]

Stanza 14

En rouvrant mes yeux pleins de flamme	Upon opening my flame-filled eyes
J'ai vu l'horreur de mon taudis,	I saw the horror of my hovel,
Et senti, rentrant dans mon âme,	And felt, penetrating my soul,
La pointe des soucis maudits;	The spearings of my cursed worries.

The poet opens his eyes (now both eyes) and finds himself back in his hovel, weighted down with pain as Adam and Eve had known after their fall to earth.

> And the eyes of them both were opened, and they knew that they were naked; and they sewed fig leaves together, and made themselves aprons (Genesis 3:7).

The flame of the Promethean adventure and the visions of anterior lives, grandiose heights, and subliminal depths linger on, making the poet's earthbound existence that much more abrasive. As the eye of God followed Cain, keeping him forever in turmoil, so the poet-architect bears his guilt, dissatisfaction, and torment with dignity (Genesis 4:15). In an *imitatio Christi* the poet-architect feels the sharp points of the crown of thorns (a reference to the rose in stanza 7); like St. Francis of Assisi, he experiences the five wounds of Christ as multiple needles spearing him. Malediction and culpability insinuate their way into his flesh.

Stanza 15

La pendule aux accents funèbres	The clock with its funereal accents
Sonnait brutalement midi,	Sounded midday brutally
Et le ciel versait des ténèbres	And heaven poured down its gloom
Sur le triste monde engourdi.	On the sad benumbed world.

The poetic vision fades. The world of reality has taken precedence. The "clock" with its pendulum sounds out linear time as the hands and numbers on its face spell out the march of hours and minutes in concrete and visceral terms. Time as an object now swells and deflates in regular beats similar to the human heart. The pendulum, a mechanistic replica designed to reflect the cosmic tempi, moves in unrelating vibrations—its hands, like cutting pages, pierce the flesh as did the stigmata (stanza 14).

The clock strikes "brutally" with "funereal accents." It sounds out the poet's destiny. The limitless beauty felt so intensely in the previous verses yields to the constricting atmosphere of earthbound existence. The only crystals now visible are those embedded in the clock and the only sonorities now audible are those transmuted into pain. Distances lessen and speed heightens; the concentration of sound nearly deafens.

"Midday" strikes; six of the twelve hours have passed. Instead of the "irridescent" rainbow linking the poet with the cosmos in feelings of joy and plenitude, heaven pours down its gloom. Desolation as well as spiritual and physical negativity enclose the poet-architect in their embrace. And amid degradation he lies virtually paralyzed and deadened by the *spleen* engulfing him. The clock continues its journey and the six doubles into twelve. The cycle of *renovatio* resumes as the very mystery of poetic creation is eternalized.

NOTES

[1]Charles Baudelaire was born on April 9, 1821. His father, a painter of sorts, to whom he had been very close, died when Charles was only six years old. His mother, much to his chagrin, married Commander Aupick in 1828. Charles' hatred for this stern, unbending gentleman knew no bounds. Baudelaire was sent to the Collège Royal de Lyon in 1833 where he experienced the meaning of "solitude" and "isolation." In 1836 he was transferred to the College Louis-le-Grand and proved to be an excellent student. He began writing poetry at this juncture and his bent for the ways of the dandy took root. In 1840 he began a liaison with Sarah, a young prostitute, and it is believed that he contracted syphillis from her. Interested in the exotic and distant, in 1841 Baudelaire set out on a boat trip to Calcutta, but by the time he reached Capetown he was invaded by a feeling of *ennui* and returned to Paris. At the age of twenty-one he inherited a substantial sum from his father's estate and began to lead what has been called a relatively "happy" existence for the next three years. He became friendly with Hugo, Gautier, Sainte-Beuve, and Jeanne Duval, the mulatress who was to become his mistress. Baudelaire's most productive years began in 1846 with the *Salon;* followed by *La Fanfarlo* (1847), and *Flowers of Evil* (1857), as well as translations of the works on Edgar Allan Poe. Despite these publications and others, Baudelaire was debt-ridden. By 1863 his health had become a source of worry. He wrote little, wandered a great deal, and was submerged in feelings of pessimism. The ravages of syphillis took their toll. Baudelaire succumbed on August 31, 1867.

[2]Baudelaire accepted Joseph de Maistre's view of suffering and evil. Punishment, blood, and destruction, wrote this theocrat who believed the world should be united under the absolute spiritual rule of the pope, served a positive function in life. Only through suffering can purification come to pass and humanity be purged on its sin and guilt. Baudelaire reiterated this view in *Mon coeur mis a nu,* where he states that the victim in a given situation must sacrifice himself consciously and with pleasure, knowing that his action is being accomplished for the spiritual good of humanity—a real *imitati Christi.* By exercising one's will in what might

be called today an example of supreme masochism, salvation and redemption may be earned for all involved. Victim and Executioner are
one and work is harmony.

[3]Jean Brun, *Héraclite*, p. 131.

[4]Charles Baudelaire, *Oeuvres complètes*, p. 1278.

[5]Edouard Schuré, *The Great Initiaites*, pp. 234-268.

[6]Serge Hutin, *Les sociétés secrètes*, p. 19.

[7]Serge Hutin, *L'Alchimie*, p. 19.

[8]See chapter Louis Lambert.

[9]Georges Poulet, *Qui était Baudelaire*, p. 38.

[10]*Oeuvres*, p. 338.

[11]*Ibid.*, p. 324-5.

[12]*Ibid.*, p. 342.

[13]Gaston Bachelard, *Le Droit de rêver*, p. 70.

[14]Charles Baudelaire, *Correspondence génerale* I, p. 6.

[15]Gaston Bachelard, *L'eau et les rêves*, p. 9.

[16]*Héraclite*, p. 126.

[17]*Oeuvres*, p. 1162.

[18]*Ibid.*, p. 880.

[19]*Ibid.*

[20]*Ibid.*, p. 881.

[21]Emile Grillot de Givry, *Illustrated Anthology of Sorcery, Magic and
Alchemy*, p. 92.

[22] Emma Hawkridge, *The Wisdom Tree*, p. 361.

[23] C. Kerényi, *The Gods of the Greeks*, p. 41.

[24] Schuré, pp. 234-68.

[25] C. G. Jung, *The Structure and Dynamics of the Psyche*, p. 456.

[26] *Oeuvres*, p. 1236.

[27] Hutin, *Les Sociétés secrètes*, p. 75.

[28] *Oeuvres*, p. 1163.

[29] *Ibid.*, p. 882.

[30] *Ibid.*, p. 883.

[31] *Ibid.*, p. 883.

[32] *Ibid.*, p. 1606.

[33] *Ibid.*, p. 1167.

[34] *Ibid.*, p. 1221.

[35] *Ibid.*, p. 1213.

[36] *Ibid.*, p. 1154.

[37] *Ibid.*, p. 1185.

[38] *Ibid.*, p. 1161.

CHAPTER 10

Victor Hugo—"What the Mouth of Darkness Says": The Dark Night of the Soul

*Blest night of wandering
In secret, where by none might I be spied...
(St. John of the Cross. "In an Obscure Night")*

Victor Hugo[1] described himself as "a dreamer who walks alone on shore, a visionary surrounded by desert."[2] His acute sense of isolation and powerlessness during his political exile (1851-1870), first on the island of Jersey and then on Guernsey, brought on a religious crisis. There is "nothing as terrible," he wrote as being ejected on an island—stark, bleak, and stormy.[3] Cut off from France, ruled by "the despot" Napoleon III, and from his own political aspirations, Hugo's affective and powerfully energetic personality, now unable to exteriorize itself, was driven inward, stimulating and expanding his visionary powers. "What the Mouth of Darkness Says" (1854) is a poetic transposition of Hugo's "dark night of the soul;" a revelation in a series of spectacular archetypal images of an entire "cosmogonic system," which, he wrote, had "been hatching within me for twenty years."[4]

During the long years Hugo spent away from his native land, he developed what might be called today the psychology of the exile. Rather than cause protracted states of depression or morbid passivity, or both, as was the case of many who suffered his fate, his despair triggered off a counterpoise; it developed within him a *mana* personality: a new spiritual orientation in which the multitude of mystical ideations to which he had been exposed throughout his life suddenly took on form and meaning. Hugo's religious crisis led to the coalescing of a mystical credo. The strength this doctrine gave him, in addition to his condition of introversion, filled him with renewed energy. He felt himself imbued with superhuman strength and experienced what psychologists term a state of inflation. He was convinced that he had the vision of a seer, the wisdom of a messiah, and the optimism of a utopist.

"What the Mouth of Darkness Says" is optimistic in essence, reflecting the romantic belief in the perfectibility of man. It delineates the phases in man's ascension (and Hugo's by projection) from the creation of the human species to his reintegration into God. Hugo stressed the value of evil and of human suffering as steps leading to man's redemption, concluding with an apocalyptic vision of the world divested of antagonism and blending harmoniously into the cosmic whole. Hugo thus saw his dream fulfilled.

"What the Mouth of Darkness Says" is included in *Contemplations,* labeled by Hugo as the *"Memoirs of a Soul."* It is just that: the disclosures of a man cut open, the outpourings on a primitive and instinctual level of spiritual notions. Hugo was not cerebral as Baudelaire; nor was his rational function as highly developed as Diderot's. Hugo *felt* his way into ideas and events. The visceral experiences always came first; then contact with the surroundings both near and distant. Once he sensed an empathetic relationship with these objects and forces, tensions grew and images cascaded forth in abrasive colors, in jagged masses, in animal and divine forms—all engraved in fluid and rhythmic cadences. His was an animated universe in which sky, sun, earth, water, and rock were charged with incandescent power, like an endless flow of electric currents. When Hugo's vision assumed apocalyptic dimensions, he became a Titan divested of identity and of personal life; he slipped into the mythical and cosmic spheres. "None of us has the honor of having a life of his own. My life is your life, your life is mine, you live what I live; destiny is one. Take, then, this mirror, and peer into it."[5]

"What the Mouth of Darkness Says" is apocalyptic literature. The belief in a higher kingdom and the hope in a better future, in the establishment of a new world that is different and frequently antipodal to the present one, has been called into being throughout history whenever terrestrial existence becomes overly oppressive. Apocalyptic works flourished, for example, when the Hebrews were taken into captivity by the Babylonians. The Book of Baruch recounts the horrendous plight of an enslaved nation and the promise of future deliverance. The Book of Daniel, replete with dreams and visions, was written at a time when the Seleucids', encouraging cruelty and suffering, dominated Palestine. The Book of Revelations, which predicted the second coming of Christ and the establishment of a Messianic kingdom, was written by an unknown author when a prisoner of Rome on the island of Patmos. In the Middle Ages people believed in the second coming of Christ during their lifetime, thus relieving them from the dread of upheavals, famines, and the plague.

Hugo's apocalyptic visions as incised in "What the Mouth of Darkness Says" were subjective manifestations of his excoriating confrontation with his existential situation and with his self. The Greek word *apokalupsis* means "uncovering," and Hugo's poem is a veritable *katabasis eis antron*. The shearing-off of superficial layers, which he had unconsciously borne during his years in France as the leader of the Romantic group and as one of the successful writers in contrast to so many failures, led him to discover the *homo duplex* living within him. There were two Hugos: the thinker and the seer. The thinker represented the man who conformed to society and functioned in it, adapting when need be to exigencies of all kinds. The seer, or visionary, may be considered that aspect of Hugo which saw beyond the world of appearances into the very mystery of creation, into the heart of the unknown—those sacred spheres that led him "right on the edge of the infinite." When tragedy struck Hugo, as it had on more than one occasion (with the untimely death of his daughter Leopoldine in 1843, with his exile from France), the seer in him took precedence. The pain engulfing his heart forced a step inward—into the "universal abyss." There he tapped the absolute, the inaccessible, the nontemporal domain, thus bringing him into contact with the pleromatic realm and visionary power.

Since it is via the image that Hugo expressed the breadth and scope of his feelings and ideations, the meanings of "Mouth" and "Shadow" (Darkness)[6] in the poem's title must be scrutinized. These visualizations set the tone of a drama that takes place on the island of Jersey under a bleak sky, a turbulent ocean, and a black sun. Assimilated subjectively, these life-forces are all animated: they breathe, possess a soul, and become, during the course of the poem, extensions of the poet himself.

The *mouth,* an orifice that both takes in and expels food, is also the source of vocal utterances. It is an organ that includes visceral and spiritual factors. The Egyptians pictured the mouth with a solar disk inside; also as reminiscent of the eye and the iris. In the Old Testament the mouth, an organ of the mind and body, is associated with speech and fire (its roundness with the sun), the two characteristics that distinguish man from animal. The Zohar looks upon the mouth (or the word) as one of the

most important factors in the creative process. In the Gospel
of St. John we read: "In the beginning was the Word, and the
Word was with God, and the Word was God" (1:1). The very
notion of language itself has been considered by the mystics as
an example of God's thought, as the voice that transforms the
inaudible or undifferentiated into the understandable.[7]

The mouth in Hugo's poem symbolizes that divine force
which flows through the universe and motivates the transformatory process: the amorphous thought-feeling as it enters into the
created world. Such alteration of content occurs when feeling
becomes articulate, when instinct takes on value, and the will becomes conceptualized. As the spokesman in the poem, the
mouth is an expression of the thinking or rational faculty (or
solar force), the organ which enables the poet (Hugo) to evaluate
his subjective and objective situation and discern in abstract
terms what he experiences in such a tremulous manner.

Because the mouth is an opening, a maw, it may be considered an area leading to the irrational domain. Instincts, in
the form of words, may erupt from the mouth at any moment,
disrupting the solar or cerebral ideations enunciated. The onslaught of violent images may be ejected unexpectedly, uproot-
ing values and altering shapes, textures, and colors. The mouth
is that sacred or magic area from which either the Dionysian or
the Apollonian side of man may become heard.

The *shadow* in Hugo's poem reveals the secrets of the universe to the poet. As the spokesman of God, he is the unidimen-
sional translator of the amorphous into the concrete message.
Comparable to the Holy Ghost or to the Egyptian Kamu-tef,
the forces which injected semen into Mary and into Isis, he
brings gnosis to the poet. As a mediumistic figure, the shadow is
sacred since he is forever in touch with divinity. He may therefore be likened to a shaman who is also in touch with spirits and
capable of revealing messages through dreams or other spiritual
devices.[8] According to theosophist doctrine the shadow figure
represents the vital energy (psychic or nervous) that permeates
nature and flows through the envelope of flesh in which man's
spirit is imprisoned. Such a feat is possible, according to metaphysicians, because spirits are made of subtle matter and are
therefore not limited by the laws of material beings.

In terms of Hugo's personal psychology the shadow was a seer aspect of the poet; that transcendental force in him which was capable of experiencing the depths of existence in relation to the present, past, and future. Hugo's belief in the power of his shadow was not merely on an unconscious level; it became a living reality for him. During his stay on Jersey he received the visit (in September 1853) of the once beautiful and still charming Delphine de Girardin who was, at this time, dying of cancer. She proved to him that tables could move and talk, and she converted him to spiritism. But Hugo was not alone in his belief. He had illustrious predecessors: Abraham, Saul, Peter, Christ, St. John of the Cross, St. Theresa of Avila, St. Francis of Assisi—all of whom had indulged in augury, levitation, apparitions, exorcism, ecstasy and experienced the stigmata.[9] There were, Hugo believed, arcane messages in the universe for those able to receive them. Almost every night Hugo communicated with such notables as Euripides, Moses, Christ, Dante, Shakespeare, gaining from them extraordinary insights, which he felt in turn obliged to reveal to mankind.[10]

It is via the shadow (that primitive and transcendental force within Hugo) that he experienced the memory of past events and nature's most archaic aspects as volatile entities capable of expressing what is eternal in the cosmos. In that the shadow is a projection of Hugo, we may consider "What the Mouth of Darkness Says" as a kind of dialogue between Hugo the poet and the universe at large—between man and God.

1. *God in the Manifest Universe*

The poem opens on a decor detailed in firm and massive brushstrokes. The shadow (darkness), as Hugo's double or as a Holy Ghost figure, is "somber" and "tranquil." He extends his hand and takes the poet by the hair, and in so doing his hand grows larger and thus seemingly more powerful. He guides the poet to the top of the "dolmen which dominates" that particular section of the island of Jersey. The atmosphere is somber, austere, and reminiscent in its starkness and isolation of the remote areas where oracular pronouncements were made in antiquity: high rocks or long crags beside stormy oceans. Here the Delphic oracle or magicians, such as Merlin, evoked good and evil spirits. Excitement is generated by the loneliness of the area and its proximity to wild seas, empty heavens, and the hardness and cutting edges of rocks. Such an environment aroused and then liberated a force within Hugo that had been repressed prior to his stay in Jersey. Spinoza had written in the fifth part of his *Ethics* that once a feeling of emotion has been articulated or conceptualized, the energy implicit in the word or image slackens and disappears.[11] Such was the dynamism implicit in the first section of "What the Mouth of Darkness Says": emotion first; then its release in the image-word.

The image of the *dolmen* (a large stone the Celts and Druids used for religious purposes) stands out so massively on the horizon that it sets the emotional tone for the entire poem: the Shadow, the Poet, the universal abyss, the cape. Stones in general and dolmens in particular symbolize the presence of some divine force or emanation. From earliest times stones have been considered sacred, for instance, the Greek *omphalos,* the Hebrew *beth-el* (House of God). In Genesis we read: "And this stone, which I have set for a pillar, shall be God's house" (28:22). Stones are durable as opposed to the wandering or ephemeral nature of thoughts and words or even the vegetal world, which is subject to decay. The shadow, as a bridge between mortal and divine spheres, takes the poet to the top of the rock and from this height will impart his secrets to him.

The stone may be equated with God's all-seeing eye at this juncture in Hugo's poem. In Zechariah we read:

> For behold the stone that I have laid before Joshua; upon one stone shall be seven eyes: behold, I will engrave the graving thereof, saith the Lord of hosts (3:9).

For Hugo the stone represented the force that penetrates deep into the fabric of being and cuts through the world of matter, experiencing the very heart of mystery. Like the sun, it is the source of light and intelligence, the element which endows the poet with superhuman vision, the solid material which gives him the necessary strength to draw upon. The stone-eye absorbs the landscape and takes in its nutritive element; thus it excites and titillates while it increases awareness. The stone-eye upon which the poet now stands enables him with the aid of the shadow,[12] to communicate with the world beyond.

The fact that the shadow grips the poet's hair is significant. Hair, frequently associated with strength, represents power, as in the Samson legend. Therefore the poet's virile spirit will be contacted. His head, the part that has been likened to man's divine half ever since Platonic times, will be the focal point of the poem. The shadow's hand, gripping the poet's hair, denotes activity. Hands relate to things of this world; they grasp and hold. They are manifestations of inner feelings and unconscious thoughts. Hands, like the voice and facial expressions, are exteriorizations of a psychic condition. They also are used in connection with God: in the Hebrew religion amulets of five fingers stand for God's blessing; in the Islamic religion the hand of Fatima accords good luck; in Roman tradition the *manus* symbolizes authority: and in Catholic rituals, the Pope or priest blesses with his hand. Consequently, the shadow, an already spiritual figure, becomes an active force in the poet's development and his creative process.

The atmosphere in the opening lines—the ocean, the dolmen, the mouth, the shadow, the hand, the hair—is one of frenzied expectation. Everything seems ready to come to life under Hugo's baton. The universe pulsates, breathes, sees, listens. Secrets invested in the lowliest to the highest forms are soon revealed.

> Everything speaks: the air which passes and the Halcyon which glides,
> The blade of grass, the flower, the seed, the element...
> The storm, the rolling torrent of black loam,
> The rock in the waves, the animal in the mouths...

The world is a giant arena, an edifice erected to magic and mysticism. Like primitive man, Hugo saw the universe animistically in a virtual *participation mystique*. The objects about him, upon which he projected, were transformed into a group of hierophants, empowered with divine force. Unlike the more cerebral and controlled poets (Gautier, Nerval, Baudelaire), Hugo experienced the world about him viscerally. Thereby he created a series of empathetic currents and crosscurrents and increased the dimension of his rapport with objects and nature. The tension of the heaving ocean, for example, or of the sky stretching infinitely before him, or of the rock etched in the distance, created a responding note in the poet's very being. The interplay of energy between himself and the objects he described released repressed fears and pain, relaxed him, and increased the depth and contentment of communion. To some poets an infinite universe of ocean and sky would usher in a sense of fear and terror, rootlessness and loss. With Hugo the opposite was true. It imbued him with additional power and made him conscious of his ability to confront these elements—either antagonistically or in harmony with them.

2. *The Creation*

Hugo's psychology of the exile becomes most apparent in his adumbration of the Creation myth. He saw God's Creation as the result of a kind of "retreat" of God into Himself rather than an exteriorization of Himself. This concept, which resembles the views of the Lurianic Kabbalists, themselves the product of expulsion in fifteenth-century Spain, has been described as "the deepest symbol of Exile possible."[13] As pariahs divested of security, they sought to create a new beginning. Unable to express themselves outwardly, they turned inward to experience redemption and a sense of fulfillment. The Godhead's "retreat" in His creative effort is considered a projection of the psychological state of the exiles of that period.

Prior to Isaac Luria (1534-1572) the universe was thought to have been created by projection of God outside of Himself: "His creative power out of His own Self into space." The Creation was considered a step downward from perfection. Since God was absolute and perfect, he had to blend something imperfect with Himself in order to bring forth the manifest world. Had he not brought in this extra element (matter), the Creation would have been indistinguishable from Him. Lurianic Kabbalism altered this view. The doctrine of Creation known as *Tsimtsum*, was due to God's voluntary "contraction" or "retreat" into Himself. By "abandoning a region within Himself, a kind of mystical primordial space," he was able to "return to it in the act of creation and revelation." Once God had withdrawn into Himself, the possibility of existence outside of the divine (that of evil) became possible.

The creation of light was invested in Adam Kadmon (primordial man). But the intensity of the light that flowed through him was so great that the vessel shattered. The "breaking of the vessel" (*shivirat ha-kelim*) scattered the sparks throughout the lower and material, or demonic, spheres, referred to at times as "the depth of the great abyss." Redemption means the healing of the schism between the created and the uncreated world—the restoration of the fallen sparks (Tikkun), or souls, into God. Therefore man must take it upon himself to separate light from darkness (spirit from matter) during his present lifetime or in another incarnation.[14]

Hugo, like the Lurianic Kabbalists, created a withdrawal into himself—introversion due to feelings of intense solitude. It is from this inner domain that he set his own cosmic (or creative) process into motion; that he discovered the central point which mystics label "the point of creation"—the progressive manifestation of his own essence. Without his exile and the magnitude of his own suffering, "What the Mouth of Darkness Says," one of Hugo's most extraordinary poems, might never have been written.

Hugo's concept of the biblical Fall is also comparable to the Kabbalistic dictum, for it is only after a fall into matter that consciousness or awareness comes into being and the possibility of redemption becomes a reality. Before Adam and Eve ate of the apple, they lived in a paradisiac state, unaware of conflict, of night and day, of life and death. They disobeyed God's orders after the serpent had assured them they would not die as God had threatened. (In fact, since they had never experienced death, they had no notion of its meaning.)

> For God doth know that in the day ye eat thereof, then your eyes shall be opened, and ye shall be as gods, knowing good and evil (Genesis 3:5)

Adam and Eve were promised gnosis. They could then be, they thought, on a par with God. The resultant Fall made them conscious of the fact that they were no longer living in an "unconscious" or Edenic state, but rather were cast out into the world of antagonisms—into life. Burdened with feelings of suffering and joy, notions of identity, they would now be compelled to struggle and fight for survival. They were given the burden of choice, the responsibility of their acts, and the power to carve out their own destinies.

Hugo, it might be said, went through a similar fall. Before his exile he had known fame and adulation in France, which was, for all intents and purposes, his Garden of Eden. His departure from his native land may be equated with Adam's and Eve's fall into matter. Rather than remaining in servitude in France (either in an unconscious paradisiac state or consciously by obeying the oppressive laws promulgated by Napoleon III), Hugo chose the hero's path—departure and difficulty. It was in Jersey that he became acutely aware of his true mission in life and that he experienced his messianic role as a vital force. The feelings of alienation and solitude, which had incized themselves so deeply within his psyche, were no longer intellectual concepts but bruising currents that compelled him to assess his situation and look within for the strength necessary to further his creative life. During his exile Hugo's poetic writings reached their greatest depth and philosophical dimension. "What the Mouth of Darkness Says" is an expression of his earthly and spiritual battles and the choices he would be compelled to make. And the shadow warned him of his arduous task: "Prepare yourself, mournful brow, for funereal sweats."

3. *The Chain of Beings and the Concepts of Progress*

Hugo was an optimist by nature. His cosmological system reflects his positive views: just as there is a hierarchy in nature, so there is one in the social sphere.

After the Creation took place, the single World-Soul became double; the divine sparks blended with matter; Adam and Eve were cast out of paradise and conflict took root. Evil and good were set in opposition to each other and a ranking of natural phenomena came into being: angels, spiritual essences, "imponderable" creatures were born—from the highest to the lowest of forms. The universe, then, was replete with masses of species ascending and descending the ladder of Creation.

Man differs from the rest of nature, Hugo posited, because he alone is endowed with the mental ability to rise to a more beautiful existence with each incarnation. The tree, the vegetable, the flower, and the pebble can only long to become reimmersed in totality or divinity. Because innate matter has no imagination, it is unconscious of its action. It experiences flux, it strives toward light and awareness, but it has no capacity to direct its destiny.

Life in Hugo's romantically optimistic view is a "sublime ascension;" it is "slow" and is accomplished "by degrees"—from the realm of mystery, terror, and perdition to the domain of divinity—but it is a certainty. To situate and root his vertical vision Hugo refers to a ladder throughout the poem. When on the top, he rises beyond the world of matter and sees into infinite distances in his "invincible" and "admirable" march to the divine realm. When at the bottom, with inanimate life, he experiences imprisonment, solitude, and pain in a world without God.

The ladder images inject a quality of spasmodic motility; the images qualifying the objects and people enumerated in their ascent and descent appear and disappear in quick succession. The tableau, therefore, ranges from heights (stars, sun, angel, sky, summit, azure) to depths (abyss, precipice, void). The greater the activity, the more violent the forms. Hugo's visual affectivity may be compared to Herbert Read's description of Blake's "Illustrations of the Bible"; they have "a magnificence and boldness in their design, a wild energy in their invention, a bare force of color."[15]

Because of the perpetual motility in Hugo's imagery, one may label it *action verse:* brutal frenzy is forever injected into lines such as "The Hydra Universe twists its star-scaled body," thus encompassing spacial immensities and multiplicity of flaming lights. What John Ruskin wrote concerning Joseph Turner's painting is also applicable to Hugo's frenzied strokes: "In a wildly magnificent enthusiasm, he rushes through the ethereal dominions of the world of his own mind—a place inhabited by the *spirit of things.*"[16] Hugo seems to be intent upon hurling himself into the heavens, which at first are seen as comforting and understanding forces, but which moments later pour down their wrath in bolts of lightning, blinding, cleaving, and maiming in their trajectory. Emotions are also expressed in a variety of shifting color tones and spacial configurations: exacerbation, irritation, anger, and love with black, red, yellow, cinder; fear and isolation in images delineating vast expanses: void, plenitude, the infinite.

Hugo's optimistic belief in the ascending stages in cosmic development—from the pebble to divinity—is a natural outcome of Judeo-Christian metaphysical concepts. It is antithetical, however, to the Greek idea of the cosmic plan. Heraclitus, Pythagoras, Plato, and Aristotle believed that situations on earth occur and reoccur in cyclical manner; that the Trojan War was fought and would again be fought; that Socrates died and would again die. These philosophers spoke of events in terms of cycles or *aeons* and not of eschatological concepts. The notion of the eternal return is implicit in their cosmological structure. If change does occur, it represents a fall from a relatively ideal primitive state and is tantamount to a degeneration rather than to progress. Political states do not improve. On the contrary, they deteriorate, they become corrupt. In a hierarchized vision of the universe such as the Greeks conceived of it everything in the manifest world is an inferior replica of the perfection that exists in the superior sphere.

Hugo's concept of progress, then, stems from Judeo-Christian tradition and the birth of eschatological consciousness (discussed in chapter 8). For the Christian the Creation was a unilateral unfolding. It had a beginning and an end, that is, a progression toward a paradisiac future and the establishment of the new Jerusalem as promised in Revelation. The birth of Christ was a unique event. He died once. In The Epistle of Paul to the Hebrews we read:

> So Christ was once offered to bear the sins of many; and unto them that look for him shall he appear the second time without sin unto salvation (9:28).

For the Christian time is irreversible. Time progresses continuously toward a goal that gives it its reality and significance. The Christian world, in direct opposition to the Greek view, exists within time and must have an end. Its beginning takes root in the Creation and its end in the apocalyptic visions of the Last Judgment and Redemption. The periods between the Creation, the Fall, and the Last Judgment occur only once, and are neither eternal nor infinite. For the Christian the past is related to the future and emerges directly from it. The Greeks, on the contrary, believed in astral fatality and in the "hierarchical superiority and circular domination of heavenly bodies."[17]

The Judeo-Christian concept of progress (as stated previously), also embraces the notions of post-Cartesian thinkers: for instance, Condillac believed in the progress of man from the lowliest manifestation to the highest; Leibniz conceived of the monad as alive in a variety of stages of development, from the infinitesimal inanimate form to the perfect monad—God, the Infinite. Reason was to help man extend his field of vision; mathematics and science were to conquer the world. Man was perfectible.

Also influential in the formation of Hugo's ideas concerning social and human progress was the age-old concept of utopia as adumbrated by St. Augustine in City of God, Francis Bacon in *New Atlantis* and François Rabelais in *Gargantua and Pantagruel;* and as developed by Jean-Jacques Rousseau in his myth of the noble savage, an innately good fellow because he followed the natural order of things.[18] The nineteenth century saw the growth of visionary socialism and the establishment of "perfect" agricultural communities, ideas of which Hugo was a partisan. Charles Fourier stated in his *Theory of Four Movements* (1808) and *Treatise on Domestic Agricultural Association* (1822) that if man channeled his natural passions, harmony and progress would result. He suggested dispensing with government and believed that the individual should be morally responsible for his acts.[19] Other utopists also made their impact on Hugo: Louis Blanc, considered the father of state socialism, and Robert Owen, who asserted that man's character was modeled by his environment and could become a more positive force in a society based on cooperation. More important in influencing Hugo was Saint-Simon's moral-religious cult. In *New Christianism* (1825), Saint-Simon state his belief in the brotherhood of man and contended that industrial and scientific leaders should guide society toward a better social order. He advocated socialist views, a federation of the nations of Europe, the abolition of hereditary rights, and disarmament. While in exile, Hugo too had visions of a society based on harmony and mutual appreciation of each other's efforts and beliefs. He looked forward to the day when persecution and pain would no longer be a reality; when "the United States of Europe, Peoples-Brothers" would come into being; when "liberty and fraternity" would become meaningful; when "today's lugubrious night" would vanish."[20]

Hugo's views of progress were subjective and humanistic,

the result of an affective rather than a cerebral approach to life.
He had a big heart and was capable of pity and of emotional outbursts at the sight of a hungry child, a cast-off girl, and of pover-
ty-and-disease-stricken families. In his poem "Oceano Nox,"
in *Rays and Shadows* (1840), he described the widows and
children of fishermen who were left destitute and despairing.
One of his most extraordinary outcries against social injustice
is to be found in "Encounter" where he lashes out at the rich
always taking advantage of the poor, adding to their already outrageous human condition. However, Hugo looked forward to
harmony in the existential domain with the betterment of man's
social condition in time.

4. *Evil as a Positive Force*

How did evil come into existence? How did suffering?
pain? Why are some people punished and others not? Why are
innocent children maimed and killed?

> And first of all what is justice?
> Who renders it? who makes it? where? when? at what time?
> Who is weighted with fault? and who is to be chastised?

The notion of evil (discussed in the chapter on Descartes)
has preoccupied man since earliest times. The Egyptians looked
upon this force as active in the existential world. They personified it in the god Set, Osiris' brother. The Greeks did likewise,
and called him Typhon. The Muhammedans named him Iblis.
The Hebrews and Christians labeled him Satan. According to
St. Augustine, evil stemmed from a *privatio boni* and possessed
no substance as such. The Gnostics asserted that the Demiurge
was the creator of evil, and earthly existence necessitated a constant struggle to wipe out such an element. The Illuminists
suggested that certain disciplines and ascetic practices would
diminish the power of evil, which would disappear entirely once
man had become reintegrated into divinity. The Kabbalistic
concept of Tikkun (the gathering of the light scattered throughout the cosmos after the breaking of the vessel and the emergence of evil as an element in life) places the burden of rising
to divinity for the most part on man. Man thus aids in the transformation process. The Kabbalists, and mystics in general,
believed that man must actively bring about his redemption;

that evil is an obstacle placed in man's path so that he may, if he wishes, overcome it, thus strengthening his will by dint of effort.   Man, unlike inert matter, has the burden of choice. If he perpetrates evil, he becomes conscious of his act. He then combats such tendencies within him and society. It is in the power expended by his will that he earns expiation and purification, thus ascending in the hierarchy of being. He is, to a certain extent, the molder of his destiny. Such a view is diametrically opposed to Buddhist doctrine and to its Occidental counterpart in the philosophy of Schopenhauer. Evil, suggested Schopenhauer and the Buddhists, is the result of man's desire. It is desire that compels him to act, that drives him to disappointment and satisfaction, therefore to perpetual suffering. Man must suppress his will by exercising his reason in order to annihilate desire and thus lessen pain.

Like the Kabbalists and mystics, Hugo believed in overt activity of man to better his lot on earth. He further posited, as they had, that without evil man would be unable to understand good, that antagonism and polarity are facts of life. To live in a binary world forces one to choose a way. Choice implies decision, which in turn forces responsibility upon the individual for his acts.[21] It is the power of choice that distinguishes man from animal.   The animal "leans toward the earth," it strives toward divinity, but it cannot expiate, according to Hugo, nor see.   Although the animal has the capacity to experience pain, it is not conscious of it. It knows God only in terms of light and feels an inescapable longing to merge with this force. The animal suffers from its estrangement from God but does not know why it experiences such pain. Its suffering has no merit, claims Hugo, because an animal cannot differentiate between good and evil, nor can it perpetrate evil.   It cannot commit a crime and thus cannot expiate or be redeemed.   Souls within the phenomenological world, even the pebble, seek to cross the zone of blackness to light, blindness to vision, of descent to ascent, and of imprisonment to freedom.[22] What is novel in Hugo's doctrine is his belief that inert matter (a stone) is capable of longing to return to divinity and undergoes a kind of "thoughtful mineralization process" that helps it ascend the ladder of creation.

Buddhist and Schopenhauerian thinking considered life a vale of tears; Hugo did not. Although he did go through periods of intense despair and melancholia in 1843 he wrote in *Autumn*

Leaves "Alas! to be borne into life longing to die," he did not wallow in such negativism. This kind of ennui had given birth to the *mal du siècle* as exemplified in Chateaubriand's hero René in the outpourings of Lamartine, and in the stoic resignation of de Vigny. Hugo's view of evil as an active and dynamic force to be combated on an individual and collective basis not only helped him survive his exile but also imbued him with energy and strength—the desire to become an invincible force in his country's destiny.

> Free, he knows where good ends, where evil begins;
> His actions are his judges.

In several flamboyant passages in "What the Mouth of Darkness Says" Hugo lists the cruelties perpetrated by men such as Emperor Tiberius, whose excesses terrified the world, and Sejanus, his minister, and equally vicious, who met a well-deserved horrendous death. Madmen strike pitilessly and tyrants oppress, "Horror is followed by Horror" throughout history: for instance Nimrod, Delilah, Clytemnestra, Ganelon. Such souls are punished as they descend to the abyss. Hugo's concept of descent should not be equated with the Christian notion of hell. His doctrine, an adaptation of Hindu credo, implies perpetual reincarnation into lower forms. Nor in the final analysis is the victim the one to suffer, rather the perpetrator of the crime. "It is he. The vile oppressor, the somber and mad tyrant" who will be "nailed in the shadow to the depths of matter." To rise or to descend is up to man. Strength and vision must be his guide; humanity and love must be the motivating forces of his existence.

5. *The Messianic Doctrine*

Whenever needs are great and whenever oppressive forces invade society, the demand for a Messiah emerges. Hugo considered himself just such a figure, divinely chosen to fulfill an obligation. The concept of the poet-Messiah was not Hugo's invention; it was part of Romantic doctrine. Lamartine, de Vigny, and Hugo believed the poet to be a superior being whose mission it was to become the political and spiritual leader of his people. A tragic figure during his political exile, Hugo, like a messiah, was convinced that his personal sacrifice was for the good of the French people. His image would save them from ignominous shame and they would be strengthened by his martyrdom; he would set the example for them to emulate. Hugo had chosen his destiny and was responsible for his acts.

As Messiah, Hugo received God's revelations from the shadow. Like the messiah in general, and Christ in particular, he saw himself as a martyr, a redeemer, a perpetrator of miracles, a being whose function it was to better man's earthly lot. In his poem "The Sages" (1854) he lists eighty superior beings (among them Pythagoras, Socrates, Moses, Christ, Aeschylus, Bonaparte, Dante, Shakespeare, Beethoven) who helped shape man's destiny. Their messages were cumulative and enabled each generation to come closer to the perfect state of happiness. No single person has the definitive answer, Hugo declared, he can only help solve certain aspects of specific problems, thus helping man progress slowly until eventual illumination takes hold.

At certain intervals in history, goodness takes precedence over evil; at other moments, the forces of destruction dominate. The messiah's goal is to help reestablish harmony for eventual union with God. Once goodness reigns on earth, the world of disparity will vanish. Light invades the cosmos and "Job resplendent" emerges in a world dicated by love. The banished are welcomed and blessed. What had been severed, in a final apotheosis will be unified: Christ and Belial will be accepted into God's realm.

Hugo set the character traits necessary for the messianic figure. He must be frightened by nothing, neither by the vastness of the universe nor by the pain of the human condition. Although man's agony may fill the poet-Messiah with "mute horror" and his soul may quiver at certain sights, his courage must never wane and his heart must never yield to weakness nor succumb to evil. The poet-prophet must be invincible once he has chosen his destiny. He must also be wise and perceptive, and he must know how to command attention and take the lead. "It is time that men of action should take the rear seat, and the men of ideas the front. The summit is the head. Where there is thought, there is power. It is time that the genius steps in front of the hero."[23]

Greater responsibilities increase the difficulties heaped upon the messianic figure. De Vigny demonstrated this fact in his poem "Moses." As the leader of a people who departed from a land they knew, to an unknown wilderness where anything could happen, Moses assumed the burdens of his people. Since he was superior to the masses, he could communicate with no one and lived in utter solitude. During the forty years spent in the desert, the Hebrews, with Moses at their head, struggled to rid themselves of their slave mentality. The strength given to Moses by God, in addition to his own will and ability to cope with the eventualities confronting him, made him conscious of the immense battle facing him. Consciousness therefore imposed great weight upon him. Christ, a messianic figure for Hugo, was the incarnation of light and wisdom. His sacrifice was complete. He warred with evil in the world, with darkness, and with matter.

Leaders or messianic figures are always scapegoats for the discontented, for everything that malfunctions in society. Hence, they must bear the burden of castigation and vilification as well as the antipodal ideations—admiration, devotion, and idealization. Unless blessed with wisdom and balance, to be the chosen one is to either bend under the sting of revilement or to suffer the immeasurable joys of inflation.[24]

As a messianic figure, Hugo succumbed to the state of inflation. Such an extreme is not uncommon to one living as intensely as he did and on such a primitive (instinctual) level. Inflation ensues when the ego (the center of the conscious personality) identifies with the Self (the "ordering and unifying center of the total psyche") and no separation exists between the two. The individual experiencing a state of inflation feels no disparity between himself and the world about him, no identity or separatedness from the universal flow. He cannot objectify. In such a primeval state of wholeness he has the illusion of being able to perform miracles and of arrogating to himself that which belongs to God. Such was Hugo's psychological state during his exile. He saw himself as an Olympian force chosen first to suffer, then to mediate between God and man, and finally to confront God in his very sanctuary.[25]

As God's chosen one, Hugo felt, as did other messianic figures, that love and admiration were destined for him. In Deuteronomy we read:

The Lord did not set his love upon you, nor choose you, because ye were more in number than any people; for ye were the fewest of all people: But because the Lord loved you, and because he would keep the oath which he had sworn unto your fathers, hath the Lord brought you out with a mighty hand and redeemed you out of the house of bondmen, from the hand of Pharaoh king of Egypt (7:7-8).

Love and admiration, however, are demanding of the recipient of such emotions. They imply obligation and devotion to a cause. Therefore the messianic figure must divest himself of his personal and subjective goals in order to fulfill the mission expected of him. A transformation takes place: from mortal to immortal, from follower to psychopomp. As a collective figure, he also becomes the recipient of collective anguishes and needs.[26]

In his state of inflation Hugo did not consider the needs of his wife, his children, or even of his mistresses. They were subservient to his visionary obsessions, to his metaphysics, and to his social destiny as a leader of man. Those chosen by God (or by themselves) are distinct and unique; as such they are lonely men who cannot really relate to the average person or bend to the multitude. For some the burden of being God's favorite is immensely difficult to bear. Moses shied away from the ordeal of being God's favorite: "O my Lord, send I pray thee, by the hand of him whom thou wilt sent" (Exodus 4:13). Hugo, though angered at first, then despairing at his exile (his own choice), with the passing of months became energized by the uniqueness of his situation. He tried to assimilate and evaluate the scope of what he believed to be his God-given mission. Inflated at the thought of earning greatness and immortality as a leader of mankind, he thrived in the isolated atmosphere of Jersey with its somber and rugged coast. He believed the obstacles placed before him—anguish and torment—were a test of his will and courage; and they were the very elements that enabled him to rise above the common lot and become one of the greats of humanity.

Significantly, the image of the eye, although used throughout "What the Mouth of Darkness Says," is particularly meaningful when associated with the messianic spirit. When linked to the man of vision, the eye becomes an instrument capable of expanding consciousness and of perceiving the meaning of power of divine intelligence that radiates about the universe and permeates the poet, forcing him into activity—into clarity. "And everything is the eye from which this extraordinary look emanates." Every facet of the universe is under perpetual observation, consumed by a cosmic eye that taunts, follows, haunts, embraces, loves, chatises, animates, and dulls. It is the eye of God—the eye of Hugo, the messiah or madman, wandering about bewildered, sorrowful, and finally ecstatic. Like a giant lung that takes in the entire universe as it inhales, and rejects it as it exhales, the poet's eye gives birth to visualizations of all types: terrifying dreams, monstrous forms, living phantoms, impalpable angels, erotic and spiritual sensations. The poetic eye floats, dilates, threatens, questions, and angers. It sees into the secrets forbidden to man; it has, like Prometheus, stolen fire. Never in repose, it is imbued with an obsessive desire to encompass the world: to feed on it, experience it in all of its infinite manifestations. Hugo seems at the very edge of insantiy. The irrational now holds dominion.

Because Hugo's poetic eye had become so powerful, his verses are considered eidetic, as are the works of Shelley, Coleridge, Hogarth, and Blake.[27] So vivid, so acute, so bold was his visual memory and his power to recreate the concrete forms, harmonies, proportions, textures, and gradations of color tones represented in the poem, they were almost duplicates of the original image. Hugo had always experienced great sensitivity in the optic sensorial nerves. Coupled with his intuitive nature and his hyperactive imagination, he came to see and feel beyond the world of appearances, dependent upon contingency and inconstancy, right into the heart of the ordered world. In so doing he injected feelings into the objects upon which he projected, endowing them with conceptual values and emotions. When enumerating, for example, such cruel men as Octavius and Attila or when describing the worms eating away at Cleopatra's cadaver, he drove into these images his immense anger, hatred, bitterness, and disgust. Tactile sensations swell and grow from Hugo's storehouse of images. Whether he depicted animals (bear, tiger, wolf, owl, raven) or inanimate objects (stone, thistle, thorn, mandragora) or recesses in the earth (caves, abysses, voids), visceral reactions are transformed into concepts.

As revealed in "What the Mouth of Darkness Says," Hugo believed that human life is a phase in an existence that will end, after many incarnations, in a final reintegration of the manifest world into God. Suffering and evil are part of the human experience. Because they are forces to be surmounted, thus paving the way for salvation and progress, they are strengthening agents and positive entities. The turmoil and despair rampant in earthly life has to be alleviated as much as possible by dint of effort on the part of individuals and collective figures such as the superior men (geniuses or sages), who appear in almost every generation. They are divinely inspired or chosen to point the way so that the rest of humanity may follow.

Hugo, along with other utopists and mystics, envisaged an ideal realm—a type of paradise—where disparity would no longer exist and love would be the motivating force. Such a uroboric domain, however, is of necessity incompatible with life on earth; it might be said that Hugo indulged in his own brand of escapism. His idealism and his faith in progress, as well as his faith in the reign of happiness on earth, seemed, as the century rolled on and the magnitude of human suffering increased rather than decreased with the growth of the industrial society and the progressively more devastating wars, like a cry from the wilderness— one which would soon fade into oblivion. Existential existence requires binary opposition and choice. There are times during a life—and Hugo was experiencing this interlude—when the paradisial sense of repose becomes necessary for survival. Hugo longed for this moment when he wrote "What the Mouth of Darkness Says." It was his *dream*!

NOTES

[1]Victor Hugo was born in Besançon on February 26, 1802, the youngest of three brothers. His father, Joseph, was in the Imperial Army. His mother, Sophie Trébuchet, was a forceful and independent woman. Hugo's childhood was spent in Corsica, Italy, Spain, and France. In 1814 he settled down in a boarding school in the suburbs of Paris and there discovered his bent for literature. Two years later he wrote in one of his school notebooks: "I want to be Chateaubriand or nothing." A literary career of magnitude began with *"Odes and Divers Poems"* (1822), *Han d'Islande* (1823), *The Orientals* (1829), *Notre Dame de Paris* (1831), *Hernani* (1831), *Ruys Blas* (1838), to mention but a few. On February 25, 1848, after the Revolution of that year and the abdication of Louis-Philippe, Hugo was named mayor of the eighth district of Paris. On June 5 he was elected deputy from Paris to the Constituent Assembly and by 1849 was deputy to the Legislative Assembly. Two years later, on July 17, he addressed the Assembly and denounced the Prince-President—the future Napoleon III. Events followed in quick succession. On December 2, 1851, Hugo became a member of the Resistance Committee, set up to take steps to prevent what was foreseen as a coup d'état led by Louis Bonaparte. The future Napoleon III was declared *hors la loi*. He won the day, however, and expelled Hugo along with seventy-two of the people's representatives from France. Hugo left Paris for Brussels, on December 11, disguised as a worker. Then, on August 5, 1852 Hugo took up residence on the island of Jersey in a cottage called Marine-Terrace. When expelled from Jersey in 1855, after writing a "protest" against the expulsion of certain French exiles from England derogatory to the queen, he and his family moved to Guernsey where they remained at Hauteville-House. On August 18, 1859, Hugo rejected Napoleon III's amnesty. "When liberty will return," he declared, "I will return." His volume *Chastisements* (1853), a collection of poems he wrote during his exile, earned him a formidable success in France. The intensity of his hatred for "Napoleon le Petit" was expressed in violent terms—as opposed to his passion and admiration for Napoleon I, "le Grand." Hugo returned to Paris in triumph on September 5, 1870. Napoleon III had capitulated to Bismarck; the

French Republic had been declared. By February 9, 1871, Hugo was
elected deputy from Paris to the National Assembly. He left France
again during the Commune and went to Belgium, then on to Luxem-
bourg. In 1873 he returned to Paris where he remained active, idealistic,
and a great humanitarian until the end of his life on May 22, 1885.

Hugo had become so beloved a figure that his funeral, on June 1,
was declared a national ceremony. His body was placed in the hearse of
the poor and driven from the Arch of Triumph to the Panthéon. Nearly
all of France paid their respects to him.

[2]Victor Hugo, *Actes et paroles* II, p. 6.

[3]*Ibid.*

[4]Victor Hugo, *Correspondance* II, p. 205.

[5]Victor Hugo, *Oeuvres poétiques* II, p. 482.

[6]The literal translation of the title "Ombre" is "Shadow" although I took
the liberty of translating it "Darkness". Hugo, a constant reader of
Virgil, remembered the Latin *umbra* (*Aeneid*, VI) which designates full
darkness.

[7]Gershom Scholem, *Major Trends in Jewish Mysticism*, p. 216.

In the Kabbalah, the Sefiroth (the ten spheres of divine manifestation) is
defined as the names which "He gave to Himself."

[8]Mircea Eliade, *Shamanism*, p. 103.

[9]Yvonne Castellan, *La Métapsychique*, p. 10.

[10]Maurice Levaillant, *La Crise mystique de Victor Hugo*, p. 100.

[11]*Scholem*, p. 260.

[12]Le Spectre who utters the revelation may be translated as The Ghost.
Hugo thought he received many a visitation from ghosts, while at Jersey.

[13]*Ibid.*, pp. 260-267.

[14]*Ibid.*

[15]Herbert Read, *The Meaning of Art,* p. 173.

[16]*Ibid.,* p. 174.

[17]Henri-Charles Puech, "Gnosis and Time," *Eranos Yearbooks* III, pp. 40-51.

[18]The wise Diderot was perceptive enough to see the dangers involved in an oversimplification of complex situations and a flagrant overevaluation of natural man.

[19]The best-known community based on Fourier's ideology was Brook Farm (1841-1846) in Roxbury, Mass. Such well-known writers and philosophers as W. H. Channing, N. Hawthorne, and M. Fuller became members. Emerson was one of the few who looked upon this venture with skepticism.

[20]Denis Saurat, *La Religion ésotérique de Victor Hugo,* p. 148.

[21]Victor Hugo, *William Shakespeare,* p. 328.

[22]Charles Renouvier, *Victor Hugo le Philosophe,* p. 49.

[23]*Ibid.,* pp. 50-65.

See Hugo's poem "Ibo."

[24]Rivkah S. Kluger, *Psyche and Bible,* pp. 13, 30.

[25]Edward Edinger, *Ego and Archetype,* pp. 12-36.

[26]Kluger, pp. 13-33.

[27]Herbert Read, *Education through Art,* p. 43.

For further reference see:

Jacques Bousquet, *Les Thèmes du Rêve dans la littérature romantique* (Paris: Didier, 1964).

Henri Peyre, *Victor Hugo* (Paris: Presses Universitaires de France, 1972).

CHAPTER 11

*Joris-Karl Huysmans—Down There: Satanism
and The Male Psyche—The Black Mass and
The Female Principle*

*Everything, yea the whole world is full of Satan
and his angels, the streets and the market-place
and the baths and the stables no man is without
his demon.*

(*Tertullian*, De Anima)

The image—not the dream—is the most arresting quality of Joris-Karl Huysmans'[1] novel *Down There* (1891). Excoriating and ugly masses, these images delineate for the most part the forces of evil as expressed in the masculine phenomenon of Satanism and in its feminine counterpart, the Black Mass.

The plot of *Down There* is intriguing. Durtal, the protagonist, is searching for a style that would conciliate the Naturalist's precision of detail and emphasis on documentation and his own need for a mystical experience. Durtal has seen Matthias Grünewald's (c. 1480-1528) painting "The Crucifixion" in the Cassel museum and knows instantaneously that he has found the formulas that would answer his aesthetic and spiritual needs. In Paris he decides to write a biography of Gilles de Rais, a man he considers "saturated with mysticism." A companion in arms of Joan of Arc, Gilles later became one of the greatest Satanists of all time. Durtal's forays into the medieval era, while writing Gilles' biography, intrude into the present when he encounters a whole network of contemporary Satanists. Meanwhile he has received a series of anonymous love letters. These excite his curiosity and arouse him sexually—in the manner of a succubus. When he discovers the identity of the woman, Mme. Chantelouve, the wife of a friend, they have relations and both are disappointed. They realize that illusion is greater than realization. To dispel his torpor, Mme. Chantelouve takes him to a Black Mass, herself an adept of this kind of erotic-mystical experience. Durtal is traumatized by the events he witnesses. He concludes that despite the pride nineteenth-century man takes in what he regards as "progress," little evolution has really been accomplished in terms of man's relationship with himself, with others, with the supernatural, and with Christ.

Huysmans had always been preoccupied with the question

of evil. He equated women with evil. Early in his life he had been hurt by his mother and as a result had grown to distrust women, whose power over him he feared. He felt evil to be on the march in his era, which he considered ugly, sordid, mediocre, and materialistic. Huysmans had lost faith in the credo of Naturalism and Positivism and their scientific attitudes toward life. Isolated from the security of the prevailing values, unable to find an answer to his own inner chaos, he seemed set adrift, dissociated from his age and from individuals. What had once seemed right was no longer so. What had previously been looked upon as good, now seemed evil. A solitary, pessimistic individual, Huysmans experienced life in a negative manner.

His absorption in the notion of evil, as well as of cruelty and suffering, is evident in his approach to the pictorial domain that plays a significant role in *Down There*. Huysmans was haunted and mesmerized by the macabre and monstrous beings in the paintings of Odilon Redon; and Félicien Rop's satanic etchings attracted him because they depicted "the supernatural of perversity."[2] The impact of Grünewald's "The Crucifixion" Huysmans felt numinously. Durtal, the hero of *Down There*, experienced his reaction to the Isenheim altarpiece as follows:

> He shuddered in his armchair and closed his eyes as if in pain. With extraordinary lucidity he revisualized the picture, and the cry of admiration wrung from him when he had entered the little room of the Cassel museum was reechoing in his mind as here, in his study...[3]

Huysmans virtually entered Grünewald's emotions as represented in "The Crucifixion": pain, suffering, ecstasy, anger, evil, mortification, and love—the polarities of the life experience. Color, form (distortions), and composition became instruments of emotion enabling Huysmans to live out man's potential for evil as well as his need for sacrifice through projection into Christ's crucifixion. It is no wonder that Christ is described viscerally in cruel and sanguinary terms.

> Dislocated, almost ripped out of their sockets, the arms of the Christ seemed tramelled by the knotty cords of the straining muscles. The laboured tendons of the armpits seemed ready to snap. The fingers, wide apart, were contorted in an arrested gesture in which were supplication and reproach but also

benediction.   The trembling thighs were greasy with sweat.
The ribs were like staves, or like the bars of a cage, the flesh
swollen, blue, mottled with flea-bites, specked as with pin-
pricks by spines broken off from the rods of the scourging and
now festering beneath the skin where they had penetrated.[4]

In Grünewald's "Crucifixion," Huysmans nailed down his
views concerning man's propensity for evil (murder-cruelty-
sadism) and for sacrifice (mortification-masochism), two sides
of the same coin. He unified in a single image the underlying
themes of *Down There:* Satanism, a product of the male psyche,
and the Black Mass, a manifestation of the female unconscious.

1. *Satanism and the Male Psyche*

What is the etiology of Satanism?   From what concept
does this destructive ritual stem?   Why did Huysmans embody
this concept in the person of Gilles de Rais?

The concept of Satan, or the Devil, is archetypal. It is,
therefore, an image or a force that stems from the collective unconscious. On a human level Satanic principles are equated with
evil.   Good and evil are opposite poles of a moral judgment.
Such binary opposition exists only in the world of manifestation.   Religions throughout history have varied in their attitudes
toward these two finite concepts.   In that God is infinite and
immanent (the All) in Judaism, He incorporates both polarities
within Him.   In Exodus (34:5-7) we are made privy to His thirteen attributes and their opposite extremes: love and hate, kindness and punishment, etc.   The Christian, however, conceives
of Christ as all good (all light, all spirit); a doctrine that rejects
the notion of evil as implicit in the Godhead.

In early Judaism, evil (or anything connected with this
cosmic power, such as demonic spirits, which were creatures
of the Lord and thus part of Him) was under the control of
divinity.   In Deuteronomy we read: "thou mightest know that
the Lord he is God; there is none else beside him" (4:35). Under
the influence of the Persian and Hellenistic ideations, the concept of evil became concretized in Satan, Belial, and Beelzebub.
Satan, as the son of God, was the "adversary" (in the Hebrew
meaning), the "accuser," the one to inject feelings of suspicion

into Job and thus instrumental in his suffering. In this regard Satan was both finite and infinite: finite in his malevolent attitude toward Job, and infinite as a negative principle in God Himself. The confrontation that took place among the three forces involved—Job, Satan, and Yahweh—may be conceived as a concretization of antagonistic principles within the God-head itself. Psychologically, it is an archetype in projection of the human psyche.[5] In Jeremiah we are again told that evil cohabits with the principle of good in Yahweh.

> Then the Lord said unto me, Out of the north an evil shall break forth upon all the inhabitants of the land (1:14).

In Zechariah, Satan has evolved. He has become more detached from God (3:2). In I Chronicles we read: "And Satan stood up against Israel, and provoked David to number Israel" (21:1).[6]

Because the divine was whole, man who projected his un-conscious onto Him likewise remained a totality. Although con-flict within him existed—as it must since it is a fact of life—the schism was never irreparable since a *coniunctio* was always pos-sible within the Godhead itself.

With the increasing influence of Persian, Hellenistic, and Gnostic doctrines, binary opposition between good and evil reached its most crucial form. Christ became the concretization of absolute good and light. Satan, or the Anti-Christ, now severed from the Godhead, represented evil, dark, and material forces. Evil in this context became the "adversary" of Christ, and therefore of God.[7] The split was exemplified in the Mani-chaean heresy (among others), which led St. Augustine to write his tract against the Manichaeans, whom he knew well since he had been a member of their sect before his conversion in 378 by St. Ambrose. Evil, he declared, neither existed as a substance nor as a reality in a God-created world since God was all good and was incapable of creating evil. St. Augustine, as mentioned previously, relegated evil to a *privatio boni,* with no substance of its own. Thus the Christian God was divested of his dark side and became, in actuality, a divided figure, that is, representa-tive of only one aspect of worldly life and by an extension of man's unconscious. A dualistic formula is expressed in II Thessa-lonians: God's earthly or eschatological manifestation in Christ and Satan's in the Anti-Christ.[8] The conflict between opposing forces became inevitable. The Christian God, it is written in Romans, shall crush Satan.

> And the God of peace shall bruise Satan under your feet shortly (16:20).

To "resist" the Devil indicates the strength of the Christian faith (I Peter 5:9) as well as the Christian's intelligence and understanding of Satan's ways.

> Lest Satan should get an advantage of us: for we are not ignorant of his devices (II Corinthians 2:11).

St. Paul was a firm believer in ascetic practices. Such disciplines, he felt, could compel man to evolve and accordingly rid him of his demoniacal ways.

> To open their eyes, and to turn them from darkness to light, and from the power of Satan unto God, that they may receive forgiveness of sins, and inheritance among them which are sanctified by faith that is in me (Acts 26:18).

In Christ, then, man experiences only one half of his nature. His evil, or earthbound, side is relegated to infernal regions; or worse, in some cases is nonexistent. The result may be seen, psychologically, as an imbalance or split within the psyche. The alchemists had attempted to remedy the schism in the notion of the *lapis philosophorum*—a *complexio oppositorum* onto which they could project.

The question now arises as to what the Christian was attempting to control (or to annihilate, as the case may be) within himself and the Godhead when divesting Satan (or what he represented) of his reality.

In that Satan (or the Devil or animal in man) stands for "adversary," the spreader of chaos, doubt, and confusion, his intrusion into events implies that the status quo based on a divine "rational" order, on "wisdom," is being threatened.

That entity (or Satan) by its very existence is, then, attempting to destroy the smooth-running *Zeitgeist*, and therefore must be exterminated. Psychologically, such a force can be termed irrational or instinctual because of its unpredictable nature and because it has not yet been made cognitive. The unexpected, however, is not only inherent to man, but is also a universal principle. To seek to reject such a force, that is the disruptive side of life, is not to acknowledge man's passionate nature. What is man's fate, then, when his "irrational" side is forever being annihilated? In such a frame of reference, what is basic to him is in effect being destroyed. In many cases, however, the instinctual forces, rather than being destroyed, simply become repressed and imprisoned in the unconscious. The natural response to imprisonment is rage. Blocked within the psyche, these negative powers become more and more powerful. Every now and then these contents break out, uncontrollably, as in wars or persecutions—Satanism and the Black Mass—as personal or as mass phenomena.

Man's irrational, instinctive, or earthly side (*physis*) when working in harmony with his cognitive side (*logos*) enables him to experience punishment, confusion, and pain, but in a productive manner, enlarging his frame of reference and leading toward increased creative potency. The dichotomy between good and evil is not eclipsed; the energy, resulting from the tension of opposites, allows growth. It is interesting to note that in Tibetan Buddhism evil is never destroyed in the cosmic domain; nor do Tibetans attempt to annihilate this force in the human sphere; they merely try to diminish its power. The Oriental looks upon evil as part of the life force that must be experienced.[9]

Metaphysically, duality or opposition in nature causes activity just as friction generates a form of energy and electricity. If opposition is nonexistent, then so is action. Motion, looked upon as perpetual combat or destruction, is a process that is implicit in the cosmic flow, in life. There arises, on the other hand, an equally strong drive for unity or synthesis from such antagonism between opposing entities in the universe. Unity predominates in the phase of preexistence known as the void, before creation and a differentiation occur. Since life as we live it daily implies a state of differentiation and activity, oneness is incompatible with it.[10]

Man's nature, and the natural world in general, is antagonistic and ambivalent, and for this reason the play of opposites
as witnessed in such divinities as Osiris-Set, Eros-Anteros, Ahri-
man-Ahura Mazda, to mention but a few, has been experienced
since the dawn of mankind.[11] Let us recall that Mephistopheles
was that force that has always remained associated with nature
and had led Faust into the Realm of the Mothers and finally
toward salvation and redemption.[12] Mephistopheles said in
Faust:

> I am that power which always wants to do evil, and yet always
> creates good.

To reject man's earthbound nature by condemning it and to
concentrate merely on his godly side is to bring forth a top-heavy
being whose illusions and delusions may cause him to topple,
crumble, and finally grovel in the most turbid of mires. He is,
in effect, cut off from life and from nature—his own nature and
life. When instincts are properly tended to, understood, and
accepted as part of man's humanity, they may act in consert
with the other facts of his personality, and in so doing become
positive forces, as occurs frequently in the creation of a work
of art. When unattended, they crave for what is rightly theirs.
They become virulent and destructive, as in Satanic cults or
Black Masses.

Satanism was not the invention of medieval times. It was
a natural expression of a schism that took place within the
psyche centuries before. It flourished, for example, during the
Merovingian period under Louis the Pious along with sorcery,
necromancy, black magic, and ritual murders. Monasteries
were perpetually troubled by the intrusion of devils and phantoms of all sorts. Peter the Venerable (1092-1156) wrote of the
"diabolical invasion at Cluny"; Bernard of Clairvaux (1090-
1153), the mystic, was well known for his successes in exorcism.
Some Knight Templars confessed to their Satanic practices.
Under the reign of Philippe le Bel, trials of sorcery, black magic,
witchcraft reached epidemic proportions. The Carmelite Pierre
Ricordi was judged and tortured for invocating a demon by

constructing out of his own blood and saliva a wax effigy of the woman he sought to lure to him. In the fourteenth century the *autos-da-fé* in Toulouse were considered sufficient punishment for making a pact with the Devil. James Sprenger and Henry Kramer, two Dominican Inquisitors appointed by Innocent VIII to rid Bavaria and Saxony of magical attempts to invoke the Devil, described in *Malleus Malleficarum* the horrendous methods of burning and torture used to accomplish the task, which led to the deaths of hundreds of people. Condemnations continued unabated throughout the Renaissance. One of the greatest proponents of the occult was Catherine de Medici, who had her personal magician with her at all times. Her son, Henri III, practiced black magic in a tower at Vincennes. Nor was the "Age of Reason," the seventeenth century, devoid of such frightening practices. La Voisin, who indulged in Satanism, necromancy, and goety, boasted of clients drawn from the highest social ranks. In 1668 Father Mariette celebrated his diabolical rites first in the church of Saint-Séverin and afterward at Saint-Germain. Similarly, in 1631 the well-known case of demonic possession at the Loudun convent took place. It was there that the mother superior declared herself possessed by the demon Astaroth and accused Father Grandier of having sent other demons, among them Asmodée, Leviathan, Uriel, Behemoth, to wreak havoc on her convent.[13] Many cases of Satanism were reported in the registries during the eighteenth century. Young nuns were cured of diseases by priests practicing the black art. Venerable figures such as Pierre Vaillant, Cagliostro, Count Saint-Germain practices magnetism, hypnotism, cartomancy, and so on.

Huysmans singled out Gilles de Rais (1404-1440) above all others for examination with regard to his Satanic practices. For Huysmans' hero, Durtal, Gilles de Rais is a true mystic and Satanism is part of his credo. "From lofty Mysticism to base Satanism there is but one step. In the Beyond all things touch. He carried his zeal for prayers into the territory of blasphemy."[14] Gilles' extreme religiosity and patriotism, which is suddenly transformed into the perpetration of the most ignominious acts, is understandable to Huysmans' protagonists "from a pious man he suddenly becomes Satanic, from an erudite and placid man, to a violator of small children, a strangler of boys and girls."[15] A mystic is one who transcends the polarities within him and experiences thereby a *coniunctio.* Gilles was forever attempting to reconcile the opposites that tore at him and at times chose good at other instances evil, to attain his goal.

For the mystic the cosmos is monistic; all is related and interrelated. In this transcendental domain duality is nonexistent, good and evil exist only in the finite sphere. It is not surprising then that poets and novelists such as Baudelaire and Barbey d'Aurévilly, and modern writers such as Genet, attempted to reach the world of absolute via evil: degradation and violation of established values and the immersion in the most execrable acts.

Gilles de Rais was born in the castle of Machécoul in Brittany, a region that has been since earliest times a favorite haunt of Satanists (perhaps because of the menhirs and dolmens).[16] Early in life, Gilles had displayed a highly volatile personality, a will to power and a need to dominate.[17] Shortly after his marriage to Catherine de Thouars (1420), which brought him great wealth, he joined forces with Joan of Arc. He rode at Joan's side, protected her during the dramatic events that lead to the coronation of the dauphin, later Charles VII, at Rheims, and then received the great honor of being made Marshal of France.

After the excitement of military life had subsided, Gilles returned to his castle at Tiffauges. Inflamed and dilated at the thought of having helped fulfill divine will in the military sphere, this man, as Durtal declared, now found another outlet for his excitable temperament. He expended his energies in a life of unparalleled luxury and debauchery. He could boast of a bodyguard of two hundred men; a private chapel where High Mass was sung daily; his own personal clergy fitted in exquisite vestments; an open house providing gourmet delights for quantities of people; a remarkable library; artists hired to decorate the palatial domicile.[18] As to be expected, Gilles' funds diminished and he sought occult means of replenishing his stock of gold.

It was at this juncture that he began his experiments in witchcraft, magic, and alchemy. He studied the procedures of such great magicians and alchemists as Albertus Magnus, Raymond Lulle, Nicolas Flammel, and Abraham-Juif. He indulged at first in ceremonial magic and later set up an elaborate laboratory in the castle where he began cooking his own metals. He emulated Béroalde de Verville's technique as forwarded in

Moyen de Parvenir. He heated the metals of his choice in ovens in accordance with the twelve prescribed operations: calcination, solution, separation, conjunction, putrefaction, and projection.[19] Unlike the famous Nicolas Flamel, who had succeeded it was said in transmuting half a pound of mercury into silver and then into gold, no matter how hard Gilles tried, his experiments were unsuccessful. Impatient, he sent for the famous Italian alchemist and Franciscan priest Francesco Prelati. Together they began their most sinister practice—human sacrifices. Durtal wrote: "under the impulsion of a perverted mysticism, to the most sophisticated of cruelties, the most delicate of crimes."[20] Due to the fact that Gilles had witnessed so much bloodshed during the Hundred Years' War in his battles against the English and because he was familiar with the cruelties perpetrated by the French in the name of Christ when they exterminated the heretical sect, the Albigensians in the thirteenth century, human sacrifices did not seem repugnant to him.

Gilles had over fifty children kidnapped. They were taken directly to Tiffauges castle and either killed outright or tortured or the object of perverted sexual practices before being strangled. Their blood was then drained and mixed with a pasty substance, thus constituting the consecrated host. Sometimes the host was blended with exrement. Pure blood was used as the eucharist in wine.[21]

Together Gilles and Prelati would offer the hearts of their victims to Satan or his aides, Beelzebub and Belial, in accordance with prescribed rituals. Prelati traced a circle, a cross, and various occult letters; then he recited magic formulas and prayers to Satan. After Gilles stepped into the sacred area where the rest of the sacrificial ritual took place, it is said that he was "possessed" by a "demoniacal fury."[22] His joy at watching and participating in the cruelties involved—even in vampirism—brought him extreme pleasure. In fact, in his final confession he said "I was happier in the enjoyment of tortures, tears, fright, and blood than in any other pleasure."[23]

In 1440 Gilles was brought to trial and confessed his sins. Before he was burned at the stake, he spent his last days in passionate and frenetic lamentations and prayer.

Huysmans stressed Gilles' propensity for Satanism, but he

also discussed contemporary Satanic rituals, thus deflating the reader's propensity for hubris. His friends and readers, therefore, would not be able to look back smuggly upon those "dark" and "ignorant" ages—those so-called Middle Ages. Heinous crimes were being perpetrated by Satanists all over Europe during Huysmans' era too. Although he disguised some of the names in *Down There,* easily discernible are Father Van Haecke, who indulged in Satanic practices until his death in 1912, and the notorious Joseph-Antoine Boullan, who did likewise until he died in 1895. Huysmans looked at his era rather objectively: with admiration for the great progress made in the domain of science. But in terms of answering the enigma of life and death, man is no more advanced at this juncture than he had been centuries before. What are nonmaterial beings? Do they exist? Do souls float about as do microbes? germs? "Space is peopled by microbes. Is it more surprising that space should also be crammed with spirits and larvae?"[24] Nor have scientists been able to explicate the process of intuition, coincidences, hallucinations, and prophecy—all expressions of matter in transformation. The world of the occult remains an enigma to this day.[25]

What is the meaning of Satanism on a psychological level and why was Huysmans obsessed with the notion of evil?

Outbreaks of Satanism as a personal or mass phenomena may be looked upon, psychologically, as an expression of the shadow. As the word indicates, the shadow "contains inferior characteristics and weaknesses which the ego's self-esteem will not permit it to recognize."[26] When the shadow remains unconscious, its unacceptable contents are frequently projected onto individuals or groups. Persecutions may follow. Such activities, psychologically, demonstrate an attempt on the part of individuals (or of the collective) to destroy what they believe threatens them, that is, lives inchoate within them, and which they seek to annihilate. Heresies, for example, in the Middle Ages were considered expressions of evil since the doctrine they forwarded was antithetical to the "true" faith. This kind of thinking may be labeled a negative shadow projection.

As a collective phenomenon, evil may be observed in such people as Gilles de Rais, Caesar Borgia, and Adolf Hitler; as collective activities, in witch-hunts, Satanism, and the Inquisition. When the shadow is projected upon a person, that individual becomes the Devil for all intents and purposes. It takes the masculine form in most cases, since, in patriarchal societies, the male element is the strongest and thus to be most feared. In olden days the collective shadow (the evils of the community) was projected or heaped onto a goat by a priest; the animal was then sent out into the wilderness and the clan was purged of its sins. The evil of the community supposedly disappeared with the animal. But so did the pain that facing and trying to resolve tensions and problems necessarily entails. By merely rejecting an unpleasant situation, one escapes a conflict that could have had salutary effects. Similarly, Christ was a scapegoat. He took upon himself the sins of the world and was condemned as an "evil force." Examples of this kind of "scapegoat" psychology also appear in the pictorial domain: in the wood engraving by Cranach the Elder "The Torments of the Damned" and in "The Last Judgment" by Brueghel the Elder and also by Hieronymus Bosch.

When the collective shadow is experienced affectively, and with little or no discernment, it becomes contagious and destructive. The tension of opposites has disappeared and the individual permits himself to be engulfed or "possessed" by the shadow. He loses his capacity to differentiate and is no longer responsible for his actions. He lives in a darkened realm. Such was the situation of Gilles de Rais when he indulged in Satanic orgies.[27]

As long as Gilles de Rais was on the side of Joan of Arc, and thus the prevailing *Zeitgeist*, little conflict ensued within his unconscious. His passions were working for what society considered the right cause; his faith seemed infinite. As soon as the climate changed and the goal had been attained, a slackening of tension emerged and conflict followed. The solidarity he had experienced with the group broke up. A sense of alienation ensued. When he retired to Tiffauges and attempted to lose himself in debauchery, all went well until his affective outlet ended. Impoverished, he again experienced the terrors of loneliness. He took up Satanism, which relieved him once again of the fright that comes with a confrontation with the self. Finally, after his trial and condemnation, his "passionate" religiosity overwhelmed him and remained with him until the end, thus obliterating any possible emergence of lucidity.

In that the shadow is an expression of characteristics rejected by both the individual and the collective, it may be associated with regard to the Christian psyche, with instinct, or with the Devil. It is understandable, then why the individual is forever attempting to stamp out this aspect of himself, which he despises, and frequently via ascetic practices when, in fact, he should more readily accomplish his goal were he to accept instinct as a fact of life and integrate it into his psyche. Whenever instinct, or the Devil, is subjugated rather than experienced for its own right, destruction is most frequently the outcome.

Gnostics, alchemists, and mystics (e.g., Jakob Boehme) understood the need man had for Satan in the religious psyche; so did Milton, who called it the true *principium individuantionis*.[28] For them the Devil was the instigator of action, the one who injected doubt and a desire to transcend the world of opposites, thus a desire to create. William Blake wrote: "Good is the passive that obeys Reason; Evil is the active springing from Energy. Good is Heaven. Evil is Hell."[29] He understood that life is a dynamic process; that creation cannot exist without conflict. *The Marriage of Heaven and Hell* was a creative manifestation of Blake's intense need to reconcile the tension of opposites within his own being. Baudelaire's "Litanies of Satan," Hugo's "The End of Satan," Barbey d'Aurévilly's *Les Diaboliques*, and Hoffmann's *The Devil's Elixir* are examples of artists who also attempted to face the shadow problem within their own psyche. Indeed, in his preface to *Les Diaboliques*, Barbey d'Aurévilly wrote: "The author believes in the Devil and in his influence in the world."[30]

The same may be said of Huysmans and his protagonists in *Down There*. By personifying instincts in the various characters peopling his novel, the reader views Huysmans' chaotic instinctual domain. The Satanic fantasy (and the clusters of rituals centering around Satan in *Down There*) symbolizes one of the most archaic features of the unconscious, contents not yet understood by consciousness. Satan is one half of the totality—the other being God. The pull of such dual images or forces within the psyche is manifested in many world religions and philosophical credos, such as Christ and the Anti-Christ, Zarathustra (the ideal being) and the ugliest man (whose function it was to disorient and to hurt the superman). The greater the split between the polarities (good and evil), the greater is the individual's insecurity and the more powerful becomes the irrational. Consequently, to be overly fascinated with purity and perfection, as is the Christian ideal, made it impossible to assimilate the Devil within the psyche. Therefore, a way had to be found to unify what was disparate. St. Augustine conceived of the concept of *privatio boni,* which did not lessen the Devil's hold upon humanity.[31]

Nietzsche wrote of the dangers involved in depotentiating instinct. He spoke of the "denaturalization of natural values." And he said: "We must liberate ourselves from morality in order to be able to live morally."[32] To codify morality is to ossify it, to transform it into an absolute. Because of the rigidity of the attitude, morality, after a while, turns into its opposite frequently thus paving the way for a state of *enantiodromia,* as was the case of Gilles de Rais. If morality is looked upon as an end unto itself, it may become an evil. To seek perfection (or its opposite) indicates a repression of one or the other. In some cases dissociation between a conscious set of moral precepts, or a conscious adaptation and an unconscious rejection of it, brings about a dissociation of the psyche. Only by reconciling and accepting the good and evil within the human being (natural man), rather than repressing one or the other, can an individual come to terms with such factors. If man has a *reservatio mentalis* and refuses to confront the Devil in himself—that is, the factor which doubts, which irritates, which is the adversary—then he comes under its dominion.[33]

To be tyrannized or "possessed" in the Middle Ages meant to be under the sway of demoniacal forces. Today, psychologically, it indicates the fact that one is under the spell of a powerful complex ("splinter psyche"), a "split-off"; in other words, when unconscious negative contents are not integrated into the total psyche and become autonomous entities within the subliminal world, each goes its own way. Such was the situation with the deeply disturbed Gilles de Rais and Durtal (and by extension Huysmans). The psychic totality had become fragmented and split up into various complexes. Each "split-off", or "miniature complex," developed a strange fantasy life of its own, and each of abnormal proportions.[34] Fantasies of this type may be regarded as "toxins" because they do not fit into the conscious mind harmoniously. They resist all attempts on the part of the will to cope with them. In the case of Gilles de Rais, he veered from one extreme to the other, from "passionate" piety to immersion in evil—both in an attempt to transcend his human condition.

Gilles' affective reactions (whether in prayer, confession, or in the perpetration of the most sinister sexual and brutal acts) are par for the course when under the dominion of a complex. Complexes may be looked upon as having a type of electric current: they possess emotional charges and feeling tones. The affects from a complex are sometimes so great, they are capable of acting physically upon a person. Respiration, blood pressure, and the circulatory system may be altered, depending upon the power of the complex over the individual. Gilles in moments of extreme piety or cruelty virtually stopped breathing for seconds, his face was inundated with sweat, and his movements became the product of extreme passion. During these moments, occurring in cases of psychosis, deep-rooted complexes were breaking through into consciousness; they erupted with great violence and invaded the entire personality.[35]

It is interesting to note that blood plays a vital role in Huysmans' descriptions of Satanic acts as well as in his pictorial representations in *Down There*. Blood may be associated with mystical communion. To shed this source of life, then, should not be looked upon as a completely destructive act. On the contrary, blood sacrifices are as old as mankind. In ancient times animals were killed and burned in an act of reverence to the gods for reasons of fertility. It was thought that the earth had to "drink" blood in order to become productive and powerful once again.[36] Gilles who, according to Huysmans, was "saturated with mystical ideas,"[37] believed implicitly in this dictum. The alchemical process and the magical rituals in which he participated (and the sacrifice of children) were to bring him riches and fulfillment. Such activities would permit him, on a psychological plane, to do away with his feelings of impotence as a mortal and become a godlike figure. Hadn't Satan promised such an outcome to Adam and Eve in the garden of paradise?

Durtal regarded the gore perpetrated by Gilles de Rais at

Tiffauges and the cruelties associated with the Crucifixion at Golgotha as sacred acts. These mysteries enabled the protagonists and the author to leave, at least momentarily, the contemporary world, thus giving vent to the disdain they felt for their times. In so doing, they succeeded in joining forces with a mythical past, reentering the eternal pleromatic realm.

By participating in the dramas of Satanism with its sadistic and sacrificial aspects, Huysmans (via his hero Durtal) perhaps felt he would earn sanctification, salvation, and redemption. Shortly after completing *Down There,* he attempted to experience the opposite polarity—the good through sacrifice, a type of crucifixion—and became an oblate and a dolorist.[38]

2. *The Black Mass and the Female Principle*

In one form or another women have been associated with the forces of evil. Their infernal, dark, chthonic, devouring, hostile, and terrifying characteristics have been manifested in such beings as Medea, Gorgon, Hecate, Cybele, and Agave. As *vagina dentata* types, they have been described as castrators and destroyers of man; as "spirit" or "deadly mothers," they send insanity or "moon sickness" to man; as succubi, vampires, man-eating Lamias, and witches, they drain the male of his life-force. Women were looked upon as impure, as instigators of orgies and leaders of Sabbaths. Perhaps the most famous is a depiction in *Faust* on the summit of Blocksberg. Artists also featured women in their evil aspects: Dürer drew "The Witch"; Goya painted the "Transformation of the Sorceress" in which he depicted witches that had been changed into bats; and a witch riding a goat is sculpted on the western doorway of the Lyons cathedral. Writers such as Baudelaire, Hugo and de Vigny emphasized women's destructive characteristics. And Barbey d'Aurévilly envisaged women as the source of evil.

Symbolically, women have been associated with nature and the material world; imagistically with the body, vessel, earth, and cave. In this regard, they are antipodal to the spiritual values inherent in the male. According to Judaic-Christian focus they are thereby considered inferior and damned as representatives of flesh and instinct. In Judaism, Christianity, and Islam, the woman is blamed for man's fall, for Eve's so-called seduction of Adam.   Jules Michelet wrote: "A strong and dynamic religion, such as paganism, the Greek religion begins with the sibyl and ends with the sorceress."[39]

In Judaism, Islam, and Christianity, women were secondary citizens.   They were certainly reproved in the Christian religion. Women were forbidden to serve Mass or enter into the mystical spheres of the Church.   Because of such an extremist attitude, women were either looked upon as objects of worship (Virgin Mary) or as evil beings (lustful, sensual, and so on).   To sanctify or to idealize women, Michelet pointed out, is to denigrate the real, flesh-and-blood human being and to repudiate her as a partner in life.[40]

As mentioned earlier, Huysmans was revolted by women and unconsciously feared their power over him and his need of them.   A misogynist, his overly negative reaction to women verged on the pathological, and therefore he could not experience their positive side, only their threatening aspects.   Scholars and psychologists have blamed this state of affairs on his mother's remarriage; her neglect of him after the birth of her other children; and on his unfortunate liaison and his own sexual impotency.[41]   Huysmans' one-sided attitude toward women was manifested in the character of Mme. Chantelouve.   It is she who in *Down There,* takes Durtal to the Black Mass.

Durtal regards Mme. Chantelouve (her name means "singing she wolf") as a succubus.   In fact, he describes her as "a succubus of the bedchamber."[42]   She is thus a forbidding and dangerous force.   She prevents him from concentrating on his work and encourages his capacity for daydreaming; she arouses him sexually to the point of distraction and in this respect is eminently pagan: a natural, spontaneous force, a kind of *Hexe,* a woman of the Apocalypse.

As a female demon, Mme. Chantelouve incizes her way into Durtal's conscious and unconscious life.   Let us recall that female demons played a far greater role in Christianity than they did in Judaism.   Relatively unimportant and powerless in early Judaism, because of its monotheistic outlook, demonology gained in significance in medieval Kabbalism, a doctrine that had been influenced by Christianity's dualistic formula.   Kabbalism had been looked upon by some as a more emotional—the more feminine—

side of Judaism.

The most famous she-demon in Kabbalistic literature was Lilith. Huysmans refers to this figure in connection with Mme. Chantelouve several times. Lilith, it has been posited, is an outgrowth of the Sumerian (2400 B.C.) incubi-succubi group of demons who came to men at night and copulated with them.[43] According to the Kabbalah, Lilith was Adam's first wife. Both she and Adam were made of clay. When Adam wanted to make love to her, it is said that she objected. "Why should I lie beneath you," she questioned, "when I am your equal since both of us are created from dust?" Adam attempted to dominate her, but she protected herself by uttering the "magic" name of the Lord, after which she rose into the air and flew away to a reputedly sinful area near the Red Sea. Here, Lilith began leading a life of ill repute and gave birth to countless demons. She refused to return to Adam despite the fact that God had sent three angels after her; however, she struck a bargain with them and agreed not to harm any babes if the names of the three angels in question were written on amulets. Later on, Lilith became enamored of Adam, but marriage was not impossible since Eve had already become his wife. Both had been expelled from the Garden of Eden and Adam and Eve had decided to do penance for their crime. For 130 years they gave up all sexual relations and indulged in mortification of the flesh. It was during this period of continence that Lilith coupled with Adam and bore him demon children. Male spirits came to Eve who in turn procreated.[44] The offsprings of these unions were the succubi and incubi that so plagued the devout during the Middle Ages: Bodin, St. Thomas Aquinas, St. Augustine, St. Bonaventure, Pope Innocent VIII, to mention only a few.[45]

The Zohar describes Lilith as follows:

> She roams at night, and goes all about the world and makes sport with men and causes them to emit seed. In every place where a man sleeps alone in a house, she visits him and grabs him and attaches herself to him and has her desire for him, and bears from him. And she also afflicts him with sickness, and he knows it not, and all this takes place when the moon is on the wane.[46]

As a succubus, Mme. Chantelouve was a seductress of the

most dangerous type. She had the power of destroying men. Her very beauty and her tantalizing qualities made her more powerful and more dangerous than any male demon. Dominated by Mme. Chantelouve's charisma, Durtal lost all control over his emotions. He was obsessed with her attributes, a slave of her sensuality. However, when he realized the sexual act, Durtal experienced disgust and revulsion at his own flesh-oriented needs.

> She revolted him, horrified him. Was it possible to have so desired a woman, only to come to—that? He had idealized her in his transports, he had dreamed in her eyes—he knew not what! He had wished to exalt himself with her, to rise higher than the delirious ravings of the sense, to soar out of the world into joys supernal and unexplored. And his dream had been shattered. He remained fettered to earth. Was there no means of escaping out of one's self, out of earthly limitations, and attaining an upper ether where the soul, ravished, would glory in its giddy flight?[47]

Try as she would, Durtal could not escape his earthbound condition. Only through the dream could he accomplish this end: "To love at a distance and without hope; never to possess; to dream chastely of pale charms and impossible kisses."[48] Mme. Chantelouve was also disillusioned by the real world. She preferred possessing men in her fantasy world to making love in the existential domain: "I have possessed Byron, Baudelaire, Gérard de Nerval, those I love... And you would be inferior to my chimera, to the Durtal I adore, whose caresses make my nights delirious."[49]

Mme. Chantelouve believed the Black Mass—that mystic-erotic experience—enabled her to transcend her human condition. The Black Mass, wrote Michelet, was and is a means of "redeeming Eve, damned by Christianity."[50]

The Mass in the Roman Catholic liturgy is considered a living mystery. It incorporates the idea of sacrifice (slaughter, a gift offered to God) and the meal ("consecrated" food and wine, partaken by those present and by God who made Himself present).   In Karl von Weizsäcker's version (1875) of I Corinthians, 11:23-27) used by C. G. Jung to describe the sacrament of the Mass we read as follows:

> ...Lord Jesus...took bread, gave thanks, broke it, and said: This is my body for you; do this in remembrance of me. And after he had supped, he took the chalice also, and said: This chalice is the new testament in my blood. As often as you drink, do this in remembrance of me. For as often as you eat this bread and drink this chalice, you declare the death of the Lord, until he comes.[51]

The height of the Mass occurs with the transubstantiation: when the bread and the wine become the body and the blood of Christ. It is at this moment that Christ-God enters the human sphere, after which he returns to the realm of the absolute.[52]

In the Black Mass we have a complete reversal of the ritual. The fact that women participate in this mystery is in itself a contradiction.   Let us recall that in the resolutions of the Councils of Laodice[53] and Carthage,[54] women were forbidden to serve or participate in the ritual of the Mass.   The Black Mass ceremony takes place (with varying procedures, depending upon place and time) as follows: An inverted cross is placed above the altar.   The name of Satan is written on the consecrated wafers, which are triangular in shape.   Usually they are made with ergot, bread, urine, menstrual blood, or semen.   Black candles are placed around the altar and a protective pentagram is drawn around it.   The altar itself is draped in black.   A woman frequently a virgin, lies nude on the altar and a black chalice is placed on her abdomen.   The priest, frequently nude under his chasuble, which is embroidered with special symbols of either gold or silver, officiates. After placing the gold paten and chalice on the nude woman, the priest then kisses the sacrificial spot *"uel extra uel intra corporale."*[55]   Latin prayers to Satan are then enunciated with utmost reverence, after which the blood sacrifices begin: some children are sacrificed outright by strangulation and others are mutilated at the altar, their blood drained with great solemnity during the ceremony.   An incredible orgy becomes the finale of this mystery of mysteries.[56]

Huysmans describes various Black Masses in history: one at which Father Guibourg officiated for Mme. de Montespan, who lay naked on the altar, praying for Louis XIV's eternal love; others for Mme. d'Argenson and Mme. de Saint-Pont, and for many other illustrious ladies. Huysmans also relates Catherine de Medici's bouts with the Black Masses and those delineated by the Marquis de Sade in *Justine,* celebrated in the convent when Juliette became a member of the "Society of the Friends of Crime."

Huysmans claims to have witnessed Black Masses and outlines the one Durtal and Mme. Chantelouve attended in great detail. The facts introduced into Huysmans' erotic-mystical delineations were inspired, or so it has been claimed, by actual priests who indulged in such religious perversions: Father Joseph-Antoine Boullan and Father Van Haecke. The latter was a modern counterpart of Gilles de Rais. Father Boullan was an even more sinister figure who indulged in Satanic practices and officiated at Black Masses. He boasted of the fact that his religious congregation met at Versailles and there practiced a variety of occult and perverted acts. His liaison with the converse Sister Adèle Chevalier Boullan considered the highest type of spiritual love. He claimed to have cured sick nuns and other women who consulted him via autohypnosis and autosuggestion. He knew how to arouse their fantasy world and provoke their dreams or hallucinations, enabling them to experience sexual relations, they believed, with Jesus Christ. He suggested certain poses and procedures condusive to such relationships.[57] Boullan, with whom Huysmans corresponded, affirmed that Black Masses were practiced all over Europe and with passionate reverence—with as much excitement, fervor, and faith as they were in the Middle Ages.[58]

Father Boullan is portrayed in *Down There* as Doctor Johannes, a master exorcist "the most learned in the occult sciences."[59] More sinister, however, is Huysmans' secondary character, the Chanoine Docre, a most formidable master of the depraved occult arts. It was he, Huysmans asserts, who fed consecrated hosts to white mice and had the image of the cross tatooed on the soles of his feet so that each time he took a step he would stamp on the image of Christ.[60] Far more subtle than Gilles, Docre did not "strangle children, just suggested suicide."[61] He was also a master poisonmaker and used all types of toxic materials on the participants of his Black Mass. He even filled fish with hosts so that the fish, a symbol of Christ, would look grotesque.[62]

The Black Mass described by Huysmans may be looked upon, psychologically, as an expression of hysteria. Huysmans was acquainted with Jean Martin Charcot's discoveries regarding this age-old disease and incorporated some of his conclusions in *Down There.*

Hysteria, one of the most complex of mental ailments, dates back to ancient Egypt. It was considered a women's illness (the word *hysteria* comes from the Greek meaning "womb") and was diagnosed as the wandering of the womb about the body. The cure consisted in fastening and steadying this part of the anatomy. Little knowledge concerning this disease was gained since the time of Hippocrates, who was the first to write about it. During the Middle Ages the doctors considered hysterical persons "possessed" or demon-ridden; but rather than attempting to heal the illness, the victims were either burned at the stake or tortured for what was thought to be their sinful nature. Galen was the first to understand the psychogenic aspects of this sickness, in a primitive manner to be sure, but at least he was ridding it of its theological interpretation. Carlos Piso, in the sixteenth century, diagnosed hysteria as a mental sickness affecting not just women but men as well. Thomas Sydenham, a century later, looked upon it as a mental condition. Charcot proved this theory with his experiments in the treatment of hysteria by hypnosis.[63]

Freud, Breuer, Charcot, Janet, and Bernheim approached the question of hysteria from a clinical point of view. Freud described the etiology of hysteria, claiming that it resulted from a trauma or "psychic wound", in childhood and was usually due to repressed sexuality. He later broadened his views concerning the disease. Fantasies, which could have been traumata, arouse excitement that would under normal circumstances be abreacted. With the hysterical patient, however, the release of affective fantasies is not possible. The "retention of the excitation" or the "blocking" or "repression" of the affect does not permit the psychic energy to be released. Hence it is transformed into a physical system. The goal of the psychiatrist is to release this pent-up energy and in so doing transmute "affects from the symptoms."[64]

Hysterical symptoms may therefore be considered "symbolic representations of repressed unconscious events." These strong emotions cannot be discharged or expressed because the contents of the fantasies are incompatible with the conscious outlook. The energy is then diverted into the wrong channels (somatic), resulting in symptoms (conversion). Some people have psychological predispositions to fantasies and traumas that accrete in potency with the passage of years. "The patient constructs in his imagination little stories," writes Jung, "that are very coherent and very logical, but when he has to deal with reality, he is no longer capable of attention or comprehension."[65]

Under the stay of hysteria, particularly of a mystic-erotic nature, such as Huysmans described in the Black Mass, any kind of adaptation to the outer environment becomes impossible. Women whose psychic life may revolve around sexuality are particularly prone to such split-offs from the existential scene. Dreams and wishes are related to the fulfillment of an inner obsession or compulsion. Mme. Chantelouve and Durtal are such people. They experience sexual fulfillment in their fantasy life. As long as they live out their passion in the world of the imagination they have no need to confront reality, or to adapt to it—and eroticism can have full sway. When both face the actual world in terms of sexuality, they are revolted.

After the Black Mass and once "reality" returned, Huysmans wrote, Durtal was wringing with "disgust"; he was "asphyxiated" by the aroma of flesh. The events described below were so antithetical to his existential attitude that as soon as he was exposed to the goings-on in the actual world, he sought to flee.

> ...Another sprawling on her back, undid her skirts, drew forth a rag, enormous, meteorized; then her face twisted into a horrible grimace, and her tongue, which she could not control, stuck out, bitten at the edges, harrowed by red teeth, from a bloody mouth.[66]

Durtal could not bear the tyranny of the polarities within him: his lust for flesh and his immersion in the material world on the one hand, and his cognitive hatred of these very things on the other. He felt himself "shudder." As for Mme. Chantelouve, she confessed that "these scenes shatter me. I am in a daze. I must have a glass of water."[67]

The hysterical outbursts occurring during the Black Mass, thus enabled Durtal, but only temporarily, to transcend the everyday world. As soon as consciousness returned, he was again filled with excoriating frustrations, inner antagonisms, and dissatisfaction with his own being and with his wordly lot.

Satanism and the Black Mass are expressions of a conflict experienced by certain types of Christians in their attempts to heal the breach within their psyche, the one created by the polarities of good and evil. Huysmans explored the paths of evil in the Satanic experience via Durtal and Mme. Chantelouve in the Black Mass. Neither foray into the domain of the so-called "absolute" proved efficacious. Corroded with guilt, with feelings of inadequacy and disgust, Huysmans decided to opt in both the existential and fictional worlds for the opposite *way*. He became exceedingly devout; he went to a Trappist monastery for a time and ended his days as an oblate. Even in this sphere of extreme spirituality, however, he felt the continuous pull of that demonic force within him—that entity which questions, doubts, and disturbs.

NOTES

[1]Shortly after Huysmans' birth in 1848 in Paris, his father became ill and his mother spent long years caring for him. When his father died in 1856, Huysmans was deeply depressed. His mother's remarriage (to a Protestant) he considered an act of betrayal to his father's memory. The birth of his half sisters increased his sense of neglect and the rancor he felt against his mother. After passing his baccalaureate, he accepted a job at the Ministry of Interior and took a mistress who later gave birth to another man's child. He then entered the army and fought the Prussians. A civilian once again, he followed his bent: writing. *Marthe* (1876) delineates the life of a prostitute. Huysmans' style was to be naturalistic henceforth. His mentor was Zola, to whom he dedicated his novel *The Vatard Sisters* (1879). *En Ménage* (1881) is a morose work, more of a psychological analysis than a study of the environment's effects upon the protagonists. Humanity is considered with bitterness; life is rendered absurd and ridiculous. Huysmans' misogyny is full-blown in *A Vau-l'Eau* (1882). Only the world of art offered him some semblance of contentment and feelings of relatedness. He admired the works of the Impressionists Renoir, Monet, Pissarro, Berthe Morisot, Degas and also lauded Forain. During the Exhibition of the Independents (1881) he recognized Gauguin's genius. Gustave Moreau's canvases "evoke the fairy-like visions, the bloody apotheoses of former ages."

Huysmans became more and more introverted with the passing of years. A difficult person to begin with, his morbidity, his disgust with things of the flesh, his short temper, and his nervousness alienated him progressively from society. He despised his era and believed that mankind had not progressed since ancient times, despite the invention of electricity. Man had lost contact with nature and was devoid of a mystical credo, of depth, and of understanding.

Psychologists have labeled Huysmans' obsessive denigration of women and of the flesh as the outcome of feelings of sexual impotency. It has also been forwarded that Huysmans had contracted syphilis in his youth and had never been cured of it. His unfortunate liaisons did not add to his *joie de vivre*.

Against the Grain (1884) was labeled by Arthur Symons "the breviary of Decadence." Its hero was introspective, forever searching for unusual sensations in jewels, music, paintings, and so on. Huysmans eventually broke with the Naturalists because he felt the stress they placed on environment and documentation neglected the psychological side of life. He discovered his personal method of expression in *Down There* and labeled it "spiritual naturalism." Huysmans was converted to Catholicism and spent nine days among the Trappist monks. His last volumes, *En Route* (1895), *The Cathedral* (1898), and *The Oblate* (1903), deal with his search for holiness and his need for penitence in a background of extraordinarily rich symbolism. Huysmans died in 1907.

[2]Robert Baldick, *La Vie de J. K. Huysmans*, p. 180.

[3]J. K. Huysmans, *La-Bas*, p. 10. *Down There* (trans. Keene Wallace), p. 12.

[4]*Ibid.*

[5]Rivkah S. Kluger, *Satan and the Old Testament*, p. 52.

[6]Geo Widengreen, "The Principle of Evil in the Eastern Religions," *Evil*, p. 24.

[7]C. G. Jung, *The Archetypes and the Collective Unconscious*, p. 322.

[8]Victor Maag, "The Antichrist as a Symbol of Evil," *Evil*, p. 61.

[9]C. G. Jung, *Psychology and Alchemy*, p. 252.

[10]C. G. Jung, *The Practice of Psychotherapy*, p. 257.

[11]C. G. Jung, *Mysterium Coiunctionis*, p. 69.

[12]Liliane Frey-Rohn, "Evil from the Psychological Point of View," *Evil*, p. 181.

[13]François Dumas, *Histoire de la Magie*, p. 449.

[14]*La-Bas*, p. 50; *Down There*, p. 52.

[15]*Ibid.*, p. 49; p. 51.

[16]Emile Grillot de Givry, *Illustrated Anthology of Sorcery, Magic and Alchemy*, p. 72.

[17]W. D. Wyndam Lewis, *The Soul of Marshal Gilles de Raiz*, p. 54.

[18]Montague Summers, *Geography of Witchcraft*, p. 391.

[19]Lewis, p. 123.

[20]*La-Bas*, p. 46; *Down There*, p. 48.

[21]*Ibid.*, p. 57; p. 60.

[22]Dumas, p. 207.

[23]*La-Bas*, p. 155; *Down There*, p. 158.

[24]*Ibid.*, p. 129; p. 131.

[25]G. Encausse (Papus), *L'Occultisme et le Spiritisme.*

[26]Edward Edinger, "Outline of Analytical Psychology," p. 8-9.

[27]Psychologically, one may forward the opinion that Gilles' ego (the center of his conscious personality or that factor which adapts to both consciousness and the unconscious) has never been strengthened and the emotional shock (or trauma) of finding himself isolated from the prevailing concepts increased his sense of insecurity and, consequently, the chaotic state within his unconscious.

[28]*Psychology and Alchemy*, p. 313.

[29]H. G. Baynes, *Mythology of the Soul*, p. 879.

[30]Jules Barbey d'Aurévilly, *Les Diaboliques*, p. 40.

[31]C. G. *Aion*, p. 42.

[32]Liliane Frey-Rohn, p. 156.

[33]Baynes, p. 279.

[34]C. G. Jung, *The Psychogenesis of Mental Disease*, p. 56.

[35]Erich Neumann, *History of the Origins of Consciousness*, p. 288.

[36]*Ibid.*, p. 55.

[37]*La-Bas*, p. 44; *Down There*, p. 46.

[38]A dolorist is one who believes in the utility and the excellence of pain.

[39]Jules Michelet, *La Sorcière*, p. 31.

[40]*Ibid.*, p. 126.

[41]Baldick, p. 89.

[42]*La-Bas*, p. 88; *Down There*, p. 91.

[43]Raphael Patai, *The Hebrew Goddess*, p. 210.

[44]*Ibid.*

[45]*La-Bas*, p. 132; *Down There*, p. 135.

[46]Patai, p. 221.

[47]*La-Bas*, p. 175; *Down There*, p. 178.

[48]*Ibid.*, p. 178; p. 181.

[49]*Ibid.*, p. 146; p. 149.

[50]Michelet, p. 31.

[51]C. G. Jung, *Psychology and Religion: West and East*, p. 204.

[52]*Ibid.*, p. 221.

[53]*Ibid.*, p. 369.

[54]*Ibid.*, p. 391.

[55]Summers, p. 443.

[56]Kathryn Paulsen, *The Complete Book of Magic and Witchcraft*, p. 30.

[57]Baldick, p. 189.

[58]Pierre Cogny, *J. K. Huysmans A la Recherche de l'unité*, pp. 139-147.

[59]*La-Bas*, p. 256; *Down There*, p. 261.

[60]*Ibid.*, p. 187; p. 190.

[61]*Ibid.*, p. 187; p. 190.

[62]*Ibid.*

[63]Niel Micklem, "On Hysteria: The Mythical Syndrome," *Spring*, pp. 148-151.

[64]C. G. Jung, *Freud and Psychoanalysis*, p. 130.

[65]*Ibid.*, p. 98.

[66]*La-Bas*, p. 242; *Down There*, p. 248.

[67]*Ibid.*, p. 244; p. 250.

CHAPTER 12

Arthur Rimbaud—"After the Flood":
From Chaos to Cosmos

Authentic life is not taken over either from men or from God, rather it can be fulfilled only out of itself, and is nothing whatever other than fulfillment.
(Martin Buber, Pointing the Way*)*

"After the Flood," a prose poem included in Arthur Rimbaud's[1] *The Illuminations* (1886), is a genuine psychodrama. It reenacts the plunge for freedom experienced by many adolescents who live in the imprisoning atmosphere of an authoritarian mother and a conventional and restrictive society. "After the Flood" is a subjective and symbolistic poetization of the biblical legend of Noah. It takes us through several phases of Rimbaud's life on both a personal and a collective level: his birth, childhood, adolescence, and future. In that "After the Flood" is a creation myth, it enabled the poet to participate in an *illo tempore,* thus opening the flood gates to his rich fantasy world. The water and the moon are the main protagonists in Rimbaud's psychodrama. Although each makes its presence known throughout the poem, it is the circuitous and deceptive manner in which the moon—the Great Female archetype—imposes her authority throughout the work that becomes crucial. In contrast to the Romantics, such as Nodier, the moon is no longer viewed as an endearing and reflective force. Rimbaud seems to anticipate the growing power of women in society and is frightened by it. He decries the moon's ascendancy as a negative influence (she empowers storms and rain, causes drownings and shipwrecks), even in terms of her positive attributes (she always provides a counterforce when indulging in her bloodthirsty activities, and the crescent moon took the form of the Ark in the Noah myth, saving humans and animals). The very fact that the moon perpetuates life and preserves the illusion that man may one day unravel her mysteries is for Rimbaud a supreme example of her destructive nature.

In Genesis the Flood destroyed all living creatures as punishment for man's wickedness; only Noah, his family, and pairs of the animal kingdom were permitted to survive in a floating ark. No sooner had the primeval waters been released, than chaos reigned; the rhythms of the universe were unleashed, its very structure washed away. A flood according to biblical traditions thus is a sweeping, cataclysmic force that destroys all barriers and dissolves the elements: earth, water, air, fire. According to the alchemists (Rimbaud had been attracted by their works) water in an ebullient state transforms solids into liquids and disparate particles into a single "circulatory process," forcing the component parts to return to the all-embracing monad, or the *quinta essentia*.[2] Alchemy is related to the Noah myth in that Noah's son Shem (or Chem plus the Arabic article *al*) was to have been, according to certain traditions, the originator of this science. Alchemists associated water, not being a fixed agent, with energy and illumination—the "fiery water" or the "secret fire." Stoics alluded to it as "primal warmth". Heraclitus referred to it as the "ever-living fire"; the Gnostics regarded it as a magic and nourishing substance called *mana;* and Thales posited that all comes from water. Homer referred to Oceanus as the "source of the gods" and "the source of all things."[3] Some philosophers, namely the nineteenth-century Lorenz Oken, believed that as a child emerges from the uterine waters, so the sea is a giant uterus, and from it all is born.[4]

For Rimbaud, water at flood level is the fluid chaotic mass, the visceral element that arouses the creative process. Like blood that flows through the body, water circulates throughout the cosmos, adapting to the universal rhythmic movements and individual needs. It therefore becomes a vehicle for adventure, for the excitement of foreign lands—for the unknown. Its power annihilates the status quo, reshuffles natural forces, and strikes hard and brutally at whatever binds man to the phenomenological world and those opaque curtains that prevent perception. Its dynamism parallels the poet's swift, vertiginous, and rebellious nature. Psychologically, flood waters symbolize the "autonomous" upsurge of undifferentiated libido pouring out from the unconscious in image sensations and image energy. This cataclysmic entity is frequently associated with Icarus-like youth, impatient to enact their heroic deeds, to conquer the world or themselves.

In his struggle with and use of this powerful element, Rimbaud becomes a shaman, a seer, a master of ceremonies, in whom the sacred has been made manifest. As a *spiritus creator,*[5] he uproots reason, transcends matter, disorients the senses. His emotions once kindled, his nature grows abrasive, his instincts scalding. In Rimbaud's famous "Letter of the Seer" (May 15, 1871), a type of *ars poetica*, he declares that the real poet "must be a *seer*, must make himself a *seer.*" In order to achieve this goal he must experience life in a new way.

> The Poet makes himself a *seer* by a long, immense, and reasoned
> *disordering* of *all the senses.* He searches himself for all forms
> of love, suffering, madness; he exhausts all the poisons in him-
> self and keeps only their quintessence. During this time of inef-
> fable torture he needs all his faith, all his superhuman force,
> while he becomes above all the great sick one, the great crim-
> inal, the great damned one—the supreme Sage!   Because he
> reaches the *unknown*!...
>
> The poet then is really a stealer of fire.

The poet, Rimbaud declared, must be beyond good and evil. He
must be capable of experiencing all aspects of life, that is, eternal
ideas, feelings, concepts, even a dissociation of the ego. "For I *is*
another," Rimbaud wrote.   The poet is a vessel, an instrument
chosen by a universal soul to create his work.   He is no more
aware of why he has been selected to accomplish this task than a
piece of brass is deciding to become a trumpet.   To achieve his
goal "reason" must be dismantled, inhibitions freed, constraints
destroyed.   The poet's task is arduous. He must degrade himself
and wallow in the most sordid of conditions; he must suffer the
ignominies of soul and body—a dismemberment.   Rimbaud's
doctrine called for anguish and pain so that a new language,
fresh feelings, and sensations could be reached.   In *Illuminations*
and *A Season in Hell* Rimbaud conducted daring experiments in
vocabulary, rhyme, and rhythm.   He renewed the poetry of his
day, which he considered worn and devoid of inspiration: "I
created all the feasts, all the triumphs, all the dramas. I tried to
invent new flowers, new constellations, new skins, new languages.
I believed I had acquired supernatural powers," he wrote in
A Season in Hell.

For Rimbaud the flood waters symbolized a giant *awaken-*
ing. He experienced them not only in terms of his creative instinct but as a psychic happening as well, enabling him to gain insight into his own primitive nature and contact a language he
had all but forgotten, that of *organic life.* The flood image could
be described as a "latent sensation" in that it emerges with
authority and confronts, brutalizes, and vitalizes.   The libido it
releases acts as a transformative agent binding the disparate
parts of the poet (body, mind, soul) like a "plant which needs

earth and sky, sustenance and form" to flourish.[6]

AFTER THE FLOOD

1. *Aussitôt que l'idée du Déluge se fut rassise, un lièvre s'arrêta dans les sainfoins et les clochettes mouvantes, et dit sa prière à l'arc-en-ciel à travers la toile d'araignée.*

As soon as the idea of the Flood had subsided, a hare paused among the sainfoins and the swaying bellflowers, and said his prayer to the rainbow through the spider's web.

Not the actual Flood, Rimbaud specifies, but the "idea of the Flood" is of import to the poet. Thus a telepathic connection between the idea and the word is set up. To Swedenborgians such a relationship indicates an interplay between certain harmonies and cacophonies implicit in the visual designs of the actual vowels and consonants making up the words, and the ideas engendered by them. As components or as tonalities, words are looked upon in this instance as microcosms, aspects of an original universal language before man's fall.[7] The poet who knows how to manipulate these mysterious elements in his work and experiences a correspondence with them in nature becomes a master. Eliphas Lévi wrote, "Man is the earth's thaumaturge, and by his verve, that is to say, his intelligent word, he disposes of fatal forces."[8] The idea as an abstract notion is likewise a powerful stimulus in that it is accompanied by the archetypal image of the flood and thus is endowed with psychic energy. Hence it is an agent of transmutation, a "natural instinct embodied in a mental form."[9]

On the other hand, the association of idea and flood is antithetical: the idea is a product of consciousness, of cognition; the flood, of the unconscious. The image of the flood precedes its "rational construction." It fuses with the intellect only after it has lived for a time in an embryonic state in the oneirosphere. Only with the pulsating waters that finally flood consciousness does the idea become concretized in the word. Rimbaud's introduction of the word idea into the flood image creates an unstable atmosphere, one of perpetual oscillation between cognition and instinct, an organic correspondence between water and air.[10]

By using the word *subsided,* Rimbaud minimizes the grandeur and reduces the spaciousness of the giant cosmic event, the
Flood. In French the verb *asseoir* ("to sit down"), personifies
the image, whereas the English translation cannot capture this
effect. As the Flood literally sits down in Rimbaud's poem, it
gives the impression of being fatigued from its travail and, like
an animal, must pause before going on with its work. The unexpected fixing of this cyclical and impetuous event, the stoppage of the flood waters in space and time, shocks by its very
suddenness.

The stoppage of motion disrupts the rhythmic patterns set
up by the unleashing of feelings and sensations; it also underlines
the disparity in size between the tiny hare and the immense
flood waters. The initial onslaught has come to a halt. A reflective quality permeates the atmosphere as the hare "paused
among the sainfoins and the swaying bellflowers." A momentary
atmosphere of peace is ushered into the scene as the poet seems
to experience "the universal law of equilibrium and harmony
resulting from the analogy of contraries."[11]

Hares are known for their speed, their fleetness, and their
dexterity. They are animals that procreate freely, and in early
Christian art were associated with lust and fertility. A white
hare was frequently placed at the foot of the Virgin Mary to
indicate her dominion over the sensual nature of man.[12] The
image of the hare as used by Rimbaud comprises the speed of
the flood as a creative factor and its intense stillness resulting
from its containment in the act. The duality of the image reinforces the rhythmic extremes within nature and the poet and
paves as well the way for zones of repose.

The hare is endowed with other qualities. It symbolized
the Demiurge among the Algonquin Indians and the prototype
of the Master of the Universe among the Mongols. Osiris was
sometimes represented as "the Great Hare," as an aspect of
"elemental existence." In that the hare is a type of craftsman
ordering the physical world into being and in conformity with
rational patterns, Rimbaud may have looked upon it as a positive
force. For the Gnostic, however, the *Demiourgos* is an evil being,
the creator of the material world that prevents man from experiencing the fullness of divinity. If the image of the hare in Rimbaud's poem thus acts as a barrier and if the poet does not seek

further than the peaceful image that comes into focus in this line, it may spell negativity for him.[13]

The word "sainfoin" comes from the Latin *sanus* and implies "wholesome" or "healthy"; the suffix *faenum*, meaning "hay," introduces the earth and fertility principles. The prefix of "sainfoin" is sometimes confused with the word *saint*, thus adding a religious connotation to the line. The rose-and pur-purine-colored flower of this leguminous plant injects the atmosphere with color and thus emotions concomitant with these joyful and spiritual hues. The hare stops in awe at nature's infinite riches. A lust for life, reminiscent of Van Gogh's sense of abandon when he first began painting in Arles, may be associated with this image.

Because the word *bell* is implicit in "bellflowers," a further emphasis on religion may be discerned. Rimbaud had been brought up in a devout home and had gone through a period of passionate commitment to the church. Bells are made of metal and are vaulted in aspect, thus comparable to the ancients' concept of the shape of heaven. The hanging position of the bell has mystical significance: objects suspended between heaven and earth are endowed with celestial characteristics. As the bell-flowers sway in the wind, they sound out their song and fill the expanse with divine overtones, spreading their message as a censer does its perfume. Wind, which in Rimbaud's poem moves the bellflowers, in biblical literature is considered as spirit (*nous, pneuma*) and endows man with life and a soul.[14] Hence, the wind's function is similar in the poem as body and soul become one in the new creation that has just come into being. The swaying of the bellflowers sets up a countermovement in opposition to the stillness of the hare and the initial onslaught of the primal waters, thus creating a virtual cosmic symphony.

Flowers represent the transitory nature of life and thus they partake in the death and resurrection cycle. Used already during antiquity in funeral pyres and during feasts, flowers are constant reminders of humans to enjoy life as it unfolds—in the eternal present. But man—and Rimbaud is no different from others—has since earliest times attempted to break out of the constrictions imposed by nature to create his own order. In his bout with Utnapishtim (the prototype of Noah), Gilgamesh is promised that the secrets of life will be disclosed to him in a plant.

> Gilgamesh, something secret I will disclose to thee,
>   And give thee thine instruction:
> That plant is like a brier in the field;
>   its thorn, like that of the rose, will pierce thy hand.
> But if thy hand attain to the plant,
>   thou wilt return to thy native land.[15]

No matter what the dangers or restrictions placed before man, he longs to *know.* Rimbaud too, in his wild, restless, brutal way, sought to break through the mask of social (and literary) structure to discern truth. The hare, likewise, attempts to pierce "through the spider's web" by prayer to experience the rainbow as a living force.

Prayer is a *rite de sortie* and a *rite d'entrée.* Because it does away with constrictions that bind people to the world of matter[16] and stirs that "archaic heritage" within man, prayer is considered a transformatory ritual enabling one to experience cosmic consciousness. Once contents are aroused within the psyche through this spiritual experience, which is an energetic process, the doors to the unknown are forced open and images arise autonomously from man's most primitive layers. In these depths he comes to terms with the God within him or his self, thus constellating fresh points of view. The archetypes that flow into consciousness through prayer release new energies, infusing individuals with the strength and power to forge ahead. Prayer, an effective device for all peoples in all stages of development, fills individuals with a kind of animal strength, as though repressed instinct had suddenly been permitted to flow unrestricted.[17] Prayer is a link between the individual and the cosmos; between past, present, and future; it is an anabasis and a katabasis. Like the flood, it either opens up a giant and terrifying void—chaos—or a stunning pastoral image—cosmos.

The hare prays to the "rainbow," thus binding prayer with light. In the Zohar such an accord is described as follows: "Prayer, which ascends from the bottom, illuminating the lamps of the All-High, thus lights shine in heaven, and this is how all worlds are blessed."[18] The rainbow is a bridge linking God to man, the temporal to the spiritual.[19] In the Noah myth God placed a sign of agreement in the heavens in the form of a rainbow.

> And God said, This is the token of the covenant which I make
> between me and you and every living creature that is with you,
> for perpetual generations:
>
> I do set my bow in the cloud, and it shall be for a token cove-
> nant between me and the earth.
>
> And it shall come to pass, when I bring a cloud over the earth,
> that the bow shall be seen in the cloud:
>
> And I will remember my covenant, which is between me and
> you and every living creature of all flesh; and the waters shall
> no more become a flood to destroy all flesh.
>
> (Genesis 9:12-15)

The "spider web," or cloud, hiding the hare from heaven,
may represent the barrier of illusion separating the sense world
from the spiritual realm, or inner from outer reality. The spider
web is also a protective device that enables man to function as a
separate entity, preventing his submersion in the divine flow.
A spider has fascinating characteristics and thus adds complexity
to Rimbaud's image. The spider is both an aggressive and creative force since it weaves its web from its own substance. It is
cyclical, as is life, alternating ceaselessly between death and rebirth. Woven in spirals toward a central point—that of Creation
or the mystic En-Sof from which all emerges and all returns—the
web is a mandala image. In the Christian faith the spider frequently symbolizes the Devil because it weaves a trap for the fly
just as the Devil forever attempts to ensnare man.

Rimbaud's image indicates the hare's desire to pierce
through the opaque network of fibers, rhythms, and sensations
cast in front of it. In its capacity as a demiurge the hare emerged
from primal waters, attempts through incantations to reject the
constraints imposed upon it. It refuses to be caught in the
spider's web, to be victimized and "robbed" of life.[20] But
dangers await the hare as do all those who attempt to transcend
their condition. These heroic or Promethean figures are in peril
of being caught up in the cosmos' sinister aspects. Nietzsche
wrote, "Man is a rope stretched between the animal and the
Superman—a rope over an abyss."[21]

2.   *Oh! les pierres précieuses qui se cachaient,—les fleurs qui regardaient déjà.*

Oh! the precious stones that were hiding—the flowers that already looked around.

Once the flood waters had subsided, nature came into being again. Along with the flowers in varied brilliant colors, the rainbow in pastel tones, and the spider web in shimmering and irridescent hues was born a more sturdy and durable element—"precious stones."

Stones denote unity and strength. Unlike biological entities (flowers, animals, people), they are not subject to quick change. They therefore have come to symbolize a kind of continuity and indestructible strength within nature itself. Consequently, once the "cold-blooded" waters of the unconscious had subsided, light (or the rational principle) penetrated, exposing the treasures (or precious stones) in each individual and force in nature. The same idea was expressed in the biblical tale where "the tops of the mountains" became visible (Genesis 8:5), that is, differentiation occurred, and man began to reason.

Rimbaud's stones are "precious." And since they contain some hidden and mysterious quality, they may be likened to hierophanies. Although stones seem hard and unfeeling on the surface, Orpheus proved that when he played his lyre, the sweetness of the tone could move them. In the Deucalion myth stones are equated with bones as a source of life. Zeus had destroyed the "degenerate" people on earth and Deucalion, upon his father's suggestion, had constructed a wooden chest for himself and his wife, which landed on Mt. Parnassus. Deucalion asked an oracle how life could be restored, and it told him to throw the bones of his mother behind him. Deucalion misunderstood the directives and thought the oracle had said stones. From these stones there arose a new generation.[22]

Stones are associated with arcane knowledge. In the Zohar the seven liberal arts had been inscribed on the seven stone tablets at Hebron, remnants from an antediluvian era. It was also said that Adam's descendants recorded the information gathered from the stone tablets in hieroglyphics on two of the stones and that Noah found one of them at the foot of Mt. Ararat, upon which had been inscribèd the astronomical record.[23] Because stones have been linked to specific religions (the stone that contained Mithras before his birth, the stones used as a *katabasis* in Gilgamesh's search for the plant of immortality), they have come to represent a mystery. To the Hebrews, the stone represents the solidity of the divine message: "And this stone, which I have set for a pillar, shall be God's House" (Genesis 28:22); to the Christians Christ is "the chief corner stone" (I Peter 2:5-7); to the Masons, the Temple of Solomon is "the perfect stone."[24]

For Rimbaud "the precious stones that were hiding" represent the mystery buried within the earth, which is only partially revealed to man in the form of the stone jutting out from the earth's crust. Like the rock, Rimbaud's verse is buried within its own recesses; but when it emerges, it is sturdy and as enigmatic as rock. Within its inner core (of the line of poetry and the stone) lives a soul that breathes and discerns. As *vates,* the poet sees beyond the outer core, the mask, right into this natural entity that is in itself a *complexio oppositorum:* the stone (verse) possesses the fluidity of water, the volatile nature of fire, and is made permanent through cohesion. Consequently, the stone is the poem, the body of thought (ideas, sensations, feelings) given form. The stones are "precious" because like jewels (idea word) they have been cut, faceted, polished, and set into the human spirit in fixed configurations. In Paul Valéry's words: the poet now infuses order, balance, and harmony into the stone, giving it the worth and the perfection of a magnificent Doric column.[25]

"The flowers that already looked around" implies the existence of a natural hierarchy. Although they belong to the vegetable world, flowers understand the mystery of God's immanence. As they look about, thereby displacing space, their aroma blends into the air, their colors tint the atmosphere; their verticality personifies the human form, paralleling man's desire to penetrate the higher spheres of existence. Important too is the religious association to flowers. In Greek mythology, flowers came to be linked with the *puer aeternus:* Tammuz, Attis, Adonis, Hyacinth, Narcissus. These deities died young and had never developed into full manhood. They had been prevented from doing so by the mother figure: the *vagina dentata,* a castrating force.[26]

The *puer aeternus* also refers to the child-god celebrated in the Eleusinian Mysteries, the "child of nature" like Dionysus-Iacchus or Dionysus associated with Eros, mentioned by Ovid in his *Metamorphoses*. This "divine youth" or "redeemer" element is intrinsic of the death-and-resurrection cult. The deities live to die and to be reborn.[26] Only by means of their dismemberment can "Mother Earth" be replenished and satisfied.[27]

According to psychologists the *puer aeternus* become either a homosexual or a Don Juan. Frequently they suffer from a messianic complex, at other times from megalomania. These gods (or men) live through the woman (or the male partner) and cannot grow firm roots into the soil (the world); therefore, they exist in a state of perpetual psychological incest with the mother (whom they either love or seek to destroy). They are thus appendages of the mother and, like an evanescent force, a dream, live ephemerally, as does the flower. In that the *puer aeternus* or "divine youth"is related to seasonal vegetation, his pattern of existence is circular or cyclical.[28]   Van Gogh, interestingly enough, likened the flower to life in its circular aspect: "Life is probably round."[29]

Water is the generative principle in Rimbaud's image, bringing life's dual aspects to the fore: the transitory (flower) and sturdy-durable (rock) factors. Time during such creative moments seems, paradoxically speaking, to have been suspended and so the entire vision is experienced in an eternal present. Although each segment of activity or inactivity in the line is experienced as an entity unto itself, the composite image is viewed by the poet in terms of a "rhythm of ideas" and a "rhythm of things"—a kind of tuning into the cosmic course. At once reversible and irreversible, the poet's time enables him to become integrated into the very heart of the myth. The spatial immensities of the initial "flood idea," contrasted with the minuteness of the hare and flower images, create rhythmic interchanges between the microcosm and the macrocosm, man and divinity—the ego and the self. Henri Michaux phrased this duality in his *News From Foreign Lands* in terms of anguish: "Space, but you cannot conceive of this horrible inside-outside element which true space is."[30]   Such space-spanning arouses Rimbaud's personal and collective unconscious, enriching thus the source of his creativity.

3. *Dans la grande rue sale les étals se dressèrent, et l'on tira les barques vers la mer étagée là-haut comme sur les gravures.*

In the filthy main street butchers' stalls rose, and barges were tugged toward the sea rising up in tiers as in engravings.

From the pagan joys of nature we now come to the sordid ugliness of the industrial society with its machines, its dirt, and its limitations. The "filthy main street" takes Rimbaud into the very heart of bourgeois society: its puritanical ideas, religious bigotry, and regressive sense of morality as opposed to the cleanliness, release, and beauty of nature. The city is associated with the feminine principle in that it both contains and protects its inhabitants. Its "filthy main street" cuts through this enclosed body like an axis, dividing what had once been whole; such as the infant being born, then the adolescent breaking away from the mother for the first time and considering her an impure force.

The "butchers' stalls" may be equated with man's instinctual self. The butcher cuts and treats meat, and prepares it for human consumption, thus preserving man's life by partaking of the earth principle. A dialectical interchange is set up: to kill is to preserve life. In the Noah legend we read: "Every moving thing that liveth shall be meat for you; even as the green herb have I given you all things" (Genesis 9:3). Meat also injects a leveling factor into the picture as opposed to nature's hierarchical plan: all men must eat. Symbolically speaking, to reject meat is to do away with life and by extension with the spirit.

Because meat is vital to man's survival, religions are filled with dismemberment images: Osiris, Dionysus, Christ. The bodies of these divinities were either swallowed or chewed or taken in through the Host to celebrate the sacramental meal. In Greece during the ritual of the Thesmophoria (when Pluto took Persephone to the underworld), the worshippers ate swines' flesh, thus symbolizing the partaking of the god's body; in Meiningen even today the flesh of pigs is eaten on Ash Wednesday and Candlemas, the bones kept and then put into the field or blended with the seeds in a bag, thus assuring fertility for the year; in Mexico the Aztecs used to kill and then eat their god

Huitzilopochtli in effigy, thus communing with him; and in Japan the Ainu ate their god in the form of millet.[31]

To eat the flesh of a god either symbolically or actually, is to assimilate, absorb, and thus to take into oneself the god's being. The sacramental feast is a way of binding people together, of expressing "brotherhood", thereby strengthening one's ties with the collective. Each time the Christian takes Communion, he "reactualizes" the mystery,[32] thus once again experiencing primordial time and returning to his origins—a *regressus ad uterum*. Christ said:

> For my flesh is meat indeed, and my blood is drink indeed. He that eateth my flesh, and drinketh my blood, dwelleth in me, and I in him (John 6:55-56).[33]

To eat the body of God is an aggressive act. Chewing, masticating, swallowing, and digesting, are activities that require the taking in of an outside substance by the individual, thereby perpetuating life's force. Paradoxically, although the eating of flesh in common is basic to Catholicism—the Catholic is also taught to revile the flesh and to consider it unclean. Gnosticism, Illuminism, Neoplatonism (among many sects) believed the body (instinct) envelope prevented the soul from reintegrating into divinity. Therefore anything carnal, beastial, or sensual was looked upon as unworthy and repulsive.

Although he rejected overtly the aesthetic aspects of Christianity, Rimbaud still clung to its imagery. He blamed its doctrine for having been instrumental in destroying natural instinct; for having established an "inhuman" credo; for having divested man's capacity for joy; for having split man right down the middle: spirit to be sought, flesh to be reviled. Kierkegaard had attempted to repair the schism between body (sinful) and mind (spirit and all important) that had alienated man from nature (an extension of the physical world) and from self by returning to primitive Christianity prior to the imposition of the body interdict. Nietzsche, aware of the cleavage within man's psyche, sought to return to the Grecian cults existing before Plato's time: the Dionysian mysteries, which were celebrated in ecstatic and frenzied rituals. He wrote in *Thus Spake Zarathustra:* "I conjure you, my brethren, remain true to the earth, and believe not those who speak unto you of superearthly hopes! Poisoners are they, whether they know it or not."[34]

Rimbaud was caught up in a similar dichotomy: spirit versus body. His mother's rigid, authoritarian, and puritanical view had served to create an abyss within him. Like Nietzsche, Rimbaud attempted to reach out beyond good and evil and become that superman, that destroyer of convention and limited morality. The titanic element within him became full-blown. He dared—like Zarathustra, who exclaimed "What good is my reason."[35] Rimbaud countered in *A Season in Hell*, "I am not prisoner of my reason." He would become that "venturer," that "adventurer."[36] He would embark on those "unexplored seas!" Reason alone—without body—stultifies!

Rimbaud fought with all his might for release from the dominion of the *vagina dentata:* by extension the city and society. His extraordinary energy enabled him to thrash outward, to breathe in life to its fullest, to eat meat—raw and cooked—to celebrate his own sacramental meal. Only by experiencing extremes (vice and virtue) could he become the poet-seer he sought to be. In *A Season in Hell* he spoke out his doctrine: "Do I still know nature? do I know myself?—*No more words.* I bury the dead in my stomach. Cries, drum, dance, dance, dance!" Rimbaud not only demanded freedom, he also had to experience all the cruelties life has to offer: crime, fire, infamy, damnation; otherwise "true life is absent." Infamy must be turned into glory, cruelty into charm. Like his Scandinavian ancestors, he had to drink blood, pierce his side, and become ugly. Only then would he begin to understand and become the poet able to express the inexpressible: "I fixed vertigos."[37]

For Rimbaud poetry was not simply a matter of talent nor of inspiration or revelation. It required a concerted act of the will on the poet's part; it had to be an aggressive and cruel instrument. The poem, like Prometheus' theft of fire, had to disregard conventional form, sensation, ideology. It had to bring chaos with its birth. Cartesian logic had to be dismembered like the meat in the butcher shop, then digested, and then expelled in fresh and provocative forms.

"Barges were tugged toward the sea rising up in tiers as in engravings." In this image Rimbaud literally breaks out of his environment; he is outwardbound. Barges, used to transport freight from one land to another, are like idea-sensations cutting through well-worn paths and hackneyed ideological concepts; they reverse the normal and disrupt the pat. As the barges make their way into the open sea, the energy they create by displacing water may be likened to the circulatory patterns of the various arteries of the body—interpenetrating every part of the individual in question and the cosmos by extension. Like in his poem "Drunken Ship", Rimbaud senses feelings of release and the joy of discovery as the barge makes its way into the unknown.

"The sea rising up in tiers" may be likened to various levels of consciousness, with the dangers implicit in each. The ship's course or the poet's adventure places him in constant peril: the waves might sink the barge, his unconscious might overwhelm his consciousness. But water (or the unconscious) is also a perpetual storehouse of treasures that enriches the traveler with the myriad sights seen; consciousness enables him to differentiate and to sift the material emerging from the oneirosphere, thus helping him create his masterpiece. Rimbaud's barges would either be a Ship of Death or Noah's Ark.

The water "rising up in tiers" is a perfect metaphor to describe the various stages of the neophyte's initiation into life or into the poet's arcane world. The tiers may also be compared to the various layers in a tree or the many geological stratas in the earth, and therefore form both an anabasis or a katabasis. These tiers or levels are compared to "engravings." The art of engraving requires knowledge, discipline, and a variety of steps to complete the process. Rimbaud was familiar with it since he had spent some time with Forain, Gill in Paris and also knew the works of Cranach, Dürer, Rembrandt, and Goya. Moreover, engraving had become a popular art in the nineteenth century. Millet etched scenes of peasants at work in *The Gleaners;* Géricault, Gavarni, Delacroix, and Daumier completed hundreds of engravings and etchings. Like the engraver, the poet must confront matter. Only in this manner can corrosive sensations, images which society labels distorted and shocking, be born. The poet must also allow life to *engrave* itself upon him: he must, therefore, experience terror, fear, anguish, and suffering as had the great artists of the past who had entered their primal worlds: Bosch, Brueghel, Grünewald, Giotto. Tranquility and security are not the instruments alotted the hero who seeks to cut out the new from the well-worn. As Christ said:

> Think not that I am come to send peace on earth: I came not
> to send peace, but a sword.
>
> For I am come to set a man at variance against his father, and
> the daughter against her mother, and the daughter-in-law
> against her mother-in-law (Matthew 10:34-35).

4. *Le sang coula, chez Barbe-Bleue,—aux abattoirs,—dans
les cirques, où le sceau de Dieu blêmit les fenêtres. Le
sang et le lait coulèrent.*

Blood flowed, at Bluebeard's,—in slaughterhouses,—in
circuses, where the seal of God whitened the windows.
Blood and milk flowed.

Tranquillity and security become unacceptable to Rimbaud.
Let blood flow—in the sacramental meal, in butchershops, in
war—let men and animals be slaughtered, for only dismemberment leads to the path of *renovatio*. The poet, therefore, must
make himself vulnerable to pain. Blood sacrifices are *de rigueur;*
they denote the intensity of faith. Before the Exodus, the
enslaved Hebrews sacrificed the paschal lamb; its blood was
smeared on the doorsteps of their homes to prevent the angel
of death from killing their firstborn. And "the blood shall be
to you for a token upon the houses where ye are; and when I see
the blood, I will pass over you, and the plague shall not be upon
you to destroy you, when I smite the land of Egypt" (Exodus
12:13). The idea of blood as a protective force Rimbaud expresses in the image, "where the seal of God whitened the windows."

Blood is also linked to castration and death rituals, thus to
fertility: after Attis castrated himself violets sprang from his
blood; Joseph of Arimathea gathered up in the Holy Grail
Christ's blood after the crucifixion which led to redemption.
The spilling of blood (in communion or war, for religious or
poetic sacrifice) dazzles and dazes Mother Earth, who sucks the
blood in deep swallows. As it travels through the recesses of her
realm, nourishing her every step of the way, a new growth
and a new sensibility come into being. Rimbaud, the adolescent, the poet, is now experiencing this same sense of fulfillment.

In the allegory of the pelican as rendered by Alfred de Musset in his poem "May Night," this bird (Christ) claws open his own flesh so that his children may feed freely upon him, thus giving them the necessary nourishment and energy to live through their existence. The pelican is the sacrificial agent which allows himself to bleed to death for his family (and for society); he is the poet who is bled by society which feeds upon him. Rimbaud the poet is both a sacrificial agent (pelican) and a destroyer of the status quo, the feminine principle (Bluebeard).[38]

"Blood and milk flowed." The pelican gives of his blood as a mother gives of her milk. Blood and milk are nutritive and life-giving agents, whether considered from a physical or from a spiritual sphere. Blood is linked to milk in alchemical tracts as well as in the work of the Gnostics, such as in *Odes of Solomon*, where the father, an androgynous figure, gives blood, milk, and semen.

> A cup of milk was offered to me: and I drank it in the sweetness of the delight of the Lord. The Son is the cup, and He who was milked is the Father: and the Holy Spirit milked Him: Because His breasts were full, and it was necessary for Him that His milk should be sufficiently released; and the Holy Spirit opened his bosom and mingled the milk from the two breasts of the Father; and gave the mixture to the world without their knowledge.[39]

The Gnostic Clement of Alexandria looked upon father's milk as *logos;* the Stoics' regarded it as *logos spermatikos*, as the creative force of the word.[40]

Rimbaud's allusion to blood in terms of Bluebeard, a venerable alchemist, indicates a negative attitude to the mother archetype. Like Bluebeard, who murdered his wives because he could not dominate their curiosity, which he felt represented an eternal threat to his well-being, so the poet must be weary too of those maternal forces that purport to be eternally nutritive.

When associated with wine in the religious service, blood is linked to the vine and to the earth. When Noah began taking care of the vine, he became a "man of the ground" and was no longer the "pious one."[41] When he drank wine, he experienced his own type of "disorientation of the senses." In Genesis we read: "And he drank of the wine, and was drunken; and he was uncovered within his tent" (9:21). Blood is thus linked with drunkeness and ecstasy, and with orgiastic and instinctual ways, as in the Dionysian rituals. Although Christ is associated with wine in the sacramental offering (the drinking of his blood),[42] there is also a Dionysian element within Him, as exemplified in the "miracle at Cana."

> I am the true vine, and my Father is the husbandman.
> Every branch in me that beareth fruit, he purgeth it,
> that it may bring forth more fruit...
> I am the vine, ye are the branches (John 15:1-5).

The "miracle at Cana" is comparable to "the miracle in the temple of Dionysus" as viewed in "The Damascus Chalice," which features Christ amidst the vine, and in this respect is reminiscent of the statues of Dionysus in similar poses.[43] It has been posited that during the early days of Christianity Christ still represented the lusty, physical Greek God Dionysus as well as the "bodiless" spiritual entity—the all-*white* being— the Christ of later centures.

Because blood is linked to wine, it encourages "the sacramental vision of reality," permitting those who imbibe it entry into limitless areas and participation in the most profound stratas of the sensual world. As mescaline made the primal area of being accessible to Aldous Huxley, so the "universe of a diminished conscience vanishes."[44]

In that blood nourishes, sustains, revitalizes, and is also a mysterious force, it represents the *elixir vitae*, the alchemists' *aqua permanens*, and for Rimbaud that exquisite burgeoning of energy which knows no bounds: "Hunger, thirst, screams, danse, danse, danse, danse!"[45] That power enabled him to become the superman; that stimulant gave him the power to dissociate himself with the visible world.

5. *Les castors bâtirent. Les "mazagrans" fumèrent dans les estaminets.*

Beavers did their building. Glasses of black coffee steamed in the cafés.

Beavers are active animals; they are builders. They live in streams and lakes, and in colonies. They are noted for their fur and for the intricate construction of their huts (both above and below water), protections against ever-present enemies. Beavers chip away at trees with their incisor teeth and use the pieces they gather for food as well as to build their houses. To Rimbaud these animals represent bourgeois society, the established order, ossified religious ideologies. These stereotyped eager beavers are imitators who live in such a circumscribed manner that they come to represent the collective, and as such the lowest strata. "I hate all trades," Rimbaud wrote in *A Season in Hell.* "Masters and workmen, all ignoble peasants."[46]

"Glasses of black coffee steamed in the cafés." This line ushers in a conventional and an exotic quality. Conventional it is because the coffeehouse was a gathering place for gossip, talk, and gamble. Will's coffeehouse in London boasted of having had Dryden, Swift, Goldsmith, and Hogarth as its habitués; Le Café de la Régence in Paris had offered Voltaire, Diderot, d'- Alembert, and many others hours of relaxed chatter. Just as the collective gathered in the "filthy main street," many others including the élite—gathered in coffeehouses. Coffee also a- rouses exotic images: fantasies of distant lands, tropical realms, an archaic past. Coffee was grown in Ethiopia, the Congo, Liberia, Yemen, Sumatra, Egypt, and Turkey. It was brought to Arabia in the fifteenth century and to Europe by the middle of the seventeenth. Ironically, Rimbaud himself was to become a coffee exporter.

Black coffee represents the alchemist's *massa confusa,* the chaos or flooding of matter when differentiation is obliterated. The allusion to alchemy is further underscored with the word *steamed,* giving the impression of an alchemical brew when the essence of the element—or the God hidden within the blackness of matter—is extracted. Like the *bain-marie* of the alchemist, the vessel in which distillation takes place—the *solve et coagula—* so the dissolution of inferior elements also comes to pass. Each moment during the cooking process represents another phase of the inner-soul state. Like the *grand oeuvre of the alchemist,* so the brewing of coffee proceeds from lower to higher forms, from brute to purified matter. It is through the flame (fire, flood, passion), the active, volatile element within man and nature, that the coffee's aroma blends into the atmosphere and its essence is extracted and imbibed in liquid form. Like Communion wine or the Host or prayer, the parishioner experiences inner strength from this numinous force.

The glasses which contain the steaming coffee are comparable to the alchemist's *kerotakis,* the enclosed vase in which pieces of copper and other metals were vaporized. Allusions may also be made in this regard to the *philosophical egg,* a kind of symbol of the world. To extract the quintessence from the blend required great care in following the intricacies of the heating process so that the proper fusion could take place.[47] Thus in life, the masses who viewed the brewing coffee were unaware of the process going on, of the numinous experience about to be lived—they lived peripherally, on the outside of things, enjoying the fruits of the creator's toil.

Glass may well define Rimbaud's personality. It is hard, brittle, cutting, abrasive, and usually transparent (though not always). As Rimbaud cut his way through freedom, hurting his "dragon" mother in the process, he created a world as pure as crystal, as beauteous as dawn, and as prismatic in its countless reflections. "O purity! purity. It is this minute of awakening that gave me the vision of purity!"

Glass and crystals are comparable. In Revelation we read about "a sea of glass like unto crystal" (4:6). Glass may look like or be made of crystal, bringing to mind the "precious stones" earlier in the poem. In ancient Rome rock crystal was supposed to be congealed ice. Saint Gregory wrote:

> Crystal may be gathered of water. Water is of itself fleeting; but by strength of cold it is turned and made stedfast Crystal. Men know that it is of snow or ice, made hard in space of many years.[48]

The fact that glass is usually transparent indicates a *coniunctio* for the mystic: matter exists, yet does not seem to. Because of its beauty, clarity, transparency, and reflective power, glass, like water, has the ability to mesmerize; because of its sparkling nature, it has been likened to stars, thus representing diffusion in a cohesive object, multiplicity in oneness. The glasses containing the black coffee in Rimbaud's image is a feminine symbol—a containing vessel—from which all must be extracted, imbibed, and thus released.

6.   *Dans la grande maison de vitres encore ruisselante, les*
     enfants en deuil regardèrent les merveilleuses images.

In the still dripping big house with glass panes, children
in mourning looked at the marvelous reflections.

The entire atmosphere of the "big house" with the rain
"still dripping" on the "glass panes" extends the previous image
of the steaming coffee glasses and at the same time captures the
foggy and misty climes of northern France with the spray released from the barges as they make their way into the open sea.
Fog and mist, which circulate in these images, prevent one from
seeing clearly, like the "spider's web," at the beginning of the
poem, that blocked the sky's clarity and curtained the sun's
rays, thus diminishing the universe's light. To live in a "fog"
is to lighten man's task; it is to accept the conventional, the
uninspired, the well-trodden road. To break out of these dismal
surroundings requires combustion, breakage, and terror. "Isn't
it because we cultivate mist" that the modern world lacks the
sagacity of Oriental ways, that "poisons" are the rule of the
day—for both the soul and the mind?[49]

The "big house" refers to city dwellings as well as to the
constructions of beavers. Temporal abodes indicate man's and
animal's need to enclose and protect, to acquire some kind of
security and permanence in imitation of nature's immortality.
But Rimbaud, a believer in flux, danger, destruction, unpre-
dictability, and excesses, sought to break out of the secure but
imprisoning realm and to jump into the waters of life. "I am
escaping," he wrote in *A Season in Hell.*[50]

The "children in mourning" may refer to himself when
young. Like the stone, the house represents "a corner of the
world."[51] For the child this domain is his universe. Within its
walls time and space are experienced like a theatrical round.
The child is at the heart of the drama. He is the master of his
own ceremonies as he directs the forces and objects about him.
He is not as yet fossilized; his fantasy still reigns supreme as he
alters notions and things to suit himself. When a child looks at
picture books, each page floods his imagination with dreams and

excitement; when he gazes out of the window, reason has not halted his creative activity. Rimbaud's childhood was similar. However, his home was a prison and the window represented release. Reading and pictures triggered off his power of forming mental pictures.

Rimbaud is in mourning now: bleak, black, disconsolate. Although it had never been happy, he mourns the death of his childhood, a time when he found release in his ability to fantasize. Like other children, he sees the "marvelous reflections," even a watery self-image. The reflective quality of Rimbaud's symbols (glass, water, rainbow, pane) throughout lightens and enlivens the somber atmosphere of the poem and also creates the effect of multiplicity, choice, futurity—consisting in the child's innumerable possibilities in life. The child, not yet dazzled by his own image as was Narcissus, longs for the world beyond the window, for there the dream takes hold: "This inspiration proves that I have dreamed!"[52] The child's capacity for whimsy is limitless, like the fountain in the Noah myth: "The fountains also of the deep and the windows of heaven were stopped, and the rain from heaven was restrained" (Genesis 8:2).

7. *Une porte claqua, et, sur la place du hameau, l'enfant tourna ses bras, compris des girouettes et des coqs des clochers de partout, sous l'éclatante giboulée.*

A door slammed, and, in the village square, the child waved his arms, understood by weather vanes and cocks on steeples everywhere, under the glittering downpour.

The slamming of the door changes the mood of reverie and enchantment. A sudden stoppage of communication takes place, halting the undulatory rhythmic effects and inciting counterpoint rhythms. The slamming of a door may result from an act of aggression. The onomatopoeic French word *claquer* serves to cut off all access to the outer world. It deafens, divides, "knots," seals, and impedes dispersion of forces into cosmic spheres.

The child attempts to keep the door open to prolong his imaginative orgy. The mystic will try to untie the knots in order

to experience the ineffable, "the flood of the divine stream."[53]
The fine artist is aware of the fact that the door of his unconscious must be closed at certain periods, thus permitting consciousness to fulfill its task of differentiating the flood of material with which it is faced. To liberate oneself completely, psychologically speaking, would overwhelm man's consciousness
and his capacity to sift the outpourings of sensible forms or
images from the collective unconscious. Water without a dam
inundates. Rimbaud's eidetic power also had to be tempered.

The "village square" which may be round, rectangular or
triangular, is unually placed in the center of a community.
This center point is comparable to the café or "the filthy main
street," a gathering place of the multitude. It is here that ideas
are exchanged, activities indulged in. Churches are frequently
built in these central areas, and in this regard may be looked
upon as mandala images or as points of contemplation where
natural self-healing may occur. Psychologically this central
image introduced into the poem at this juncture implies a withdrawal from extremities or the affirmation of an introverted
attitude, reminiscent of the house image and the slamming of
the door.

The "child waved his arms" as he stood in the square in a
gesture of abandon and joy—in full communion with the natural
forces around him. Because so many look toward the child as
the hope of the future, divine children or child heroes have been
replete in the history of all civilizations: Moses, Apollo, Hercules, Hermes, Dionysus, Christ, and so on. These children are
primordial figures, *filius ante patrem.* They represent unity
and plurality: the beginning and the end; *renatus in novam
infantiam:* pre-and post-consciousness.[54]

The spontaneous manifestation of this child archetype in
Rimbaud's poem may indicate an undeveloped factor emerging
within his own psyche, a pre-conscious happening, a connecting
principle coming to the fore and linking him with his past, present, and future. The child is an embryo, the storehouse of
potentials. For the alchemist the child was like the philosophers'
stone in that within him lived all possibilities. Christ said:
"Verily I say unto you, Except ye be converted, and become as
little children, ye shall not enter into the kingdom of heaven"
(Matthew 18:3). Unless the unsophisticated, spontaneous, fresh,

and unspoiled content in human beings is given free expression, new or original forms cannot come into being. Meister Eckhart's vision of the "naked boy" and the "Radiant Boy" of the English ghost stories are emanations of the *puer aeternus.* Goethe's Faust in Part II became a young boy and member of the "choir of blessed youths" before completing his life's sojourn as Doctor Marianus.[55]

"Weather vanes and cocks on steeples" are symbols of ascension, elevation, and spirituality. A working relationship thus exists between the boy who waves his arms in the square and the weather vanes blowing in the wind: he is "understood" by these objects. As the child looks, waving his arms, his lungs fill with a sense of infinity—verticality, spaciality—and he is enraptured. The wind (*nous,* spirit) that blows high above the building and pours down from the heavens in the form of sparkling rain, nourishes the child's fantasy world. Like celestial crystals or the mystic's *scintillas,* the rain freshens the atmosphere with new concepts and attitudes.[56]

The heights and lows of Rimbaldian imagery indicate a desire to hurtle through the air. Like the prisoners in Plato's allegory of the cave, so the child—like Icarus who still lives in an undifferentiated realm—dreams of communing with the sky, of flowing wildly through nature, the possessor of infinite power.

8. *Madame *** établit un piano dans les Alpes. La messe et les premières communions se célèbrèrent aux cent mille autels de la cathédrale.*

Madame *** installed a piano in the Alps. Mass and first communions were celebrated at the hundred thousand altars of the cathedral.

The "Madam" in the poem may refer to Rimbaud's mother who never understood him and against whose unbending nature he rebelled. In a letter (September 24, 1870) to Rimbaud's teacher, Georges Izembard, after her son's flight from home, she wrote: "Is it possible to understand the foolishness of this child, he, ordinarily so wise and so tranquil? How could such folly have come into his mind?" Rimbaud introduced the word *Madame* in other poems, in 1872 for example, in "Madame

Stands Too Straight in the Prairies" and in "The Seven-Year-Old Poet."

The image of the personal mother and the maternal principle in general runs through Rimbaud's idea-vision. The word *installed* in connection with the piano on top of the Alps indicates the imposition of a home environment with all of the security and restrictions therein implied. The piano, an instrument appealing to the intellect (the Pythagorean mathematical concept of the music of the spheres) and to the senses (tones, rhythms, cadences, etc.), is placed on a mountain top, indicating the poet's desire to break out of the family structure or out of poetic conventions. Although Rimbaud's mother would never have thought of placing a piano on a snowcapped mountain, and the very mention of such an idea would seem grotesque, the juxtaposition of these notions indicates his own imprisonment within the eternal feminine force: this authoritative, structured woman that lived with him in such a destructive way. Rimbaud's rejection of conformity, the fact that he hung around cafés in dirty rags, his use of scatology, were all designed to destroy what he despised—mother, city, society—the *vagina dentata type.* But, by the same token, he had perhaps become a prisoner of his own negative ways.

The image of the Alps, representing not only verticality (implicit from the outset of the poem), but iciness and remoteness again as well, Rimbaud's desire to liberate himself from a previous outlook; it also reveals an intense need to experience communion with the universe and is reminiscent of the child waving his arms in the village square. Mountain imagery figures in most religions: Mt. Sinai, Mt. Tabor, Mt. Meru, Mt. of Olives, Mt. Caf, and so on. Mt. Meru was the abode of Indra the "swashbuckler" god who embodied cosmic energy and heroic qualities and was the most "human" of the Hindu divinities. His mountain lay at the center of the earth, between heaven and earth in the Himalayas, and was associated with the polar star.[57] Rimbaud's mountain like Indra's is snowcapped; it is condusive to meditation, and to poetic creativity because of the piano. These polar heights indicate crystal-clear vision for miles around, thus clarity of insight. The mountain also injects a sense of power over the world. To scale it is a difficult task because of the dangers awaiting the climber, and is ensnaring due to the shimmering crystals that blind and mesmerize. Yet, in Rimbaud's

vision the child in him is painfully aware that he too will be entrapped in the dynamics of a pattern he is powerless to alter—
that is, the stages of life: birth, childhood, adolescence, middle
and old age.   The more he attempts to subjugate his fears, the
greater is his hatred for society and for himself.   Contrary to
Julien Sorel's flight to high mountains in Stendhal's *The Red and
the Black,* and Sorel's identification with the eagle and with
Napoleon, Rimbaud could not experience the ecstasy that comes
with weightlessness.   He was a prisoner of his own needs and
thus was unable to reach the higher planes of discernment.   He
could not complete his *rite de passage* because he could never
comprehend the metaphysical truth as stated in the *Rig Veda;*
"he who understands has wings."[58]

Mountain imagery is important in the Noah myth and as
such was meaningful to Rimbaud because of his identification
with it. In Genesis we read:

> And the waters prevailed exceedingly upon the earth; and all
> the high hills, that were under the whole heaven, were cov-
> ered (7:19).

> And the waters decreased continually until the tenth month:
> in the tenth month, on the first day of the month, were the
> tops of the mountains seen

> And it came to pass at the end of forty days, that Noah opened
> the window of the ark which he had made:

> And he sent forth a raven, which went forth to and fro, until
> the waters were dried up from off the earth (8:5-7).

Similar images of hills, mountains, and windows, are present in
"After the Flood." The raven, like the weather vanes and steeple
cocks the child sees in the square (line 7), was used as a recon-
noitering agent by Noah. He sent it out to assess the situation,
to find out whether dry land had emerged. For Rimbaud, they
pointed to the four corners of the earth, they told him where
the wind was emerging from and where it was to go.

"Mass and First Communions were celebrated at the hundred thousand altars of the cathedral." This sentence expresses
the eternal repetition of man's needs in terms of ritual and

prayers. The sameness of life becomes an impasse for the poet-creator. Were the conventional world to be circumvented, would not the new, the original, likewise follow a pattern eventually? Would man always be hampered by his physical and spiritual limitations? Nietzsche answered this question: *"I teach you the Superman.* Man is something to be surpassed. What have ye done to surpass Man?"[59] Rimbaud, in the ebullience of youth, could not take time out to meditate upon the question of whether he could succeed in breaking out of man's vicious cycle. He had not yet learned—as was Icarus' fate—that time is an active factor in paving the way to understanding.

9. *Les caravanes partirent. Et le Splendide-Hôtel fut bâti dans le chaos de glaces et de nuit du pôle.*

Caravans departed. And the Hotel Splendide was erected in the chaos of ice and of polar night.

Caravans transport wares from one land to another. They denote a remote time in history, an archaic civilization. The Queen of Sheba, for example, arrived in Jerusalem from Yemen with her caravans filled with precious goods. Rimbaud's caravans are leaving the village square, the center of the metropolis. The poet now seeks to exteriorize his vision. He wants to send the precious wares within him out into the world for all to see. The Hotel Splendide, a conventional tourist hotel, is a meeting place, like the village's main square or street, but on an international and national level. The frenzy of activity in this kind of hotel, with the hustle and bustle of foreign merchants trying to sell and buy wares, lends a chaotic atmosphere to the image.

Rather than reminding one of the warmth engendered by activity, the hotel's location on the "chaos of ice and of polar night" is reminiscent of the piano "installed" on the Alps. There is a frozen, deathlike quality in such glazed imagery. In contrast to the ebullience and burning interchange of the blood images in the early stanzas, the poet's sensations are now fixed and congealed; the warmth of passion, immobilized in thoughts, is buried in the black night. Inaction is now the rule. The ice, the snowcapped mountains, the crystal glasses, the "glittering downpour," the "white windows," the "precious stones" are like so many moods solidified in some archaic past.

The juxtaposition of white (the Alps) and black (the polar night) is terrifying. The tops of mountains are usually associated with light—whether spiritual or physical. But Rimbaud's peaks are chaotic and icy. The animal in him has not been subdued and his spiritual realm is still antipathetic, he has not yet come to terms with instinct and has not yet come to accept the "divine," the "rational" restricted order imposed upon him by the female society.

10. *Depuis lors, la Lune entendit les chacals piaulant par les déserts de thym—et les églogues en sabots grognant dans le verger. Puis, dans la futaie violette, bourgeonnante, Eucharis me dit que c'était le printemps.*

From that time, the Moon heard jackals howling through the wilderness of thyme—and eclogues in wooden shoes grumbling in the orchard. Then, in the forest, violet-hued, burgeoning, Eucharis told me that it was spring.

In the preceding image the heavens were black. The rational principle, as viewed in the "chaos of ice," was no longer clear nor valid, but rather muddled, indicating that some kind of impasse had been reached. To relieve the infinite darkness of polar night, the moon begins to dominate the scene. Rimbaud capitalizes the moon, thus according it the importance of a divinity.

Like the polar night, the moon is a cold body. It lives only through reflection. In its reflective capacity it is attached to the imagination, to the psyche in man, and thus has the power to dictate over the phenomenological world. The moon does not glow in the harsh, brilliant masculine way of the sun, but rather in the more feminine, eerie, and mysterious manner of the unconscious prevailing in the existential world. It is Rimbaud's archaic past, dominated not by water at this point, but by an even more powerful influence, that which affects water, the most primitive force within his unconscious—the Great Mother archetype in her triune aspect: celestial, terrestrial, and infernal.

It is only the moon's infernal aspect that holds Rimbaud spellbound. Associated with the darkness of the moon was Hecate, the Greek night deity that reigned over the lower world and tantalized men, aroused ghosts, and haunted crossroads and graves. Her companions were hounds and hares (the animal mentioned in line 1). She inspired infernal passions and frightening fatal relationships. In his poem Rimbaud mentions "jackals howling through the wilderness" when viewing the moon in the sky. Aggressive and carniverous animals, the jackals (wild dogs) travel in the dark in packs. They were sacred in ancient Egypt and personified in the jackal-faced god Anubis, the accompanist of the dead during their "night-sea journey." Jackals represent those dark, frightening, yet divine forces that hold sway in man's unconscious. Like instincts they are ferocious when unfed.[60]

The moon is a fecundating force, and overabundance can cause wilderness. A "wilderness of thyme" implies a state of utter loneliness and alienation from nature. The "wooden shoes," symbolizing the peasants, always grumbling and dissatisfied with their lot, are no more endearing to Rimbaud than is industrial urban society. Rimbaud could only feel an affinity with nature in the raw, unspoiled and untarnished; but not with the "prosaic" or conventional nature of those who earned their livelihood from the earth, for they too had as limited a relationship with it as those who lived in the dirty cities.

Forest symbolism—associated so frequently with the unconscious, the Great Mother, the vegetal and primeval world—no longer inspires fear and trembling. Because of his existential experiences Rimbaud had come to terms with this instinctual realm. Considered by some as safe and protective forces, the house and city are destructive insofar as Rimbaud is concerned. The forest, looked upon as a regressive and frightening area, is the seat of the poet's burgeoning forces. Now lit by the rays of the moonlight, the forest has become a differentiated area. The blackness of death has been transformed into the lighter hues of rebirth.

It is the blackness of the polar night—or what the Greeks called "melancholia"—that Rimbaud experiences the death of his former attitude and the burgeoning of new forces. He feels as though he has imbibed *soma*, the drink "brewed from the moon tree," which for some is a source of illumination, for others, intoxication and madness.[61]

The "violet-hued" colors discerned in the forest are active

forces. Like the deep color of blood, they take on the *mana* function and become catalyzing agents. Violet is the color worn by bishops of the Catholic Church and, like red, it is a regal, violent, and ardent tonality representing unsublimated forces within nature. It is in turbulence and not in peaceful calm that Rimbaud will experience a burgeoning.

"Eucharis told me that it was spring." Eucharis was Calypso's most beautiful nymph. According to Fénelon she did not want to release Telemachus, Ulysses' son. Spellbound by her beauty, Telemachus remained a prisoner of his emotions. Eucharis, then, represents the alluring female figure; like Calypso, she is a cold-water, fishlike entity who reigns over man. It was Minerva, under the features of Mentor (the intellect or male principle) who succeeded in separating the young hero from this death-dealing female. Rimbaud's image of renewal as announced by Eucharis is far from being an optimistic one: to experience life on her terms—that is, as her prisoner—is to give up any possibility of growth and independence. On the contrary, it is to agree to castration. In that there is an association to be made between the nymph Eucharis and the Eucharist, Sacrament, one might say that to imbibe the body and blood of Christ in Communion would likewise lead to cyclical sameness—or an imprisonment—and not to the superhuman characteristics hoped for by youth.

It is the moon's force that prevails: the female element as it functions in its dark, passionate atmosphere, encouraging the growth of aromatic herbs (thyme), sweet-smelling flowers (violets), but destructive as well in the form of howling jackals and Eucharis, who entraps and ensnares man by prolonging the illusion that through subservience to her man will find fulfillment.

11. *Sourds, étangs;—Ecume, roule sur le pont et pardessus les bois;—draps noirs et orgues,—éclairs et tonnerre,—montez et roulez;—Eaux et tristesses, montez et relevez les Déluges.*

Gush forth, pond;—Foam, roll above the bridge and over the woods—black palls and organs—lightning and thunder—rise and roll—Waters and sorrows, rise up and release the Floods again.

The flood waters "gush forth" once again and "foam

mounts as the *rite d'entrée* begins its final phase. Rimbaud
has called upon confusion to engulf him. He is now compelled
to face the elements (earth, water, fire, air) existentially—as
matter, instinct, energy, spirit—not in terms of the outside
world but as they function within him. The one who emerges
from this difficult trial may experience an inner transcendental
light, thus becoming one of the elect, a *voyant*. The psychic
experience Rimbaud undergoes may be likened to the chaos
cultivated by the shaman, which leads to the "foundations of a
new sensibility."[62] It has been described as follows:

> ...a mysterious light that the shaman suddenly feels in his body,
> in the interior of his head at the very centre of the brain, an
> inexplicable guiding light, a luminous fire which makes him able
> to see in the dark, literally as well as figuratively, for now he is
> able, even with his eyes closed, to see through the darkness and
> see things and events of the future, hidden from other beings.
> In this way he can see into the future as well as into the secrets
> of others...it is as though the house in which he is were suddenly
> lifted up; he can see very far in front of him, right through the
> mountains, exactly as if the earth were one great plain and his
> sight reached to the ends of the earth. Nothing is now hidden
> before him. Not only is he now able to see a long way, but he
> can also discover the stolen souls, whether they are guarded,
> hidden in strange distant places, or whether they have been
> carried away up on high, or down below into the land of the
> dead.[63]

A neophyte has to die and return to the source of life, to pre-
natal darkness, to the void, in order to be reborn. Only within
this blackness can light be seen. Darkness in this instance is the
very *principia vitae* of all that exists. Isaiah wrote:

> And I will give thee treasures of darkness, and hidden riches
> of secret places, that thou mayest know that I, the Lord, which
> call thee by thy name, am the God of Israel (45:3).

The blackness of the turbulent waters has brought sorrows
to the poet. Rimbaud has withdrawn into his self; he has adopted once again an introverted attitude. The key to the change
may have occurred with the mountain symbolism, continued
with the "wilderness" in the pastoral scenes, and the haunting
and mysterious sojourn of the moon. But all initiations must be

secret. Aristotle justified the rule of concealment surrounding the rituals at Eleusis and Samothrace because he felt the lessons to be learned during certain ordeals in life cannot be transmitted to others—they belong to the domain of experience. The cerebral disciplines were not the vital factor, rather, the influx of new feelings brought to consciousness as a result of such trials.[64]

The antithetical color effects (red, black), the harsh and deafening sonorities (thunder, foam, rolling), and the violence of the lightning that sears and cuts through the very fabric of the image, brings to mind Dürer's statement concerning art: "For art truly is hidden in nature; he who can tear it out, has it."[65]

Transformation engenders sorrow, and though blood symbolizes both the death of one attitude and the birth of another, each alteration of feeling, sensation, and ideation is now experienced by the poet in sorrow.

12. *Car depuis qu'ils se sont dissipés,—oh! les pierres précieuses s'enfouissant, et les fleurs ouvertes!—c'est un ennui! et la Reine, la Sorcière qui allume sa braise dans le pot de terre, ne voudra jamais nous raconter ce qu'elle sait, et que nous ignorons.*

For since they have vanished,—oh! the precious stones burying themselves, and the opened flowers!—what boredom! and the Queen, the Sorceress who kindles her coals in the earthen pot, will never be willing to tell us what she knows, and what we do not know.

The poet-creator is tired of the continuous effort expended to bring forth the new; he even wonders whether life's eternal cycle of death and rebirth is not just another illusion. Once the *mystai* (poet) has experienced his depths, he either finds new fields to conquer or follows the same trajectory he already knows which would surely lead to boredom. New moons are like old moons. Even the "opened flowers" bore Rimbaud. The enthusiasm and energy which accompany each new beginning are followed by despair at the finale. In the past, man worshiped nature and perceived its living soul beneath the material form—

346 *Dream and Image*

the laurels, myrtle, and hydrangeas, were associated with goddesses such as Aphrodite, Hera, and Artemis—and the world at large seemed vital and vigorous. In time, nature was "sterilized" and its force paled. Once catalyzing agents, flowers worked on the spirit and body of man. Now, whether flowers are in full bloom or not is of little importance to the poet.

He even tires of the Queen, "the Sorceress who kindles her coals in the earthen pot." Like a female alchemist, she keeps cooking her materials; she remains the magician, the master of ceremonies she has always been; the Lamia, or nightmare, who sows her demoniac power and brings about pain, suffering—suffocation. A feeling of resentment against this "queen of heaven" or "queen of the earth and mistress of the field" is sounded but with less anger than in the previous stanzas. Whether the poet experiences this female force in her nymphlike disguise, as Eucharis, or in her "deathly womb," as the breeder of cities and forests, or as a "devouring whirlpool," the maker of floods, he no longer fears her power, but is bored by her ways.[66]

But despite Rimbaud's heroic pretenses, his one-sided attitude toward the moon as a castrating force, as a modifier or transformer of nature, is evident in the image of the "kindling coals." It is the moon who lights the fire, who provides the pot or cauldron, who generates the warmth, the life, that magical force. It is Rimbaud's task to rob her of her power. "I am the stealer of fire." Fire, expressed linguistically in such aggressive words as *furor, ferg, wut, menos,*[67] becomes the bone of contention between these two cosmic principles: the female archetype as envisaged in the moon image and the masculine transcendental principle as viewed in the solar hero—or Rimbaud. The moon as sorceress has become the "master of fire" the "swallower of live coals." Hence, she kindles the energy leading to religious ecstasy—once the proud privilege of the shaman and priests. She now reigns supreme.

The earthen pot in which she kindles her coals is a *kratophany* (the manifestation of an impersonal life-force).[68] It implies in terms of Rimbaud's personal psychology those spiritual and sexual forces which are in the process of being liquefied, alchemically speaking, only to be solidified and congealed once the floodgates have been closed.

The female principle as represented in the moon image is no longer viewed as a source of beauty and gentleness, as the early Romantics and even some Symbolists had conceived of it. A new moon has come into being for Rimbaud; the precursor of twentieth-century woman. Such a female force he looks upon as a witch, a vampire, a ghoul, a spectator. It is she who brings about the "abysmal side of life." Her womb has been turned into a giant maw, a devouring agent, a flesh-eating and blood-letting force.[69] The blending of masculine (coals) and feminine (pot) symbols in the sacrificial cauldron may be looked upon as premonitory vision of the reordering of sexual structures within contemporary society. It is in the earthen pot that the sorceress regulates the heat of the coals, thus permitting the embryo to evolve into maturity.

The impenitent youth had rebelled against the edifice he despised. He had experienced the Flood in terms of his own inner existence. His energies burst forth in aggressive and tangled imagery, in universal themes, such as in the Noah myth. A fighter and destroyer, Rimbaud's trials had led him to consider society as a composite of mediocre beings and no longer a unity, each individual hopelessly embroiled in his own sordid and petty nature, each fearful of facing his smudged soul, and thus created a world of illusion. The poet thought he could escape the vicious round that was life in his artistic creation—a palpable expression of self or the eternal within man. During these moments of awareness or of empathy between subject and object, the veil of solitude that cloaked the poet and the pain engendered by the creative process vanished; the burden of loneliness became a little less difficult to bear. Rimbaud pursued this *dance macabre* through his own murky waters, blackened mountain peaks, and quivering forest imagery, but always under the surveillance of the moon principle. In his poetic frenzy he discovered that the moon would never reveal her mysteries; that what he had under-stood to be discovery or revelation was merely a distorted re-flection of what she had decided to disclose. He would never be made privy to her arcana. His meanderings into the world be-yond would always be limited, and the glow and energy that pro-voked him to pursue his insights would, by their very repetition, become a bore. The moon fostered the illusion of rebirth and perpetuated the myth of increased illumination and evolution in order to blind man—thus helping him survive with the aid of a crutch. As for the bellicose young man, he had grown wan with awareness. He dreamed no more. He rejected the unconscious because "I am no longer."[70]

NOTES

[1]Arthur Rimbaud was born in Charleville on October 20, 1854. His parents were not well matched. Mme. Rimbaud was devout to the point of bigotry, parsimonious, prudish, and exacting. Conversely, her husband was easygoing, friendly, and had a joyous disposition. Captain Rimbaud left home permanently after the birth of their fourth child in 1860. He played no role in his childrens' lives thereafter and died in 1878. Rimbaud makes no direct allusions to his father in his writings. Rimbaud's homelife was painful. His mother, always in financial difficulties, was obsessed with discipline. She not only divested her children of all freedom, but also demanded they follow the strictest of schedules. Rimbaud was a docile student at the College of Charleville. He was an omnivorous reader and enjoyed adventure stories and fairy tales. When he took his first communion he was imbued with deep faith. Rimbaud found intellectual companionship in his teacher, Georges Izembard, who considered him brilliant. They discussed literary matters and Izembard, a poet, encouraged him to write poetry. When the Franco-Prussian war broke out in 1870, Izembard returned to his home in Douai. Rimbaud remained with his family. Feelings of dissatisfaction and restlessness increased, so did his hostility toward his mother. By August 28, 1870, he could no longer bear the tight atmosphere and got on a train for Paris. Without money and without a ticket, he arrived in the metropolis and was promptly arrested. Since he refused to give his name, he was incarcerated in the Mazas Prison where he remained a week. He wrote to Izembard who arranged for his release and sent him the necessary funds to return home. Rimbaud returned to Charleville, but not for long. On February 25, 1871, he again left for Paris. Rimbaud wandered about the city in search of work as a poet. He ate out of garbage pails and slept under bridges. On March 10, he returned to Charleville. Rebellious, he sought to scandalize his mother and his compatriots. He refused to work. Dirty and unkempt, instead, he hung around cafes, accepting sous from anyone who would hand them to him. Charles Bretagne, a customs official whom Rimbaud met in a cafe, introduced him to books on magic, demonology, alchemy and on the occult. Rimbaud was fascinated and not only read those he had

borrowed from Bretagne, but also volumes on the Kabbalah, on Buddhism, and on Illuminism in the public library. It was Bretagne who put Rimbaud in contact with Verlaine. Rimbaud's entry into Verlaine's life and their sexual relationship served to disrupt the older poet's marriage. Verlaine abandoned his wife to follow Rimbaud. They went to England where Rimbaud began writing his *Illuminations*. In December 1872 he left suddenly for Charleville. When Verlaine became ill, Rimbaud returned to London and began *A Season in Hell*. While the two poets were in Brussels, during a quarrel Verlaine shot Rimbaud in the wrist and was condemned to two years in prison at Mons. Rimbaud was disheartened. He finished *A Season in Hell* and wrote no more. The rest of his life he spent traveling to Germany, Italy, Austria, Egypt, Arabia, Cyprus, the Sudan, and Abyssinia working at various odd jobs among them as coffee exporter, gunrunner, and foreman in a building gang. He developed a tumor on his right knee and went to the hospital in Marseille where his leg was amputated. He then returned home; but his malady progressed and he died on November 10, 1891, in Marseille at the age of thirty-seven.

[2]Marie Louis von Franz, *Creation Myths*, p. 223.

[3]*Iliab*, XIV.

[4]C. G. Jung and C. Kerenyi, *Essays on a Science of Mythology*, p. 47.

[5]Mircea Eliade, *Myths, Dreams, and Mysteries*, p. 137.

[6]Gaston Bachelard, *L'Eau et les rêves*, p. 4.

[7]Gwendolyn Bays, *The Orphic Vision*, p. 198.

[8]Eliphas Lévi, *Dogme et rituel de la haute magie*, p. 33.

[9]C. G. Jung, *Psychological Types*, p. 557.

[10]Jeanne Bernis, *L'Imagination*, p. 13.

[11]Lévi, p. 14.

[12]George Fergusson, *Signs and Symbols in Christian Art*, p. 20.

[13]J. E. Cirlot, *A Dictionary of Symbols*, p. 139.

[14]Genesis: "And the Lord formed man...and breathed into his nostrils the breath of life; and man became a living soul." (2:7)

[15]Gilgamesh did acquire the plant after an extraordinary plunge into deep waters. "In his age, Man becomes young again.
I will eat of it and return to the condition of my
youth."

But Gilgamesh lost it shortly thereafter, as it should be since no mortal is allowed to penetrate the mysteries of life.

Joseph Campbell, *The Hero with a Thousand Faces*, p. 187.

[16]C. G. Jung, *Mysterium Conjunctionis*, p. 522.

[17]C. G. Jung, *Symbols of Transformation*, p. 177.

[18]Jean-Pierre Bayard, *La Symbolique du feu*, p. 50.

[19]The rainbow also figures in Ezekiel and is likened to the experiences of envisioning God: "As the appearance of the bow that is in the cloud in the day of rain, so was the appearance of the brighteness round about. This was the appearance of the likeness of glory of the Lord. And when I saw it, I fell upon my face, and I heard a voice of one that spake." (1:28).

In Revelation the vision of God's throne was preceded by the rainbow. "And he that sat was to look upon like a jasper and a sardine stone: and there was a rainbow round about the throne, in sight like unto an emerald." (4:3)

[20]C. G. Jung, *Civilization in Transition*, p. 354.

[21]*The Philosophy of Nietzsche*, p. 29.

[22]Eliade, p. 169.

[23]In another legend mentioned in the Zohar, the book was made of precious stones and within its pages were recorded the seven charms that God had given to Adam.

[24]The Grail was cut from an emerald that had fallen from Lucifer's forehead. In this case the stone represents "exile" and, like man, has fallen

from paradise into matter and must be redeemed and restored to divinity.

Hervé Masson, *Dictionnaire initiatique*, p. 299.

[25]Martin Buber, *The Knowledge of Man*, p. 161.

[26]Erich Neumann, *The Origins and History of Consciousness*, p. 44.

[27]Marie Louise von Franz, *Puer Aeternus*, p. I, 1.

[28]Neumann, pp. 44, 28.

[29]Gaston Bachelard, *La Dialectique de la durée*, p. 208.

[30]*Ibid.*, p. 130.

[31]James George Frazer, *The New Golden Bough*, pp. 450-457.

[32]Eliade, p. 31.

[33]See also Mark 14:23-24; I Corinthians 11:25; Matthew 26:26.

For the Christian *to know* is to come into contact with the spirit—the divine realm. For the Hebrew *to know* (*da'at*) means to experience both spiritually (in terms of the intellect) and physically. Body and mind, therefore, work in harmony. Sensual joys and sexual fulfillment are part of life, and both aspects of man exist in God.

[34]Nietzsche, p. 28.

"Despisers of life are they, decaying ones and poisoned ones themselves of whom the earth is weary: so away with them."

[35]*Ibid.*, p. 29.

[36]William Barrett, *Irrational Man*, p. 195.

[37]Arthur Rimbaud, *Oeuvres complètes*, p. 243.

[38]See Huysmans section for further information on Bluebard.

[39]Edward Edinger, *Ego and Archetype*, p. 232.

[40]*Ibid.*, p. 40.

[41]*Mysterium Coniunctionis*, p. 79.

[42]"For this is my blood of the new testament, which is shed for many for the remission of sins." (Matt. 26:27-28)

[43]C. G. Jung, *Psychology and Religion: West and East*, p. 253.

[44]Buber, p. 99.

[45]Rimbaud, p. 224.

[46]*Ibid.*, p. 220.

[47]Serge Hutin, *L'Alchimie*, p. 90.

[48]William T. Fernie, *The Occult and Curative Powers of Precious Stones*, p. 201.

[49]Rimbaud, p. 240.

[50]*Ibid.*, p. 239.

[51]Gaston Bachelard, *La poétique de l'espace*, p. 24.

[52]Rimbaud, p. 220.

[53]Gershom Scholem, *Major Trends in Jewish Mysticism*, pp. 131, 78.

[54]*Essays on a Science of Mythology*, p. 27.

[55]*Ibid.*, p. 78.

[56]*Mysterium Coniunctionis*, p. 491.

[57]*New Larousse Encyclopedia of Mythology*, p. 326.

[58]Eliade, p. 105.

[59]Nietzsche, p. 29.

[60]E. O. James, *The Cult of the Mother Goddess*, p. 215.

[61]Esther Harding, *Woman's Mysteries*, p. 168.

[62]Eliade, p. 79.

[63]*Ibid.*, p. 83.

[64]Serge Hutin, *Les Sociétés secrètes*, p. 19.

[65]Buber, p. 152.

[66]Erich Neumann, *The Great Mother*, p. 168.

[67]*Myths, Dreams, and Mysteries*, p. 147.

[68]*Ibid.*, p. 70.

[69]This destructive aspect of the female has had its place in all religions, in India, for example, in the dragon goddess Kali. In Calcutta worshipers still indulge in blood sacrifices to her to such an extent that temples and natural religious sights have been turned into "slaughterhouses" by the devout.

  Neumann, p. 152.

[70]Rimbaud, p.

The translation of "After the Flood" was made by Enid Rhodes Peschel. *Arthur Rimbaud, A Season in Hell, The Illuminations*, p. 108.

CHAPTER 13

Stéphane Mallarmé—Igitur or Elbehnon's Folly: The Depersonalization Process and The Creative Encounter

All that is visible must grow beyond itself, extend into the realm of the invisible. Thereby it receives its true concentration and clarity and takes firm root in the cosmic order.

(*The* I Ching)

Stéphane Mallarmé's *Igitur*[1] is a dream meditation carried
on in silence and with quiet determination. It is an initiation
into the most solitary regions of the human soul, a depersonalized area which mystics have referred to as the primordial point—
where Nothingness becomes Something, the Void is transformed
into the Creation, *Igitur* is a tale that unfolds in a circumscribed
area: a room, a stairwell, and a tomb. There is no escape: no
window, no sky. The atmosphere is closeted, limited, stifling,
constrained. Only one path is open: downward into the corridors of time to contact the primordial race of poets from whom
the modern creative spirit gains sustenance.

Mallarmé described his inner meanderings while writing
Igitur as a kind of death. "I have just spent a terrifying year:
my Thought thought, and I have reached pure Conception.
What my being...has suffered during this long agony is unre-
latable; but, fortunately, I am perfectly dead, and the most
impure region where my Mind can venture is the Eternity of
my Spirit. This solitary entity accustomed to its own Purity is
not even obscured by the reflection of Time."[2]   In view of
Mallarmé's statement and *Igitur's* story line, which delineates
the steps leading to the tomb, certain critics have interpreted
this work as Thanatos-oriented. But for Mallarmé, death does
not mean an end in the sense of a finale, rather, the termination
of a specific *way* and the beginning of a new orientation. His
description of his willed introversion accompanied by depression
indicates, from a psychological viewpoint, a withdrawal of libido
(psychic energy) from external objects or events. Psychic energy
is then driven into the unconscious. Such inner focus acts as a
compensatory device for the individual unable to cope with an
intensely creative drive. By turning inward, he represses his
psychic energy, thus violating the ego and activating latent or
dormant factors within the unconscious. A reshuffling of these
contents via an introduction of renewed energy, thrusts fresh
forms, sensations and images into consciousness thus making
new conceptualizations available. Marciglio Ficino, among many
creative people, wrote about his excoriating bouts with depres-

sion-introversion that he underwent prior to and during moments of great creative foment. *Igitur,* therefore, is not to be considered Mallarmé's suicidal journey as some critics have intuited, but rather an iconographic and verbal expression of the artist's heroic struggle to give birth to the unknown.

Igitur was not published during Mallarmé's lifetime. It was discovered in 1900 by Dr. Edmont Bonniot and printed in 1925. The word *déchet* ("waste") had been written on the work, which meant for Mallarmé unfinished or unusable material set aside for some future date. Probably written between 1867 and 1870, *Igitur* reveals Mallarmé's obsessive fear of spiritual and literary sterility. This psychosis, which drove him deeply into his own "abyss," blocked him for a while as an artist. Unable to communicate with others on a meaningful level, he went through months of insomnia, extreme fatigue, and the tension accompanying such an unnatural state. Mallarmé was very much aware of the demands he was making on himself and on his family sacrificing the mortal man living in a mortal world in favor of his eternal self in the work of art. He accepted isolation and loneliness during this period as a way of life, as a way of overcoming what he considered his creative impotence. "*Igitur,*" he wrote, "is a tale in which I want to confound that old monster Impotence... If it is [the tale] completed, I shall be cured; *simila similibus.*"[3]

Throughout the harrowing period of his descent into self, Mallarmé was terriorized by his own condition and described himself as living in a collective world; as perhaps going insane. In a letter to his friend Eugène Lefébure he wrote, "(I have spent moments approaching madness interspersed with equilibrating ecstasy)...I am in a state of crisis which cannot last... I am emerging from the absolute."[4] He confessed he had been losing contact with reality; that he was living outside of the phenomenological world, that his identity was splintering, scattering to the wind, and that he felt utterly helpless trying to prevent the further dismemberment of his psychological being. Mallarmé described the horror which accompanied the awareness of such progressive disintegration. To his friend

Henri Cazalis he wrote that he had to have a mirror placed before him on the table while writing, otherwise "I would become Nothingness again." He could no longer distinguish his personal from his impersonal self. "This is to tell you that I am now impersonal and no longer Stéphane whom you used to know—but an aptitude the spiritual Universe uses to develop itself through what had once been me." Because of the "fragility of my terrestrial apparition, I can yield only that part of me which is absolutely necessary to my development."

Mallarmé's progressive depersonalization created a kind of schizophrenic state. His emotional condition was so aggravated by his withdrawal from the workaday world that each time he began writing he had an outbreak of "hysteria" or uncontrollable anguish (a nervous irritability arising from the strain of protracted thinking). To avoid such abreactions he made it a policy to dictate all letters to his wife.[5] Because hysteria (the word in Greek means "womb") was considered a female ailment until the nineteenth century, it might be said that Mallarmé was reacting in a volatile and affective way in the existential world while conserving a masculine cerebral attitude throughout his creative descent.

Igitur is the narration of "a rather long descent into Nothingness," at the end of which "only Beauty exists—and it has only one perfect form, Poetry."[6] Mallarmé understood, as had the ancient hierophants, that his pain had to be endured if his ontological search were to be productive. To discover the mystery of the spheres of existence entails psychic death. "My mind had to be invaded by the Dream, it refused to function in an exterior fashion...it was going to perish in permanent insomnia; I implored the great Night to descend and it granted me my wish by bringing increased darkness. The first phase of my life is ended. Consciousness, satiated with protracted shadows, awakened slowly forming a new man, and must recapture my Dream after the latter's creation. This [state] will last several years during which time I shall have to relive the life of humanity as a whole, from infancy on, while becoming conscious at the same time of itself."[7]

The greater Mallarmé's withdrawal from the world of reality, the more hermetic *Igitur* became. His text is like an arachnean web. It represents through words the interrelatedness

of phenomena; the permutations necessary to travel from the
world of sense perception to the nonperceptual continuum
existing outside of the visual and temporal space-time concepts.
Iconographies, rhythms, sonorities, silences, ellipses, alliterations,
metaphors, inversions, syntheses, contradictions, antitheses, and
repetitions are but a frew of the literary vehicles used by Mallarmé to set up an ever-widening circular pattern within the text
itself designed in part to arouse infinite sympathetic vibrations
in the protagonist as well as in the reader, thus expanding consciousness. *Igitur*, therefore, takes on the power and density
of a ritual or an incantation, evoking the auditory sense as does
the Hindu mantra, the energies by posture and gestures as does
the mudra, and the visual vortices of geometrical designs (the
mandala) as in the yantra.

Igitur is the name of Mallarmé's hubris-ridden hero. He,
like Prometheus, Orpheus, Dionysus-Iacchus, and Christ, experiences his Dantesque quest into the inner lobes of the brain where
he divests himself of identity and reaches that area where nowhere is everywhere. It is from these pyramidal depths that he
recounts with extreme lucidity his spiritual rebirth in the work
of art. In a preliminary note to *Igitur*, Mallarmé stated: "The
Tale is addressed to the reader's Intelligence which itself functions as its director."[8] The text, then, is a mind-oriented work;
an inquiry into the domain of unacquired knowledge as opposed
to what has been learned cognitively. As Chang Tsai wrote:
"Man strives toward that which is hidden, and when a physical
form is not present...[he focuses] back toward the cause of the
thing manifested."[9] *Igitur* is Mallarmé's return to the original
"essense of the mind" or psychic structure behind what might be
called the "acquired structure of consciousness."

Mallarmé's description of *Igitur* lends extra weight to the
word *Conte* ("Tale") because of the capitalization of the letter
C.[10] In so doing he makes an association with the word *compter*
("to count") thus emphasizing the numerical values implicit in
the work Numerological associations were important for Mallarmé because of his studies in mysticism and alchemy where
numbers were used for mantic purposes. Numbers, as ordering

devices, are one of the most ancient representatives of man's spirit and intellect, as well as being attributes of matter.[11]

According to Rolland de Renéville, the adverb *igitur* was taken from Genesis: "Thus the heavens and the earth were finished, and all the host of them." (*"Igitur perfecti sunt coeli et terra et omnis ornatus eorum'* (2:1). Certain mystics believe that this sentence refers to the creation of angels by God, that is, the manifestation of the creative powers emerging from deity (Elohim). Adverbs are defined as "an indeclinable part of speech" that modify verbs, adjectives and other adverbs; they "usually express time, place, manner, condition, cause, result, degree, means, etc."[12] Igitur, the adverb, is a multifaceted entity that influences the entire sentence. Symbolically, Mallarmé's protagonist is likewise a radiating force. Like a spider (an image to which Mallarmé has recourse throughout the work) whose energy is transmitted to every area of the web, so Igitur too modifies the impact and import of the words used by the very substance of his own being.

Igitur's name is composed of six letters. This number, numerologically, symbolizes the spirit of servitude. In Genesis we read that God created the world in six days: "Six days shalt thou labor." Six being a perfect number (when adding its halfs, its thirds, and its sixths, it reforms itself), Igitur thus expresses the notion of totality. Heaven is described in the Zohar as a complete unit and as having six sides, "which extend from the supernal mystic essence, through the expansion of creative force from a primal point."[13] The idea of wholeness is also evident in the six-pointed star, the Magen David, symbolizing interlocking triangles, a Hebraic, Masonic, and alchemical symbol.[14] The six may also refer to the directions of space (two-dimensional) and thus to the maintenace of equilibrium as well as to mantic procedures in the *I Ching,* the trigrams and hexagrams being symbols "of the original psychic structure common to all mankind."[15]

Elbehnon, the second name given Mallarmé's hero, is a combination of *El* (meaning "divinity") and *Behn* ("son"). The protagonist then is either the son of God or of an angel. (God may also be understood as self or the transcendental factor in man and son as the ego.) The word *angel* comes from the Greek *angelos;* in Hebrew, *malakh* signifies "person sent" or "Messenger." In both the Old and New Testaments angels were either helpful or detrimental forces. In Genesis, angels married the daughters of men and their descendants carried within them godly aspects (6:2). In Revelations, angels made up the "armies of heaven." Angels lack individuality. Despite their personal names, their functions, and their hierarchical rank, they are neither male nor female. They are intermediary beings who travel between God's realm (that of the mind or spirit) and the phenomenological world (matter and body). Jesus was considered such a mediator by Christian Gnostics: God's son came to earth to liberate those who believed in him.[16]

Like an angel, Igitur is a transmitter, a messenger, a link between the infinite or divine realm and the finite and terrestrial sphere: outer and inner world, the poet and his work. In a letter to Villiers de l'Isle Adam, Mallarmé wrote that he had finally "understood the intimate correlation between Poetry and the Universe, and so that it would be pure, conceived of the idea to extract it from the Dream and from Chance and to juxtapose it to the conception of the Universe."[17] Igitur then is a descendant of a race of angels who were and are poets. In that angels are for the mystic objectivizations of God's vision and are "comparable to transparent envelopes of diverse colors," they are like "glittering and pure lights" finally freed from temporal form. [18]

There are eight letters in the name Elbehnon. Eight represents the numerical equivalent of infinity, eternity, fullness, and justice. It is, therefore, something and nothing.[19] Ideographically, eight is a composite of two equal circles and, like the double triangle (six), represents a *conunctio oppositorum*, thus lending a sense of spiritual wholeness to the name. Because according to Gnostic belief there are seven spheres in heaven, the eighth being that of divinity which begins with the termination of the cosmos, Elbehnon belongs to the godly realm.[20]

Mallarmé must have wanted to arouse a sense of mystery when choosing such names as Igitur and Elbehnon. He perhpas intended to inject a feeling of awe, of the sacred into his creative endeavor as had the ancients during their mystery rituals. In Egypt the notion of the "concealed name" was important since it hid within it the *ba*, the soul (or double), of the individual. The Kabbalistic concept of the secret name of God, the "four-foldedness of the letters of God's name, YHWH,"[21] stimulated feelings of sublime plenitude. Igitur then may be looked upon as that "nameless one" referred to in Malarmé's text as "the personage,"[22] an arcane force.

That Mallarmé should have inserted the word *Folie* between two angelic principles (Igitur and Elbehnon) indicates his desire to break out of the circumscribed concepts of revealed religion or the norms heretofore associated with the poetic process. The word *folly* indicates madness and the irrational domain, but is also an allusion to the medieval acting group known as "Les Enfants Sans Soucis," or the Company of Fools, which included the Prince of Fools, the Mother of Fools, etc. (Fool in old French means *folie*.) This company of Fools spoke openly against church and state whenever the spirit moved them. Because they were considered "mad" or "fools" and spoke a kind of gibberish when situations so warranted, they were not called into account for their aberrations as were other theatrical groups made up of "normal" actors and actresses.[23] So Igitur-Elbehnon also sought to break out of the well-trodden domain, both visually, linguistically, and imagistically.

Igitur is divided into five cyclical schemes:

1. Midnight
2. He leaves the room and loses himself in the stairwell
3. Igitur's life
4. The Dice-Throw
5. He lies down in the tomb

1. *MIDNIGHT*

"Midnight" recounts the protagonist's *état d'âme* as he prepares to descend the stairs leading into his tomb. He experiences the objects around him (mirror, draperies, furniture, clock) as living entities. Time is arrested in these presences which, as mysterious beings, reveal the interrelatedness of time, spirit, and space. An open book lies on the table. Its "pallor" stands out as does the enigma surrounding its existence. It is associated with night and with the "silence of an ancient word." Igitur now defines himself as the "hour that must render me pure." A dream (*chimère*) reflects light as does the now closed book. The light of an ancient idea, not yet born, seeks to come into being. The hour of Midnight sounds like an echo. "Goodby, night that I was, your own sepulcher, whose surviving shadow was metamorphosed into Eternity."[24]

Midnight indicates the existence of an isomorphic relationship between number, time and psychic state. According to Pythagoras, numbers are the basis of reality: that is, an awareness of reality may be expressed by numbers.[25] Each number, therefore, is not only significant in itself, but corresponds also to a whole series of entities in the universe.[26] There is, then, a relationship between the visible world (man's spatial-time scheme) and abstract events understood mathematically when incorporated into substance. The nonperceptible continuum that transcends man's three-dimensional universe may thus be concretized in numbers.[27]

Psychologically, numbers are archetypal contents: they arouse energy, rhythms, patterns, and foment a dynamic process. They are "idea forces," that is, the concretization or development of virtualities or possibilities in space; they are also experiences or shapes that lie latent in the unconscious until consciousness experiences them in the form of "images, thoughts, and typical emotional modes of behavior."[28] In the conscious domain numbers are "quantitative;" in the unconscious they are both "quantitative and qualitative," thereby arousing all kinds of sensations and feelings. As ordering devices used by man since the beginning of time, numbers are manifestations of his desire to conquer the world of contingency as well as the one that lies beyond his dominion. In that numbers lend order to what might be considered chaotic, they give a sense of security to those in need of it, and in this regard are considered "archetypal foundations of the psyche."[29] It is understandable that an entire book in the Old Testament should be called Numbers because within its pages are enclosed generations of souls leading back to the beginning of time, thus giving historical continuity to the Jewish people. The tracing of Christ's lineage back to David is likewise an attempt on man's part to experience his ancestral soul in its original form. Thus in Igitur's

quest to seek his ancestors—"the race of poets"—he is trying
to stablize and lend continuity to a world dominated by chance
and disparity.[30]

Midnight indicates the center of the twenty-four-hour
cycle, the halfway mark, the end before the zero hour. Representing the twelve signs of the zodiac, it stands for a totality:
the twelve months of the year, the twelve disciples, the four
seasons of the year multiplied by three,[31] and the twelve names
of Surya, the Hindu god identified with the sun. Since midnight preceeds dawn or rebirth of the day, it took on great
significance in many ancient mystery religions.[32] The Kabbalists offered special prayers at midngiht signifying a spiritual
"catastrophe" on a cosmic level. In that twelve in its semi-
circular and circular effect stands for completeness, it ushers
in moods of repose and dynamism, activity and passivity, the
one and the two or God and his Creation, being and nothingness, the image and its reflection. As unmanifested contents of
the unconscious, twelve as a duality exists in the form of "basic
intuitions" or an unexpressed "aggregate of all sense impressions
upon individuals."[33] Igitur's very life—his intellect—depends
upon certain phases in which numbers are concretized: "Certainly a presence of Midnight subsists," or "revelatory of Midnight," or "And from Midnight remains the presence of the
vision of a chamber of time," or "It is the pure Dream of Midnight." Midnight becomes, then, the pivotal point in Igitur's
descent, his expanding consciousness.

An analogy may be made between Igitur's descent and the
ritual exercises outlined in *The Secret of the Golden Flower*.
In this ancient Chinese document individuality is dispersed
when consciousness of self as an individual entity no longer
exists, when each isolated thought seems dissociated. Such
dissolution of the ego was Igitur's goal as it was in a similar
way for the yoga who could experience *super consciousness*
during certain periods in time—when knowledge of the self
and the nonself (that part of the individual which is freed from
the self) were known simultaneously.[34]

For Igitur time is concretized. It exists in the objects
inhibiting his room: the furniture, clock, mirror, draperies.
Time in this sense means the eschatological time of the finite
world. Because this kind of time cuts, divides, bruises, and

is instrumental in the death-and-rebirth cycle, it is linked with emotional characteristics. In that time is an abstract notion ("It is the pure Dream of Midnight") and viewed cyclically, it is, as Aristotle proclaimed, circular and not divided into arbitrary schemes such as past, present, and future, numbers of hours, etc. Cyclical or mythical time is fluid and experienced as psychic energy in its qualitative and quantitative form. For Igitur, therefore, "The hour has not disappeared in the mirror..." it has imposed itself in the form of a visual image, a psychic experience, a constant reminder of man's mortality and his ephemeral nature.

Time may be looked upon as non formal, spaceless entity, an *illo tempore* where everything is possible: the flow from one (God or the center point of Creation) merges into the circular zodiacal combination of signs (or the Indian wheel of life which is linked to twelve). Orphics related time to space. The first principle of their cosmogony was Time (or Cronus); then came Chaos (symbolizing the infinite) and Ether (the finite). The interplay of these forces organized matter in the form of an egg with Night as its shell.

Igitur chose midnight as the moment to act, to form the egg with Night. Midnight: this point in space-time was considered the central point of creation. Aristotle called it "the unmoved mover;" the Hindu Shri-Yantra spoke of it as the creative center or "form in expansion;" the Kabbalists' doctrine was Tsim-Tsum or the central point into which God withdraws in order to create. It is within this area (twelve) in space (Igitur's room, stairwell, tomb) that the infinite, absolute, void, the purest of areas—that sterile ground—may be experienced.

Until this point Igitur had not "disappeared into the mirror," that is, his goal of dispersion or superconsciousness had not yet been achieved. Duality still existed. The *mirror* image, used so frequently by Mallarmé in *Igitur* and other works, is of great significance. When likened to the Narcissus myth it becomes a vehicle for self-contemplation. Mallarmé spoke of it in a letter (May 17, 1867) as a "dream pool where we never fish for anything else but our own image, without thinking about the silvery scales of the fish!"[35] The mirror may also be considered a device that reflects unconscious memories: a type of moon image as opposed to the sun disk. As a dynamic force it not only reproduces but also abosrbs the image, distorts it, and underlines its feminine or passive characteristics.   In a letter to Villiers de L'Isle Adam, Mallarmé described the virtues of the mirror: "and you would be terrified to learn that I have experienced the Idea of the Universe via sensations alone (and that, for example, to secure an ineffable notion of pure Nothingness, I had to impose the sensation of absolute void in my mind).   The mirror which reflected Being was most frequently that of Horror and you can guess that I am expiating most cruelly the results of this unnamed Night diamond."[36]

The mirror had for Mallarmé prophetic faculties. It was a hierophany, an aid to the discovery of the point of creation.[37] The darkness in Igitur's room was relieved every now and then by the glimmer of light radiating from the mirror. It was through this vehicle and other "presences" in his room that he would experience the *epoptai*, the vision of things beyond, arousing within him feelings of excoriating fear and ineffable ecstasy.[38]

Draperies which also became realities for Igitur are examined: their function in his life. "Time," de declares, "has not been buried in the draperies." Draperies, curtains, or wall coverings in general may be regarded as partitions between two worlds (God and man), two states of being (death and life), two existential attitudes (illusion and reality), two time schemes (eschatological and cyclical), two worlds (multiple and the one), two character traits (passive and active), and two attitudes toward the work of art (creative and sterile). As such they are composites of opposites; divinities vested with immortality. The mirror and the drapes were fetishes for Igitur, enclosing within their folds or recesses certain mysterious powers that he had to transcend in his initiatory process.

Because time "has not disappeared in a mirror, has not been buried in the drapes, evoking furnishings by its vacant sonority," it has become a kind of storehouse for energy, increasing the dynamism between Igitur and the world about him. The word *evoking* recalls the preceding mirror image and in so doing underlines the reverberations and reflective capacity of the drapes in the world of sense perception. Although words such as *vacant* and *sonority* may at first glance appear antithetical, for the mystic they are not: *vacant* in the sense of "empty" and *sonority* in terms of "noise" are quite compatible.   In

Tantric yoga, for example, such space is believed to have "its sound" because matter is "sonorous," vibratory, dense, and filled with energy.[39] Indians, therefore, tune their instruments "to silent sounds." The Pythagoreans spoke of numbers as associated with "the music of the spheres;" the Spanish Kabbalist Abraham Abulafia wrote of "a harmonious movement of pure thought, which had severed all relation to the senses," and which he compared to music.[40]

That time and the objects associated with it (mirror, draperies) are experienced in terms of vacancy and sonority indicate a difference in Igitur's levels of consciousness. Igitur is in the process of absorbing the various images he sees around him, integrating these into his being (soul), thereby increasing his understanding of their impact upon him. The word *ameublement* (furnishings) is of paramount importance. It is a composite of *âme* (soul) and *meuble* (from the word *mobile* meaning "furniture"). The linking of these two worlds, the physical and the spiritual, indicates a fluidity in both the inner and outer spheres, an interchangeability therefore in levels of consciouness.

The mirror, drapes, and furnishings surrounding Igitur may be looked upon as presences capable of evoking sensations and thoughts. In that objects reflect ideas, they become, psychologically, what the viewer projects into them and react to the quantum of energy believed to be inherent in them. In this sense one may say that psychic energy is personified in objects, which then have the capacity to arouse and irritate the viewer. Objects become hierophanies for Igitur. They are endowed with sacred values and are important factors in his initiatory progress. It is not Igitur as a person that counts in Mallarmé's narrative, it is his being as manifested in the thoughts and emotions emerging from him.[41] These thoughts are "objective essences" or form-ideas (*archetypes*) that become concretized in the furnishings (*ameublement*).

Segments of the past will be experienced by Igitur as eternal presences in such words as *recollect, gold, simulate, absence, nul*, and *reverie*. To *recollect* recalls the mirror and lunar reflections or previous states and images referred to by Igitur, a contemplative being. For the Gnostic and Kabbalist, to recollect indicates a "gathering" in process; for the Buddhist, "indwelling." Such introversion, then, will be Igitur's way, the clue being given by the word *recollect*.[42]

Gold not only sheds light, like the sun or moon rays, but is also the source of wisdom, the divine mind for the Hermetist. Igitur seeks to discover the source of gold within himself, and in order to do so wanders through every aspect of existence, like the hierophant through darkness.[43] For the alchemist gold is his ultimate achievement. It represents gnosis, the philosophers' stone, divine illumination and intelligence. It is not only superior to all metals, but to all spheres of existence as well, spiritually speaking. It is the glorified fourth state of the alchemist that makes possible the realization of what had heretofore been the amorphous quantity of infinite possibilities. In that the rays cast by gold flicker, they are mobile forces which filter throughout the universe. In Hindu doctrine, light is associated with movement in the person of Savitar, "the principle of movement." He is the cause of light, wind, and darkness, and is endowed with golden eyes, hands, and tongues.[44] Gold in its cognitive, spiritual, material, and divine ramification not only shine throughout *Igitur,* but because of its motility adds to the dynamism of the tale.

To *simulate* brings to mind the "absence" of an object and the desire to recapture its presence or essence via illusion. But time is not an empty illusion, nor is it merely a reflective device. For Igitur it is a creative force in and of itself, comparable to a jewel's hardness, purity, and light-giving quality.

The word *null* refers to the jewel's lack of identity, its zero aspect, its undifferentiated nature. It is a world *in potentia* like the mind and psyche of the poet prior to the creative act. It is the realm in which beauty and purity exist in the raw, the dream before it has taken form—the domain of mystery. If meditated upon, the jewel becomes a void, instrumental in the Orphic descent. If gazed into, it enables the individual to withdraw to the point of creation within himself, experiencing disassociation with the outside world.

Reverie when associated with the jewel arouses the notion of reflection and recollection, those irrational spheres—in Igitur's case the world of folly. It is in this domain that the spirit in man seeks release; wants to abandon itself to its souvenirs, delusions, and illusions, thus enabling it to roam freely and contentedly about space. In a letter to Henri Cazalis, Mallarmé wrote of this particular aspect of dream and matter: "I want to experience the spectacle of matter, conscious of being and yet plunging forcibly into the Dream, which...isn't."[45]

Mallarmé now brings into focus two other notions: "marine and stellar" worlds so complex in their bejeweled nature that within their being "could be read the infinite conjunctions of chance." *Marine* and *stellar* in this context signify a *hieros gamos*, the marriage of two elements: sky (air) and water (liquid). The latter, rich in terms of fish and potential treasures, has been associated with the unconscious, those primal waters which existed prior to the Creation, that formless and mysterious nothing, the zero of eternity, the Orphic egg.[46] Stellar regions symbolize diffusion, the intellectual light force struggling against the world of darkness; consciousness making its way through unconscious regions. Stellar and marine reflect images arousing a variety of emotional levels: air or stellar, associated with the mental being, with spirit or wind (*nous*), an area from which divine beings descend (angels) or humans ascend (Jacob's dream). In Hermes Trismegistus' Emerald Table it is stated that "It ascendeth from the earth to heaven, and descendeth again to the earth, and receiveth the power of the higher and lower things."[47] Because of the remote nature of stellar regions, they give the impression of lacking individuality.[48]

When projecting upon stellar regions, Igitur sought to become diffused, dissociated, multifaceted, thereby impersonal and eternal. The marine world aided him in experiencing the realm of possibilities with him—all the poems he would be able to create once he had abolished chance and had become master of his *heimarmene* (fate and divine providence). The dynamic structure set up by the polarity of marine and stellar stresses the duality within the phenomenological world: image and reflection, the one and the multiple, darkness and light, liquid and air, etc.[49]

The word *chance* in "the infinite conjunctions of chance" is of prime importance. Chance is Igitur's bitter foe. It symbolizes all that is uncontrollable, anti fate, the zero, the infinite. It represents the world of possibilities from which his creation (the poem) will be extracted. For the Kabbalist the world of chance is the En-Sof (God without limits), "where nothing can be predicted and yet must be postulated."[50] It is the world against which Prometheus battled, which Orpheus attempted to transcend, which stands as a constant reminder to man of his subservience to the laws of probabilities. Igitur sees the world of chance (disorder, multiplicity) outside of himself reflected in the mirror, fragmented in the stars, diffused in the furniture and draperies—as so many reflections of his own inner chaotic realm that he seeks to rework, reorder, recreate in a single all-encompassing conjunction or conjunctions.

A conjunction, gramatically speaking, is an invariable word that seeks to link together two words or two prepositions of the same nature. In astronomy when sun and moon are in conjunction, darkness clothes the world. For the alchemist it is a marriage of the constellations "where the greatest marvels appear." For the Orphics musical conjunctions are revealed in octaves, chords, harmonies, and in spiritual and psychic affinities. For the Kabbalist man is a conjunction: "Man in the world combines brain and membrane, spirit and body, all to the more perfect ordering of the world."[51] Psychologically a conjunction may be regarded as an acausal connecting principle in the universe. C. G. Jung labeled such a principle synchronicity. Kepler, in his *Harmonices Mundi,* expressed the idea of conjunction or "instantaneous perceptual awareness in a timeless present of actuality."

> Inasmuch as the soul bears within itself the idea of the zodiac, or rather of its center, it also feels which planet stands at which time under which degree of the zodiac, and measures the angles of the rays that meet on the earth; but inasmuch as it receives from the irradiation of the Divine essence the geometrical figures of the circle and (by comparing the circle with certain parts of it) the archetypal harmonies (not, to be sure, in purely geometrical form but as it were overlaid or rather completely saturated with a filtrate of glittering radiations), it also recognizes the measurements of the angles and judges some as congruent or harmonious, others as incongruent.[52]

Kepler was convinced that the outside world could be determined by inner contemplation, that within man there existed the idea of the zodiac (for Igitur, the twelve), that is, the cosmos at large.

The same may be said of Igitur. The more deeply he descended into his own nature, the greater was his comprehension of the outer world in its quintessencial form. With increased unity between inner and outer corpus, he hoped to be able to experience the "omega point" or objective consciousness—a state of meditation according to the Buddhist during which time all "fixed positions" are overcome—intellectual, sensual, emotional, or psychological. In this state Igitur would be in a position to create the poem of poems—his legacy to mankind.[53]

Igitur is a living intellect or hopes to become one—a being divested of temporality and existing in a state of "reciprocal nothingness." At this time he experiences himself as a propeller of energy, a point in which energy is both concentrated and generated onto outer and inner objects. He becomes a dehumanized being, a two-way transformer which manifests itself in lower and higher frequencies, depending upon the objects and conceptualizations upon which Igitur focuses his brain waves.

He is the "revealer of Midnight," states Mallarmé, thus reiterating the fact that time for Igitur is a living presence, a pure being, experienced in an eternal present, concretized in objects (room, mirror, furniture), in active concepts (vacant, sonority, absent), in numbers (infinity, conjunctions, null), in the cosmos (marine and stellar), and in the multiple and the simple. The word *revelatory* is particularly significant for the Gnostic and for hermetic philosophers whose works Mallarmé had studied. Knowledge of divinity is revealed for members of these sects by secret means or formulas.[54] In Luke we read: "For there is nothing coveted, that shall not be revealed; neither hid, that shall not be known" (12:2). The one who struggles, digs and sacrifices, shall gain gnosis, and only he will have understanding. The same may be said for Igitur's ascesis: only by repeated efforts and a tortuous struggle will treasures be revealed.

Igitur's room may be seen as a priosn, a walled-in area as in Plato's Allegory of the Cave (*Republic*). It is also a private and personal domain where thoughts, feelings, and sensations are enclosed; a virginal area with no access to the outer world. As an image of containment, a type of fetish for Mallarmé, it may be considered a repository for riches. The room also takes on the hermetically sealed quality of the alchemist's vase, thus enhancing its mystery. It is within Igitur's room that the furniture "arrested time," thoughts glimmer and shudder, the intellect takes on the depth and power of something sacred and divine. It becomes the holiest of areas as does Solomon's temple (Kings VI:5, 6, 8) for the Mason, "the vault of the second death," the area where the initiate's second being is reconstructed.

It is in Igitur's room that vague, imprecise thought begins to take on weight. The word *thought* viewed in terms of its French root *penser* (Latin *pensare* or *peser*), "to weigh" gives it substance and dimension. Thought then may be weighed; it is mobile in that it *shudders;* visible as it is *luminous;* eternal because it circulates in time (as waves: liquid, sound, electric); endowed with feelings in that it is *calm,* narcotic-like as in the domain of pure ego, the state Igitur longs to experience.

By repeating the same or slightly altered forms of words throughout his text, Mallarmé achieves a narcotic effect, recalling the circular movement of the mandala. In so doing, the reader loses his way but, according to the Buddhist, discovers a new inner state of wholeness. Words such as *conjunction, unique, infinity, constellation, marine, nothingness, essence,* etc. are used with ever-widening meanings and associations and form concentric visual patterns, one frequently canceling the other out in descending or ascending folds. Moreover, Mallarmé's repetition of words, images, cadences, rhythmic structures, and sonorities resound in his work like so many "divine Breaths" or "Buddha breaths"—like mantras that are supposed to contain the power and resonances of the universe at large.[55]

Mallarmé writes of the "fall of time" (or "of the hour") that may be likened to Adam's fall into matter, necessitating a redemption and regeneration. The fall is a necessary disciplinary stage for the mystic since only through humiliation and darkness can illumination come about. Igitur will have to destroy life as he knows it. He will have to experience the disintegration of his ego to reach that inmost point of creation. To willingly seek one's own destruction, to be aware of the consequences involved (the possibility of submersion or insanity) is a terrorizing experience. It requires heroism, tenacity, and a will of iron. Igitur was equipped with this inner strength.

Darkness invaded Igitur's room. Blackness is propitious to growth according to ancient mystery religions (Eleusis, Pyramids,

Dionysus-Iacchos, Orpheus, Mithra, Christ)—light vanishes in caves or in hidden rock formations in order to give birth to a more brilliant and rarefied illumination: "The future is in a state of gestation in the tomb of the past, an interior and hidden realm, inaccessible except to the initiated worthy of supreme revelations."[56] It is in the realm of darkness that the seed takes root and germinates. It is also in the mysterious *ameublement* (soul and mobile) of the brain that the idea comes into being, that, according to the *Book of Formation*—the *Sepher Yetzira*—it is transformed into sound (voice), and that the "impenetrable" becomes "comprehensible." In his room (his "Interior Palace") with its arcana (furnishings, mirror, draperies) Igitur experiences the mystery of unity and exteriorizes it for the reader (or makes it conscious to himself) in the finite world.[57] Matter fuses (whether in concrete form or as an idea, sensation, or impulse) in the room; an intimacy between the elements takes place—as in the vaulted areas of the mind, the inner temple of the soul. In this circumscribed domain, Igitur's *pure I* emerges, that nonpersonal and mythological essence floats into existence and takes on its funnel-like or messenger-oriented function. Igitur now becomes the transmitter of the infinite into the finite, the eternal into the mortal sphere, the unwritten poem into the fixed verse.

Igitur's thought *shudders* and *trembles*. Its mobility will soon diminish in amplitude when used in conjunction with *deaden* (French *amortir*, from Latin *mors, mortis*). The emergence of thought into the manifested world will soon be lost in *forgetfulness* (*oubli*), recalling Plato's theory of recollections: birth preceeded by immersion in the River Lethe (forgetfulness), thus wiping away the memory of anterior existences and divesting man of immortality—a divine attribute. For Plato and Mallarmé thought consists of recollection: the emergence of one facet of a potential condition or infinite possibilities. Thought is a reshuffling of matter from a preformal structure into a new combination or an example of what the god Phanes represented in Orphic mysticism: the "eternity of the world-creating principle."[58]

Igitur is no *pantocrator*. He needs the existential world of duality to create opposition, a condition antithetical to somnolence that he will later, in good Hegelian tradition, experience in the synthesis, in the idea, in the created work. Igitur also requires another force: the female with her "languishing hair" set around a "face illuminated with mystery." Hair is a sensual image—a fetish for Mallarmé—representing a conflict between the real sensual woman and the unreal or imagined spiritual idealization of the female principle in all of her purity and beauty. Baudelaire's associations to hair, which Mallarmé knew well, bring to mind perfume, dream, and escape into the pleromatic realm. The word *hair* (*chevelure* in French) also has astronomical connotations: it is the luminous *way* a comet leaves when traveling through the skies, or, expressed metaphysically, light piercing darkness, the idea shooting through matter. The hair that surrounds the face in Igitur's view is made up of strands and filaments and is comparable to material used to make paper, a book, or the web of a spider, images Mallarmé used throughout *Igitur*. The Hindu refers to Shiva's hair as the threads from which "the material of the world was woven or the "lines of strength" of the manifested world.[59]

The *eyes* of this mysterious female apparition are described as *null* and resembling a *mirror*. Eyes are doors to the soul, to light, spirit, and understanding. Plato considered eyes as the source of intelligence: "the Mind's Eye."[60] The eye is man's sun. It is the "radiation" and "dissipation" of "spiritual consciousness." Eyes may also be viewed as in Redon's paintings: depersonalized, transcendental, collective, and mythical forces devoid of all individuality except for their presence in time. In this respect they are terrifying because they are beyond human comprehension and control, resembling stellar powers that determine man's fate from the outside. Like mirrors, eyes are also reflectors and transmitters, messenger angels bridging the gap between inner and outer worlds—divine and mortal realms.

The mysterious face with eyes looked upon as *null* is now compared to the "host's mirror," thus adding another mediating entity to the already long list. A *host* is somebody who receives and gives hospitality, who symbolizes in the rite of communion the body of Christ, who takes on reality as an agent of transformation. In the cosmic sphere "all the hosts of heaven" include the sun, moon, stars, and the twelve signs of the zodiac (II Chron. 33:5). Igitur, like an everpresent eye, whether focusing on that "presence of Midnight," the "mysterious furnishings," the "shuddering" thought, or the luminescent and darkened hues, becomes his cosmic host, this mystical and existential being whose function it is to receive and transform in an ever-mobile world.

As Igitur's depersonalization process pursues its course, he becomes less and less involved in matter as the finite world thinks of it and closer therefore to the mystic center, the irradiating point where revelation of the spiritual essence can be gleamed. It is for this reason that he can speak of the "pure dream of Midnight" and "the recognized Clarity." Purity exists in the dream despite the fact visualized thought is a material entity. The dream has gone through the process of gestation just as man has: from the single cell animal to the multicelled body, or from chaotic or unintegrated matter to formed and cohesive matter. Everything in Igitur's room (curtains, table, thought, etc.) is visible in its formed and preformal state. Therefore, whether it is animate or inanimate, formed or formless, it vibrates, shudders, breathes, or moves about in a variety of dimensions. The clock for example, exists as the "presence of Midnight" for Igitur. It breathes as does the human heart when it sounds; it is part of the eschatological time and sphere and is likewise a remembrance of past time or cyclical concepts in that its vibrations live on indefinitely; its form may be transformed, but its face is a concretization of an inner state of wholeness or non-perceptual continuum.

The "pure dream of a Midnight" has vanished, but its "Clarity" was "recognized," that is, its dream or visualization can be recalled (reco-naître, re-cognized, regained, reborn) because its remains are eternal and are lodged in the depth of being, "plunged in shadow," where evolution takes place. The notion of "plunging" into something brings to mind water images, initiation rituals as well as a sense of abandon, delight, and folly, and of danger when one rushes into something new, different, or strange. The ordeal implicit in the initiation may be survived, one may be cleansed and renewed, but one may also drown in the endeavor. For Igitur a plunge into the "shadow" would enable him to overcome his excoriating sense of "sterility." The very act of leaping is aggressive; it requires strength and agility; the fall creates a chaotic situation and arouses what is dormant. In the domain of the idea Igitur is plunging more deeply into his unconscious and there triggers off a multitude of sensations and images, thus disrupting the peace and calm of infertility.

An "open book" lies on the table. This book, a *conjiunctio* of cosmic forces, encompasses everything. In his *Autobiography* Mallarmé writes: "a book which is a book, architectural and pre-meditated, and not a collection of inspirations dictated by chance even if these inclusions were to be marvelous."[61]

The book on Igitur's table is part of the decor; it is exterior to him as are the curtains, clock, the furniture. Yet, within its pages are contained the secrets of existence: though open it is closed and embedded in night, though verbal it remains silent, though palpable it is amorphous. The book in question is surely a hermetic work since it professes "ancient words." Mallarmé may be referring to the work of Thoth (the Tarot) or the book of magic by Albertus Magnus, the thirteenth-century Dominican philosopher who was considered the world's greatest magician; or the innumerable volumes of magical and mystical tracts by Nicolas Flamel, Nicolas de Cusa, Paracelsus, Orpheus, and more.[62]

The "ancient words" contained in the book although described as "pale" may have been an allusion to the *Book of the Dead* or other religious works in which the words contained had the power to assist the dead in their night sea journey to the land of the blessed. Each individual, the Egyptians believed, possessed two names, an external and a hidden one. If the arcane name was known, the individual could order it about and it would do its bidding, if not, he remained helpless. Each word in the book likewise has an inner and outer value. Once the secret message is gleaned, the word yields to the creator's will, expanding in power and significance.

The book may also be associated with the previous image of the hair and a later reference to the spider and its web. In Sanskrit *sutra* means "thread," and a book "may be formed by an ensemble of sutras, as material is formed by an assemblage of threads." In ancient China knotted cords were the most primitive way of writing. The symbol of weaving (paper, spider) not only represents writing, but all the worlds as well, thus making up universal existence. In the Upanishads, the Supreme Brahma is defined as "That substance upon which the world is woven," or as a spider's web in the Hindu system.[63]

Mallarmé's book is then the prototype of all texts, the one

which contains everything. As Igitur's meditation centers around the book (or the ego, psychologically speaking, as differentiated from the body), an abstract or spiritual entity, his body is slowly freeing itself from the sense world. Such an image in the mystical sense has been expressed in the concept of "the untying of the knots" in order to allow pure thought to flow freely. It is at this juncture that midnight—the divine meeting place of duality—is equated with pallor, sterility, and purity. The ego, inherent in the book, merges with the environment. The transformation then occurs when the following words are sounded: "I was the hour which must render me pure."

Mallarmé's struggle with feelings of sterility and nothingness, and the void that accompanied the writing of *Igitur*, nearly cost him his sanity. He described his state to Henri Cazalis: "Discouragement dominates me daily, I am dying of torpor. I shall emerge from this besotted, annulled. I feel like knocking my head against the walls to awaken myself."[64] Mallarmé, influenced by Hegel as scholars have suggested, had driven his hero Igitur to the state of nothingness or to "the point of departure," the negative (shadow) or yet undefined primal state, the unrealized condition that contains everything else. It is the poet's function and thus Igitur's, to transform (in the Hegelian sense) this original and unknowable mystery of matter into being, thus giving it conscious form and making it accessible to man. The book on the table, therefore, which represents everything the poet strives for, everything that transcends contingency, must be experienced in its totality and its mystery.

Just as the book is a microcosm of the macrocosm, a prototype of everything that is and is not, so Mallarmé also believed that all the myths of antiquity were likewise modeled from one pattern.[65] The book then is the center, the egg in Orphic mysticism, the seed and its potential—the mystery and source of life.[65] The book will predict Igitur's destiny: its secrets will reveal the fact that he, like Orpheus, will experience dismemberment in the supreme sacrificial act in order to recreate himself into that higher spiritual being whose essence is nowhere and everywhere. Such a process entails the following: Igitur must pass into the land of the dead and remain in a dark cavelike area where he will experience, both physically and emotionally, the terrors connected with his passing from one sphere of existence to another—death and resurrection.

As Igitur continues shedding his finite nature, he becomes "the hour which must render" him pure or the word, that is, the idea that contains all ideas—the manifestation of the infinite. A similar notion is presented in John in reference to the divine: "In the beginning was the Word, and the Word was God and the Word was with God, and the Word was God." Such is divine *Logos* and man's capacity to grasp it in his own terms. Igitur's identification with the hour (or time) must be considered in this context as an identification with the word, that is, another aspect of the multiple (reflective) images used by Mallarmé to represent the world of infinite possibilities.

The "ancient idea" that had died many years ago "now shines" for Igitur reflected by the chimera." The *chimera* refers to the ancient Greek fire-breathing monster and symbolizes the volcanic character in man. The transparency and clarity of Mallarmé's chimera—or dream (an illusion as well) clarifies the idea and reveals its fabulous and/or monstrous essence. But the chimera is also that entity "in which the dream agonized," introducing the notion of combat (in Greek *agon* means "combat"); thus denoting action, a struggle against death, fall, decline, and a desire for rebirth or immortality. Agony is also assoicated with the word *antagonism* in the next clause ("to terminate the antagonism of the polar dream"). The friction aroused in Mallarmé's text by words such as *agony* and *antagonism*, is set against the vision of a "polar dream" implying ice, whiteness, coldness, and immobility in congealment. The introduction of the word *pole* brings to mind the earth's rotation around a central axis or the notion of midnight that divides the twenty-four hour circadian cycle. Pole also implies diffusion and differentiation. The action in these clauses is mainly volatile, as is the heating of the alchemist's oven when transformation of the elements is about to occur.

The book is now closed. Night enfolds the scene and the "vacant gesture" is called upon to end the conflict between the world of chance (the existential domain) and the realm of infinite potentialities. The world of contingency is again evoked by Igitur: "the pure fire of the clock's diamond," an ornament that scientillates and is the "sole survivor and jewel of the eternal Night." The diamond on the clock represents purity but also the evolutionary process in nature—or man as he strives to perfect himself, the poet in his agony to create his all-encompassing poem. Diamonds begin in the earth as carbon and achieve their purity and beauty with the passage of centuries through the transformatory process—as the word in the mind. In Sanskrit diamond (*dyu*) means luminous being: an object which is hard, radiant, and in this respect enduring as is the written word.

The clock's face contains the diamond: it is also part of its mechanism and adds to the mysterious nature of the clock's presence. Because of the luminescent quality of the diamond the clock remains visible despite the darkness surrounding it. The fluid nature of the passage of time paves the way for the clock's entry into the dimensionless world of the *unus mundus.*

Like the diamond that scintillates, the clock reverberates and echoes, recalling past words, anterior existences, and profounder spheres. The obscurity that clothes the atmosphere of shimmering illuminations and eternal sounds may be equated with matter, the maternal and germinal forces, those preexisting in primal chaos (*obscurum per obscurius*), the path leading back to the mystery of origin before the *fiat lux.* The light images (diamond, scintillas, fire, glimmer) may be equated with solar light or fire symbolism, the transformatory agent for the alchemist; the basis of life for Heraclitus and the libido for the psychiatrist; part of the purification ritual for the hierophant. The battle between light and dark Igitur now wages transforms him into a type of Promethean figure who steals fire from Zeus in an act of defiance. Or will Igitur take after Empedocles who attempted to transcend the basic dualism of the human condition by plunging into the vital heat and thus ending his existential existence?

The doors to the tomb open, thus unlocking Igitur's passage to the primeval realm. There he will experience matter in its undifferentiated form, that is, the four elements: earth, water, fire, and air—as one. Igitur descends and in so doing asserts himself; he acts overtly as had the Creator when forming earth from the void and light from darkness. Like "the Spirit of God" Igitur's shadow now divested of its personal accounterments (his psychological identity and physical body) passes into another dimension. Not Igitur's voice remains audible, but its echo (its duration or prolongation); its trajectory in the finite world, its impersonal and eternal spirit as in the reflected night. Mallarmé's metaphysics may be expressed as follows: the shadow is to night what the word is to the echo, what the poet is to the poem, what the created world is to God's domain.

2. *HE LEAVES THE ROOM AND LOSES HIMSELF IN THE STAIRWELL*

Igitur dos not slide down the circular banister, but slowly makes his way into each of the spirals. The mystery grows more intense with every state in Igitur's evolucion. He is like those ancient mystae in Orphic mysteries who, unlike the hierophants at Eleusis and Cabiri, could enact their rituals at home, not necessarily in sanctuaries or in temples.[66]

The circular stairs are like rungs in a ladder leading inward, cutting through the geological folds or levels of consciousness. In this mazelike area Igitur first loses himself, then becomes acutely aware of his duality, and finally opts for complete loss of identity. He fumbles and mumbles; he agonizes because he is forever hearing gasps, pants, fluttering of wings, or seeing shadows, reflections, and terrifying apparitions—chimeras. The more he loses sight of his own personality, the more he floats into oneness and weightlessness.

The circular effect of the stairs may be looked upon as crystallized energy and thus as a catalyzing agent, prodding, pushing, encouraging Igitur in his descent.[67] It may also be reminiscent of the Gnostic symbol of the ouroborus (the snake eating its own tail), representing eternity and associated numerically with the number eight, of Elbehnon. For Igitur we may view the stairs as a positive factor in his life despite the fact that he experiences a type of vertigo or narcosis throughout his descent. He becomes the instrument of his aggressive energy and intends, like Faust, to experience fulfillment by leaving the realm of the personal unconscious and entering into the transpersonal domain of the collective unconscious.

Shadow, obscurity, and night descend upon Igitur as he enters the inner folds. Time seems to have been condensed into a type of chemical substance: the hours fall as they pass, they sound, they feel, they multiply. Mallarmé's concept of time may now be considered *atomistic* in the manner of Leucippus and Democritus. For these philosophers reality was made up of "indivisible" atoms called *eidolon* in their materialized form. Dreams and hallucinations also consisted of individual atoms grouped together in certain forms, attracted to each other by atmospheric conditions. These eidola or visual perceptions were likewise regarded as thought perceptions; in either case they could influence the person projecting upon them. Igitur encounters these atom-visual-thought images in his descent; he confronts them in rhythmic and affective encounters and is possessed by them in the emerging dream visions.[68]

The spider web is the image Mallarmé now uses to express in the ever-deepening circular journey, Igitur's growing distaste for the world of multiplicity. The mazelike appearance of the web has frequently been compared to matrices or thought patterns, every idea being reflected and related to another in its concreteness—form and substance. The spider, like the divine force, restructures the universe from itself. Mallarmé had compared himself to a spider in a letter to his friend Théodore Aubanel. He declared having experienced his own center "where, like a spider, I am master of the principle threads leading out of my mind, and by means of which I shall weave marvelous laces at each point of conjunction, which I sense, and which already exist in the heart of Beauty."[69]

The spider, as all else in the universe, is double. It obeys a fixed set of rules that is ingrown, hereditary, and part of its physical makeup: "radical threads will always intersect the laterals at equal angels;" it also exhibits a spirit of independence on its subjective way, each web being subject to the permutations of the environment (the depth and size of the wall or corner upon which the web is woven, etc.)[70] Igitur experiences the same duality: he enters the mazelike stairs or the lobes of his brain structure as would any individual according to fixed patterns, but then uses his own ingenuity in creating and seeking his goal.

Igitur, like the poet and the spider, is a spinner of thoughts, a weaver, an aggressive force, a performer or agent through which energy flows. He is not the source of the vibrations he senses all about him but the vessel, the garment through which these networks or arrangements manifest themselves. Like the spider Igitur-poet uses his threads or filaments, those substances, objects, or entities common to all human beings, but he uses this qualitative energy in his individual way. The manner in which his thoughts, feelings, and sensations are aroused, their graphic arrangement, makes for his originality. The spider web is a visualization of a process of evolution from the point of creation to its developed form; it resembles a mandala in that it encloses levels of energy that heighten and diminish. Each intersection of the web may act as a point of meditation for the individual observing it. The word in the poem also may be considered as a mandala, and certainly was in so far as Mallarmé was concerned. Each word was a cross-web of metaphors, a point of contact linking it with the entire *verse*—and with the uni*verse* at large.

The spider as the creator of a web of illusion has been associated with Maya—the phenomenological world, earth, the feminine principle. Like the world it builds and destroys in eternal permutations, its threads are perpetually generated and regenerated in an endless death and rebirth mystery: In that Athena was the patron goddess of the weavers in Greece and by extension the spider was sacred to her, it may be compared to this goddess of wisdom and intellect. It is through the intellect that the poet-spider weaves his web and counts and recounts his creative experience. Each word reflects the life he lives, its fiber and texture, and therefore his universe.

Igitur becomes that spider with tentacles that reach out into the cosmos. Yet he is, paradoxically, man as he is his creation as yet unmanifested in the work of art because within his being live all poems, all creative principles. The whispering he hears as he climbs down the stairs into his tomb are like many sensations: *grazing, panting, scansions.* The sounds, rhythms, and palls of energy Igitur feels throughout this stage of his initiation are not only audible but also become visceral forces, impeding and helping his journey inward. The variety of noises evoke the clock mentioned in the previous section, a bird, a human voice, a heartbeat. A landscape that transcends the human sphere comes into being. Like recitations, prayers, mutterings, dirges, and incantations, these auditory vibrations are experienced by Igitur as is a new language: at first incomprehensible, then slowly revealing its complex mysteries. It is written in *The Book of Formation* that "the whole creation and all language proceeded from one combination of letters."[71] It is this arrangement Igitur-poet-spider seeks to find in his own death and resurrection.

The word *scansion* used in *Igitur* is of great import. It indicates a metrical analysis of the structure of verse; it is also a way of marking a universal beat. An analogy may be made with the human heart as it pumps the blood throughout the body. Scientifically one may associate its rhythm with the implosion and explosion of the sun and the creation of the universe.[72] Metaphysically it is comparable to the giant inhaling and exhaling of the universe associated with the Buddha breath or the creative process. In Orphic tradition the division of one into many and back again follows a primal rhythm. Orphic musicians controlled the universe (stones, animals, people) via music in its aural and rhythmic manner.[73]

Scanning for Igitur evolved a condition of harmonious polarity that may be explained according to Hegelian view by thesis, antithesis, and synthesis. Such polarity is inherent in the universe and varies only in the interpretation given the integration and differentiation process, or on another level, the universal repetition of growth and decay. The question arises as to the value or direction of such perpetual movements: Plato looked forward to the reign of justice, Lebniz to universal harmony, the Hebrews to the coming of the Messiah, the Christians to the kingdom of God—Mallarmé, an agnostic, to the birth of the poem.

Igitur experiences the scanning process in his descent; its rhythms help him fuse with the world of objects about him and in so doing attract or repel certain combinations of atoms that encapsulate him in the form of audible or palpable energies.[74] Igitur having become a composite figure—dehumanized—is able "to relive," in Mallarmé's words, in a conscious way the life of "humanity since infancy." Igitur's being encompasses his ancestors, his race (physical, spiritual, and psychological characteristics), and those poets whose beings have been forgotten in the corridors of time. Because Igitur is inhabited by so many other beings now emerging from anterior existences, he decides to look at himself once again in the mirror. He no longer sees a human form before him, but rather a bird flying about, possibly one of his former incarnations or a manifestation of some superior being emerging at this point in time from some marginal existence.

The bird image may symbolize man's spirit, his intuitive

nature, his soul. It has been evoked from time immemorial—
from Cromagnon times in the Lascaux cave paintings to Plato's
concept of it as "divine intelligence."[75] Birds are mobile and
ascend into the air, thus standing for evolution in enlightenment.   In Igitur's sphere of existence they certainly signify all
these things, but because they emanate from a higher state of
being, they indicate the entry of the angel into the thickening
web. Igitur feels the fluttering of wings brushing against him, a
dragging quality that ushers in moods of joy, abandon, and
constriction.   Since wings cast shadows in their flight, they
endow the atmosphere with a kind of impressionism and an
excitement in the interplay of these light and dark forces. Because wings are placed on the heels of the Greek god Hermes (or
the Egyptian Thoth) one might conclude that the knowledge
contained in The Book of Divination lying on Igitur's table
(the Book of Thoth or Tarot) is linked to the divine element
(hermetic philosophy) contained in the bird image. More important, perhaps, in understanding Igitur's quest is the fact that
the bird image is linked to a myth that became a favorite with
alchemists: the Phoenix that burns itself in a pyre and is reborn
again from its own ashes.

Igitur's vision now floats back into time. It becomes more
explicit. He sees himself living in his own mind and experiences
a growing awareness of self. The doors to the tomb become
visible; each one represents a different aspect of gnosis—acquired
knowledge and eternal knowledge (as contained in the book on
the table which is a manifestation of the uncreated or that which
exists *in potentia*). Igitur hears the infinite void pulsating about
him; he sees apparitions hovering around and experiences their
impact upon him. His vision grows so acute that it bothers him.
Everything seems too clear, too light. Igitur seeks to escape
into his "uncreated anterior" world, the shadow he was. Yet,
he is intent upon shedding the disguise he had been obliged to
wear (his body) so as to experience "the heart of the race he feels
beating within him."

As Igitur's identity fades, memories of past incarnations appear and disappear in faint and powerful glimmers; heartbeats
intrude upon the cosmic flow; opening and shutting doors lead
to the tabernacle where his demise and transformation is to take
place. As Job expressed it: "Have the gates of death opened
unto thee? or hast thou seen the doors of the shadow of death?"

(38:17)   Similarities with Christ's resurrection as related in Matthew come to mind: "for the angel of the Lord descended from heaven, and came and rolled back the stone from the door, and sat upon it" (28:2).

Images of glass, mirrors, and vials intrude upon the scene as Igitur prepares for his death. Barriers vanish. A new language makes its presence known: a composite of all utterances, all thoughts—the word or the core of mystery. It is not the word *per se* that takes on meaning, but its power as a vehicle in the meditative ritual, thus helping Igitur descend into his preformal state. Each word (whether created or uncreated) has its own mystical logic, each contains within its form the deepest secrets of the universe. For Igitur-poet, a correspondence exists between the word of man and the work of divinity, the poet as architect of his building—God as the transcendental force making such construction possible.

To succeed in using this new language that exists in the intellect or in the mind's eye, necessitates a severing of connection with the sense world—a limiting force of nature. Once the knots have been untied and Igitur can break out of the constrictions imposed upon him, he will experience the "music of pure thought!"[76]

3. *IGITUR'S LIFE*

Before blowing out the candle that now becomes visible to the reader Igitur tells his ancestors about his *ennui*—his quest for the absolute. He has lived according to clock time. But because his ancestors enabled him to become aware of another time—the eternal or cyclical cosmic experience—he now considers clock time a heavy, "stifling" force, an obstacle preventing him from attaining his goal. The mirror becomes a way of measuring his progress into transcendental time. He gazes at his image reflected in the glass, he watches it diffuse and die before him. He reworks this same image in the objects about him by "opening" or seeing into them so that they in turn will "pour out their mystery," their memories, their silences. He stares at the clock and its vanishing hours. He no longer feels bound by the fear of disappearing into eternity. He had placed his hands before his eyes at first so as to block out the vision of his progressively

disintegrating being. Now he removes his hands from his eyes
and observes himself unto his depths in the mirror: his own
"phantom" expands in size and power as it absorbs "what remained of sentiment and pain in the mirror." The shadow,
now immense, feeds on all the concrete objects in the room;
as for Igitur's decomposing form, it reaches out into the objects in the room and imposes its diffused self onto them. A
monstrous being emerges from these forms, which will be eternalized in his mind in an "isolated and severe attitude."

Mallarmé's use of the mirror in section 3 differs considerably from its meaning in section 1. Here it is reminiscent of
certain rituals in Mithraic practices based on the hierophant's
desire to fuse consciousness with a supraconsciousness. Celsus
(175 A.D.) wrote that the initiate lying on a couch in the center
of an octagonal room would stare at the mirror placed in front
of him and in so doing his corporeal being would be diffused
(dismembered) in the myriad reflections emanating from all the
other mirrors placed about the room. The hierophant thus felt
duality within his own being and from this conflict evolved to
the point of being able to sense his own soul.[77] Igitur seemed
to be enacting a similar ritual using not only the mirror, but
also the draperies, the clock, and the book, whose presences were
all reflected in the mirror. They were like many alien forms
which by their very purity, objectivity, and durability worked
upon his being, destroying it little by little.[78]

Igitur had become an acosmic, transmundane figure living
in a nonmundane body and world. His situation was untenable.
He had reached an impasse. It is at this juncture that he enters
the memory of his ancestors, thus reactivating something that
had been dormant within him and releasing him by the same
token from his existential existence. This last phase of Igitur's
transformation may be explained in terms of physics. Professor James V. McCornell, of the University of Michigan, wrote
the following concerning the possibility of "memory   transfer-
ence with regard to the flat worm which is the lowest organism
(with a synoptic-type nervous system) on the philogenetic scale,
demonstrating an ability to learn..." He wrote:

> Hyden, the Swedish biologist, was one of the first to theorize
> that ribonucleic acid (RNA) might be the complex molecule
> which served as the chemical mediator of learning. Hyden

reasons that if DNA, which is considered exceptionally stable
and unchangeable, encoded an organism's 'racial' memories,
perhaps RNA, which is known to be much more malleable,
could act to encode an organism's individual memories; hence
RNA would be what is now called the "memory molecule."[79]

Thus, it is believed that when an individual dies physically, the
"personal memory" also comes to an end, but "the form of recorded information may not."

It is Igitur's desire to recall his poet-ancestors, either in
terms of Platonic "idea-essences" or archetypes (inherited forms
of knowledge transmitted by images), thus linking the time-space
factor concretely. The proof that energy (idea is energy) cannot
be destroyed is thereby given. When therefore Igitur views the
draperies and furniture in his room as monstrous chimeras, they
are not only aspects of himself he sees in projection, but or-
ganisms living in a transformed state in concrete objects as well,
therefore, particles of his own being.

A psychological term used for the dissolution of Igitur's
ego (identity) into exterior objects is schizophrenia. Verbal and
visual descriptions of schizophrenic patients in their rapport with
the world outside of themselves resembles Igitur's terrifying
state of depersonalization. It is no wonder that Mallarmé feared
insanity.

4. *THE DICE-THROW*

Igitur is still dissatisfied. Although he has blended into the
object around him, he has not yet merged with the absolute.
Only by the act, by throwing the dice, can he accomplish his
goal—fix chance in the number or the idea it represents. But he
wonders whether even by acting he is really the author of his act,
or is it chance (the collective will) exteriorizing itself within him
and obeying the laws of cosmic causality. Igitur nevertheless
shakes the box, "*Le Cornet est la Corne de licorne—d'unicorne*"
("The Dice-box is the Horn of the Unicorn"). In French the
words *Cornet* and *Corne* may signify "Horn," *licorne* and *unicorne* mean "unicorn"; thus Mallarmé's play on words and their
ramifications.

Igitur's act (throwing the dice) may be defined as an attempt to discriminate between what is of import to him and what is imposed upon him at this particular moment, or as a synthesis of antagonistic forces: thesis, antithesis, and synthesis. Unlike Parsifal who did not ask the question (or act) concerning the mystery of the Holy Grail, thus proving himself incapable of taking his own destiny into his hands, Igitur opts for the opposite road. He makes the supreme gesture and throws the dice, thereby resolving his quandry and thereby destroying the possibility of creating the absolute: of experiencing beauty or the ideal. But by the same token his act is an affirmation of his personal will, his identity, and his future. Igitur's struggle against the ineffable that was his drama—between being and nothingness—was decided the very instant his act took place. His hero is comparable to Job's confrontation with God: "Though he will slay me, yet will I trust in him. But I will maintain my own ways before him." It is not the Judeo-Christian God Igitur faces but the mystic's all, the infinite.

The word *hasard* in French comes from the Arabic *az-zahr* ("dice-game"), which symbolizes man's rejection of the law of probabilities. Since time immemorial man has been attempting to break its power or discover its secrets through numbers, religious devices, and so on. Igitur is such a thaumaturge. He too seeks to be a master of ceremonies, thus controlling destinies and the creative process. His gesture enables him to transcend the human condition just as the poet each time he sets down a word on a page fixes chance, thus controlling it. The world of infinite possibilities has just emerged into the world of phenomena and is no longer experienced as pure possibility but realized in the number showing on the dice—or the word in the poem.

Igitur casts his dice as the devotees of *I Ching* throw their coin or the geomancers their bones. The dice-box to which Mallarmé has recourse is made out of a unicorn's horn, a fabulous medieval animal with a horse's body and a horn in the center of its forehead. This animal was looked upon as both a symbol of chastity, since only a virgin could tame it, and pure energy, the *spiritus mercurialis,* an aggressive force (a transformatory agent that could alter the consistency of matter). The unicorn, like Igitur's chimera, lends a mythological atmosphere to the passage, thus integrating past into present and enlarging still more the infinite ramifications of Mallarmé's thought.

Igitur closes the book, blows out the candle, and gets into the tomb where he lies down on the ashes of his ancestors. For the mystic breathing refers to God's spirit as well as to the "withdrawal of sensorial functions which become reabsorbed into thinking matter."[80]   Therefore when Igitur blows out the candle, he has extinguished his life. He crosses his arms. Such an image is a graphic expression of a space-time synthesis: the vertical (hierarchical aspects of spiritual and physical man) and horizontal (amplitude of his human personality).   By crossing his arms Igitur expresses in one gesture the multiple aspects of man in his "integrality" and as an "ensemble of possibilities."[81] Because the cross is not strictly a Christian symbol but existed in Egyptian, Indian, and Hebrew times, it lends an atemporal note to the scene, as though Igitur's ancestors were alive at this moment in time and making their presences known via a visualization.

For the alchemist the image of the man lying in the tomb of his ancestor's ashes indicates the experiencing of the quintessential essence of being.   Ashes are regarded as matter rid of its impurities, as the stage that follows mortification, death, and the decomposition of metals and chemicals—as "the seed of gold" that will germinate and give birth to the new being—or the soul restored.   Ashes also represent the principle of continuity and permit man to contact anterior existences through this entity.

The Orphics considered the tomb to be the body that acts as the prison for the soul. Only after death (the disintegration of the flesh) can the soul be liberated.[82]   In this sense Igitur has been freed from matter and can experience the purity of eternity.   In so dong he knows the absolute but at the same time forgets human speech. After consulting the *grimoire* (the magic book) as well as human thought (look at the light reflected in the chimera), he understands that the casting of the dice was foretold and resulted in the negation of chance. The fact that Igitur forgets speech during his transformatory process is another indication of his vanishing identity (his individual mode of expression) and that he recalls the original or primordial language embedded in matter through the *grimoire* indicates his passage from one phase of existence to another.   For the Pythagorean and Kabbalist, the original or primordial language is God's word before His spirit was embedded in matter.   Such words have divine qualities to them, unsuspected power that remains incomprehensible for beings living in the temporal realm.

Now that Igitur experiences the infinite, he realizes that chance is a finite concept, that his act was "useless" because it does not exist in the pleromatic, uncreated realm. He is dissatisfied. He still seeks to discover that point where both worlds merge, making the infinite and finite accessible to the one who succeeds in his goal.

5. *HE LIES DOWN IN THE TOMB*

Igitur takes the last step in his mystical quest. There he lies "On the astral ashes, those of his indivisible family." He drinks what he calls "the drop of nothingness which the sea lacks." The vial is empty and Mallarmé adds, only folly remains; "the purity of the castle." Even Nothingness has vanished.

An affinity now exists between *ashes* and *astral,* both are alchemical terms. Paracelsus spoke of the astral or stellar regions as intermediary points between physical and spiritual beings. Each person has an astral body that may be looked upon as a kind of double and, under certain circumstances, can manifest itself in the phenomenological world. This astral body, which spiritualists call *perspirit,* lives on after death on an astral plain in a kind of invisible world that is also situated between one sphere and the next. The disincarnated spirits reside in the kindgom of the dead awaiting reincarnation. Because, according to occultists, everything that is visible in the phenomenological world is a reflection of what exists in the astral plane, life on earth is a mirror image of what it is above. It is in the astral plane, then, that time is obliterated, that premonitions and hallucinations occur. It is in this area that Igitur experiences his death—that is, he is dead to the living but alive to the spirit or divine intellect within him.

The "poor personage" in the tomb has now reached the longed-for state of detachment described by so many mystics and alchemists in their tracts. The body, now diffused and integrated into the world about him (the concrete objects, the sound and rhythmic patterns about him), now liquifies, that is, experiences another form. The drop of nothingness has been drunk. Such an image indicates a shift of form in the transitory process of life.

Water, according to the Orphics, indicates the demise of the soul;[83] for the Gnostics it incorporates the world of matter or darkness. Heraclitus wrote, "Death for the soul is to become as water." But the god Soma, in Hindu cosmogony, was experienced as a plant whose juice was extracted and given to believers who then gained victory over death. Soma also took the form of a bird considered "the prince of poets." In this connection *soma,* or liquid, would be looked upon as the very lifeblood of inspiration, the essence of life.[84]

It is no wonder that Mallarmé had recourse to the drop of liquid which is associated with the creative principle. The empty vial or alchemical vessel containing the liquid, may be considered a female matrix as was the dice-box. The vial, now purged of impurities, exists as a void, a vacant and sterile entity. No human thought, feeling, or sensation remains to mar its pristine purity.

Nevertheless, "folly" is "all that remains of the castle." The alliteration between *fiole* (vial) and *folie* (folly) stresses the fact that when liquid is imbibed new realms may be reached. Drunkenness, as is baptism or any initiatory ritual requiring the taking in of liquid, releases man from the circumscribed domain, and from his fear of stepping into the unknown. In his madness Igitur is divested of everything that remains in the castle, that is, his body and his head. The castle (as well as the vial and the dice-box) are enclosed and containing objects. They are then both protective and imprisoning devices depending upon the attitude affixed toward them. Medieval knights journeyed from castle to castle to perform their songs, their feats of battle, and to rescue damsels in distress. The alchemist as well as the Kabbalist viewed the castle as an inner temple, a holy place— "the Mansion of the Beyond, the Other World."[85]

"Nothingness had departed," therefore the deepest level of consciousness known to the mystic—the one devoid of images and sensations—had come into being. The state of Nirvana or "self-annihilation" has been born. Such a condition does not imply death in the Occidental sense, but rather indifferentiation, the sphere where conflict, contrast, duality, and movement are absent. The Hindu looks upon the world of duality as transient and antipathetic. Only the *absolute* is of import when multiplicity has vanished. For the Hindu absolute non-duality is reality.

> Therefore the non-dual position does not conflict with the dualist's position. This unborn (changeless, non-dual Brahman) appears to undergo modification only on account of Maya (illusion) and not otherwise. For, if this modification were real, the Immortal (Brahman) would become mortal.[86]

Only when Igitur lies on his ancestors' ashes does he experience the emptiness of nothingness and purity of being. In this mental form he knows absolute nonduality. "Through the mind alone is Brahman to be realized. There is in it no diversity." Such a state of nothingness should not be considered a negative condition, but rather as the experience of fullness.

> Where one sees nothing else, hears nothing else, understands nothing else—that is the Infinite. Where one sees something else, hears something else, understands something else—that is the finite. The Infinite is immortal, the finite mortal.[87]

Igitur has attained superconsciousness that has put him in harmony with universal principles. The mystery has been revealed to him in the tomb—his inner palace. Igitur has not become the very substance of his great work; he has made himself master of his own being and destiny.

Mallarmé experienced the ineffable. In a letter to Eugène Lefébure he wrote: "Beauty has finally found its *co-relative phases* in the Universe."[88] Mallarmé had entered the cosmic dream state and Igitur was his transcription in graphic and verbal patterns of his journey into supra-consciousness.

NOTES

[1]Stéphane Mallarmé was born on March 1, 1842. He lost his mother at the age of five from tuberculosis. He and his two year old sister, Maria, were cared for by their maternal grandparents. His father remarried a year after his wife's death. Stéphane was sent to an elegant parochial school and there chided because he was not a member of the nobility. He developed an inferiority complex and became introverted. His unhappiness and loneliness were manifested in a hostile and aggressive attitude. His sole confidante and companion was his sister who died in 1857. Two years later his sadness was to be increased with the passing of the girl he "loved," Harriet Smyth.

In 1861 Mallarmé discovered Baudelaire's *The Flowers of Evil.* This book influenced the young man enormously: Baudelaire's morbidity, his attraction and cultivation of *ennui,* of the dream, his desire for the Ideal and the Infinite, his terror of the abyss, impressed Mallarmé. His first poems "Placet," "Le Guignon," "Le Sonneur," were published in 1862. After he became fascinated with Edgar Allan Poe's mystical works; the esoteric ideas of Villiers de l'Isle Adam. Mallarmé was developing his own credo: just as music, mathematics, and the sciences have their hieroglyphics which unless understood are useless and meaningless, so poetry must remain out of reach for the untutored. Readers must experience poetry as they do an initiation into a religious or occult society. Poetry must have its arcana. It must be "closed" to the masses and remain accessible only to the elite. Like the ancient mystery schools whose priests belonged to the highest of orders, so poetry should be a hermetic art—a sacred one.

Mallarmé married Marie Gerhard in 1863. He took the position of English teacher at the Imperial College of Tournon. He was disappointed in his career, in the climate which crippled him with rheumatism. The most terrifying notion of all was the feeling of poetic sterility which overcame him. It caused him nights of insomnia and of anguish which he later referred to as his "nights of Tournon." Despite his depression he completed poems such as "Azur" (1864), etc. Mallarmé was searching for a new poetic way. He followed Poe's dictum: it was "the effect produced in a poem" which was of import. Mallarmé rejected facile rhyme schemes; cheap emotions and the dream for him was not to be an escape mechanism. He had recourse to ellipses, he cut his phrases, inverted verb and subject, substituted one idea or sensation for another.

Mallarmé's teaching experience failed: from Tournon he moved to the Lycée de Besançon (1866), to the Lycée d'Avignon (1867). By 1871, his wife, his daughter Geneviève, his son. Anatole, moved to Paris. He accepted a teaching position at the Lycée Fontanes (Condorcet) and continued his writings. Influenced by Hegel and the occultists and mystics (Fourier, Lavater, Plotinus, Boehme, Paracelsus, Egyptian and Greek mystery religions, Lévi, the Kabbalists, and alchemists), Mallarmé's verses became more and more esoteric.

In 1875 Mallarmé moved to 87 Rue de Rome in Paris where he began receiving on what came to be known as his famous "Tuesdays." Verlaine, Manet, Zola, Mendès, Banville, Debussy, Villiers, Huysmans, Valéry, Claudel, and others visited him. A cult was built around Mallarmé. His friendship with Mary Laurent, Manet's former mistress who became his neighbor on the Rue de Rome, enabled him to counterbalance the suffering of his personal life (the death of his son in 1879), the humiliations he experienced as a teacher, the intense tasks he set himself as a poet.

Mallarmé died as he had lived, quietly, in his modest country home at Valvins, on September 9, 1898, from a lung ailment.

[2]Stéphane Mallarmé, *Correspondance 1862-1871*, p. 240.

[3]*Ibid.*, p. 313.

[4]*Ibid.*, p. 273.

[5]*Ibid.*, p. 301.

[6]*Ibid.*, p. 273.

[7]*Ibid.*, p. 301.

[8]Stéphane Mallarmé, *Oeuvres complètes*, p. 433.

[9]Charles Poncé, *The Nature of the I Ching*, p. 12.

[10]*Oeuvres complètes*, p. 427.

[11]Marie Louis von Franz, *Number and Time*, p. 45.

[12]*The Living Webster Encyclopedia Dictionary,* 1973.

[13]*The Zohar,* I, p. 65.

[14]Gershom Scholem, *The Messianic Idea in Judaism,* p. 270.

   The origin of the hexagram is unknown. For the Hebrews, the six-pointed star is a pictorial representation of the first two triads of the Sefiroth; for the Mason, part of his evolution and initiation; for the alchemist, union of water and fire (the reverse triangle) as well as the double triadic principles of sulphur, mercury, and salt.

[15]Poncé, p. 17.

[16]Hans Jonas, *The Gnostic Religion,* p. 133.

[17]*Correspondance,* p. 259.

[18]G. Encausse (Papus), *L'Occultisme et le spiritualisme.*

[19]Jean-Pierre Richard, *L'Univers imaginaire de Mallarmé,* p. 184.

[20]Jonas, p. 261.

[21]Scholem, p. 56.

[22]Eliphas Lévi, *Dogme et rituel de la haute magie,* p. 175.

   Twenty-two letters exist in the Hebrew alphabet: Mallarmé's title Igitur *La Folie d'Elbehnon,* omitting the "or" in the title adds up to twenty-two. Eliphas Lévi believed that twenty-two was the sign of Thoth, the Egyptian sun god, later incarnated into man and known under the name of Hermes Trismegistus (the three times great) originator of alchemy and the inventor of hieroglyphics.

[23]See Lewis Spence, *An Encyclopedia of Occultism,* p. 281.

[24]*Oeuvres complètes,* p. 435.

[25]Franz, p. 11.

[26]Edouard Schuré, *The Great Initiates,* pp. 305, 311.

[27]*Ibid.*, p. 191.

[28]Franz, pp. 204, 62, 18.

[29]*Ibid.*

[30]*Ibid.*, p. 45.

As functions of the mind and psyche, numbers are active forces symbolizing contents that have not yet reached consciousness. They may take the form and force of energy that may then be transformed into sensations of pleasure or pain and will, therefore be important factors in shaping one's destiny. (See Poncé, p. 26.)

Numbers have been used in mantic procedures in the *I Ching*, by throwing coins or yarrow stalks; in geomancy where grains, pebbles, and other objects are counted; in gambling games. (See Franz, p. 45.)

[31]The twelve names of Surya, the Hindu god identified with the sun. *New Larousse Encyclopedia of Mythology*, p. 332.

[32]René Guénon, *Le Symbolisme de la croix*, p. 68.

[33]Franz, p. 19.

[34]Thomas Hopkins, *The Religious Life of Man*, p. 66.

[35]*Correspondance*, p. 245.

[36]*Ibid.*, p. 259.

The mirror stands for duality and multiplicity of being for Mallarmé. Such a notion is of ancient vintage and is present in the Gnostic "Hym of the Pearl" discovered in the apocryphal Acts of the Apostle Thomas. "As I now beheld the robe, it seemed to me suddenly to become a mirrow-image of myself: myself entire I saw it it, and it entire I saw in myself, that we were two in separateness, and yet again on in the sameness of our forms..." (See Jonas, p. 115 for discussion of it.)

[37]*Zohar*, p. 389.

Mallarmé viewed the mirror as had the ancient Spanish Kabbalist: "This degree is the sum total of all subsequent mirrors, that is, of all external aspects related to this one degree. They proceed therefrom because of the mystery of the point, which is in itself an occult degree emanating from the mystery of the pure and awe-inspiring ether."

[38]Walter F. Otto, "The Meaning of the Eleusinian Mysteries," *Eranos Year-books* II, p. 33.

[39]Ralph Metzner, *Maps of Consciousness*, p. 51.

[40]Gershom Scholem, *Major Trends in Jewish Mysticism*, p. 133.

[41]Georges Poulet, *Les Métamorphoses du cercle*, p. 443.

[42]Jonas, p. 59.

The Gnostics speak of the sparks of light or scintillae which were dispersed after the fall and must be restored to divinity in order to bring about primordial unity.

[43]Alice Raphael, *Goethe and the Philosophers' Stone*, p. 80.

[44]*New Larousse Encyclopedia of Mythology*, p. 332.

[45]*Correspondance*, p. 207.

[46]Metzner, p. 90.

[47]Jonas, p. 256.

[48]*Ibid.*, p. 259.

The Babylonian astrologers considered stars as fixed and impersonal powers that ruled the cosmos in a structured and orderly manner. Yet it is from these same regions that the Pythagoreans determined the equivalent of astral order and the Stoics created their *heimarmene* (fate and divine providence).

[49]In the Vedic Creation myths as in the Judeo-Christian Egyptian and Greek sources, one is fascinated by the similarity of the colorful oppositions mentioned. "This (world) was darkness, unknowable, without form, beyond reason and perception, as if utterly asleep. Then the august and self-existent Being, he who never unfolded, having unfolded this (universe) under the form of the great elements and others, having

shown his energy, appeared to scatter the shades of darkness."

Zohar, p. 387.

[50]*Ibid.*

[51]Gershom Scholem, *Zohar,* p. 29.

[52]Metzner, p. 2.

See Pierre Teilhard de Chardin, *The Phenomenon of Man,* 0. 420.

[53]Metzner, p. 158.

Buddha was asked what "opinions he *held*." "No opinions," he answered. "To *hold* an opinion is to remain fixed and not be fluid." According to Buddhist philosophy one must be able to "stand firmly on a moving point," that is, possess a mobile attitude toward everything or experience a conjunction of opposites.

[54]Jonas, p. 45.

[55]Metzner, p. 45.

Just as the Indian mantra—O M—is believed to contain the force and vibratory pattern of the universe as a whole, thus imbuing it with the force to generate psychic heat, so for the mystic and for Mallarmé the sound of a letter, word, etc. is also endowed with physical, aural texture, enabling it to flow through the atmosphere as energy makes its way through the body and thoughts inroads in the mind.

[56]Alex Meller, *Dictionnaire de la Franc-Maçonnerie,* p. 90.

[57]Guénon, p. 88.

[58]Franz, p. 256.

[59]Guénon, p. 187.

[60]B. Jewett, *The Works of Plato,* p. 270.

[61]*Oeuvres complètes,* p. 663.

[62]Jérome-Antoine Rony, *La Magie*, p. 45.

[63]Guénon, pp. 178, 187.

[64]*Correspondance*, p. 111.

[65]*Oeuvres complètes*, p. 1164.

In *Les Dieux antiques* Mallarmé tried to reduce the many myths of antiquity and of a variety of nations to a common denominator. See the work in its entirety.

[66]*Eranos Yearbooks*, II, p. 70.

[67]*The Secrets of the Golden Flower*, p. 30.

[68]Franz, p. 197.

Let us recall that Paris and Helen (*Faust*, Part II) were considered eidola and as such were reincarnated. Such a feat is explained today in scientific terminology by nuclear fission.

[69]*Correspondance*, p. 225.

[70]Arthur Koestler, *The Act of Creation*, p. 38.

[71]Rabbi Akiba Ben Joseph, *The Book of Formation*, p. 20.

[72]Guénon, p. 89.

[73]Jean-Claude Pilloux, *L'Inconscient*, p. 10.

[74]The depersonalization process has been delineated by the alchemist Agrippa von Nettesheim in terms of a duality of spheres in the universe and is considered a creative principle.

[75]In Ezekiel we read: "And when they went, I heard the noise of their wings, like the noise of great waters, as the voice of the Almighty, the voice of speech, as the noise of an host: when they stood, they let down their wings." (1:24)

[76]Scholem, p. 133.

[77]Raphael, p. 146.

[78]T. Witton Davies, *Magic, Divination, and Demonology*, pp. 8-9.

[79]Poncé, p. 7..

Quoted from *New Scientist*, vol. 21., pp. 458-468.

[80]Louis Gardet, *La Mystique*, p. 24.

[81]Guénon, p. 75.

[82]*Eranos Yearbooks*, II, p. 39.

[83]Jonas, p. 117.

[84]*New Larousse Encyclopedia of Mythology*, p. 331.

[85]Guénon, p. 84.

[86]Boris Vysheslawzeff, "Two ways of Redemption," *Eranos Yearbooks* VI, pp. 17-18.

[87]*Ibid.*, p. 20.

[88]*Correspondance*, i, p. 246. (May 17, 1867).

CONCLUSION

After journeying through some of the dreams and images writers encountered before composing their works or incorporated into their novels and poems, one may begin to understand the vital role the oneirosphere has played in the creative process. The altered states of consciousness experienced by these creative individuals as a result of their powerful dreams and images put them in touch with the pleromatic world, the *unus mundus* that fed them, so to speak, both quantitatively and qualitatively. Whether topics such as Cartesian hubris, Racinian obsessions with regard to good or evil, Cazotte's prophecies, Diderot's scientific investigations into monism, Nodier's and Nerval's views of the feminine principle, Balzac's thinking man, Gautier's parapsychological experience, Hugo's hallucinatory cosmogony, Baudelaire's unity in the work of art, Huysmans' preoccupation with Satanism and the Black Mass, Rimbaud's passage from chaos to cosmos, or Mallarmé's creative encounter were broached—they bear a common stamp, that of eternity. Certainly the substance and impact of the themes adumbrated have altered in intensity and in scope with the passage of time. Questions such as good and evil which preoccupied seventeenth, eighteenth, and nineteenth century man, are, generally speaking, no longer excoriatingly troublesome. The woman's image has altered too. Contemporary society for the most part no longer sees her as Nodier and Nerval had: as a divinity capable of alleviating man's anguishes. For many today, she has been reduced to lifesize. She has become humanized. The very nature of the transformative process and the concomitant change of emphasis with regard to certain problems and relationships enables one to observe man's evolution and/or devolution. Such differences in stress should not necessarily be viewed in a hierarchical sense—either in terms of improvement or regression—but rather as a shifting in orientation and in values. The extreme optimism of a Descartes or of a Hugo with regard to man's glorious future has been somewhat mitigated today. Man no longer really believes he will

ever discover the answer to life's problems. He has become
increasingly aware of his finiteness and the infinite nature of the
universe. His frenzy for gnosis, so active during the industrial
and scientific revolutions and still a very potent force, has
nevertheless simmered down a bit. Man has taken into account
the double-edged nature of discovery and so-called progress:
with every positive achievement a negative step comes into
being. In other terms, the greater man's conquest of nature,
the more powerful is his destruction of this life-force—whether
in terms of pollution, the ozone layer, or the diminution of
natural resources. Yet, like Prometheus, man strives, and he
must strive to experience life in all of its manifestations and as
completely as possible. Such is his destiny.

The writer, like the prophet in many ways, senses man's
quandaries through his works before the general public becomes
aware of them. He experiences the unknown because his oneirosphere responds more powerfully to the deepest layers within
himself, to the collective unconscious made visible or comprehensible to him via archetypal forms. It is therefore of extreme
importance to study and understand the contents emanating
from the oneirosphere of writers as well as of all creative individuals. They seem to be the forerunners of what *is to be.*
The dreams and images of Descartes, Racine, Diderot, Cazotte,
Nodier, Nerval, Balzac, Gautier, Hugo, Huysmans, Baudelaire,
Rimbaud, and Mallarmé studied in this volume thus should not
be looked upon simply as individual offerings or as the artistic
revelations of one person, but as myths, as that collective cultural material that lies hidden in a mysterious inner realm, concealed by opaque curtains, which the creative artist makes visible
in his own subjective way. Dreams and images are to be consulted, analyzed, and experienced as living forces by contemporary readers, for within them lives man's history—past, present, and future—incized in his visions.

> He revealeth the deep and secret things: he knoweth what
> is in the darkness, and the light dwelleth with him (Daniel
> 2:22).

BIBLIOGRAPHY

Adam, Charles, *Vie et oeuvres des Descartes* (Paris: J. Vrin XII, 1957).

Adam, Charles and Paul Tannery, *Oeuvres de Descartes* (Paris: Leopold Cerf, 1908).

Akiba, ben Joseph (Rabbi), *The Book of Formation* (New York: Ktav Publishers, 1970).

Aquinas, Thomas (Saint), *Summa Theologiae* (New York: McGraw-Hill Co., 1963).

Augustine, (Saint), *The Confessions* (New York: Liveright Publishing Corp., 1943).

Bachelard, Gaston, *L'Eau et les rêves* (Paris: Jos[Corti, 1942).

—, *La Psychanalyse du feu* (Paris: Gallimard, 1949).

—, *La Poétique de l'espace* (Paris: Presses Universitaires de France, 1958).

—, *Le Droit de rêver* (Paris: Presses Universitaires de France, 1970).

—, *La Dialectique de la durée* (Paris: Presses Universitaires de France, 1972).

Baldick, Robert, *La Vie de J.-K. Huysmans* (Paris: Denoël, 1958).

Balz, Albert, *Descartes and the Modern Mind* (New Haven: Yale University Press, 1952).

Barbey d'Aurévilly, *Les Diaboliques* (Paris: Garnier-Flammarion, 1967).

Baron, Salo, W., *A Social and Religious History of the Jews* I (Philadelphia: Jewish Publication Society, 1952).

Barrett, William, *Irrational Man* (New York: A Double Anchor Book, 1962).

Baudelaire, Charles, *Oeuvres complètes* (Paris: Pleiade, 1961).

—, Correspondance générale I

Bayard, Jean-Pierre, *La Symbolique du feu* (Paris: Payot, 1973).

Baynes, H. G., *Mythology of the Soul* (Baltimore: The Williams and Wilkins Co., 1940).

Bays, Gwendolyn, The Orphic Vision (Lincoln: University of Nebraska, 1964).

Béguin, Albert, *L'âme romantique et le rêve* (Paris: Librairie José Corti, 1967).

Bernis, Jeanne, *L'Imagination* (Paris: Presses Universitaires de France, 1969).

Birch, Una, *The Disciples at Saïs* (London: Methuen, 1903).

Blanchot, Maurice, *L'Espace littéraire* (Paris: Gallimard, 1955).

Block, Haskel, "Mallarmé the Alchemist," *Australian Journal of French Studies*, II-III, 1969.

Bonnefoy, Yves, *Rimbaud par lui-même* (Paris: Seuil, 1966).

Boorsch, Jean, *Etat présent des études sur Descartes* (Paris: Les Belles Lettres, 1937).

Brun, Jean, Héraclite (Paris: Seghers, 1969).

—, *Empédocle* (Paris: Seghers, 1966).

The Teachings of Buddha (Tokyo: Kzenkyusha Printing Co., 1970).

Buber, Martin, *The Knowledge of Man* (New York: Harper Torchbooks, 1966).

—, *Pointing the Way* (New York: Harper Torchbooks, 1963).

Campbell, Joseph, *The Hero with a Thousand Faces* (Princeton: Princeton University Press, 1973).

Careil, Foucher, de, *Oeuvres inédites de Descartes* I (Paris: Auguste Durand, 1959).

Castellan, Yvonne, *La métapsychique* (Paris: Presses Universitaires de France, 1966).

Cellier, Léon, *L'Epopée humanitaire et les grands mythes romantiques* (Paris: Société d'édition d'enseignement supérieur, 1971).

Chastel, André, "La Légende de la Reine de Saba," *Revue de l'Histoire des religions,* tome 120-124, juillet-août, 1939-1941.

Cogny, Pierre, *J. K. Huysmans à la recherche de l'unité* (Paris: Librairie Nizet, 1953).

Cohn, Norman, *The Pursuit of the Millenium* (New York: Oxford University Press, 1970).

Cohn, Robert Greer, *Toward the Poem of Mallarmé* (Berkeley: University of California Press, 1965).

—, *Mallarmé's un Coup de dés an exegesis* (New Haven: Yale University Press, 1949).

—, *The Poetry of Rimbaud* (Princeton: Princeton University Press, 1973).

Davis, T. Witton, *Magic, Divination, and Demonology* (New York: Ktav

Publishers, 1969).

Descartes, René, *Discourse on Method and the Meditations* (Middlesex: Penguin Books, 1972).

—, *Oeuvres et lettres* (Paris: Pleiade, 1953).

Dhotel, André, *Rimbaud et la révolte moderne* (Paris: Gallimard, 1952).

Dictionnaire des symboles (Paris: Seghers, 1973).

Diderot Interpreter of Nature (trans. Jean Stewart and Jonathan Kemp) New York: International Publishers, 1943).

Diderot, Denis, *Oeuvres* (Paris: Pleiade, 1951).

Dumas, Alexandre, *Mes Mémoires* V (Paris: Calman-Lévy).

Dumas, François, *Histoire de la Magie* (Paris: Belfond, 1970).

Edinger, Edward, *Ego and Archetype* (New York: Putnam's Sons, 1972).

—, "An Outline of Analytical Psychology" (unpublished).

Eliade, Mircea, *Shamansim* (Princeton: Princeton University Press, 1972).

—, *Myths, Dreams, and Mysteries* (New York: Harper Torchbooks, 1960).

Encausse, G. (Papus), *L'Occultisme et le spiritisme* (Paris: Felix Alcan, 1902).

Etiemble, R., *Le Mythe de Rimbaud* (Paris: Gallimard, 1954).

—, et Gauclère, Yassu, *Rimbaud* (Paris: Seuil, 1966).

Europe, Rimbaud, mai-juin, 1973.

Fellows, Otis and Diana Guiragossian, *Diderot Studies* XVII (Genève: Droz, 1973).

— and Norman L. Torrey, *The Age of Enlightenment* (New York: Appleton-Century Crofts, 1942).

Fergusson, George, *Signs and Symbols in Christian Art* (New York: Oxford University Press, 1973).

Fernie, William T., *The Occult and Curative Powers of Precious Stones* (Blauvelt: Rudolf Steiner Pub., 1973).

Fowlie, Wallace, *Mallarmé* (Chicago: University of Chicago Press, 1962).

Franz, Marie Louise von, "The Dream of Descartes," *Timeless Documents of the Soul* (Evanston: Northwestern University Press, 1968).

—, *Puer Aeternus* (New York: Spring, 1970).

—, *Creation Myths* (New York: Spring, 1972).

—, *Number and Time* (Evanston: Northwestern University Press, 1974).

—, *Interpretation of Fairy Tales* (New York: Spring Publications, 1970).

Freud, Sigmund, *Standard Edition of the Complete Works,* XXI (London: Hogarth Press, 1961).

Frey-Rohn, Liliane, "Evil from the Psychological Point of View," *Evil* (Evanston: Northwestern University Press, 1967).

Fraisse, Paul, *Psychologie du Temps* (Paris: Presses Universitaires de France, 1957).

Frazer, James George, *The New Golden Bough* (New York: Criterion Books, 1959). (ed. Theodor H. Gaster)

Gardet, Louis, *La Mystique* (Paris: Presses Universitaires de France, 1970).

Gardner, Davis, *Vers une explication rationnelle du coup de dés* (Paris: José Corti, 1953).

Gascar, Pierre, *Rimbaud et la Commune* (Paris: Gallimard, 1971).

Gautier, Théophile, *Contes fantastiques* (Paris: José Corti, 1962).

Gilson, Etienne, *Etudes sur le rôle de la pensée médiévale dans la formation du système cartésien* (Paris: J. Vrin, 1951).

Givry, Emile Grillot de, *Illustrated Anthology of Sorcery, Magic and Alchemy* (New York: Causeway Books, 1973).

Gouhier, Henri, *Descartes* (Paris: Librairie philosophique, 1949).

Guénon, René, *Le Symbolisme de la croix* (Paris: 10/18, 1957).

Harding, Esther, *Women's Mysteries* (New York: G. P. Purnam's Sons, 1971).

Hawkridge, Emma, *The Wisdom Tree* (Boston: Houghton Mifflin and Co., 1945).

Hill, Brian, *Such Stuff as Dreams* (London: Rupert Hart-Davis, 1967).

Hopkins, Thomas, *The Religious Life of Man* (Dickinson Pub. Co., 1971).

Hugo, Victor, *Correspondance* II (Paris: Albin-Michel, 1950).

—, *Actes et paroles* II (Paris: Albin Miche, 1938).

—, *Oeuvres poétiques* II (Paris: Pleiade, 1967).

—, *William Shakespeare* (Paris: Flammarion, 1973).

Humphrey, George René, *L'esthétique de la poésie de Gérard de Nerval* (Paris: Nizet, 1969).

Hutin, Serge, *Les Sociétés secrètes* (Paris: Presses Universitaires, 1970).

—, *L'Alchimie* (Paris: Presses Universitaires de France, 1971).

Huysmans, J. K., *Là-Bas* (Paris: Le Livre de Poche, 1966).

—, *Down There* (trans. Keene Wallace) (New York: Dover Publishers, 1972)

James, E. O., *The Cult of the Mother Goddess* (London: Thames and Hudson, 1969).

Jonas, Hans, *The Gnostic Religion* (Boston: Beacon Press, 1967).

Jowett, B., *The Works of Plato* (New York: Tudor Publishing Co.).

Juin, Hubert, *Charles Nodier* (Paris: Pierre Seghers, 1970).

Jung, C. G., *The Archetypes and the Collective Unconscious* (New York: Pantheon, 1959).

—, *Psychology and Alchemy* (London: Turledge and Kegan Paul, 1953).

—, *Symbols of Transformation* (New York: Pantheon Books, 1956).

—, *The Psychogenesis of Mental Disease* (New York: Pantheon, 1960).

—, "A Letter on Parapsychology and Synchronicity," *Spring,* 1960.

—, *Freud and Psychoanalysis* (Princeton: Princeton University Press, 1961).

—, *Memoirs, Dreams, Reflections* (New York: Pantheon, 1963).

—, *Mysterium Coniunctionis* (New York: Pantheon, 1963).

—, *Civilization in Transition* (New York: Pantheon, 1964).

—, *Psychological Types* (London: Pantheon, 1964).

—, *The Practice of Psychotherapy* (New York: Pantheon, 1966).

—, *Alchemical Studies* (Princeton: Princeton University Press, 1967).

—, *The Structure and Dynamics of the Psyche* (Princeton: Princeton University Press, 1969).

—, *Psychology and Religion: West and East* (New York: Pantheon Books, 1959).

— and Kerenyi, *Essays on a Science of Mythology* (Princeton: Princeton University Press, 1969).

Jung, Emma and Marie Louise von Franz, *The Grail Legend* (New York: Putnam's Sons, 1970).

Keeling, S. V., *Descartes* (Oxford: Oxford University Press, 1968).

Kerenyi, C., *The Gods of the Greeks* (New York: Grove Press, 1960).

Kluger, Rivkah, Scärf, *Psyche and the Bible* (Zürich: Spring Pub., 1974).

—, *Satan and the Old Testament* (Evanston: Northwestern University Press, 1967).

Koestler, Arthur, *The Act of Creation* (New York: Dell Publishing, 1973).

—, *The Roots of Coincidence* (New York: Random House, 1972).

Koyré, Alexandre, *Entretiens sur Descartes* (New York: Brentano's, 1944).

Lattimore, Richmond, *The Odyssey of Homer* (New York: Harper Torchbooks, 1965).

Lefèvre, *La Pensée de Descartes* (Paris: Bordas, 1965).

Levaillant, Maurice, *La Crise mystique de Victor Hugo* (Paris: José Corti,

1954).

Lévi, Eliphas, *Dogme et rituel de la haute magie* (Paris: Niclaus, 1967).

—, *The Key of the Mysteries* (New York: Samuel Weiser, 1971).

Lewin, Bertram D., *Dreams and the Uses of Regression* (New York: International Universities Press, 1958).

Lewis, Geneviève, *Le Problème de l'inconscient et le cartésianisme* (Paris: Presses Universitaires de France, 1951).

Lewis, W. D. Wyndam, *The Soul of Marshal Gilles de Raiz* (London: Eyre and Spottiswoode, 1952).

MacKenzie, Norman, *Dreams and Dreaming* (New York: The Vanguard Press, Inc., 1965).

Magg, Victor, "The Antichrist as a Symbol of Evil," *Evil* (Evanston: Northwestern University Press, 1967).

Magny, Claude Edmonde, *Arthur Rimbaud* (Paris: Seghers, 1966).

Mallarmé, Stéphane, *Oeuvres complètes* (Paris: Pléiade, 1945).

—, *Correspondance* 1862-1871 (Paris: Gallimard, 1959).

Maritain, Jacques, *Le Songe de Descartes* (Paris: Buchet Chastel, 1932).

Martin, Kingsley, *French Liberal Thought in the Eighteenth Century* (Boston: Little Brown and Co., 1929).

McKeon, Richard, *The Basic Works of Aristotle* (New York: Random House, 1941).

Meller, Alec, *Dictionnaire de la Franc-Maçonnerie* (Paris: Pierre Belfond, 1971).

Masson, Hervé, *Dictionnaire initiatique* (Paris: Pierre Belfond, 1970).

Metzner, Ralph, *Maps of Consciousness* (New York: Collier Books, 1971).

Merdowski, *The Epic of the Kings Shab-Nama the National Epic of Persia* (Chicago: Chicago University Press, 1967).

Michaud, G., *Mallarmé* (Paris: Hatier, 1971).

Michelet, Jules, *La Sorcière* (Paris: Garnier-Flammarion, 1966).

Micklem, Niel, "On Hysteria: The Mythical Syndrome," *Spring,* 1974.

Molainville, Herberlot de, *Bibliothèque orientale.*

Naudon, Paul, *La Franc-Maconnerie* (Paris: Presses Universitaires de France, 1971).

Nerval, Gérard de, *Oeuvres* II (Paris: Pléiade, 1961).

Neumann, Erich, *The Great Mother* (New York: Pantheon Books, 1953).

—, *Depth Psychology and a New Ethic* (New York: G. P. Putnam's Sons, 1969).

New Larousse Encyclopedia of Mythology (New York: Prometheus Press, 1959).

Nietzsche, Friedrich, *The Philosophy of Nietzsche* (New York: Modern Library, 1937).

Nodier, Charles, *Contes* (Paris: Garnier, 1961).

Ostrander, Sheila and Lynn Schroeder, *Psychic Discoveries Behind the Iron Curtain* (New Jersey: Prentice-Hall, Inc., 1970).

Otto, Walter F., "The Meaning of the Eleusinian Mysteries," *Eranos Year-*

books II (New York: Pantheon Books, 1955).

Pappas, John, "Science versus poetry," *Thought,* No. 179, Winter, 1970.

Paulsen, Kathryn, *The Complete Book of Magic and Witchcraft* (New York: New American Library).

Patai, Raphael, *The Hebrew Goddess* (New York: Ktav Pub. Co., 1967).

Peyre, Henri, *Victor Hugo* (Paris: Presses Universitaires de France, 1972).

Percival, Harold W., *Masonry and its Symbols* (New York: The World Pub. Co., 1952).

Pfeiffer, Robert H., *Introduction to the Old Testament* (New York: Harper and Row, 1948).

Pilloux, Jean-Claude, *L'Inconscient* (Paris: Presses Universitaires, 1970).

Poincaré, Henri, *The Foundations of Science* (New York: The Science Press, 1929).

Poncé, Charles, *The Nature of the I Ching* (New York: Award Books, 1970).

Pongracz, M. and J. Santner, *Les Rêves à travers les ages* (Paris: Buchet/ Chastel, 1965).

Pomeau, René, *Diderot* (Paris: Presses Universitaires de France, 1967).

Plessner, Helmuth, "On the Relation of Time to Death," *Eranos Yearbooks* III, (New York: Pantheon, 1957).

The Works of Plato (trans. B. Jowett) (New York: Tudor Publishing Co.)

Poulet, Georges, *Etudes sur le temps humain* (Paris: Plon, 1949).

—, *Qui était Baudelaire* (Geneva: A. Skira, 1969).

—, *Les Métamorphoses du cercle* (Paris: Plon, 1961).

Puech, Henri-Charles, "Gnosis and Time," *Eranos Yearbooks* III (Princeton: Princeton University Press, 1957).

Racine, Jean, *The Complete Plays of Jean Racine* (trans. by Samuel Solomon) (New York: Random House, 1967).

Raphael, Alice, *Goethe and the Philosophers' Stone* (New York: Garret Pub., 1955).

Read, Herbert, *The Meaning of Art* (New York: Praeger Pub., 1972).

—, *Education Through Art* (New York: Pantheon Books, 1974).

Renouvier, Charles, *Victor Hugo le Philosophe* (Paris: Armand Colin, 1900).

Richard, Jean-Pierre, *L'univers imaginaire de Mallarmé* (Paris: Seuil, 1961).

Rony, Jérome-Antoine, *La Magie* (Paris: Presses Universitaires de France, 1968).

Rimbaud, Arthur, *A Season in Hell the Illuminations* (trans. Enid R. Peschel) (New York: Oxford University Press, 1974).

—, *Oeuvres complètes* (Paris: Pléiade, 1954).

Romanciers du XVIII siècle (Paris: Pléiade, 1965).

Rosenfield, Leonora Cohen, *From Beast-Machine to Man-Machine* (New York: Oxford University Press, 1941).

Ruff, Marcel, *A. Rimbaud* (Paris: Hatier, 1968).

Salomon, Michel, *Nodier et le groupe romantique* (Paris: Perrin Co., 1908).

Saurat, Denis, *La Religion ésotérique de Victor Hugo* (Paris: La Colombe,

1948).

Schuré, Edouard, *The Great Initiates* (New York: St. George Books, 1962).

Scholem, Gershom, *The Messianic Idea in Judaism* (New York: Schocken Books, 1971).

—, *Major Trends in Jewish Mysticism* (New York: Schocken Books, 1965).

Shaw, Edward Pease, *Jacques Cazotte* (Cambridge: Harvard University Press, 1941).

Spence, Lewis, *An Encyclopedia of Occultism* (Secaucus: The Citadel Press, 1960).

Starobinski, Jean, *Mallarmé et la tradition poétique française* (Paris: Les Lettres, III, 1948).

Strauss, Walter A., *Descent and Return* (Cambridge: Harvard University Press, 1971).

Summers, Montague, *Geography of Witchcraft* (Secaucus: The Citadel Press, 1973).

Teilhard de Chardin, Pierre, Le Phénomène humain (Paris: Seuil, 1955).

—, The Phenomenon of Man (New York: Harper and Row, 1969).

Trachtenberg, Joshua, *Jewish Magic and Superstition* (New York: Meridian Books, 1961).

Underhill, Evelyn, *The Mystics of the Church* (New York: Schocken Books, 1971).

Uzanne, Octave, *Contes de Jacques Cazotte* (Paris: A. Quantin, 1880).

Vernière, Paul, *Diderot* (Paris: Marcel Didier, 1951).

Viatte, Auguste, *Les Sources occultes du romantisme* II (Paris: Honoré Champion, 1969).

Vysheslawzeff, "Two ways of Redemption," *Eranos Yearbooks* VI (Princeton: Princeton University Press, 1970).

Waite, A. E., *The Holy Kabbalah* (New York: University Books, 1971).

Walzer, Pierre-Liver, *Mallarmé* (Pairs: Seghers, 1973).

Weblowsky, Zwi and G. Wigoder, *The Encyclopedia of Jewish Religion* (New York: Holt, Rinehart and Winston, 1966).

Williams, Thomas, *Mallarmé and the Language of Mysticism* (Athens: University of Georgia Press, 1970).

Wilhelm, Richard, *The Secret of the Golden Flower* (New York: Harcourt, Brace and World, 1969).

Wilmhurst, W. L., The Masonic Initiation (London: John M. Watkins, 1957).

Widengren, Geo., "The Principle of Evil in the Eastern Religions," *Evil* (Evanston: Northwestern University Press, 1967).

Zohar, The I (trans. Murray Sperling and Maurice Simon) (London: The Soncino Press, 1933).

INDEX

"About Some Phenomena of Sleep",
130
Abulafia, Abraham, 367
Abraham-Juif, 292
Aeschylus, 274
Aesculapius, 11-12, 86-102
"After the Flood", 20-21, 314-354
Akasic Record, 213-214
Albedo, 209
Albigenses, 43
Alchemists, 168-174, 207-211,
228, 296, 315, 332, 389, 391
Alembert, Jean le Rond d', 90, 96,
104
Anamnesis, 213, 226
Anaximander, 93, 110
Androgynism, 137, 138
Ange-femme, 193-195
Angel, 360-361
Annals, 242
Anselm, Saint, 29
Anthony, Saint, 187
Apocalyptic literature, 259, 260
Apollonius, 190
Aquinas, Saint Thomas, 15, 301
Architect, 245-247
*Argument Against the Manicheans
and Marcionites,* 30
Aristotle, 12-13, 88, 187, 211, 269,
345, 365
Arnauld, Antoine, 47
"Arria Marcella", 20, 204-222
Artemidorus, 13
Artificial Paradises, 229, 247
Ashes, 389

Ashurbanipal, 8
Astral Light, 214
Athaliah, 18, 62-84
Atheism, 89, 213
Atomic Energy Commission, 122
Aubanel, Théodore, 381
Augustine, Saint, 15, 30, 41, 44,
112, 270, 271, 287, 297, 301
Augustus, Emperor, 13
Aurélia, 3
Ausonius, 49, 50
Autobiography, 376
Autumn Leaves, 272

Baalism, 70
Bacon, Francis, 270
Bacon, Roger, 228
Baillet, Adrien, Abbé, 31, 32
Balzac, Honoré de, 3, 4, 19, 123,
134, 184-201, 205
Barbey d'Aurévilly, Jules, 292,
296, 299
Barges, 327-328
Baudelaire, Charles, 16, 20, 224-
255, 259, 264, 292, 296, 299,
302, 374
Bayle, Pierre, 88
Beavers, 332
Beethoven, Ludwig van, 274
Bergerat, Emile, 205
Bergson, Henri, 47
Berlioz, Hector, 206
Bernard of Clairvaux, 290
Bernheim, Hippolyte, 305

Béroalde de Verville, 292
Bertrans, Alexander, 206
Birds, 175, 383-384
Black Mass, 20, 284, 302-307
Blake, William, 17, 268, 277, 296
Blanc, Louis, 270
Blood, 298, 329-331
Bluebird, 330
Boccaccio, Giovanne, 16
Bodin, Jean, 301
Boehme, Jakob, 20, 111, 186, 192, 296
Bogomils, 43
Bonaparte, Napoleon, 190, 274
Bonaventure, Saint, 301
Bonniot, Edmont, 357
Book, 376-377
The Book of the Dead, 7
The Book of Formation, 373, 382
Borgia, Caesar, 295
Boullan, Joseph-Antoine, 294, 304
Bosch, Hieronymus, 16, 295, 328
Brihadarmyaka-Upanishad, 14
Brontë, Charlotte, 16
Breuer, Josef, 305
Breughel the Elder, 233, 295, 328
Buddha, 14, 195
Buddhism, 272, 289
Buffon, Count de, 88
Byron, George Gordon, Lord, 130, 205

Cagliostro, Alessandre, Conte, 291
Caligula, 13
Calpurnia, 17
Cardan, Jerome, 16
Cartesianism, 52, 87, 104
The Castle of Otranto, 205
Cataracts, 236
Cathari, 43
Catherine de Medici, 291, 304
Catherine de Thouars, 292

Cazalis, Henri, 358, 369, 377
Cazotte, Jacques, 19, 104-127, 131
Celsus, 386
Chamber, Ephraim, 90
Chance, 369-370
Chang, Tsai, 359
Charcot, Jean Martin, 305
Charlemagne, 15-16, 168
Charles VII, 292
Chateaubriand, François René, vicomte de, 273
Chaucer, Geoffrey, 16
Chemical Institutions, 88
Chester Beatty Papyrus, 6
Child, 334-337
Chimera, 378
Christianity, 43, 217-219, 269-270, 287-288, 326
Christina of Sweden, Queen, 37
Chuang-tzu, 14
City of God, 270
Clement of Alexandria, 330
Clyttemnestra, 273
Coffee, 332
Cogitationes Privatae, 35, 49
Coleridge, Samuel Taylor, 17, 233, 277
Collective unconscious, 4
Collyridians, 145
Colonna, Francesco, 16
Colonnades, 239
Color, 240-241, 247-248
Communion, 326
Complexes, 298
Comte, Auguste, 46
Condillac, Abbé de, 90, 95, 96, 270
Condorcet, Marie Jean de, 17, 51
Confessions, 15
Coniunctio, 78, 210, 291, 333
Conjunction, 370

Considerations on the Greatness and Decadence of the Romans, 87
Constantine I, 13
Contemplations, 259
Conversations with Eckermann, 118
Corneille, Pierre, 18
Corpus Poetarum, 48, 50
Cranach, Lucas, the elder, 295, 328
Creation, 265
"The Crucifixion", 284-286
The Crumb Fairy, 19, 130-150
Crystals, 236-237, 333
Cusa, Nicolas de, 376
Cyclopaedia, 90

Daedalus, 245
D'Alembert's Dream, 18, 86-102, 131
Daniel, 10
Dante, 16, 193, 274
"Dante and Virgil", 206
Daumier, Honoré, 328
De Genesi Contra Manicheos, 44
De Rerum Naturae, 91
De Subtilitate Rerum, 16
The Decameron, 16
Decline and Fall of the Roman Empire, 87
Deism, 88-89
Delacroix, Ferdinand Victor Eugène, 206, 328
"Delfica", 204
Delilah, 273
Democritus, 12, 91, 186, 380
Descartes, René, 4, 16, 18, 26-60, 88, 90, 94, 96
The Devil in Love, 19, 104-127, 131
The Devil's Elixir, 130, 205
The Devil's Portrait, 205
The Devil's Trill, 17, 206
Les Diaboliques, 296
Dice-throw, 387-388·
Diderot, Denis, 18, 86-102, 104, 131,

259
The Discourse on Method, 27, 39, 41, 48
Discussions Between d'Alembert and Diderot, 92, 98
Diverse Thoughts on the Comet, 88
Divine Comedy, 16
Divine Philosophy, 214
Dobbs, Adrian, 122-123
"Doctor's Dreams", 16
Dolmen, 263
Domitian, 13
Down There, 20, 284-312
The Dream, 205
"The Dream of an Inhabitant from Mogulia", 18
The Dream of Poliphilus, 16
Dreams as source of creativity, 16-17
Dreams in Arabian civilization, 13-14
Dreams in Assyrian and Babylonian civilizations, 8-9
Dreams in Chinese civilization, 14
Dreams in Egyptian civilization, 6-8
Dreams in Greek civilization, 10-13
Dreams in Hebrew civilization, 9, 10
Dreams in Roman civilization, 13
Dreams in the Bible, 9-10, 14-15
Dreams in the Talmud, 9, 10
Dürer, Albrecht, 16, 299, 328, 345
Dutoit-Membrini, 214

Eccles, Sir John, 123
Eckhart, Meister, 20, 337
The Educated Cat, 205
Eidolon, 381

Einstein, Albert, 27, 119
Elisabeth, Princess of Bohemia, 37
Emerson, Ralph Waldo, 17
Empedocles, 93, 110, 211, 213, 379
Empiricists, 46
Enantiodromia, 233, 297
The Enchanted Hand, 205
"Encounter", 271
The Encyclopedia, Methodical Dictionary of the Sciences, Arts, and Trades, 90
"The End of Satan", 296
Enlightenment, 87
Ensor, James, 17
Epicurus, 97
Essay on Dreams, 18
Essays on the Mind, 90
Ethics, 263
Evil, 30, 271-272, 285-288
Existence, 95-97
Existence of God, 29
Eyes, 276, 374

Fall of Adam and Eve, 266
"The Fantastic in Literature", 130
Fantastic Symphony, 206
Faust, 53, 112, 195, 242, 290, 299, 337
Ferchault de Réaumur, 88
Fermat, Pierre de, 18, 47
Ficino, Marciglio, 356
Fire, 170
Flamel, Nicolas, 292, 293, 376
Flowers, 319, 323
The Flowers of Evil, 224
Fludd, Robert, 111
Flus, 93-95
Forain, Jean Louis, 328
Forest, 342
Formey, 18
Fourier, Charles, 270

Franz, Marie Louise von, 31, 32, 34, 39, 40, 41, 42, 43, 44, 46, 48, 51, 134
Freischütz, Der, 206
Freud, Sigmund, 31, 32, 305
Fuseli, Henri, 17

Gabriel, Angel, 13-14
Galileo, 35, 41
Gall, Franz Joseph, 187
The Ganges, 243
Gargantua and Pantagruel, 16, 270
Galen, 305
Gassendi, Pierre, 18, 47
Gautier, Théophile, 20, 123, 204-222, 264
Gavarni, Paul, 328
Genet, Jean, 292
Géricault, Jean Louis André Théodore, 328
Das Gesetz der Serie, 119
Gestalt-theory, 96
Geulincz, Arnold, 37
Ghosts, 34-36
Gibbon, Edward, 87
Gilgamesh, 8-9, 319-320
Gill, Eric, 328
Gilles de Rais, 284, 291-299, 304
Gilson, Etienne, 40
Giotto, 328
Girardin, Delphine de, 262
Glass, 333
The Gleaners, 3
Gnosticism, 105, 112, 140, 271, 296, 315, 318, 326, 330, 391
Goethe, Johann Wolfgang von, 53, 118, 195, 214, 217, 337
Gogh, Vincent van, 319, 324
Gold, 235, 368
Goya, Francisco José de, 299,

328
The Green Monster, 205
Gregory, Pope, 15
Gregory, Saint, 333
Grünewald, Matthias, 16, 284-286, 328
Gudea, King, 8
Guys, Constantin, 224-225, 249

Hair, 374
Hamlet, 16
Hammurabi, 8
Hare, 318-319
Harmonices Mundi, 370
Harvey, Gabriel, 18, 47
The Haunted Chamber, 205
Healing dreams, 7, 11
Hegel, Georg Wilhelm Friedrich, 47, 377
Heimarmene, 214, 369
Helvetius, Claude-Adrien, 90
"The Henriade", 19
Heraclitus, 4, 91, 93-94, 110, 224, 234, 269, 315, 379, 391
Hesiod, 10-11
Hetaira, 216-217
Hieros gamos, 72, 131, 137-145, 210, 248, 369
Hildegard, Saint, 46
Hinduism, 273
Hippocrates, 12, 138
Historical and Critical Dictionary, 88
History of Charles II, 87
Hitler, Adolf, 295
Hobbes, Thomas, 37, 47
Hoffmann, Ernst Theodor, 130, 205, 296
Hogarth, William, 17, 277
Homer, 11, 315
Hugo, Victor, 3, 20, 206, 258-281, 296, 299
Huxley, Aldous, 331

Huysmans, Joris-Karl, 20, 284-312
Hymnes orphiques, 204
Hysteria, 305-306, 358

Ibn Daud, 194
Igitur, 21, 216, 356-400
Ignored Martyrs, 186
The Illuminations, 314, 316
Illuminists, 19, 104, 105, 110, 152, 271, 326
Imhotep, 7
Incubation dreams, 7, 11
The Indiscreet Jewels, 97
Infernalia, 205
Innocent VIII, Pope, 291, 301
Izembard, Georges, 337

Jacob, 9
James, Henry, 17
Janet, Pierre, 305
Jansenism, 79
Jesuits, 40, 41, 51, 90
Jesus Christ, 12, 285-288
Jeu de Théophilus, 16
Joan of Arc, 138, 284, 292
John of the Cross, Saint, 20
Joseph, 9-10, 14-15
Judaism, 286
Julius Caesar, 16, 17
Jung, C. G., 4, 36, 120, 121, 196, 211, 303, 370
Justine, 304

Kabbalah, 107, 111, 152, 195
Kabbalism, 105, 156, 235, 271, 272, 300, 301, 364, 365, 369-370, 391
Kammerer, Paul, 119
Kant, Immanuel, 26, 46

Katochoi, 7
Kekulé, F. A., 4
Kepler, Johannes, 122, 370
Kierkegaard, Soren, 47, 326
Koestler, Arthur, 52
Koyré, Alexandre, 53
Kramer, Henry, 291
Kratophany, 346
"Kubla Kahn", 17, 233-234

La Fontaine, Jean de, 18
Lamartine, Alphonse de, 273
Lamb, Charles, 16
"The Last Judgment", 295
Lavater, Jean, 187
Lavoisier, Antoine Laurent, 88
Lays, 16
Leconte de Lisle, Charles, 204
Lefébure, Eugène, 357, 392
Leibniz, Gottfried Wilhelm, Baron
    von, 26, 88, 122, 270, 383
Leon, Moses de, 20
Leroy, Maxime, 31, 32
"Letter of the Seer", 315
Letter on the Blind, 89
Leucippus, 91, 186, 380
Lévi, Eliphas, 138, 317
Lewin, Bertram, 31, 32-33, 38, 39,
    42
Lewis, Mathew, 130, 205
Life and death, 97
Light, 46
Lincoln, Abraham, 17
Liszt, Franz, 206
"Litanies of Satan", 296
Locke, John, 90, 95, 96
Logos spermatikos, 330
Louis Lambert, 19, 184-201
Louis the Pious, 290
Lucian, 242
Lucretius, 88, 91, 97
Lulle Raymond, 292

Luria, Isaac, 43, 365
Lurianic Kabbalists, 265-266

Macbeth, 16
Magic, 111-112, 242
Magnus, Albertus, 118, 237, 292,
    376
Maimonides, 194
Malebranche, Nicolas, 26, 37
Mallarmé, Stéphane, 5, 6, 21,
    216, 356-400
Malleus Malleficarum, 291
Malraux, André, 215
Mandrake, 137-138
Mani, 43
Manichaeans, 43, 287
Marie de France, 16
Marie the Jewess, 235
Mariette, Father, 291
Maritain, Jacques, 31, 37, 53
*The Marriage of Heaven and
    Hell,* 296
Martinist Order, 104, 105,
    106
Masonic order, 105, 106, 156,
    165-168
Mass, 302-303
Matisse, Henri, 3
Matthew, Saint, 14
"May Night", 330
Maya, 14
McCornell, James V., 386
The Meditations, 27
Melons, 42-44
"Memoirs of a Soul", 259
Ménard, Louis, 204
Mephisto Waltz, 206
Mersenne, Father, 35, 41
Mesmer, Anton, 186
Messianic Doctrine, 273-277
Metals, 169, 171, 231, 238
Metamorphoses, 324

Meyerbeer, Giacomo, 152
Michaux, Henri, 324
Michelet, Jules, 217, 300, 302
Midnight, 363-365
Millet, Jean François, 328
Milton, John, 296
Mirabilis Mundi, 118
The Miracle of St. Nicolas, 16
Mirkabah mystics, 20
Mirrors, 242, 365-367
Mneme, 213, 226
Mohammed, 13
Monism, 91, 110, 131, 231
The Monk, 205
Montaigne, Michel Eyquem, seigneur
    de, 16, 96
Montesquieu, Charles de Secondat,
    baron de la Brède et de, 87, 89
Moon, 137-141, 314, 341-342
Moses, 45, 74, 168, 195, 274, 275, 276
Mountain, 176, 338-339
Mouth, 260-261
Moyen de Parvenir, 292
Mozart, Wolfgang Amadeus, 121
Museum, 215
Musset, Alfred de, 330
"Myrtho", 204
Mystics, 272, 278, 291, 296
Myths, 89-90

Napoleon III, 258, 267
Natural History, 237
Nebuchadnezzar, 10
Needham, John, 88
Neoplatonism, 105, 326
Nero, 13
Nerval, Gérard de, 3, 16, 19, 123,
    152-181, 193, 204, 205, 264, 302
Nettesheim, Agrippa von, 111
New Atlantis, 270
New Christianism, 270
News From Foreign Lands, 324

Newton, Sir Isaac, 88, 119
Nietzsche, Friedrich, 26, 47, 52,
    184, 297, 321, 326, 340
Night-Pieces, 130
Nigredo, 207-208
Nihilism, 213
Nimrod, 273
Noah, Legend of, 314-315
Nocturnal Terrors, 18
Nodier, Charles, 19, 123, 130-
    150, 152, 205, 314
Novalis, 131
Numbers, 246, 359, 363
The Nun, 16

Objectivists, 47
Occultism, 111
"Oceano Nox", 271
Odes of Solomon, 330
Odyssey, 11
Oken, Lorenz, 315
Olympica, 31
On Divination, 12
On Divination through Sleep, 12
On Sleep, 12
On Sleep and Dreams, 12
On the Theory of Colors, 207
Oneirocritica, 13
Oneirosphere, 5, 21
Orpheus, 244, 376
Orphism, 152
Our Lady of Paris, 206
Ovid, 324
Owen, Robert, 270

Paganism, 204, 219
The Painter of Modern Life, 237,
    248
Paracelsus, 46, 111, 210, 376,
    390
"Parisian Dream", 20, 224-255

Pascal, Blaise, 18, 47
Pasqualis, Martinez de, 105, 166
The Passions of the Soul, 27
Paul, Saint, 46, 145, 288
Paulicians, 43
Pelicans, 330
Periods of Nature, 88
Persian Letters, 89
Peter the Venerable, 290
Phaedrus, 186, 194
Philippe le Bel, 290
Philosophical Letters, 89
Philosophical Thoughts, 89
Picasso, Pablo, 3
Piso, Carlos, 305
Plato, 4, 12, 46, 48, 52, 96, 186-187,
    193, 194, 211, 213, 269, 337, 371,
    373, 374, 383, 384
Pliny, 237
Poe, Edgar Allan, 16
Poèmes antiques, 204
Poet, 315-316
Poimandres, 214
Polytheism, 204
Poincaré, Jules Henri, 16, 26
Polidori, John, 205
Polyeucte, 18
Poulet, Georges, 31, 32, 39, 42
Prayer, 320
Prelati, Francesco, 292
Premonitory dreams, 17
The Priest's Tale, 16
Principes, 36, 48
Principium individuationis, 296
The Principles of Philosophy, 27
Privatio boni, 297
Promenades of a Skeptic, 89
Puer aeternus, 117, 323-324, 337
Puissance vitale, 188
Purifications, 214
Pythagoras, 211, 214, 246, 250,
    269, 274, 363

Rabelais, François, 16, 270
Rachmaninoff, Sergey, 16, 121
Racine, Jean, 18, 62-84
Rationalism, 52
Radcliffe, Ann, 130, 205
Rays and Shadows, 271
Read, Herbert, 268
Reason, 30-31, 186-187
The Red and the Black, 339
The Red Inn, 134-205
Redon, Odilon, 16, 285, 374
Reincarnation, 213-214
Rembrandt, 328
Renéville, Rolland de, 360
Renovatio, 210, 252, 329
Republic, 12, 48, 371
Revelations, 46
Richard, Father, 18
Richard III, 16
Ricondi, Pierre, 290
Rig Yeda, 339
Rimbaud, Arthur, 6, 16, 20-21,
    314, 354
Romanticism, 93, 273
Rop, Félicien, 285
Rosicrucians, 156
Rousseau, Jean-Jacques, 18, 88,
    92, 270
Rubedo, 209-210
Ruskin, John, 268
Ruysbroeck, Jon van, 46

Sabbaen cult, 143, 155
Sceptics, 46
Sade, Marquis de, 304
"The Sages", 274
Saint-Amant, Marc Antoine de, 18
Saint-Martain, Claude de, 105,
    106, 111, 166, 186, 192
Salon 1846, 238
Satanism, 20, 284, 286-299
Saul, 10

Scansion, 383
"Scapegoat" psychology, 295
Schelling, Friedrich Wilhelm Joseph von, 131
Schizophrenia, 358, 387
Schopenhauer, Arthur, 272
A Season in Hell, 316, 327, 332, 334
The Secret of the Golden Flower, 364
Sejanus, 273
Seneca, 187
Shadow, 261-262, 294-296
Shakespeare, William, 16, 274
Sheba, Queen of, 152-181
Shelley, Mary, 205
Shelley, Percy Bysshe, 130, 277
Shri-Yantra, 365
Sleep, 227-228
Smarra, 205
Socialism, 270
Socrates, 165, 269, 274
Soliman, 152-181
Soma, 342, 391
The Song of Roland, 15-16
Sophists, 46
Spider web, 321, 381-382
Spinoza, Baruch, 26, 37, 263
The Spirit of Laws, 89
Spiritism, 262
"Splinter psyche", 297
Sprenger, James, 291
Stella Nova, 122
Stendhal, 339
Stevenson, Robert Louis, 17
Stoicism, 213, 315, 330
Stones, 241, 322, 323
The Strange Case of Dr. Jekyll and Mr. Hyde, 17
Subjectivists, 46
Summa Theologica, 15
Sun, 141-144
Supplement to Bougainville's Voyage, 89

Swedenborg, Emanuel, 19, 104, 119, 186, 191, 192, 317
Sydenham, Thomas, 305
Symbolists, 93

Tacitus, 242
Tartini, Giuseppe, 17, 206
Teilhard de Chardin, Pierre, 3
"The Temptation of St. Anthony", 16
Thales, 231, 315
The Theban Brothers, 78
Theory of Dreams, 18
Theory of Four Movements, 270
Theresa of Avila, Saint, 20, 187
Thinking man, Legend of the, 184-201
Thought, 185-186
Thus Spake Zarathustra, 326
Thutmos, IV, 7
Tiberius, 13, 273
Tieck, Ludwig, 131
Tikkun, 271
Time, 211-212, 364-367
"The Torments of the Damned", 295
"Transformation of the Sorceress", 299
Treasures, 243-244
Treatise of the Reintegration of beings into their first properties, spiritual and divine powers and virtues, 105
The Treatise of the World, 41
Treatise on Domestic Agricultural Association, 270
Treatise on Sensations, 90
Treatise on the Passions of the Soul, 30
Trees, 239
Trembley, Abraham, 88
Trismegistus, Hermes, 214, 369

Tsimtsum, 265, 365
Turgot, Anne Robert Jacques, 51
Turner, Joseph, 268
"Twilight Evening", 249
"Two Friends", 18

Unconscious, 4-5
The Unknown Masterpiece, 205
The Unknown Philosopher, 105, 106
Utopists, 278

Vagina dentata, 64, 323, 327, 338
Vaillant, Pierre, 291
Valéry, Paul, 16, 323
The Vampire, 205
Van Haecke, Father, 294, 304
Vates, 118, 323
"The Vaux Dream", 18
Verrière, Paul, 99
Vigny, Alfred, comte de, 273, 275,
   299
Villiers de l'Isle Adam, 361, 366
Vinci, Leonardo da, 88
The Violin of Cremona, 205
The Virgin Mary, 144, 145-146
Visions, 18

Volland, Sophie, 86
Voltaire, François Marie Arouet
   de, 18, 87, 89, 94, 104
"The Voyage", 250
Voyage in the Orient, 19, 152

Wagner, Richard, 16, 53, 121,
   247
Walls, 237-238
Walpole, Horace, 130, 205
Water, 231-232, 314-315
Weber, Carl Marie (Friedrich
   Ernst) von, 206
Weizsäcker, Karl von, 303
"What the Mouth of Darkness
   Says", 20, 258-281
Whirlwind, 38
Wine, 330-331
"The Witch", 299
Women, 299-300
The World, 44

Zoroastrianism, 43

DREAM AND IMAGE

Composed in IBM Selectric Composer *Journal Roman* and printed offset by McNaughton & Gunn, Incorporated, Ann Arbor, Michigan. The paper on which the book is printed is the International Paper Company's *Bookmark,* which is acid-free. The book was sewn and bound by Howard Dekker & Sons, Grand Rapids, Michigan.

Dream and Image is a Trenowyth book, the scholarly publishing division of The Whitston Publishing Company.

This edition consists in 500 casebound copies.